The Green Web
A Union for World Conservation

Martin Holdgate

IUCN
The World Conservation Union

Earthscan Publications Ltd, London

First published in the UK by Earthscan Publications Ltd in 1999

A catalogue record for this book is available from the British Library

ISBN: 1 85383 595 1

Typesetting by PCS Mapping & DTP, Newcastle upon Tyne
Printed and bound by Biddles Ltd, Guildford and King's Lynn.
Cover design by Andrew Corbett

For a full list of publications please contact:
Earthscan Publications Ltd
120 Pentonville Road
London, N1 9JN, UK
Tel: +44 (0)171 278 0433
Fax: +44 (0)171 278 1142
Email: earthinfo@earthscan.co.uk
http://www.earthscan.co.uk

Earthscan is an editorially independent subsidiary of Kogan Page Limited and publishes in
association with WWF-UK and the International Institute for Environment and Development.

Contents

Figures and Plates

Figures

Plates

Preface
The Conservation World's Best-kept Secret

This book is about the evolution of international action for conservation in the fifty years between 1948 and 1998. The first date was chosen because in that year an International Union for the Protection of Nature was founded. Fifty years later, it has evolved into IUCN – the International Union for Conservation of Nature and Natural Resources – or, more simply, the World Conservation Union. But the story is more complicated than that. When IUPN was founded it stood alone as the only international organization concerned with nature protection in the round. The International Council for Bird Preservation, now BirdLife International, established in 1922, was its only active predecessor. None of the global environmental organizations that are household names today – the World Wide Fund for Nature (or World Wildlife Fund), Greenpeace, Friends of the Earth – existed, and there was little awareness of, and still less popular concern over, the impacts of pollution.

But since 1948, environmental concerns and bodies demanding environmental action have multiplied dramatically. Almost all governments now have departments or ministries with responsibility for environmental affairs. The 'Earth Summit' (more correctly, the United Nations Conference on Environment and Development) held in June 1992 in Rio de Janeiro was the occasion for one of the greatest gatherings of heads of state and government ever. Environment is now global business. The evolution of IUCN has to be viewed within this context of surging greenness.

Before 1948 there were, of course, numerous natural history societies and organizations concerned with safeguarding species and their habitats, creating national parks and protecting wilderness and fine landscapes – but they were national bodies. After the Second World War the United Nations and its agencies were created, and some of those agencies – notably FAO, the United Nations Food and Agriculture Organization, and UNESCO, the United Nations Educational, Scientific and Cultural Organization – promoted and supported action to develop and use natural resources wisely. They were supported by governments and had money to disburse.

IUPN (now IUCN), created in the same period with UNESCO's active backing, had virtually no resources. It was conceived as a meeting ground, a facilitator and a supporter for its members, not as an operational agency in its own right. The primary rationale was to strengthen the whole nature conservation movement by networking – through linking expert individuals and national organizations and pooling information, assuming that if IUCN helped to share the world's knowledge its national members would work more effectively, and nature would benefit.

Any book that has the story of an organization at its centre is likely to be woven of several strands. One – the most important – is a record of achievements: what has this organization done, and why has it made a difference? This, almost inevitably, demands a comparative assessment: what was the context of that achievement, and what other bodies aided or opposed it? For a networking organization, moreover, success often depends on the elements of the network – have the linkages made them better able to achieve their ends? But another strand, of especial interest to those who want to know how the achievements (and failures) came to be, is internal: who were the people inside the organization who made it all happen, and how far were they supported (or impeded) by management and finance? These strands run through this volume, and the most difficult task in writing it has been to balance them and avoid too strong a dominance by the details (and at times the absurdities) of internal management and conflict.

What are the achievements of IUCN? Although the oldest global conservation body, it is not well known. Its name rings no bells in the public mind – and when the presenters of current events programmes on television or radio want a quick comment on the latest environmental disaster or prophecy of doom, they hardly ever turn to it. There are good reasons for this. IUCN has rarely trumpeted its achievements. It remains a 'green web' and its chief legitimacy is to support its members in their own missions. Almost any conservationist you hear on the radio will belong to an IUCN member organization.

IUCN's most famous products have been assemblages of knowledge, drawn from the experts it has convened. Its Red Data Books are the most authoritative statements of the status of species – plants as well as animals – threatened by extinction, and its action plans are the best recipes for their salvation. Its Species Survival Commission, with over 8000 members, is not only the largest voluntary network of experts on species conservation in the world – it is the *only* significant network in that field. Similarly, the IUCN World Commission on Protected Areas is *the* network for the world's 'parks people' with over 1000 members from all regions. The Union has produced the basic classification of national parks and other protected areas, and the rationale behind each category, and since 1959 it has been entrusted by the United Nations with maintaining a global list of protected areas. The IUCN Commission on Environmental Law and the Environmental Law Programme have had a seminal role in the building of the 'new' subject of environmental law,[1] and all the recent world-wide nature conservation conventions either began on IUCN's drawing board, or have been influenced by the Union's efforts.

An equally important role has been the development of over-arching strategies. The World Conservation Strategy of 1980 – greatly influenced by partnership with the United Nations Environment Programme, the World Wildlife Fund (as it then was), UNESCO and FAO – was the first such document to link the conservation of nature to the process of resource development for human needs. It spelled out the concept of 'sustainable development', of which we have heard so much since. The Global Biodiversity Strategy, which was the first blueprint for integrated global action to save the world's plant and animal life, was the product of another partnership involving the World Resources Institute and UNEP.

But the greatest service IUCN provides to its members still comes through networking. The Union links small, weak but active bodies at the thorn-roots of struggle with the world's most intractable environmental problems to large, expert and affluent bodies in the developed 'North'. It is a channel for information flow in both directions. One of its great values as a forum is that it exposes governments – especially in the North – to non-governmental thinking, including the thoughts of the South, where the aid agencies of Northern governments work. Its Regional and

Country Offices are on the ground, where the problems and the members are, and they are the leaders of the Union's action for conservation and sustainable development. Its voluntary Commissions give individual conservationists an opportunity to associate with their peers around the world, contributing knowledge and gaining strength in the process. Its periodic General Assemblies, congresses, technical meetings and regional forums bring the membership together to exchange knowledge and experience.

Although many of the pioneering steps towards what we now call 'conservation' were taken in North America, IUCN was very much a European creation. It was dominated for the first part of its existence by Belgians, British, Dutch, French and Swiss. But it soon broadened to embrace North Americans, who indeed rescued the organization from bankruptcy several times. Yet there has never been a strong sense of 'ownership' of IUCN in the USA. Until recently there was also little sense of 'ownership' in the South, the developing world, because although 'southern' regions were represented from early times on its Council, the IUCN leadership was strongly rooted in the North and some of its attitudes bore the trade-marks of the colonial past.

Yet from the outset, the organization looked south. It was concerned with the need for conservation in the developing world, and with supporting new and vulnerable environmental movements that were beginning in Africa, Asia and Latin America. It '*played a crucial role through personal contacts and written material in convincing people in the South of the importance of conserving their renewable natural resources*'.[2] And it learned from the South, especially of the importance of '*a wise balance between the observance of ecological needs and those of the people*'.[3] The number of people from the South involved in the work began to increase in the mid-1970s, when a Venezuelan was appointed as Director-General, and an Egyptian became President. The World Conservation Strategy of 1980, by speaking the language of sustainable development, showed people in the developing world that this organization had something to offer them. The election in 1983 of a North American Director-General who had worked extensively in Latin America and spoke fluent Spanish was a further important southward step, into a continent that had been marginalized in the early period when African and Asian issues dominated the Union.[4]

From about 1988 'Southern' membership began to grow rapidly, and Southern Regional Councillors began to exert a powerful influence. National and Regional Committees allowed members to speak with clearer (and louder) voices. Today, IUCN is truly a worldwide 'green web'.[5] In 1998, its members were 74 states, 110 government agencies, and 743 non-governmental organizations, spanning 138 countries. Most components of the WWF family belonged, as did Greenpeace (Australia), Friends of the Earth and almost all the main national conservation organizations. The Commissions – the voluntary networks that are IUCN's most distinctive feature – involved nearly 10,000 individual specialists in 180 countries. Most of IUCN's 900 staff are now based in the developing world and most of its expenditure is managed there: most are citizens of the regions in which they work. As its fiftieth year ends, IUCN, for the first time in its history, is evolving to match, in its governance, membership and activities, the pattern of the world it seeks to serve. But the tree that has taken root in the South has yet to cast its fruits into the North and alter the concepts and approaches there.[6]

Although written to mark the fiftieth anniversary of IUCN, this book begins further back. The first chapter sets the scene by describing the early years of what became the 'conservation movement'. Chapter 2 describes, in some detail, the turbulent process that culminated in the creation of the International Union for the Protection of Nature at Fontainebleau in 1948. Thereafter the history of IUPN and

IUCN can be divided into six main stages, which form the building blocks of this story. The first, described in Chapter 3, saw the Union established and beginning its work. It extended from Fontainebleau to the fifth session of the General Assembly held in Edinburgh in 1956. In that period the first flush of enthusiasm peaked, the first programmes were set in motion, the first Commissions became active, the first Secretary-General completed his work and departed, the first financial crisis shook the Union when UNESCO's support was interrupted for a while, and the capacities and limitations of a body of IUPN's peculiar character became very evident.

The second stage, addressed in Chapters 4 and 5, was a period of strengthening science and influence. It overlapped the first stage, beginning in Copenhagen in 1954, with the election of the French biologist Roger Heim as President, gained impetus in Edinburgh two years later, when IUPN became IUCN, and lasted until the late 1960s. The office moved from Brussels to Switzerland, and the International Biological Programme attracted the attention of a large section of the world's ecological community. This was a stage of catalysis, in which a tiny IUCN Secretariat did what it could to promote worldwide conservation, and in which the Commissions were the spearheads of the Union's programmes.

The ideas and knowledge flowed, but the action lagged, and those working with IUCN knew that they were losing in the struggle against environmental degradation and the loss of species and habitats. Hence the creation of WWF, in 1961. It was the first organization to stimulate widespread public concern and to raise money from the public at large for worldwide nature conservation. It worked through supporting a mass of national and local action – at first, largely through and with IUCN, and later more directly. It has been an undoubted success, raising billions of dollars for its cause.

The 1970s brought an outburst of popular environmentalism, stimulated by widely-publicized disasters and the skilled campaigning of a new generation of activist 'green' bodies – like Friends of the Earth and Greenpeace – which sprang up alongside WWF and IUCN and caught a good deal of the popular limelight. Governments came back into the action, with the major UN Conference on the Human Environment at Stockholm in 1972 and the subsequent creation of UNEP, the United Nations Environment Programme. For IUCN it was a time of reconstruction, with a greatly strengthened secretariat, and the appointment of a professional scientist as Director-General. In this period, which lasted until about 1976 and is described in Chapter 6, the Secretariat gained the competence to manage significant field programmes as well as to support those of the Commissions – and this change from a body that was essentially scientific and a provider of expert advice to one that was operational brought its own stresses (not all of them are resolved even yet).

Stage four, between 1978 and 1984 and covered in Chapters 7 and 8, was the era of conservation strategies. It was a period of much closer cooperation with United Nations agencies, and close integration with WWF. Its high point was the launch of the World Conservation Strategy in 1980. It saw a great increase in projects on the ground, to start with as joint ventures between IUCN and WWF. It saw the establishment of a Conservation for Development Centre, which helped many countries to produce National Conservation Strategies and undertake projects. While IUCN never abandoned its commitment to traditional nature conservation, and the Species Survival Commission and Commission on National Parks and Protected Areas were leaders in their respective spheres, the promotion of conservation within wider programmes of sustainable development became a central activity.

Stage five, which developed rapidly after the General Assembly held in Madrid in 1984 and lasted until about 1994, was a phase of expansion. In the first part of the period official governmental development assistance agencies became increasingly strong supporters of IUCN, dramatically increasing the amount of project work on the ground. Chapter 9 describes the early part of this stage, which also brought fundamental changes in the relationship between IUCN and WWF. In the second part of the period, there was a global resurgence of thinking about the world environment, focussed by the 'Earth Summit' in Rio de Janeiro in 1992. Chapter 10 covers that period, which saw the launch of the second World Conservation Strategy, *Caring for the Earth*, in 1991. There was a worldwide reawakening of interest in the fate of the genes, species and ecosystems of the world, leading to the Global Biodiversity Strategy and the Convention on Biological Diversity, both involving IUCN deeply.

Stage six, the stage of regionalization, emerged from the expanding worldwide programme of the Union in the late 1980s and early 1990s and was in many ways an inevitable consequence of Rio, with its emphasis on new national action for sustainable development. Chapter 11 describes how IUCN and its members responded, starting at the General Assembly held in Buenos Aires in 1994, which 'gave IUCN back to its members'. The centre of gravity of the Union moved decisively southwards.

This book is about what IUCN has done and how it has worked. In Chapter 12 I try to distil my conclusions. One thing that stands out is that IUCN is no ordinary body. As Max Nicholson has put it:

> *'In dealing with IUCN, one must always bear in mind that there never has been, and undoubtedly never will be, any other human organization even remotely resembling it. Its peculiarities, subtleties and complexities are sometimes mind-boggling.'*[7]

At the end of a year in which my mind has indeed boggled at the complexities, one conclusion is clear. IUCN has a record of continuous, and increasing, service to the world conservation community despite recurrent crises. Like a hot-air balloon, it has been launched, to rise and sail serenely through the skies – only to descend with little warning, and strike financial rocks, often ejecting the Director-General (the chief pilot) in the process. Refuelled, recaptained and relaunched, new heights have been gained, and even more serene progress made – until the next crisis.

Few organizations have been so accident-prone. Few accident-prone bodies have such a record of achievement. And there seems to me to be a reason for this – the very complexity of the organization. Most of the crises have affected the central structure – the Council and the Secretariat. The voluntary networks, the Commissions, have been hampered when funds dried up, but resourceful leaders have almost always been able to carry on the most important work. The Council has continued to function. The General Assemblies – world congresses of conservationists – have continued to be held, in times of poverty as well as plenty. Publications, statements and recommendations have continued to emerge. And this has been due in large part to personal dedication on the part of Presidents, Director-Generals, Councillors, Chairs, Commission members and staff. If one slogan above all others characterizes IUCN down the years, it would seem to me to be:

'Continuity through Crisis'.

Martin Holdgate
Hartley, Cumbria
July 1998

Acknowledgments

Like any history, this book tries to deal in a factual way with a diversity of information. I have used published statements, and also much unpublished material in the Union's archives. I have relied on interviews with people who were deeply involved in the action. Although my personal judgement of what is most important has inevitably affected the balance of the text, I have tried to report neutrally, and that is why most of the book is written in the third person (even when dealing with my own six years as Director-General). The Preface and Chapter 12 are written in the first person to indicate that they are my own interpretations.

My debt to my helpers is immense. I have been fortunate that a number of the people who helped to create IUPN over 50 years ago are still with us, and have generously contributed both memory and documents. They include John Berry, Richard Fitter, Alain Gille, Max Nicholson and Miriam Rothschild. Mme Mady Harroy has kindly sent me an extract from the unpublished autobiography of her late husband, the Union's first Secretary-General, Jean-Paul Harroy. From a slightly later period, I have been greatly helped by Michel Batisse, Robert Bootc, Gerardo Budowski, Françoise Burhenne-Guilmin, Wolfgang Burhenne, Raymond Dasmann, Eskandar Firouz, Charles de Haes, Mohamed Kassas, Ian McPhail, Tony Mence, Adrian Phillips, Duncan Poore, Robert Prescott-Allen, Maurice Strong, Lee Talbot and Russell Train. Many of them have been kind enough to read chapters and put me right where I had strayed from the exact path.

From about 1975 the cloud of witnesses becomes vast. I have listened to many people – far more than I can acknowledge here – but am especially grateful to HRH Prince Philip, Duke of Edinburgh and long-time President of WWF International (and Vice-President of IUCN) and to Curtis ('Buff') Bohlen, Christine Buhler, Mike McCloskey, Michael Cockerell, Marc Dourojeanni, Hal Eidsvik, Pierre Goeldlin, Jay Hair, Mark Halle, Fiona Hanson, Ursula Hiltbrunner, Frits Hesselink, Luc Hoffmann, Peter Jackson, Yolanda Kakabadse, Walter Lusigi, Claude Martin, Dan Martin, Juan Mayr, Roger McManus, Jeffrey McNeely, Kenton Miller, Russell Mittermeier, Patrick Moore (a founder of Greenpeace), Anis Mouasher, David Munro, David Runnalls (an original member of IIED), Richard Sandbrook (an early leader of Friends of the Earth), Jeffrey Sayer, Hugh Synge, Estelle Viguet and Conrad von Ulm-Erbach.

Although the IUCN archives themselves are slender until about 1965, there is a vast amount of documentation from that year onwards and I have only been able to skim the surface of the reservoir of information in the basement of the IUCN headquarters in Gland. Kevin Grose and Cécile Thiéry have been most helpful guides in that labyrinth. Joanna Boddens-Hosang helped immensely by translating from the Dutch an account of the early development of the International Office for the Protection of Nature, led by Pieter van Tienhoven. John Sheail of the UK Institute for

Terrestrial Ecology, himself a professional historian, kindly supplied me with extracts from British official files now available in the Public Record Office. Ursula Hiltbrunner has extracted and supplied data and graphs of the growth of IUCN membership, Fiona Hanson has analysed the progressive growth in influence of Regional Councillors from the South, and Cécile Thiéry has provided statistics on the dramatic growth in published output. Other documentary sources are scattered widely, and I have not been able to consult many, but I am grateful to Pierre Lasserre and Michel Batisse for some papers from UNESCO, to Alain Gille for alerting me to the existence of 65 boxes of Jean-Paul Harroy's papers in the Belgian Royal Museum for Central Africa at Tervuren,[8] and to Gina Douglas, Librarian of the Linnean Society of London, where Max Nicholson's papers relating to the early years of WWF are housed.

Very near the end of the period available for this work, Fiona Hanson of IUCN sent me a copy of a Master's Thesis by Nathalie Liamine on the history of IUCN from 1948 to 1988.[9] I deliberately set this work aside, for use as an independent check on the accuracy of my researches. It has been invaluable in that capacity, and I was happy to find that Ms Liamine and I agree on almost all material points.

This whole venture has been very much the brain-child of my successor as Director-General of IUCN, David McDowell, himself a historian by discipline. He, with Jeffrey McNeely, led a steering committee which has been of immense help as a 'sounding board' and panel of friendly critics. Javed Ahmad, Director of Communications, Katherine Mann and others at IUCN headquarters have been unfailingly helpful and supportive. Finally my sincere thanks go to Elaine Shaughnessy, Head of the IUCN Publications Services Unit in Cambridge, UK, for her encouragement and help at all stages in the production of this work.

The statements in this book are my conclusions from the material I have seen. I am acutely conscious that because the time available for research and writing was short – about one year from start to finish – and I have had to weave the work in among many other commitments, the result is less complete and authoritative than I would have wished. One victim of this constraint has been an objective and thorough examination of how far the world community has gained from the existence of the 'green web', and of the benefits the members have received through belonging to it. I hope that time may allow a continuance of these researches in the future, for the subject matter is both fascinating and important to the history of our times.

1 The Springs of Conservation

The Universal Vision

Our remotest ancestors were so close to their environment that they would have found it hard to think of it as separate from themselves. When you live as hunters or fisherfolk, snatching your living directly from the wild, building your shelters from whatever the wild provides, and travelling afoot or in small boats you yourself have fashioned from branches, skins or tree trunks, your dependence on the environment is absolute, and knowledge of it is the key to survival. In such a setting, '*caring for the Earth is born when you are born*'.[1]

Human history has been one of progressive take-over of the flows of energy within natural systems, permitting ever-increasing human abundance and ubiquity. The impacts on the natural world have been immense. Early hunters altered ecosystems by fire, and by their extermination of many of the largest and slowest-breeding animals.[2] But agriculture – the taking of selected plants and animals into human ownership – had a more profound influence because it established the dichotomy between 'domesticated' and 'wild' and began the familiar struggle between the two.[3] Pastoralists slaughtered the wolves or lions that preyed on their flocks and herds, and killed the deer and antelopes that competed with their beasts for pasture. Agriculturalists attacked the 'weeds' they could not eat and guarded their crops against wild herbivores as best they could. These conflicts remain important today. In Africa, elephants and buffalo may be admired by foreign tourists, but they spell ruin to small cultivators if they invade their *shambas* overnight.

We call this process of transforming nature 'development', and over much of human history, and in most human societies even today, it is seen as something wholly admirable. Today's 'conservation movement' is, in a sense, counter-cultural because it argues that the transformation of nature has gone too far. It expresses a thought that many people still find alien – that nature needs protection *against* human society. That thought was born in the urbanized and industrialized world, where humanity has become both dominant and affluent – and has rediscovered the importance of the natural world to human welfare, human enjoyment and even human survival. But by treating people and nature as if they were separate, and by seeming at times to place wild creatures above humans, this 'Northern' protectionist thinking stepped out of line with the values of many parts of the world. One of the challenges IUCN and other conservation bodies face is how to bridge the cultures.

Reverence for nature is ancient and almost universal. Many peoples have sensed the presence of deities and spirits in the springs, the rivers, the deep forests, the wild hills and the storms. Many legends and histories reach back to that period when the world of nature was at the heart of the world of humanity, and the two could not be separated.[4,5] This ancient reverence led to special status for particular places: there have been sacred, protected forest areas (*abhayaranxyas*) in India for over 2000 years. There are other, ancient, protected forests in China and Nepal, and sacred groves in Ghana and other West African countries, while in the Pacific region the imposition of *tapu* (taboo) had the effect of creating sacred protected areas.[6,7] Asoka, Emperor of India, passed an edict for the protection of animals, fish and forests as long ago as 252 BC.[6] Among the Celts of ancient Europe, sacred trees were at the heart of religious ritual: when the Romans invaded the British Isle of Anglesey in 61 AD they destroyed the oak groves and the druids together.[8] Native Australians today look back to the roots of their culture in 'the dream time', linking place and history in a uniquely mystic way. Buddhism and Animism still recognize the holistic links between all living things, including human beings.[6]

Hunting was another ancient strand that became woven into the rope of conservation. Many peoples have developed rules that demand respect for the quarry and ensure that destructive 'overkill' is prevented.[5] The Maori word *rahui* denotes resources put off-limits to exploitation.[9] Almost mystical rituals link hunter and hunted in places as far apart as the high Arctic and tropical Asia.[5,6] European rulers – whether kings or feudal overlords – defined 'forests' as areas of land where they and their servants had sole rights to the game and were, as a consequence, able to control how much was taken, and how much was left. William of Normandy, who '*loved the stags as dearly as though he had been their father*',[10] decreed such a hunting reserve – still called the New Forest – before 1085. The Holy Roman Emperor Frederic II, who lived from 1194 to 1250, wrote a scholarly book on the art of falconry which included novel ideas about natural history and conservation.[11] In 1423 King Ladislas Jagellon of Poland is said to have promulgated a law restricting the hunting of wild horses, elks and aurochs.[12] The Mogul Emperor Babar is said to have hunted rhinos in special reserves established in the Punjab in the 15th century.[6] Several of today's famous Asian national parks, including Royal Chitwan in Nepal and Ujung Kulon in Java, were first established as hunting reserves.[6] More recently, 'game reserves' have been a feature of East and southern Africa for almost a century. The bond between hunter and hunted is reflected in modern hunting organizations – some of them members of IUCN – that are dedicated to the conservation of their quarries. The USA has been particularly strong in such organizations – perhaps in reaction to the fact that the European laws which gave a monopoly of hunting rights to landowners were rejected in the New World, and the lack of alternative controls led to wanton and excessive slaughter.[13] The importance of hunting controls is indicated by the fact that a high proportion of the world's governments have departments with responsibility for 'game' management.

In contrast, resource depletion and pollution are often thought of as recent problems. But there are signs that early civilizations were all too well aware of what happened when people got out of balance with the environment that supported them – although once they became urbanized they do not seem to have been very good at taking avoiding action. Western Eurasian settled agriculture first appeared thousands of years ago in the 'fertile crescent' along the valleys of the Tigris and Euphrates in what are now Syria, Iraq and Iran, and irrigation systems allowed a great boost to production, which supported a vast increase in human numbers and the building of great cities.[3] But problems of soil degradation, especially by salt accumulation, led to some Sumerian cities being abandoned 3700 years ago.[14,15] Too much tree-felling, followed by silting-up of the irrigation systems, seems to have underlain the decline of the Khmer culture that built the marvellous monuments of Angkor.[16] The collapse of the Mayan civilization has been ascribed to the population growing beyond the carrying capacity of the environment. Soil erosion following deforestation in Attica was condemned by Plato over 2000 years ago,[17] while only a little later Roman writers including Pliny warned that crop failures and soil loss were resulting from bad husbandry.[18] And pollution with water-borne sewage was a problem in imperial Rome, while air pollution from wood and coal smoke was a nuisance in cities such as London and Edinburgh in medieval times.[19]

The Origins of Western Conservation

Although many European rulers set up hunting reserves, nature reserves from which hunting was excluded were rare. But as early as 1569, the Swiss Canton of Glarus prohibited hunting on a mountain named the Karpfstock, thus establishing a game reserve that has been in existence for over four centuries.[20] In 1576 the Wood of the Hague was set aside by the then Prince of Orange and the State of Holland; in 1669 Colbert issued an ordinance to protect French forests and waters, although his motive was probably to secure good timber supplies for the Navy;[21] in 1826 Walton Park in England was made a bird sanctuary by its owner, Charles Waterton; in 1838 the first Czech Protected Area was created; and in 1858 Napoleon III protected part of the forest of Fontainebleau as the first nature reserve in France, albeit in response to the picturesque arguments of artists rather than the claims of naturalists.[22]

The European culture did not respect wild animals in their own right. Rooted in the Judaeo-Christian tradition, it has often been accused of interpreting Biblical references to the dominion of man over nature as a licence for unbridled exploitation. Love of animals was acceptable among saints, but a sign of oddity in the laity. Cuthbert might cherish the eider ducks of the Farne Islands, Hugh of Lincoln his swans, and Francis of Assisi proclaim the brotherhood and sisterhood of all the creation – but when Lady Glanville took an interest in butterflies this '*was regarded as so sure a sign of mental imbalance that her will was disputed on that ground*'. Even as late as 1823, the now-revered painter of birds, J J Audubon, complained that his friends regarded him as a madman![22]

The 'conservation movement' in 19th century Europe and North America seems to have sprung from three sources: the rediscovery of the romantic in nature, the scientific exploration of the natural world, and revulsion at the cruel destruction of some wild species, especially birds. One of the earliest and most influential writers was Gilbert White, whose *Natural History of Selborne*, which appeared in 1788, became the fourth most published book in the English language: it '*advocated simplicity and humility in order to restore man to peaceful co-existence with nature*'.[14,23] Jean Jacques Rousseau was especially important because he emphasized that nature was good and that the closer people were to nature the freer, happier and more honest they became.[24] His philosophical approach helped to create a new vision of human relationships with nature in Western European culture, later echoed in North America by Ralph Waldo Emerson, who wrote of nature as the first in time and in importance of all the influences on the human mind.[25] The influence of Romantic poets like William Wordsworth was also profound. In his youth, Wordsworth was overwhelmed by nature, which:

> '*To me was all in all. I cannot paint*
> *What then I was. The sounding cataract*
> *Haunted me like a passion: the tall rock,*
> *The mountain, and the deep and gloomy wood*
> *Their colours, and their forms, were then to me*
> *An appetite; a feeling and a love...*'[26]

Wordsworth wanted these beauties protected. He wrote in his *Guide to the Lakes*, published in 1810, that he hoped the Lake District would be treated as '*a sort of national property, in which every man has a right and interest who has an eye to perceive and a heart to enjoy*'.[27] Goethe, Emerson, Hardy, Whitman and many others brought a sensitivity to nature into the drawing rooms of all who aspired to be culti-vated. Essayists and keen observers like Henry David Thoreau, Richard Jefferies and W H Hudson sketched a more believable countryside. Hudson argued that nature protection must be a part of any true culture, while Thoreau, who has been described as '*the spiritual founder of the modern crusade to preserve what is left of our wilder-ness*',[28] argued that '*in wilderness is the preservation of the world*'. Books about natural history, often beautifully illustrated, by authors like Buffon, Redouté, Audubon, Gould and many others appeared on the shelves of the educated rich.

These contributions to literature were flanked and stimulated by the reports of European, and later, American voyagers. As Europe became wealthy and learned to build that first master-weapon, the ocean-going ship equipped with cannons, so its exploration of the world expanded and science, commerce and colonization marched hand in hand.[29] For the explorers of the time, and their masters at home, the world was an empty place: they respected its inhabitants only where they had civilizations and material attainments to match their own (though this did not stop the conquest of India, the destruction of the Mexican and Inca cultures, or conflict in China). Much of the Americas, Africa, Australasia and Asia were perceived of as 'uncivilized' and available for settlement by more 'advanced' Europeans, who made a virtue out of their appropriation by imposing their religion, agriculture, education and cultural assumptions.[29]

The colonists also took their familiar plants and animals with them, acclimatiz-ing European trees, shrubs, garden plants, mammals and birds in all suitable (and many unsuitable) habitats around the world.[29] These translocations have proved devastating to many native species, including Australian marsupials and New Zealand trees and native birds. On the credit side, the sharing of the staple food plants among the continents undoubtedly aided human quality of life: where would Africa be without American maize, Europe without Andean potatoes, or North America without Eurasian wheat?

Many explorers took naturalists along with them, and they brought back speci-mens of new species and published narratives of their journeys which excited popular interest. The reports of world-travelling scientists like Sir Joseph Banks (who accom-panied Captain James Cook in the Pacific), Charles Darwin, whose *Voyage of the Beagle* stands head and shoulders above the crowd,[30] and Joseph Hooker, who accom-panied Sir James Clark Ross from 1839 to 1843 and deduced that '*land in the Antarctic regions...before the glacial period might well have been clothed with vegetation*',[31] had an immense influence on perceptions of the natural world.

Science itself nurtured new insights. The Swedish naturalist, Carl von Linné (known universally as Linnaeus) laid the foundation of modern natural history by devising a concise and universally applicable system of classification of plants and animals. The intellectual world reeled from the shock of Darwin's *Origin of Species*, published in 1858.[32] The German geographer, Alexander von Humboldt, is credited by many with being first to promote the idea of nature protection alongside other ideas about what we would now call ecological inter-relationships.[12] In North America, George Perkins Marsh (whose studies extended to Europe, the Mediterranean basin and parts of Asia as well as the degraded farmlands of his native Vermont) wrote the world's first major treatise on humanity's destructive impact on the natural world: *Man and Nature; or, Physical Geography as Modified by Human Action.*[33]

In 1866, two years after Marsh's book appeared, the German scientist Ernst Haeckel first used the term 'ecology', to describe the web that linked organisms and their surrounding environment.[34] The concept evolved in two distinct – but linked – directions. One was philosophical and political, emphasizing the dependence of people on one another, and the strength of their roots in nature, and expressed in the beliefs of Monism – an optimistic, nature-based, philosophy that rejected the Christian emphasis on redemption through suffering. Monism was summed up by Haeckel in 1894:

> '*Monism teaches us that we are...children of the earth who, for one or two or three generations, have the good fortune to enjoy its treasures...to drink the inexhaustible fountain of its beauty, and to trace out the marvellous play of its forces.*'[34,35]

Later in life, Haeckel attacked Christianity for elevating humans above nature. Humanity was part of nature and nature was beauty and order.[34] His philosophy was pacifist and while '*monism began as a materialistic creed, before Haeckel's death it had moved to a vitalist position, where all was one, but all was spirit*'.[34] But the nature-based ideas put around by Haeckel and his many associates were also used to justify various back-to-the-land movements, which gained popularity in Europe in the 1920s, as part of the quest for cultural rebirth after the grief and destruction of the First World War.[34] They demanded ecological awareness, life according to ecological principles and the maintenance of ecological balances. In some ways they were forerunners of the post-Second World War green movement.

The academic ecologists were meanwhile almost literally stalking off into the wilderness.[36] They adopted Haeckel's concept of a science that would explain the workings of the interdependent 'web of life', but not his philosophy. They explored Darwin's assertion that '*plants and animals, most remote in the scale of nature, are bound together by a web of complex relations*'.[32] Thomas Henry Huxley saw evolution as a '*harmonious order governing eternally continuous progress, the web and woof of matter and force interweaving by slow degrees...*'.[37] The basic concepts of ecology – the community as a group of associated species, characteristic of a particular situation; succession, as an orderly process by which species and communities follow one another as the habitat is changed by biological or physical processes; and the ecosystem as an assembly of interacting plants and animals, together with those parts of the physical environment with which they interact – were elaborated by such scientists as Clements, Duvigneaud, Elton, Leopold, Odum, Shelford and Tansley from observations of 'natural' environments. The aim of scientific ecologists was to get as far away from human influence as possible, and study 'pristine nature'. They described the fragments of quasi-natural habitat, and the vegetation types they supported, as evidence of the nature that was there before human impact.[38] Despite

George Perkins Marsh, it took quite a long time for the universality of human impact to sink in, and longer for academic ecology to join the mainstream of social action.

The third major stimulus to conservation in Europe and North America came from the destructive exploitation of nature. The devastation of bison in the USA and of elephants and other 'game' species in southern Africa, the massacre of egrets, gulls and other species for the fashion trade and the extinction of the once abundant passenger pigeon in 1914 all fuelled demands for action. The State of Massachusetts passed a law to protect useful birds as early as 1818.[28] During the late 1860s, a group of German farmers and foresters who were worried about the ravages of insect pests following the destruction of their natural predators, formed a bird protection organization.[12] In the 1860s the shooting of seabirds off the British coast inspired the Seabirds Act of 1869, followed by three other laws to protect wild birds,[14,39] and a couple of decades later revulsion against the killing of birds to provide wings, plumes and feathers for women's fashions led to new action. This was probably the first nature-protection campaign with wide public roots: indeed women led the campaign against the slaughter of birds for other women's adornment.[22] In the USA the campaign was boosted in 1905 by the murder of an Audubon Society warden by an egret hunter: in this period egret plumes were fetching $32 an ounce – twice the price of gold.[13]

The Conservation Movement Begins

These strands were woven into national action in many countries. It took two early forms – the establishment of national societies to protect various kinds of animal, and the creation of the first national parks and nature reserves.

The Society for the Protection of Animals (later the Royal Society for the Prevention of Cruelty to Animals) was founded in Britain in 1824 and by the 1870s was campaigning against 'cruel sports'. Action for bird protection can be traced to 1845, when Dr Edward Baldamus proposed the protection of animals, and birds in particular, to the first assembly of the German Ornithological Society.[12] The Société Nationale de Protection de la Nature et d'Acclimatation de France was founded in 1854.[40] The German Bird Protection Society appeared in 1875[12] and the predecessor of the British Royal Society for the Protection of Birds in 1889.[41] In the USA, the American Ornithologists Union dates from 1883, while in 1886 George Blake Grinnell, who grew up on the Audubon estate, led the action to protect birds against plumage hunters: the eventual result was the National Audubon Society.[28] In 1886 Grinnell was also co-founder, with Theodore Roosevelt, of the Boone and Crockett Club, whose members had to be hunters, but whose mission was to conserve their quarry.[13]

Even if Wordsworth was first in print, the modern national parks movement was unquestionably born in the USA. In 1864 the Congress granted the Yosemite Valley to the State of California on condition that it was '*held for public use, resort and recreation...inalienable for all time*'. The world's first site to be defined in law as a National Park – Yellowstone – was established by Congress in 1872. It is interesting that Lieutenant Gustavus Doane, who inspected the site and advised Congress to create the Park, did not see it just as a protected wilderness. He wrote: '*as a field for scientific research it promises great results...it is probably the greatest laboratory that nature furnishes on the surface of the globe*'.[42] The trickle of parks which started at Yellowstone soon became a flood, spreading from North America to Europe and to the many parts of the world colonized by Europeans.[29] Australia established its first Royal National Park in 1879, Banff in Canada followed in 1885, and Tongariro in New Zealand in 1894 (although the mountain at its heart had been sacred to the Maori people for generations before). The oldest National Park in Africa is Tsitsikamma Indigenous Forest in Cape Province, South Africa, dating from 1890, while Europe was led by Sweden, which established six parks in 1909. Iguazu and Bariloche (=Nahuel Huapi) in Argentina were the first in South America, but date only from 1934.[43,44]

Whatever Lt. Doane had thought about research, Yellowstone was never developed in this way: one participant in its centenary celebrations in 1972 records that nobody could tell him of a single significant ecological research result obtained there.[45] Instead, the American National Parks soon became expressions of the values of John Muir, founder of the Sierra Club in 1892, who was the unrivalled prophet of the wilderness. Echoing Thoreau, Muir preached that '*while God's glory was written over all his works, in the wilderness the letters were capitalized*'.[14] His ideal national parks were large tracts of wild land with no, or few, human inhabitants (where there were indigenous people, their forced removal was seen as a necessity). The approach clearly only worked where empty space abounded or could be created: in Europe such parks were rarer and much smaller (even the Swiss National Park, established in 1914 in a part of the Alps that had previously been devastated by the metal-smelting industry, extends to only 16,887 hectares compared with the 899,139 hectares of Yellowstone or the stupendous 3,382,014 hectares of the Wrangell–St Elias Park in Alaska).[44] Arguments over what constituted a 'real' national park have run through succeeding decades, including the whole history of IUCN, but for many years it was the unpeopled 'Yellowstone model' that most nations aspired to copy.

There was a clear conceptual divide between Muir's quest to preserve natural wilderness as the most glorious expression of the divine creation and the more materialistic concept of conservation for sustainable production. That second approach was given impetus by Gifford Pinchot in the USA, but he may well have imported the concept of forest management for sustainable yield from Europe, where he had studied and where it had become the central concept of the German and French schools of forestry.[14] It had also been exported to British colonial possessions such as India. Pinchot found the almost mystic vision of Muir hard to grasp: instead he proposed three guiding principles for natural resource management: '*the use of existing resources for the present generation; the prevention of waste, and the development of natural resources for the many rather than the few*'.[14,46] As Chief Forester under President Theodore Roosevelt, Pinchot was the architect of the United States Forest Service and of a professional approach to the management of public forests.[28]

President Roosevelt was the first leader of a major nation (indeed the first leader of *any* modern nation) to put conservation at the heart of a national agenda.[28] He was a rancher, big-game hunter, camper, amateur entomologist and lifelong nature lover with '*almost an Indian veneration for trees, particularly the giant conifers he encountered in the Rockies*'.[47] He was influenced by John Muir (with whom he camped in the Sierras in 1903), and Muir was probably the driving force behind the addition of Yosemite Valley to the surrounding National Park and the creation of 53 wildlife reserves, 16 national monuments and five new national parks in the Roosevelt era.[14,28,48] But Pinchot (who had advised Roosevelt when the latter was Governor of New York State) was the President's right-hand man on conservation issues.[28]

Together they preached that conservation was '*an issue of democracy. The resources of the public domain were to be used for the benefit of all the people, not just the powerful*'.[28]

The divide between Muir and Pinchot was not absolute: Muir did accept some forest exploitation, and the two did cooperate to keep national forests in public ownership.[49] Both may well have had a hand in Roosevelt's proposal for a National Conservation Commission which was to make the first survey of natural resources throughout the USA: this foundered, however, when Congress refused funding.[14] The tripartite partnership during the last years of the 19th and early years of the 20th centuries was important because it implanted the two concepts of absolute protection of 'wilderness' national parks, and of sustainable resource management elsewhere, into mainstream American action, and this in turn had a powerful international influence.[14,50] But the debate between Muir and Pinchot has echoed down the years, and while Pinchot's concept of conservation as 'sustainable use' has dominated the approach of official government agencies, Muir's preservationism has equally impelled many parts of the non-governmental conservation movement and was taken up anew by the environmentalists of the mid-20th century.[28] The dichotomy is still apparent in IUCN General Assemblies today and runs through the whole of this history.

President Theodore Roosevelt made many statements that would be considered 'green' even today, when the value-spectrum shows such a marked 'green-shift'. Here are some extracts from a longer compilation, itself derived from numerous writings:[50]

> '*There can be no greater issue than that of conservation in this country. Conservation is a great moral issue, for it involves the patriotic duty of insuring the safety and continuance of the nation...[I] do not intend that our natural resources shall be exploited by the few against the interests of the many, nor do [I] intend to turn them over to any man who will wastefully use them by destruction, and leave to those who come after a heritage damaged by just so much...trees must not be cut down more rapidly than they are replaced...birds should be saved: the extermination of the passenger pigeon means that mankind was just so much poorer, exactly as in the case of the destruction of the cathedral at Rheims...the rights of the public to the natural resources outweigh private rights and must be given its first consideration.*'

The American concept of national parks as large natural areas, safeguarded against Man the Destroyer was clearly difficult to export to densely-peopled and much-altered regions like Western Europe. Here, landscape protection as a means of preserving the natural beauty of a peopled countryside, and nature reserves as small areas, set up to protect flora and fauna, were more prominent. A French Society for the Protection of Rural Areas appeared in 1901.[12] In Britain, the National Trust was born in 1895 from a movement to safeguard Wordsworth's Lake District, and progressively acquired areas of outstanding scenery.[51] Other voluntary bodies like the Council for the Preservation of Rural England (with counterparts in Wales and Scotland) encouraged this process. By the 1920s and 1930s the steady outward sprawl of suburbia into a countryside suffering from agricultural depression had made landscape protection the dominant conservation concern in the UK. Town and Country Planning emerged as a new discipline (one of its founders being Patrick Geddes, a botanist), and legislation was introduced to curb ribbon development along highways and impose more general statutory planning.[52] Geddes' work in turn inspired Lewis Mumford in the USA, who cried out against all-pervading urbanization.[28]

The Nature Reserves movement was, in some ways, a blend of the National Parks and Species Protection initiatives. The earliest manifestations were the sanctuary areas where hunting was forbidden, as on the Karpfstock. There was an early initiative in Germany, under Professor H Conwentz of the Prussian State Department for Nature Protection.[53] The American National Parks movement had led to the establishment of over 50 wildlife reserves before President Roosevelt's term of office ended.[14] In Britain, Charles Waterton's Walton Park bird reserve was half a century ahead of the first National Park at Yellowstone. The Society for the Promotion of Nature Reserves (SPNR) was created in 1912 by N Charles Rothschild, who was among the first to recognize the losses among wild species as a result of land use changes.[54] Between 1912 and 1915, and in some instances drawing on the support of members of the British Ecological Society (which appeared in 1913), he organized a survey of the remaining outstanding wildlife habitats in Great Britain and Ireland and identified 273 key sites.[53–55] A few of them were purchased by the SPNR and established as reserves, but Rothschild's death in 1923 contributed to the arrest of the initiative, which did not really resume until the period of the Second World War.

The Movement Goes International

As the tide of national action swelled, it spilled over to the international level, starting with birds. In 1872 the Swiss Federal Council proposed the establishment of a Commission to consider the case for an International Convention for the Protection of Birds, and the subject was discussed in 1873 at a Congress of Agriculture held in Vienna.[56] The idea was also pushed forward in Sweden by the polar explorer Otto Nordenskjold in 1880. Nothing much (except renewed talk) happened at the Second Ornithological Congress in Budapest in 1891. But in 1894 a committee was established to consider which species needed protection.[56] In 1895 the First Conference for the Protection of Birds was held in Paris – and it attempted a classification of birds into useful, wild and injurious, all from the standpoint of agriculture.[20] The follow-up came in 1902 when an International Convention for the Preservation of Useful Birds was signed by 12 European countries (not including Great Britain).[56] In 1916 the USA and Britain, and later Mexico and Japan, signed a Migratory Birds Treaty.[13]

In 1910 the Fifth Ornithological Congress decided to establish a permanent organization concerned with bird protection. A Conference for the Protection of Birds was convened in London in 1922 by an American, T Gilbert Pearson, and it was then that one of the bodies that has been a steady presence on the conservation scene for three-quarters of a century was created – the International Council for Bird Preservation (ICBP), now BirdLife International. Until the International Union for the Preservation of Nature (IUPN) was founded in 1948, the ICBP was the only fully-fledged global conservation organization.[11]

The ICBP's creators came from only four nations – France, the Netherlands, the UK and the USA – and the Committee did not meet until 1928 when 17 nations were represented at its first official assembly in Geneva. This is scarcely evidence of dynamic action or high political priority – although from the very beginning ICBP was propelled by a daunting human dynamo, Phyllis Barclay-Smith of the UK. The Committee saw the revision of the 1902 Paris Convention as a high priority, but it was 1937 before the ICBP convened a major conference in Vienna to consider a more modern International Convention which would remove the distinction of 'usefulness' and provide protection for all birds. In 1938 the International Ornithological Congress in Rouen discussed the special problems of endangered ducks and geese, agreed that reserves for migratory birds should be established in all countries, and set up a sub-committee to study the problems associated with water pollution by oil from ships – first recognition of what was to become a massive problem 30 years later. By then the ICBP had become a major force, with European and pan-American continental sections, 28 national sections and a membership involving 135 scientific and hunting associations. Bird conservation was clearly up and flying, although it was not until 1950 that the new International Convention on Bird Preservation was finally adopted in Paris.[56]

Other animals had done less well. Unrestricted hunting of 'big game' and its destruction by settlers caused alarm in Germany, Britain and the USA in the 1890s.[14] In 1900 a conference on preserving the African fauna from extinction was held in London: it even agreed the text of a Convention for the Preservation of Animals, Birds and Fish in Africa, but this never entered into force (though it was later useful as a draft). It did, however, stimulate the creation in 1903 of the Society for Preservation of the Wild Fauna and Flora of the (British) Empire (which evolved into the Fauna Preservation Society, later the Fauna and Flora Preservation Society and now Fauna and Flora International).[14] In 1901 the International Congress of Zoology met in Berlin and '*adopted a resolution in favour of the protection of all non-injurious animals belonging to the more developed species, menaced by the spread of cultivation*'.[20] In 1931 the first convention for the regulation of whaling was agreed by 11 nations – a weak agreement that set no total quotas, but did put young whales and females with young 'off limits' to commercial whalers. It was improved in 1937 and 1938, but it was not until 1946 that new machinery was set in place, and even that, as is well known, failed in its stated task.

If animals (apart from birds) did not do well at the hands of the legislators, plants received even less attention. There was a recommendation at the 1905 International Botanical Congress in Vienna that certain highly interesting plant species be safeguarded, and nothing much then happened until 1935 when the Sixth Botanical Congress in Amsterdam recommended the establishment of large protected areas, including forests closed to exploitation, and urged that foreign tree species should not be planted amongst native ones. You need only look anywhere in Europe, North America, Costa Rica, temperate South America, China, New Zealand and South Africa (and many other countries) to see how little impact this last proposal has had.

Artists as well as scientists supported international action for conservation. At the second Congrès International d'Art Public, held in September 1905 at Liège, Raoul de Clermont proposed a motion '*that the necessary steps be taken to create national parks for the purpose of saving indigenous animals, plants and minerals from destruction*'.[43] He developed his plans at an international congress for protection of landscapes in 1909, an international literary and artistic congress in 1910, and a further congress in 1911 where he submitted a draft diplomatic convention for the creation of an international bureau for the protection of regional art and for the protection of nature.[43] In 1913 he urged the creation of a standing international commission and an international bureau or office which would serve as a clearing house for documents and information concerning the protection of natural sites and monuments.[43]

There were important initiatives in America. In 1902 an International Association of Game, Fish and Conservation Commissioners was founded there. In 1909 delegates from Canada, the USA and Mexico met at the White House and recommended President Roosevelt to convene an International Conservation Conference in Washington DC, on the '*subject of world resources and their inventory, conservation and wise utilization*'.[57] Roosevelt agreed – the request clearly chimed with his personal beliefs[50] – but asked the Netherlands' government to act as host. Fifty-eight nations were invited to meet at The Hague in September 1909 – but before it could happen, Roosevelt had been succeeded as President by W H Taft who killed the project by withdrawing American support, and not long afterwards dismissed Gifford Pinchot as head of the Forest Service.[14,28,57] As many of Roosevelt's conservation policies were undone by his successors, as Pinchot was marginalized, and as John Muir aged (he died in 1914), American leadership of conservation lapsed for several decades.[28] The baton passed back to Europe.

It was picked up by Paul Sarasin, born in Basel, the son of a Swiss banker. His interest may have been stimulated by the widespread signs of environmental destruction in the Alps, which were then more densely populated than they are now, and suffered from landslides and floods following deforestation and overgrazing.[58] He was also upset by the destruction of indigenous peoples in many parts of the world.[59] Sarasin and his cousin Fritz were founders of the Ligue Suisse pour la Protection de la Nature (the 'Swiss League') in 1909, with Paul as the first President,[60] and only a year later, when the Eighth International Congress of Zoology met at Graz, he was proposing '*a Committee charged to establish an international or world Commission for the protection of nature...throughout the world, from the North Pole to the South Pole, and covering both continents and seas*'.[20,56, 57]

The Congress of Zoology agreed to establish a provisional committee, and Sarasin persuaded the Swiss Federal Council to sponsor its proposal for an international Commission, as a framework for consultation. In 1913 representatives of 17 nations (Argentina, Austria, Belgium, Denmark, France, Germany, Hungary, Italy, the Netherlands, Norway, Portugal, Russia, Sweden, Switzerland, the UK and the USA) met in Berne and agreed to establish a Consultative Commission for the International Protection of Nature. The Commission was to be based at Basel, and to assemble and publish information: in 1914 it was formally constituted, with 14 participant states. Even at this early date the delegates were at pains to emphasize that the foundation of the Consultative Commission would impose no obligatory costs on states![61,62] But the war came and put the whole venture into a troubled shade.

Sarasin did not give up. In 1921, when peace was once more firmly established, he began to press for the reconstitution of the Consultative Commission. He had made contact (thanks to the Dutch conservationist Pieter van Tienhoven) with Professor J A van Hamel, head of the legal division at the League of Nations, who advised him to make an approach to the League through the Swiss Federal Government.[63] However, the latter refused to take action, saying they thought the political circumstances unpropitious. Only seven states supported reconstituting the Commission (Austria, Canada, France, Japan, New Zealand, the Netherlands and Poland). Although a First International Congress for the Protection of Nature, again with representatives of 17 states, met in Paris in 1923 and urged that the Commission be reconvened, this too fell upon deaf Swiss ears and after Paul Sarasin died in 1929 the Commission lingered in a kind of suspended animation until 1946.[20]

Enter Pieter Gerbrand van Tienhoven, born on 19 November 1875 in Amsterdam.[63] He had, in 1905, become a member of the Board of the Society for the Promotion of Nature Reserves in the Netherlands and was one of its key figures for nearly half a century, serving as Treasurer from 1907 to 1953, and doubling as Chairman between 1927 and 1952. He was also an active promoter of bird conservation, and had been involved in protecting birds of paradise against excessive trading in what was then the Dutch East Indies. His outlook was far from narrowly European: he had many contacts in the USA (which he had visited), and had been a Dutch delegate to the meeting in London in 1922 which founded the ICBP.[63] By then he was clearly strongly committed to international conservation: in August 1924 he wrote to W T Hornaday, Director of the New York Zoological Park and crusader for North American wildlife: '*I hope we are getting nearer to joining together hands of the friends of Nature for International Protection, which is badly needed*'.[63]

Van Tienhoven was a believer in informal, unofficial, groups of the like-minded. He had been impressed by the British Correlating Committee for the Protection of Nature, established in 1924 under the auspices of the SPNR, which brought together people from various nature protection organizations.[63] In 1925 and 1926 he stimulated the creation of Netherlands, French and Belgian Committees for the Protection of Nature. In the latter year, their representatives visited London and pressed their British colleagues to join them in establishing an International Federation of Protectionist Associations. No action followed, and the ball was next bounced into the court of the International Union of Biological Sciences, at its General Assembly in 1928. A motion was adopted, favouring an International Union but in the meantime supporting the creation by the Belgian, French and Netherlands Committees of a Central Bureau of Information and Correlation. It began operations in 1928 with van Tienhoven as President, and with money from the Netherlands, Belgium and the USA.

The Bureau had a turbulent early history, riven by arguments, especially between the Belgian Board member, Victor van Straelen, and the first Director, J M Derscheid (who, incidentally, was also Secretary of the European section of the ICBP).[63] Derscheid was pushed out in 1933, to be succeeded by a Swede, Mrs Tordis Graim. In 1935 the Bureau was converted into an International Office for the Protection of Nature, constituted as a non-governmental organization financed through a separate Foundation for International Nature Protection, and steered by a General Council with members from Belgium, France, Great Britain, Italy, the Netherlands, Switzerland and the USA. The office built up an outstanding library (some of which remains as the Tienhoven Library at IUCN) and produced an 'International Review of Legislation for the Protection of Nature', but it had scarcely started before war once more spread across Europe and blighted the whole venture. In 1940 Mrs Graim returned to Sweden, and the office was transferred to Amsterdam to be directed by one of Paul Sarasin's old correspondents – Dr W A J M van Waterschoot van der Gracht.

In the inter-war years there were also several regional initiatives. In 1929 the Fourth Pan-Pacific Science Congress in Java led to the inauguration of a Permanent Committee for the Protection of Nature in the Pacific. In 1933 a Conference for the Preservation of African Fauna was held in London and dusted off the ineffective text of 1902, adopting a new Convention for the Protection of African Fauna and Flora which was signed by Belgium, Egypt, France, Italy, Portugal, Spain, the Sudan (then an Anglo-Egyptian Protectorate), the UK and the Union of South Africa. It is a sobering measure of how much the world map has changed in 60 years that these, together with Liberia and Abyssinia (Ethiopia), were the only governments that held sway on the African continent at that time (and Abyssinia was annexed by Italy in 1936). The

Convention promoted the creation of national parks and reserves, prohibited hunting from motor vehicles and aircraft, and set down other regulations to control hunting and trade in hunting trophies and in articles made from them.

The American Contribution

Although conservation lost its influence at the highest level in the USA when Taft succeeded Roosevelt, and did not emerge again in the White House until the second Roosevelt – Theodore's second cousin Franklin Delano – took up office in 1933, many individual American conservationists and many American societies continued the work.[28] The Sierra Club lost some of its steam after Muir died, but the Izaak Walton League, founded to safeguard wetlands, rivers and fishing waters, the National Wildlife Federation, the More Game Birds Foundation (later Ducks Unlimited) and the Wilderness Society all sprang up between 1920 and 1936.[13,28] By 1927 the Izaak Walton League had more than 100,000 members in 43 states.[13] Several of these societies found themselves in conflict with the US Bureau of Biological Survey (later US Fish and Wildlife Service), which was supposed to conserve game birds: in a daring conversion of poacher to gamekeeper F D Roosevelt appointed the campaigning cartoonist J N 'Ding' Darling, as chief of the Survey. He lost no time in proposing a North American Wildlife Conference, and President Roosevelt convened it in February 1936. One result was the creation of what became in 1938 the National Wildlife Federation, initially started by hunters to protect waterfowl breeding and feeding grounds.[13] A second consequence was the first National Wildlife Week, proclaimed by President Roosevelt in 1938: the proclamation called on all citizens to give thought to the need for conservation, stressing that '*only through the full cooperation of all can wildlife be restored for the present generation and perpetuated for posterity*'.[64]

Some American conservationists pressed for action abroad. In 1919 two such men, John C Merriam and Fairfield Osborn, joined with Victor van Straelen to commend the case for national parks in the Congo to King Albert of the Belgians. They pointed out that such parks could be used not only to preserve beautiful landscapes and endangered animals, but as places where what we now call ecosystems could be subjected to systematic study. The Albert (later Virunga) National Park, created in 1925, and the adjacent Parc des Volcans in Rwanda (1930), arose from that discussion.[22] All three scientists had subsequent links with IUPN, Osborn and van Straelen being among its creators and Merriam being a relative of the Union's first staff ecologist and later Director-General, Lee Merriam Talbot.

In the period between the two World Wars the scientific contribution to conservation was also building up in the USA. In the early 1920s, Aldo Leopold and M W Talbot established the first legally-designated Wilderness Area – the Gila Wilderness Area.[65] Leopold – yet another hunter-conservationist, and a founder of the Wilderness Society – had done fundamental research on the interactions between prey and predators which led him to see that species could only be understood and protected when their habitats were also understood, and that in an environment dominated by people, humans had to act to maintain ecological balance.[28] He drew his understandings together in a seminal book, *Game Management*, published in 1933.[66] The sciences of wildlife management, range management and soil conservation emerged as applied disciplines, and still underpin much of conservation today. Leopold's *Sand County*

Almanac, with its poetic and philosophical tone, had a powerful influence on how people thought about nature. He echoed Haeckel, for example in his statement that '*all ethics rest upon a single premise: that the individual is a member of a community of interdependent parts*'. He also called for a new 'land ethic' which would change '*the role of Homo sapiens from conqueror of the land community to plain member and citizen of it*'.[67]

American conservationists began to work in Asia and Africa as well as the western hemisphere. Harold Jefferson Coolidge, who was to loom so large in the history of IUCN, travelled with the Harvard Medical Expedition to Africa in 1926–27 and the Kelley–Roosevelt Expedition to Asia in 1928–29. In 1937 he organized and led an expedition that studied primates in Asia. Coolidge made the first zoological survey of north-west Tonkin and northern Laos, and was the first to point out the behavioural similarities between the pygmy chimpanzee or bonobo (*Pan paniscus*) and humans.[68–70] These expeditions were the foundation of his lifelong commitment to global conservation.

In 1930, Hal Coolidge, with other members of the Boone and Crockett Club, established the American Committee for International Wildlife Protection, composed of representatives of the most important American institutions interested in zoology and the preservation of wildlife.[68] This was stimulated partly by his own experiences in Africa, partly by the American role in the creation of the national parks in the Belgian Congo, and particularly by concern over the status of African animals among members of the Boone and Crockett Club and others who had hunted, photographed and studied them. Interest in the work of the Society for the Protection of the Fauna of the Empire led to the idea of an American body which would also support international action to protect nature. American naturalists had also been asked to help the International Office for the Protection of Nature, which was facing disaster through lack of funds.[20]

Conservation was strongly supported by President Roosevelt, who pushed forward policies for soil conservation, land management and the protection and extension of national forests.[28] At non-governmental level, the American Committee worked from 1930 onwards to build up data on the protection of nature in all parts of the world. It gave financial support to van Tienhoven's International Office.[56] It advised governments on new protective laws. It promoted the London Convention of 1933 and the Convention for the Protection of Nature and Wild Life in the Western Hemisphere, drafted in 1940. It issued some important reports on, for example, *African Game Protection*, *Migratory Bird Protection in North America*, *Nature Protection in the Netherlands Indies*, and the *Present Status of the Musk-Ox*. And it was particularly active in stimulating public interest and knowledge, issuing volumes on extinct or near-extinct mammals and on the state of nature protection in different countries. It produced books for the American armed forces in the Pacific on the environment, flora, fauna and indigenous populations of that region.

After the Second World War, the American conservation movement became even more active. The American Committee drew the attention of the State Department to the eight conventions relating to nature protection for which the USA had assumed responsibility and urged action to protect the many species in the Pacific islands, to which war had done severe damage. The New York Zoological Society – which, like its UK counterpart, the Zoological Society of London, is actually a national organization with international interests – founded the Conservation Foundation, as a springboard for wider international action.[71] American organizations were influencing conservation throughout the western hemisphere and in Asia and Africa. The

American Committee had well-forged links with van Tienhoven's Centre in Amsterdam. Personal contacts between European and American naturalists undoubtedly stimulated action on both sides of the Atlantic.

In 1944 the USA was on the brink of leadership of the international conservation movement. In October of that year, as the war was entering its closing climax, President Roosevelt proposed a meeting of '*the united and associated nations*' for '*the first step towards conservation and use of natural resources*'. He added, perceptively, in a memorandum to Secretary of State Cordell Hull that '*I am more and more convinced that conservation is a basis of permanent peace*'.[72] Had he not died before these ideas could be acted upon, the meetings that created the International Union for the Protection of Nature might well have been held on the American side of the Atlantic, the Union might have had 'Conservation' rather than 'Protection' in its title from the outset, American commitment (and finance) might have been guaranteed from the beginning, and the pattern of history might have been very different. For as Miriam Rothschild, who participated in both the Brunnen Conference that discussed the new International Union and the Fontainebleau Conference that created it, has said:

> '*the Americans were the people who really had the ideas and were thinking big. But their kind of thinking didn't gel with the Europeans. I felt that if it was really going to succeed it would be through the American approach. The Americans may have been brash, and trod on people's toes, but the Europeans were too negative.*'[73]

The Scene in 1945

Before the Second World War, international nature conservation was clearly dominated by what we now call 'the developed world'. The ICBP was the only effective international organization, and it was small and restricted its efforts to birds. As Jean-Paul Harroy put it:

> '*before 1940, those who had already seen the need to protect nature were few in number, mostly naturalists, not well linked together, effectively concentrated in Europe and North America, overwhelmingly preoccupied with the disappearance of species and without real political influence*'.[74]

In the USA the political influence had been there – while a Roosevelt sat in the White House. As it was, the death of FDR saw political support for international conservation ejected into the wilderness much as it had been when his second cousin had left office in 1909.

Europe and North America remained the dominant influences after the war. When a revived Swiss initiative finally got an international group together at Brunnen in 1947, Argentina was the only South American nation represented, while the USA, Canada, Japan and New Zealand were the only other non-European participants. But this distortion was more apparent than real, for two reasons. First, world politics were still dominated by what has come to be called 'the North'. That, after all, was where the two most destructive wars in human history started, although their battlefields spread over many distant lands. Second, in 1945, the world was still in the colonial era. Virtually the whole of Africa was administered from Europe (South Africa, although self-governing, was a British Dominion, and although Egypt, Ethiopia and Liberia were independent, the Anglo-French Suez Canal interests had immense political power in the former). All of continental South and South-east Asia was also ruled from Europe, except for Thailand (which had cleverly played the French off against the British, and so maintained its independence) and China (which, however, was torn by Japanese invasion and post-war civil strife), while the island states of the Caribbean and the Pacific were variously dominated by the European powers, the USA, Australia and New Zealand.

Against this background, the efforts of the Swiss League to revitalize action for world nature protection in 1946 seem mildly surprising. Time had moved on since Paul Sarasin's death. Switzerland had lived through the war as an island of clean, green, ordered neutrality while violence and cruelty raged about its borders. Now those surrounding lands were gripped by change, as the era of post-war reconstruction began. New ideas about conservation had emerged, especially in the USA and the UK. Despite Paul Sarasin's legacy, Switzerland would not have been thought of as the natural cradle of a new global conservation organization.

2 The Path to Union

Rebuilding for Peace

There were two priorities in the immediate post-war period: national reconstruction and the creation of a new international order to maintain peace and security. The United Nations was established in 1944. It was a union of nation-states, then seen as the essential building blocks of the global fabric. It had an Economic and Social Council, dedicated to new economic planning. Between 1944 and 1950 a series of specialized UN agencies was constituted, among which the Food and Agriculture Organization had a particular responsibility for natural resources, including forests and fisheries, while the Educational, Scientific and Cultural Organization fostered research and education of many kinds, and had direct links with the scientific world.[1,2]

UNESCO's first Director-General was the British biologist Julian Huxley. Before he took the job, he had chaired a Wild Life Conservation Special Committee which drew up new national plans for nature conservation.[3,4,5] The Committee's approach had three features which later pervaded the Anglo-American approach at international level. First, a number of leading ecologists (including Arthur Tansley, Charles Elton, Owain Richards and Edward Salisbury) were centrally involved, very much as Aldo Leopold and others had been in the United States. Second (and again paralleling the situation in America), it was accepted that conservation had to link ecological science to public policy, but it also had to make the limitations of science clear to a world that believed that technology could fix everything. And as Fairfield Osborn, then President of the New York Zoological Gardens, wrote in his pioneering book *Our Plundered Planet* in 1948, science could not '*provide a substitute for the elemental workings of nature*'.[6] Third, the British shared a new philosophy of nature protection with the Americans. The key lay in

> '*a more positive and constructive message. The backward looking word, preserve, was used less and less. Another "ordinary" English word, conserve, took its place. First in America and then in Britain, it came to imply not only protection but also the enhancement of wildlife populations. There was nothing really new in the idea of statutory land-use planning and scientific management of land and natural resources, and yet these were perceived to be the exciting dimensions of post-war reconstruction.*'[4]

In Britain, a new Nature Conservancy and a new National Parks Commission were created as part of the wider process of social and economic reconstruction. In mainland Europe the dominant concern was with rebuilding shattered towns, industries, economies and communities – aided by American funds, through the Marshall Plan. From Switzerland, Paul Sarasin's heir as Chairman of the Swiss League, Charles Bernard, and its Secretary, Johann Büttikofer, looked outwards at the turmoil of post-war activity, and felt that the threats to nature had redoubled. The Dutch initiative seemed to them to have been a victim of war, for while van Tienhoven and his Office survived, their fortunes were at a low ebb.[7] And – no doubt contemplating the flurry of activity in the United Nations – they sensed that the time was now ripe for international action. As Bernard put it: '*after this last war it was no longer considered, as in 1920, that the protection of nature was a kind of ideology which should be shelved in the face of more pressing material needs*'.[8] They prepared an initiative.

A Tour in Switzerland

An opportunity soon presented itself. In 1945, Julian Huxley (wearing his British hat as Chairman of the Wild Life Conservation Special Committee) visited the Swiss National Park in the Engadine with Eduard Handschin, Chairman of the Scientific Committee of the Swiss National Park. Huxley was impressed, and suggested that his hosts should invite a party of leading British conservationists to learn from Swiss experience.

Bernard and Büttikofer saw their opportunity and moved into action. They took over the initiative from Handschin, persuading the Swiss League to let them organize a tour in the summer of 1946 to show the British their nature reserves and the National Park. But as Charles Bernard explained in his address of welcome, they decided – without telling the British – to expand both the theme and the party.[2,9,10] Max Nicholson believes that this was very much a personal initiative by the two organizers.[10] Both men were dedicated to conservation, and Charles Bernard had a particular international perspective. A botanist and plant pathologist by discipline, after graduating from the University of Geneva he had worked for over 20 years on crop diseases in the Netherlands East Indies (now Indonesia) rising to become Director of the Department of Agriculture, Industry and Trade.[7,11] For his part, Johann Büttikofer made a major personal contribution to the rebuilding of nature conservation in Germany in the post-war period.[12]

On 30 June 17 people gathered at the headquarters of the League in Basel, and their tour took in Zernez, Cluozza, Pontresina and Lugano, before they dined at the Hotel Waldstätterhof in Brunnen and returned for a final reception in Basel.[13] Partly, no doubt, because the tour had originally been arranged for their benefit, the British sent the biggest contingent. There were six of them, and they were joined by three Belgians, two Dutchmen (one being Pieter van Tienhoven), a Czech, a Frenchman and a Norwegian.[14] Bernard, Büttikofer and Handschin made up the Swiss team. Bernard was the scientist and conservationist and Büttikofer the organizer and promoter '*always jollying people along*'.[15]

The British group were incensed when they found out how much the agenda had changed. To start with, it meant that they had so much less time in the field that the whole justification for the trip was undermined.[10,13] Worse, they found themselves thrown into discussions about a new international initiative for which they were unprepared, and which the civil servants among them should not have joined without prior authority.[10,13,16] '*The Wild Life Special Committee was in the middle of its work and we were preoccupied with getting countryside and conservation policy reorganized at home*', Max Nicholson recalls.

> '*We and the Americans – especially people like Ira Gabrielson, Fairfield Osborn and Hal Coolidge – were all internationally-minded, but we wanted to get our basic national nature conservation systems straightened out before embarking on any grandiose international ventures.*'[17]

The meeting was indeed a curious hybrid. The British wanted to see conservation in operation. Bernard and Büttikofer wanted to discuss how the Commission Sarasin had created might be revived, expanded and based at Basel.[10,18,19] The duality is evident in the itinerary. For example, on the first day they left Basel by bus at 7 am, visited a bird sanctuary, went on to the National Park Museum at Chur, and then, in their hotel, discussed international action for the protection of nature until 11 pm.[13] It was on that evening that Johann Büttikofer delivered a lengthy paper on 'the present organization of the international protection of nature' covering both Swiss and Dutch pre-war initiatives.[20]

If Bernard and Büttikofer were to succeed, they had to carry Pieter van Tienhoven with them. He was the embodiment of the Dutch movement which had culminated in the creation of the International Office for the Protection of Nature (IOPN). The Office had survived the war, with the support of the Netherlands Department of Education, Science and Protection of Culture – but it had spent most of the time taking stock of its collections, expanding them and developing a universal decimal system for their classification. It had encountered extra problems because the Director, Dr van Waterschoot van der Gracht, died in 1943.[7]

Van Tienhoven summed up the situation in 1945 in a letter to Victor van Straelen:

> '*The Office for International Nature Protection still exists, although in a dormitory state, as you will understand. We were quite worried about our archives which were stored at the Colonial Institute, where the SS was also housed, and which would have been defended like a fortress should Amsterdam have fallen victim in the final battle.*'[21]

When Charles Bernard wrote in May 1946 to invite van Tienhoven and Westermann to join the party in Basel, the future of the IOPN was on the agenda. The Dutch records make it clear that Bernard and Büttikofer were pressing van Tienhoven to move the Office to Switzerland. But van Tienhoven resented and resisted this pressure.[7] His position was more difficult because he was past 70, and unwell. The tensions ran through the tour and its attendant discussions.

Max Nicholson is clear that all those invited were more or less baffled by the emphasis on a new international conservation organization. It was not that they were hostile: they were simply unaware of any international demand for such a body and were ill-prepared to discuss it.[10] The two participants from Scotland – John Berry and Robert Grieve – had been paid for by the Scottish Office, and had some kind of brief to discuss international action for conservation, although it is doubtful if UK ministers were aware of this.[22] But the English contingent emphasized that they were present simply as interested individuals, and the official report of their visit does not even record the discussion of international conservation, dealing only with technical national park and nature reserve issues (and concluding that national circumstances in Switzerland and Britain were so different that not much could be transferred).[13] Bernard assured the group that decisions could not be taken, asserting that '*our aim is to enable each of us to state his ideas on the subject. Our conversations will be informal, as none of us has come in his official capacity. Also, there are not enough nations represented here*'.[20]

As the tour drew to its close it was obvious that the Swiss hosts wanted the meeting to draft some kind of declaration or communiqué which might give them a basis for convening a more formal meeting a year or so later, at which their plan for a new international nature protection initiative might be launched. Most of the group agreed that an international organization to coordinate and champion nature protection could be valuable. But there was no consensus on the way forward. As John Berry put it, '*an awful lot of people were pulling in strongly different directions*'.[22]

Bernard and Büttikofer were keen to revive the Advisory Commission Sarasin had helped create in Berne in 1913. They wanted to link that process to the revitalization of the International Office for Protection of Nature, and its move to Switzerland. But Pieter van Tienhoven refused even to have the IOPN discussed. His aim was its re-establishment in Brussels or Amsterdam, preferably once more under Mrs Graim's direction.[7] He felt that the Swiss '*were focussed too much on Europe and not enough on Anglo-Saxon or overseas collaboration*'.[7] But van Tienhoven did suggest – perhaps as a counter-ploy – an agreement with UNESCO that it would take an interest in the protection of nature. No doubt this appealed partly because Julian Huxley – originator of the notion of the tour – had by then been appointed as the first head of that new agency.

It was only at lunch at the Hotel Storchen in Schönenwald on 7 July – the final day – that van Tienhoven relented and agreed to the two-paragraph statement that appeared in the book subsequently published by the Swiss League.[20] John Berry reports that he was given the job of drafting: '*two of us were sent off to work in a cool basement room and write the blessed thing while the others drank champagne upstairs*'.[22] The statement read:

> '*Guests of the Swiss League for the Protection of Nature have come to Switzerland from Great Britain, France, Belgium, the Netherlands, Czechoslovakia and Norway, and at the instance of their Swiss hosts have taken the opportunity, during their tour of Switzerland, to discuss informally and without commitments the future of international collaboration as regards Protection of Nature etc.*
> *The following provisional conclusions resulted from these conversations:*
> I.   *In order to facilitate the cooperation of national societies concerned with the protection of nature and with the preservation of amenities it is desirable that there should be an active international organization widely international and representative in character, adequately financed and with adequate terms of reference.*
> II. *The national societies might well, it is suggested, consider this matter taking into account the position of the International Office for Protection of Nature and the resolutions of the First International Congress for the Protection of Nature (1923)*

(Mr Büttikofer, Secretary of the Swiss League for Protection of Nature, agreed to receive and transmit any communications on this subject which the national societies may wish to make.)

The representatives of the Swiss League stated that they hoped their Society would see its way to submit to the Swiss Government suggestions for an official initiative by that Government as regards future intergovernmental collaboration in regard to Protection of Nature.'[13,16,20,23]

Cross-cutting Initiatives

Back from the Swiss tour in 1946, Pieter van Tienhoven got on with re-establishing IOPN under Dr J H Westermann's direction, in van Tienhoven's own house in Amsterdam. It later moved to Brussels, with rooms in Victor van Straelen's Royal Belgian Museum of Natural History. Van Tienhoven remained President and van Straelen was Vice-President.[7] Bernard and Büttikofer also got busy. On 20 August they wrote to the President and members of the Swiss Federal Council urging them '*to take the necessary steps to reactivate, as soon as possible, the Consultative Commission for the International Protection of Nature instituted on 19 November 1913 at Berne, with its seat at Basel*'.[19]

They did try to keep the Dutch on side. Büttikofer met W G van der Kloot in Basel on 18 and 19 August, and visited van Tienhoven in Amsterdam, van der Kloot in the Hague and van Straelen in Brussels at the end of August.[23] But if Bernard and Büttikofer were pressing van Tienhoven to move IOPN to Switzerland, tension was inevitable.[7] Van Tienhoven wrote in February 1947 to Hal Coolidge that '*I feel rather sceptical as to such a new organization, and I am by no means inclined to insert the Office as long as we have no evidence of this organization's vitality and efficiency*'.[7]

The Swiss, for their part, '*pursued their initiatives and turned a cold shoulder towards van Tienhoven for the time being, who was very much aware of this*'.[7] Van Tienhoven's scepticism was echoed by the British, who had returned from Basel convinced that it was premature to be talking about international initiatives for nature protection.[16] They were also unhappy about the treatment of the Dutch Office. Thus G F Herbert Smith of the SPNR wrote to Max Nicholson on 11 February 1947 that

> '*the meeting of representative bodies felt that the proposed attempt on the part of the Swiss League to revive an Advisory Commission that faded out in 1914 in complete disregard of the International Office subsequently established at Brussels was most undesirable as it would only lead to rivalry between the two. My personal view is that an international organization might, but not necessarily would, serve a useful purpose, and in that event should be directly sponsored and financed by UNESCO.*'[24]

The omens were not good.

'*How then was the destined collapse of the project averted? The answer is – simply owing to the strong and sound views of Julian Huxley and his providential appointment at that very moment to head UNESCO!*[10] Huxley had taken his ideas about conservation to his new agency. He was one of those credited with insisting on the incorporation of the 'S' for 'Science' in its title, arguing at the conference that planned it that *'culture without science doesn't make sense'*.[2,25] He was also far-sighted in his recognition of the importance of what were later labelled 'environmental issues'. Writing about the purpose and philosophy of the new Agency in 1946 he said:

> *'If UNESCO is to have a real social policy, it must not confine itself to...general studies, but must also face up to particular problems which press on the modern world. Simply as illustrative examples I will mention population, the conservation of wild life and semantics. The recognition of the idea of an optimum population size (of course relative to technological and social conditions) is an indispensable first step towards that planned control of populations which is neces-sary if man's blind reproductive urges are not to wreck his ideals and his plans for material and spiritual betterment. The recognition of the fact that the wild life of the world is irreplaceable, but that it is being rapidly destroyed, is necessary if we are to realise in time that areas must be set aside where, in the ultimate interests of mankind as a whole, the spread of man must take second place to the conservation of other species...'*[26]

Huxley made his commitment clear at the first General Conference of his new organi-zation, held at the end of 1946:

> *'Delegates asked me what seemed to me silly questions: why should UNESCO try to protect rhinoceros or rare flowers? Was not the safeguarding of grand, unspoilt scenery outside its purview? However, with the aid of a few nature lovers I persuaded the Conference that the enjoyment of nature was part of the culture and that the preservation of rare and interesting plants was a scientific duty.'*[27]

Although he carried the day, events were to prove that he certainly did not have the unqualified backing of his Council or General Conference.

Bernard and Büttikofer followed van Tienhoven's suggestion and established contact with UNESCO.[7] Dr Joseph Needham, head of the Department of Natural Sciences (and later world-famous as the outstanding authority in the West on Chinese science), wrote positively on 9 January 1947 to Dr Westermann recording talks he had had with Bernard, Büttikofer and Professor Sirks of Groningen University, who represented the International Union of Biological Sciences, also considered possible custodians of international conservation. Needham's judgement was that:

> *'since the question of the Protection of Nature involves so many matters beyond the bounds of pure science (eg laws and international conven-tions about the conservation of fauna and flora, social aspects of national parks, amenities etc etc) it would seem fitting that a strong and international Protection of Nature Organization should not be incorporated within the framework of the International Council of Scientific Unions but should be something sui generis. It would occupy*

> *a status much more akin to that of such organizations as the International Meteorological Bureau, the International Hydrographic Bureau etc...*'[28]

He went on to propose that the new body should include government delegates together with delegates of specialized relevant international organizations such as the International Council on Bird Preservation and representatives of national and regional nature protection societies. He concluded: '*I should like to point out that if such a constitution is accepted, the status of the organization will be semi-governmental*', but emphasized that such an arrangement worked well with ICSU, which had signed a formal agreement with UNESCO.

Needham visited Basel for the weekend of 18 March 1947. Julian Huxley wrote to Büttikofer on the 28 March.[29] He was quite definite: '*I am hoping that UNESCO will call, in the summer of 1948, a world conference on the subject, fully representative of governments, colonial territories, international organizations and voluntary national societies.*' Accordingly, Huxley wanted to be clear about the Swiss League's plans for their Conference, to be held in June 1947 at Brunnen and now seen as preparatory to the UNESCO event. He hoped that it would '*take some steps towards the setting up of an international federation of Nature Protection bodies*', including the IOPN and ICBP. Specifically, he wanted it to pass a resolution calling for the implementation of the diplomatic Convention of 1913 and forward it to UNESCO; to pass a second resolution asking UNESCO to call a congress on international nature conservation in 1948; and to discuss the options for the constitution of the new body.

Huxley opened up a number of other important issues. He rejected the proposal of Dr G F Herbert Smith that the UNESCO congress should only involve governments. He urged due attention to regional conventions like that for faunal protection in Africa, and commended the Society for Preservation of the Fauna of the Empire (now Fauna and Flora International). And he went on to address an issue that has run like a tangled thread through IUCN's history:

> '*We should like you to be aware of the distinction we make between the respective fields of the Protection of Nature and the Conservation of Natural Resources. By the term "Protection of Nature" we mean the protection of fauna and flora, the preparation and upkeep of national parks and reservations, the correlation and improvement of game laws, the study of bird migration and its protection, the preservation of natural amenities, including scenic areas, prehistoric archaeological (but not historic) sites, natural geological monuments and so on. By the term "Conservation of Natural Resources" we mean surveys of, and regulations of access to, mineral deposits and reserves, safeguards against their undue exploitation, also soil erosion protection and land conservation, water conservancy and planned development of river basins by power production, irrigation etc., also forestry and lumber conservation.*'

It is clear that Huxley took care to see that the British, even if they thought the venture premature, did not resist it too vigorously. Max Nicholson wrote to him on 25 April 1947 explaining that the UK Government would not be represented formally at Brunnen and had been assured by the Swiss Government that other governments would not have formal representation either.[30] Huxley wrote to Smith emphasizing the need to avoid overlap between Brunnen and the subsequent conference UNESCO would be calling, reporting that the Swiss now understood that their conference would be '*purely preparatory and exploratory in character*', and saying that '*in these circumstances, it will be a pity, in our opinion, if the UK is not well represented, at least by observers*'.[31] Just before Smith left for Brunnen he received a letter from Nicholson (who was not going) 'clarifying' the line the British party were to take and saying that '*the problem is how to ensure that intergovernmental action is not prejudiced by Brunnen and that advantage is taken of the meeting to get some constructive preparatory work done*'.[32]

The Dutch also remained hesitant. It is not quite clear at what stage the Swiss began to cold-shoulder Pieter van Tienhoven, but relations had clearly deteriorated by April 1947, just two months before the scheduled Conference. Charles Bernard wrote in that month to the Dutchman, and in his response the latter explained that he had awaited the letter with apprehension, '*because it should permit the elimination of a serious misunderstanding, which, if I understand your letter, does now exist*'. Van Tienhoven emphasized his commitment to the cause of nature protection and his willingness for the IOPN to collaborate in any new organization that might be established, as well as his personal wish to work harmoniously with the Swiss League. But he was stung by Bernard's action in copying a personal letter to all the members of van Tienhoven's Council (among whom, just to complicate matters, Bernard was numbered).[33]

Victor van Straelen wrote to Bernard from Brussels more forcefully on 12 June 1947 referring to what he had understood had been agreements, and complaining that '*nothing that you announced to me has been implemented*'. He went on to argue that the dates for the Brunnen Conference had been fixed without taking proper account of other meetings in Denmark, England and Scotland.[34] Van Straelen [35] was a man of strong personality, blended with great eloquence, vast scientific knowledge and personal warmth (according to Hal Coolidge those who knew him well called him 'Uncle Victor').[36] He accused the Swiss of high-handedness, and expressed himself with characteristic vigour. Bernard responded a few days later, expressing his own astonishment at the accusations levelled against him, saying that he had on occasion contemplated abandoning his efforts, but confirming that despite opposition from the Netherlands, England and now Belgium, which made the full success of the Conference less likely, they would go ahead.[37] It is clear that he had every reason to expect a rough ride.

The Conference at Brunnen

The long-debated International Conference for the Protection of Nature was held at the Hotel Waldstätterhof in Brunnen, between 28 June and 3 July 1947.[23] There were about 80 delegates (some wearing two or three representational hats). They came from Argentina, Austria, Australia, Belgium, Bulgaria, Czechoslovakia, Denmark, Finland, France, Guatemala, Hungary, India, Italy, Luxembourg, Monaco, the Netherlands (and the Dutch East Indies), New Zealand, Norway, Spain, Sweden, Switzerland, the UK and the USA. The United Nations system was represented by the UN Trusteeship Council (responsible for promoting the independence of colonial and trust territories), together with UNESCO and FAO.[38] The International Union of Biological Sciences (IUBS), the International Office for the Protection of Nature and the International Council for Bird Preservation were also there. Charles Bernard presided, with John Ramsbottom of the Royal Botanic Gardens at Kew in the UK and M Caullery of France as Vice-Presidents and Johann Büttikofer as Secretary-General. There were seven plenary sessions in the mornings, while 'Special Commissions' and *ad hoc* groups carried on the arguments in the afternoons, evenings, and sometimes through into the small hours.

The meeting suffered from the same disharmony that had plagued the tour a year before. Although it seems a strange way to open a conference designed to reach consensus, Bernard lashed out at his critics in his opening address of welcome. '*We found ourselves repeatedly up against obstacles that we hoped to surmount*', he said. '*We have been criticized and attacked from many sides, violently, and to us incomprehensibly.*'

Bernard really let himself go.

> '*We were accused of sinister projects, the worst intentions were attributed to us. Some wrote, or suggested, or insinuated that we had imperialistic tendencies, that we wanted to have the monopoly in Switzerland of everything concerning the subject that interested us...in that Switzerland which, someone said, had never done anything for the protection of Nature.*
>
> *I notice a curious sign: nobody in fact was doing anything; everywhere the protection of nature was sleeping in calm indifference; but as soon as we launched the idea of international collaboration, as soon as we had taken the initiative – there was strenuous activity everywhere: reports were published, circulars were sent out, national and international congresses were organized, appeals for funds were made and staff engaged. A magnificent awakening which we are the first to applaud, but it seems to me that there was no reason to go against us.*
>
> *I really do not know what they suspected us of: they accused us of wanting to abolish the other organizations of a more or less international character, especially the International Office for the Protection of Nature. I have no need, Ladies and Gentlemen, to stress the puerility of these accusations...*'[8]

These may have been no more than the sentiments of an honourable man, committed to a cause, who found himself beset by suspicion at every step.[39] But the statement really did go 'over the top'. It was simply untrue to say that nothing had been happening about nature protection until the Swiss League rode down from the mountains on their green charger. A man of Bernard's international experience must have understood the need for patience, if he was to achieve his ends. It was, perhaps, as well that Victor van Straelen was not there. For he was a man of strong feelings and vigorous expression, and would not have liked being accused of puerility. Fortunately, the Dutch, in the persons of Drs Westermann and van der Haagen, set about the burial of the hatchet. They thanked the Swiss League for organizing the conference and for the publication of the record of the Basel meeting a year before. They emphasized the role of the IOPN, and its commitment to cooperate with all other organizations, for the benefit of the international protection of nature.[40]

Getting down to business, three alternative approaches were urged on the delegates.

The British, led by John Ramsbottom, put forward a proposal that closely echoed

Julian Huxley's view of things. They wanted the meeting to call on UNESCO to convene a conference in the summer of 1948 in Paris to consider the form of organization required to achieve international collaboration for the protection of nature. They proposed that UNESCO should look at the procedures which, in 1913, established the Consultative Commission for the Protection of Nature (a sop to the Swiss here), and the possible revision of the constitution of the latter to meet modern needs. The conference should discuss the constitution, structure and functions of any new organization. Finally, the UK urged that UNESCO invite not just governments but existing governmental and non-governmental national and international organizations to their conference.

The Danish delegation, led by Professor Vinding Kruse, wanted much less procedure and a lot more action. Their statement emphasized the violent changes that threatened to disturb the equilibrium between humanity and the forces of nature, the catastrophic acceleration of this process by the Second World War, and the need for urgent international action. Accordingly, the Danes resisted the postponement of the establishment of a new International Organization for the Protection of Nature, wanted the constitution of the International Organization proposed by the Swiss to be discussed immediately, and wanted that constitution to be submitted to governments, the UN, UNESCO, FAO and non-governmental organizations only after its acceptance and adoption in Brunnen. These ideas were warmly supported by Johann Büttikofer, perhaps because *'they proposed the taking over of the offices of the Swiss League, and himself as the Director General of the new set-up. Here it should be noted that Dr Bernard was throughout fully aware of the unwisdom of this move.'*[38] Presumably this means that Bernard and Büttikofer also did not exactly see eye-to-eye. Maybe that is why Büttikofer appeared to at least one participant as *'a nervous man, who never gave the impression of being very secure'.*[41]

The French team, with the IUBS, sought a middle way. The Conference was advised to recommend the establishment of an International Union for the Protection of Nature, discuss the draft constitution proposed by the Swiss League, and name ten specialists who would participate in a committee or symposium to be convened by UNESCO which would work up the constitution for submission to a further inter-governmental meeting.

In her internal report to Needham, Eleen Sam of UNESCO is blunt about the Danish proposal:

> *'The "Danish movement" to set up an organization immediately was partly due to the enthusiasm and impulsiveness of the head of the Danish delegation, Dr Kruse, and partly to the fact that some of the Central European delegates had little or no English and French and could not follow the discussions. Kruse took advantage of this to stress the UNESCO scare outside of the meetings, and also of a considerable amount of hysteria on Büttikofer's part over the incident described below.'*[38]

That 'incident' was the reading to the Conference by Dr Büttikofer of a circular letter signed by Carl Russell of the US National Parks Service which implied that UNESCO's Museums Section was already creating an International Council of Museums which would cover a range of nature protection topics. As Eleen Sam put it,

'Büttikofer put forward an angry suggestion that UNESCO's Museums Section was already intending to call a meeting in Paris on nature protection and that we were generally double-crossing Brunnen. This particular bogey took me a day of hard talking to dispel.'[38]

Anti-UNESCO feelings clearly ran high.

'Distrust of UNESCO, and insinuations that UNESCO was trying to be imperialistic in the field of nature protection was expressed strongly in almost all of Kruse's and his supporters' speeches. Kruse also alleged that UNESCO was weighed down by a cumbersome administrative machinery.'

Eleen Sam responded by drafting a statement which the Chairman, Dr Bernard, read out. This emphasized that the initiative in asking UNESCO to convene a follow-up conference was that of the Brunnen meeting and its Swiss hosts; that the work would be done by the delegates, not by UNESCO; and that the new Union would be created and run by decision of the participants.

'In brief, our intention has never been to put ourselves in UNESCO's hands, and UNESCO has never thought of doing our work. We have only hoped to have from UNESCO the collaboration and help which are absolutely essential to give us the means of working.'[42]

There was another argument over the powers of the meeting. Professor Bressou of France emphasized that the delegates to the Brunnen Conference were not qualified to act in the name of their governments. Representation of countries, and of organizations within countries, was uneven. His view was that:

'the present delegates, as technicians, should draw up a Draft Constitution, make any desirable amendments to the proposed text, and submit it in the following year to a Conference under the auspices of UNESCO, which was the most competent intergovernmental agency.'[43]

The British echoed this point, emphasizing that as at the Basel meeting 'those attending took decisions in their own names and not those of their societies'. Dr Ramsbottom added that *'of the four delegates representing the United Kingdom, two were Government officials and one a former official, yet none of them had any authority to speak in the name of the Government. They were in their private capacity.'*[44] In contrast, Professor Vinding Kruse of Denmark and those who shared his activist position considered that while the delegates were not legally competent, *'on the practical and technical side they were the most competent body to take action'*.[45]

The position of the United States was set out in a lengthy statement by George E Brewer, who, with Jean Delacour, was an observer for the American Committee for International Wildlife Protection and also represented the New York Zoological Society (which was at that time establishing the Conservation Foundation). Brewer also had links with FAO, and was to report to its Director-General, and he undertook to brief three departments of the American Government – the Forest Service, the Fish and Wildlife Service and the Soil Conservation Service. The societies Brewer represented had, he said *'authorized him to state that they believed the creation of an* *international organization absolutely essential*'.[46] But they were not sure that UNESCO was necessarily the right UN body to sponsor the action, given that its Charter (although including the conservation of cultural monuments) did not include anything that authorized it to concern itself with the broader issues of nature protection, whereas FAO had a distinct interest in the conservation of forests, soils and fresh water supplies. The US participants none the less went along with the proposal that UNESCO host the first intergovernmental meeting, so long as it was understood that it was not necessarily the appropriate agency to carry on any subsequent action.[46*]

It seems clear that the big issue – action now or recommendations for action later – never came to the vote. As John Ramsbottom pointed out,[44] a straw poll of speakers suggested that had a vote been taken, and ten delegations voted for immediate action and the rest for deferral, the result would have been deadlock. He pleaded for consensus. In the end, his views and those advanced by the French and a number of others prevailed. The British, at least, went away happy and Max Nicholson reported to the Ministry of Education on 18 July that the 'representatives of British societies' had '*secured in effect the reference back of this project on the understanding that UNESCO will call an intergovernmental conference on the subject next year*'.[47]

In the end – and after a good deal of blood-letting – the Brunnen Conference did agree on the text of a Provisional Constitution for an International Union for the Protection of Nature, gave the Swiss League a mandate to act as agent for this provisional organization, asked the League to send the Provisional Constitution to UNESCO for transmission to governments (who were to be asked whether they could accept it), and requested UNESCO to convene a congress in Paris in July 1948 to adopt a definitive constitution for the Union.[23,38] The Swiss League duly published the volume of conference proceedings in its capacity as agent for the Provisional IUPN.[23]

The Special Commissions also worked on concepts and terms. It is interesting that the word 'Union' was chosen very carefully to describe the new body. 'Organization' was rejected because it implied '*a continuing process of formation, rather than...a constituted body. "Union" would more correctly describe the structure of IUPN, which would comprise numerous other bodies*'.[38] Professor Bourdelle of France urged the need for a Commission on Nomenclature, noting that there were 85 different definitions of the terms 'nature reserves' and 'national parks'.

Equally clearly, major issues were left in the air. Eleen Sam ended her report to Joseph Needham on a cautious note.

> '*It seemed to me that on the whole this Conference's knowledge both about the problems of nature protection and about the machinery by which international bodies are set up and maintained was disappointingly limited. There was no mention at any time of what urgent proposals would need attention when the new Union comes into being.*'[38]

Not exactly the best of omens for a new body.

---

* This debate between UNESCO and FAO went on for many years. FAO questioned UNESCO's competence in ecology, and sought a role as 'executing agency' for all projects involving ecology that were financed by what became the UN Development Programme (UNDP). See also Chapter 4[1])

Onward to Fontainebleau

Third time lucky? On 25 July 1947, Charles Bernard and Johann Büttikofer addressed their own government – the President of the Swiss Confederation and the members of the Federal Council – and transmitted the text of the resolution adopted at Brunnen. They went on to explain that the establishment of IUPN would render the International Consultative Commission established in 1913 useless, and asked the Swiss Government to propose to the other states party to the Berne agreement that it be terminated.[48] Meanwhile, UNESCO got on with the preparations for the formal conference that was to draw all the strands together and create a new International Union.

The second session of the General Conference of UNESCO was held in Mexico in December 1947. It instructed its Director-General, Julian Huxley, to convene, on a date to be agreed, an international technical conference for the protection of nature. It noted that it had originally expected to do this in the United States in 1949, in conjunction with a United Nations Scientific Conference on the Conservation and Utilization of Natural Resources (the UNSCCUR Conference, planned for 26 May to 3 June 1949 at the UN temporary headquarters at Lake Success).[49] But there were objections, not least from Charles Bernard, who feared that '*a very restricted number of European representatives could manage to go to the States*'.[50] The Swiss, therefore, pressed for a meeting in Paris and urged the Government of France to convene, jointly with UNESCO, a separate international conference in 1948 to adopt a definitive constitution for the International Union for the Protection of Nature created provisionally at Brunnen.[51,52] In the end both meetings happened.

The French Government was not wholehearted. In March 1948 Bernard visited Paris and saw the Director of the Muséum National d'Histoire Naturelle, Professor Urbain, together with his colleague Professor Roger Heim. Urbain spoke at length by telephone to two government officials, M Dufay and M Dorget, respectively Director-General and Counsellor in the Ministry of Foreign Affairs. The latter questioned the proposal that the Government of France might convene the Conference because '*this would imply a commitment to contribute an annual payment towards the future activities of the Union*'. Guy Dorget also asked '*why it was necessary to create an intergovernmental organization and why UNESCO or some other existing organization could not be given responsibility for nature protection?*' Finally, since UNESCO's Conference in Mexico had instructed Dr Huxley to convene a conference in the United States, why should the Government of France take this over?[53]

Charles Bernard countered. He explained that Dr Huxley himself favoured the new proposals. It was for the conference to decide on financial obligations (if any). The new Union would be independent, but would collaborate closely with UNESCO, FAO and ECOSOC. Asked why Switzerland should not convene the conference in Berne, he said (very tactfully) that a larger country would be better, and especially France '*where the scientists were among the pioneers of nature protection*'. Dufay and Dorget were unmoved. They still thought that an existing branch of the UN could do what was needed. The French Government was unwilling to finance the proposed new Union. The three Ministries chiefly concerned (Agriculture, Education and Overseas Territories) were not agreed on the need for it. Hence Dufay could not recommend to the Minister of Foreign Affairs that France convene the Conference. With all this in contention, it was clear that more argument was needed and that the original date of July 1948 would not be practicable.[53]

It was the Muséum National d'Histoire Naturelle, in the person of Urbain, with the support of Pierre Auger, a distinguished French physicist who had succeeded Needham at UNESCO in April 1948,[54] that came to the rescue and got to work on French officialdom. By 23 May the lines had cleared. At a meeting on that day at the Museum, chaired by Professor Urbain, it was agreed that all governments would be invited '*except that of Francoist Spain, but including the military governments of Germany and Japan*'.[55] There would be a tripartite division of responsibilities for invitation – the French Government summoning other states, UNESCO handling international organizations, and the Swiss League inviting national bodies. Equally importantly, the League was to do this as agent for the Provisional IUPN, implying that the latter was already a duly constituted body, awaiting formal recognition by the world community gathered at Fontainebleau. UNESCO would duplicate the various documents. There was even a suggestion that the French Government might pay the expenses of the delegates,[55] but in the event the resources did not run to that.

UNESCO duly issued the invitations to '*the Constitutive Conference of the International Union for the Protection of Nature which will take place at Fontainebleau from 30 September to 7 October 1948*'.[56] The accompanying information sheet explains its goals. '*The essential object of the Conference is to establish and adopt the definitive Constitution of the provisional International Union for the Protection of Nature.*'[51] In the second place, there was to be a technical symposium which would look at the problems confronting nature protection, especially in Europe and Africa and which would create a Commission for Europe and Africa which would define opinions on these subjects for submission to UNSCCUR in 1949. The preparatory papers reveal that Dr Huxley was in fact thinking of three regional preparatory commissions for that meeting – the one on Europe and Africa, which could be handled within the Fontainebleau Conference, and others for the Western Hemisphere (to be linked to an Inter-American Resources Conference to be held at Denver, Colorado, in September 1948) and the Pacific and Asia (which could be tied into the Seventh Pacific Science Congress in New Zealand in February 1949).[55] Quite clearly, he did not see IUPN as taking over a worldwide role in such matters – but the agenda of UNSCCUR did fall, according to his definition, under the heading of 'conservation of natural resources' rather than 'protection of nature'.

The programme of the Fontainebleau Conference was to be divided into three parts.[51,55] First, the International Union for the Protection of Nature was to be established. After the essential formalities like the appointment of a Conference Bureau and Credentials Committee, and adoption of rules of procedure and the agenda, the proposed Constitution of the IUPN and the means of financing the Union were to be discussed. This stage was to conclude with the adoption and signature of the Constitution of the IUPN.

The second element – the first session of the General Conference (the General Assembly) of the International Union for the Protection of Nature – was to follow at once. The Bureau of the Union would be elected, the budget for the years 1948 and 1949 and the programme of work adopted, and the date and place of the next session of the General Conference decided.

The Technical Symposium for Europe and Africa was the third step. It was to review and discuss legislation and other measures adopted by governments, consider the rules of conduct to be adopted with regard to wild flora and fauna and their efficacy in furthering nature protection, discuss existing and potential conventions on fauna conservation, discuss the definition of national parks and nature reserves, consider the merging of UNESCO conferences and UNSCCUR and debate the protection of African 'big game' (a term not yet out of favour in 1948).

Because of the nature of the agenda, those sending delegations were reminded that they should include people with legal, financial and scientific expertise. They must be furnished with proper powers to sign the Act formally constituting IUPN. It was announced that the Conference would assign particular tasks to committees. The Secretariat was to be provided by the Swiss League (again as agent for the provisional IUPN) and Johann Büttikofer was named as the focal point (perhaps with the implication that at this stage he was favoured as the Secretary-General of the new Union). The delegates were requested to arrive at Fontainebleau on Wednesday 29 September so that the Conference could open on the 30th, and as a little encouragement, they were told that afterwards there would be a six-day excursion to the Cevennes, the Camargue and the forest of Sainte-Baume. It was made clear that the costs of delegates must be borne by their governments or organizations.

In the interval between Brunnen and Fontainebleau, there was obviously a good deal of toing and froing, not least about money. People like G F Herbert Smith, who wanted governments to be members of the new body, held this view at least in part because they recognized that governments had resources and the voluntary sector did not. As he wrote to Max Nicholson, '*the main difficulty is finance. Few societies have much spare money*'.[57] But more governments than the French and British were hesitant. It was reported that '*it is highly doubtful that the US Government will agree to setting up the Union as a governmental organization*'.[58] Max Nicholson appears to have advised British ministers that the UK should not be represented at government level at Fontainebleau at all '*since the advantages of British Government participation are nebulous and the disadvantages all too clear*'.[58] The Foreign Office agreed and declined the French invitation, while making clear that the British representation, although unofficial, would be '*suitably supported and informed by the Government*'.[59] They were not alone in adopting this half-and-half position.

The organizers clearly also had some problems about the draft Constitution.

> '*As we now envisage a planned Constitution different from that adopted at Brunnen, we should also submit a second draft alongside that of Brunnen. It will also be desirable to submit for study a proposal for the financing of the Union from a non-governmental angle.*'[55]

It would appear that these points of difference were shared by French, Belgian and British conservationists, and Max Nicholson, then the head Civil Servant in the Office of the Lord President (a senior Cabinet Minister), not only did some drafting himself but offered to convene a meeting of the main groups concerned with nature conservation in the British Isles in order to define their position and communicate it to UNESCO.[17,55] The alternative draft constitution eventually tabled at Fontainebleau was largely the product of the latter group, chaired by G F Herbert Smith.

The Creation of the International Union for the Protection of Nature

On the appointed day, representatives of 23 governments, 126 national institutions and eight international organizations arrived at Fontainebleau, gathering for debate in the Galerie des Colonnes. The room is long and not over-wide, flanked by columns with gilded capitals. On one wall, tall windows overlook a courtyard and the park, and not far away stands the great, sweeping, outdoor staircase, the *escalier des adieux*, from which Napoleon bade farewell to his guards, before leaving for Elba. At the end of the session, the delegates were posed on those same steps, before departing to fight nature's enemies.

The meeting followed the familiar, universal, pattern: address of welcome on behalf of the host government; address of welcome by the Director-General of UNESCO; constitution of a Credentials Committee (to find out who was entitled to vote) and a Nomination Committee; election of officers – Charles Bernard as President, Victor van Straelen (Belgium), Henry G Maurice (UK), H J Coolidge (USA), A Urbain (France) and J K van der Haagen (Netherlands) as Vice-Presidents Claude Bressou (France) as Secretary-General with Johann Büttikofer and Eleen Sam as assistants Roger Heim (France) as Chair of the Technical Symposium; appointment of Steering and Programme Committee, Financial Committee and Legal and Drafting Committee; and agreement on Rules of Procedure. Necessary tedium.

But Julian Huxley's opening speech on 30 September was not tedious, judging from his notes.[60] Indeed it was a remarkable essay in prophecy. He emphasized the value of a new technical Union, which should be professional rather than intergovernmental, and should convene experts whose knowledge should be exchanged worldwide. He stressed the importance of the regional dimension, saying '*we want regional autonomy, that is, what we say in our region goes. The only modification would be to bring in the world point of view, and world conventions*.' He emphasized that '*practical, concrete, results are needed*'. He argued that nature must be considered as a resource – which was obviously the case with fisheries, whaling, forestry or fur animals, but also applied to wildlife in general, including rare and interesting fauna and flora, fine scenery, wild country, open space and '*natural beauty in general (don't let us be afraid of the word)*'. Gifford Pinchot would have applauded.

Huxley was clear that while such resources provided the means for living, '*the end of living is not merely to live: one of the ends is enjoyment, including intellectual enjoyment; enjoyment of beauty; enjoyment of unspoilt nature in attractive countryside*'. He went on to comment (again in language far ahead of its time) on:

> '*the fascination of all these other manifestations of life which, though all products of the same process of evolution, yet are something in their own rights, are alien from us, give us new ideas of possibilities of life, can never be replaced if lost, nor substituted by products of human endeavour*'.

Turning to '*the fascination of life other than our own*', he asked:

> '*what shouldn't we lack if all wild big game were killed or reduced to zoos? If wild birds were reduced to a few species semi-parasitic on man? If all wild flowers were replaced by crops or gardens? If all primaeval forests and wild woods were cut down and replaced by scientific forestry.*'

So – what was to be done? The first need was to appeal to people and change their attitudes to wildlife, seeking to '*conserve, not just exploit*'. But conservation must always be based on scientific research and its application: there was a need for a biological service, drawing on ecology (in a second speech on 2 October to the Technical Meeting on the scientific management of wildlife [61] he elaborated on how all this should be done). Practical steps must include the setting aside of areas where wildlife and nature were paramount (these could be small nature reserves or large national parks). There should be other '*conservation areas*' where wildlife and nature are treated as equal partners with human use (a proposal taken directly from the report of his Wild Life Conservation Special Committee in Britain, and anticipating the concept of biosphere reserves).[54] There should be legislation and conventions – but these must be enforceable and enforced. There must be positive encouragement of clubs and societies.[61]

The extraordinary thing is that the same speech could be made 50 years later, with equal validity. This does not mean that much has not been done, but that the fundamental human attitudes that Huxley was addressing remain problematical today. Less depressing is the fact that this guiding philosophy has been adhered to by IUPN and IUCN and most of their member organizations throughout their 50 years of history, and that the concerns voiced are now heard throughout the world.

Back at Fontainebleau the business went as smoothly as could have been expected in such an international gathering. On 5 October 1948, most of the delegates (representing 18 governments, seven international organizations and 107 national organizations) signed the formal Act constituting IUPN.[52,62,63] The constitution was adopted, with a Preamble (drafted by the US representatives) which was described as '*a very clear definition of the present day meaning of Nature Protection*'.[63] It spoke of '*the preservation of the entire world biotic community or Man's natural environment, which includes the Earth's renewable natural resources of which it is composed and on which rests the foundation of human civilization*' and of the need to protect, restore and administer these resources wisely. The Preamble has proved remarkably durable, surviving almost unchanged through the revisions of the IUCN Statutes in 1977 and 1996.

The objectives set out in the first two Articles define clearly the kind of body IUPN was meant to be.[52] Article 1 emphasized that the object of the Union was to '*encourage and facilitate cooperation between Governments and national and international organizations concerned with, and persons interested in, the "Protection of Nature"*'. Article 2 explained that it would '*promote and recommend national and international action*' to preserve wildlife and the natural environment in all parts of the world (paying particular attention to species threatened with extinction), to broaden public knowledge about the 'protection of nature', to extend education and scientific research, and to prepare international draft agreements and a worldwide convention for 'the protection of nature'. The Union was to '*collect, analyze, interpret and disseminate information about "the protection of nature"*' and to '*distribute to Governments and national and international organizations documents, legislative texts, scientific studies and other information*'.

The structure of the Union mirrored Fontainebleau: governments, public services concerned with the 'protection of nature', international intergovernmental and non-governmental organizations and national non-governmental organizations would all be eligible for membership. It was unique as the first 'GONGO' – Governmental and Non-Governmental Organization. Although the Constitution was passed by staid bodies like the British Foreign Office (one of whose legal advisers had vetted and adjusted it in draft, and may indeed have proposed the GONGO model),[64] it had no parallel at the time (and very few afterwards).[17] There may have been four particular reasons why this hybrid status was chosen. First, it may have helped gain recognition among intergovernmental bodies like the UN agencies. Second, state members were in a position to pay significant dues. Third, if the Union had a number of state members, governments were likely to take its findings more seriously. Fourth, the hybrid structure must help cooperation across the divide between governmental and non-governmental sectors.[65]

The Union was to comprise a General Assembly, an Executive Board and a Secretariat. The General Assembly of members was the supreme body determining policy, deciding on the programme and budget submitted by the Executive Board, and making recommendations. Like that of the United Nations, it was originally supposed to meet every year but it was agreed that a two-year alternation would be more manageable (and affordable). It was not divided into governmental and non-governmental 'chambers' until the Edinburgh General Assembly of 1956.[12] The Executive Board was to run things between Assembly sessions. One main difference from today was that the Secretary-General was to be appointed by the General Assembly, but overall there has clearly been a remarkable endurance of concepts over the past 50 years.

The oddest thing about this text is its treatment of 'the protection of nature'. Despite Julian Huxley's insistence that 'protection of nature' and 'conservation of natural resources' were very different things, the semi-definition of 'protection of nature' in the Preamble to the constitution makes it clear that the term was being interpreted as something close to what the Americans and British were calling 'conservation'.[66] It was, presumably, placed in quotation marks to indicate that it was a generic term for whatever the Union was about, in default of a generally agreed definition (yet, if the Preamble is said to present this concept clearly, why not have a definition as well?). Behind that formulation, however, there was a whiff of dissent in the air.

From the beginning, some people were unhappy about the word 'Protection': the 'P' in IUPN. Probably the Americans and the British, who had taken to using 'conservation' to mean something more active than 'preservation', were in the forefront, and perhaps the linguistic problems that vex this question were the obstacle. John Berry recalls that '*I tried at Fontainebleau to make it "C" for "Conservation", and also to add "and natural resources", and asked Frank Fraser Darling to support me, but to my surprise he would have none of it saying that "our task was to protect nature". But later, the Edinburgh General Assembly in 1956 made both changes.*'[22]

Arguments apart, there is no doubt that Fontainebleau ended in a pact of peace. The constitution was safely on board, and the IUPN swung immediately into its first General Assembly. The first issue was who should lead the new organization. Huxley wanted an American, and had asked Fairfield Osborn, then Director of the American Museum of Natural History, to sound out names. '*For many reasons*', he wrote, '*it would be best that the President of the new Union should be an American*'.[67] The behind-the-scenes reason was almost certainly a wish to ensure that the new Anglo-American concepts of conservation, with their strong foundation in ecological science, dominated the new Union. The overt reason was that the President would have to be active at the Technical Conference to be held in the United States after UNSCCUR in 1949, and oversee the implementation of any decisions it remitted to IUPN. This, in turn, had financial implications, and Huxley made it clear that UNESCO's policy was to make grants to new bodies '*for a limited period to enable them to find their feet, but afterwards we expect them to be self-supporting*'.[67] For IUPN that self-support would almost certainly have to be American support. Failing an American President the British had the Duke of Devonshire waiting in the wings, though it is not clear what resources (or scientific leadership) he could have provided.

But this manoeuvre did not work. For their part, the Swiss had gone to Fontainebleau hoping that their efforts in preparing for the creation of IUPN would assure them both the Presidency, for Charles Bernard, and the Secretary-Generalship, for Johann Büttikofer.[68] There was compromise in the corridors. Swiss honour was satisfied when Bernard was elected to the Presidency. Despite his outburst at Brunnen, his energy and commitment were admired by many. He also had a lot of charm: '*he was a ladies' man. Hit it off with Eleen Sam…*'[41] Roger Heim, also deeply admired, became a Vice-President along with Hal Coolidge of the USA and Henry G Maurice of the UK (Victor van Straelen and Pieter van Tienhoven declined nomination).[68] The first Executive Board had a wide geographical spread but its members came from countries that had been active in one or more of the preceding discussions: Argentina, Belgium, Denmark, France, Italy, the Netherlands, Peru, Poland, Switzerland, the United Kingdom and the United States were all represented.[52,62] Victor van Straelen and J K van der Haagen, both closely associated with the International Office, were there. Van Tienhoven was made the first honorary member of IUPN[7] and '*took his seat at the Chairman's right, thanked the Assembly for its token of appreciation and wished the Union a long and fruitful career*'.[52] And, as a further exercise in bridge building, the first meeting of the Board (which lasted only 5 minutes!) appointed Jean-Paul Harroy, a Belgian who was one of van Straelen's protégés, as the first Secretary-General. The Conference passed a unanimous vote of thanks to Johann Büttikofer for all his work. One hopes that the grapes were not too sour, for it was well known that he had hoped for the job for himself.

Harroy himself, writing in 1988, was a little coy about the circumstances behind his sudden appointment:

'*As a result of a certain set of circumstances, at the Fontainebleau Conference…the candidate presumptive for the post of Director of the new institution had to be replaced at the last moment. I was present as the fifteenth member of the Belgian delegation. How and why did the choice fall on me?*'[69]

The answer is that it was the result of a good deal of plotting behind the scenes. The British were determined to block Johann Büttikofer, who had a very dominant Russian wife and whose political loyalties were regarded as suspect, and to stop the new Union having its headquarters in Basel. With a touch of relish, Max Nicholson wrote on 10 August 1948 to Sir John Fryer of the Agricultural Research Council that '*it is…thought that Büttikofer has antagonized so many people that there will be unanimous support for Brussels against Basel…*'. Writing to Nicholson on 12 August, Julian Huxley said that UNESCO '*agree about Büttikofer, and hope that as soon as possible another name might be found*'.[67] By that date the Belgians had virtually committed themselves to taking on the manning and running of the international office and Huxley commented that '*I am sure that the Belgians will not be willing to do more, and indeed could not very well be asked to do more, than provide accommodation and to furnish a good man as candidate for the Secretary-Generalship.*'

Harroy's credentials were in fact impeccable. He had worked on the ground in Africa, as Curator of the Albert National Park in Kivu and the Garamba National Park in Uele, in the far north-east of what was then the Belgian Congo. He had been Director of the Institute of National Parks of the Belgian Congo back in Brussels. He had written two books, one controversially entitled *Africa – the Dying Land: the Degradation of African Soils under the Influence of Colonization* and the other concerned with protecting nature. He was known to Roger Heim, who had talked to him at length when, early in 1948, he had visited Paris for a launch of his African book.[68] He had just been appointed Secretary-General of IRSAC, the Institut pour la Recherche Scientifique en Afrique Centrale. He knew the International Office for Protection of Nature well, because it was housed in the same building as the Institute of National Parks of the Belgian Congo.

Harroy was approached one evening by a Canadian delegate, Abbé Ovila Fournier, who whispered to him that he was being considered as Secretary-General. The offer became formal (although still in the corridors) next day. Through the night, Harroy worked on the text of the Statutes with Jean Baer (Swiss biologist and Professor at Neuchâtel) and Büttikofer's assistant, Marguerite Caram, born in Lebanon but a Swiss citizen, and known as 'Gogo'. Poor 'Bubu' (as Büttikofer was nicknamed), aware of his defeat, brought them sandwiches.[8] When Harroy was elected, '*while everyone applauded me, the sad Bubu crossed the meeting room with a tragic air to shake me theatrically by the hand*'.[68].

It was agreed by 25 votes to 6, with 19 abstentions, that the Secretariat would be based in Brussels, and the President of IRSAC, Professor de Bruyne, found it space in his building.[52,68] On the day after IUPN was constituted, Harroy was also appointed temporary manager of the International Office. Van Tienhoven was very pleased, noting that '*once the Union is properly housed a gradual joining of the organizations would become possible, something which is of the utmost importance to nature protection*'.[71] On 5 July 1949 van Tienhoven stepped down as Chairman of the Office, becoming Honorary Chairman; van Straelen took over the Chair, and Harroy was confirmed as the Director. '*My mandate was to incorporate it into IUPN, which as a result would inherit its valuable library*'.[69] The process which was to lead to a full merger in 1955 was under way, and an old wound was set to heal.

The new Union also did some technical work – an important demonstration that it could advance international cooperation for conservation. Roger Heim presided over the European and African Technical Symposium, which had six sessions dealing respectively with legislation and action by governments to protect nature, the scientific management of wildlife, big game protection in Africa, definitions of national parks and nature reserves, fauna conventions and international legislation and the integration of the UNESCO and UNSCCUR Conferences. It is remarkable how many of the people who were to dominate IUCN for two decades were there, in action, at the very start. It is also clear that the American influence was substantial – IUPN might have hatched in a European nest, but its flights were to be worldwide.

And the Symposium picked up education as a key. Hal Coolidge was co-sponsor of a resolution that recognized that '*one of the most effective means of ensuring the Protection of Nature is to make the world aware of the extreme seriousness of this question*', and went on to stress that the education '*not only of children and their teachers, but of the public in general*' was essential to success. They therefore called for cooperation between UNESCO and the new Union, so that plans could be prepared.[52]

The Technical Symposium also suggested the '*preparation of a World Convention to serve as a basis for future international cooperation in the field of the "protection of nature" and to assist in the development of national legislation*'. (Was this the first glimmering of an idea brought to fruition in the Convention on Biological Diversity 44 years later?) Finally, they urged the appointment of five specialist committees to give technical assistance to UNESCO in carrying out the programme for the latter's conference to be held in 1949 – dealing respectively with the African region, the European region, conservation education, nomenclature and general coordination with UNESCO.[52] The IUPN/IUCN Commission on Education had its earliest roots in that proposal.

Looking back across 50 years, and despite the in-fighting and the personalities, one can only admire the vision of the founding fathers of IUPN. Despite their differences, Bernard and van Tienhoven, van Straelen and Büttikofer, Heim and Huxley, Coolidge, Osborn, Harroy and Nicholson, shared a basic ideal. And Julian Huxley's personal commitment was clearly crucial. While this was rooted in the application of science, his vision was far broader. He believed passionately that ecology must be deployed in the service of humanity, as the foundation for social development (a theme that has remained central to IUCN for 50 years and gained global recognition at the 'Earth Summit' in Rio de Janeiro in June 1992). He recognized that the protection of nature could not be achieved in isolation, but demanded fundamental changes in human thought. That wider vision is stated admirably – indeed prophetically – in a letter written to Huxley by his brother Aldous, the well-known writer, on 25 January 1948. Aldous Huxley wrote:

'*Meanwhile I come to feel more and more that no system of morals is adequate which does not include within the sphere of moral relationships, not only other human beings, but animals, plants and even things. Do as you would be done by applies to Nature as much as to man. We have done quite monstrously badly by the earth we live in, and now the earth we live in, with its soil eroded, its forests ravaged, its rivers polluted, its mineral resources reduced, is doing so badly by us that, unless we stop our insane fiddling at power politics and use all available knowledge, intelligence and good will to repair the harm we have done, the whole of mankind will be starving in a dust bowl within a century or two. People still seem to believe that there is poverty in the midst of plenty, when in fact there is only poverty in the midst of growing poverty – and all through our own fault, through not treating nature morally.*

And the Western religious tradition has never taught that Nature ought to be treated morally. Catholic moralists still cite Genesis to justify man treating the lower animals as things. One has to go to China to find a moral system that takes in Nature as well as man. Lao-tsu and Chuang-tsu are quite clear on the subject. Tao is immanent on every level, from the material, through the organic, to the mental and spiritual, and it is as sacrilegious to outrage the Nature of Things on the lower levels as on the higher.

The Taoist doctrine of wu-wei, or equilibrium – of the balance which it is wrong and fatal to upset – is basically identical with what modern conservationists teach. We need to philosophize and poetize the conservationist's doctrine and to incorporate it into the general thought and sentiment of our age. As things stand, hardly any attention is paid in schools or universities (outside the specialist fields) to the practical and, much less, to the philosophical implications of conservationism on the one hand and our current destructionism on the other. It seems to me that there is here an important task for UNESCO to undertake. If we don't do something about it pretty soon, we shall find that, even if we escape atomic warfare, we shall destroy our civiliza-

tion by destroying the cosmic capital on which we live. Our relation to the earth is not that of mutually beneficial symbiosis; we have become the kind of parasite that kills its host, even at the risk of killing itself.'[72]

When the delegates left Fontainebleau in October 1948, some to return home, and some to tour the lovelier regions of France, no doubt many among them hoped and trusted that the infant International Union for the Protection of Nature would indeed be in the lead in the battle against human self-destruction. But some must also have wondered how this could be achieved, when despite the high ideals and rhetoric, they had made scanty arrangements for its financing.

3 The Union Established

The First Steps

The Union that emerged from Fontainebleau was a compromise. While it was constituted as a governmental and non-governmental organization, a number of governments had, quite deliberately, made sure that the intergovernmental element would not predominate, and that they were not committed to injecting money into it. The Secretary-General was only employed by IUPN part-time. The leaders of the new body had '*more enthusiasm than experience*'.[1] The first problem was how to make its mark while operating with the slenderest and most uncertain of resources. The second was how to make a body that was a creature of 'Northern' culture, with founders largely from Europe and North America, into something truly global.

Jean-Paul Harroy had to start from scratch because the Swiss League did not transfer the archives covering the Basel and Brunnen meetings and the preparations for Fontainebleau.[2] His chief task was to secure enough funds for essential expenses, including travel to meetings abroad. 'Gogo' Caram reproached him for his parsimony, and the salaries paid to the tiny office were extremely meagre, but one reason was his determination to produce as many publications as possible, as a basis for the expansion of the Union.[2] Building on the meetings at Basel, Brunnen and Fontainebleau, and on the database assembled by van Tienhoven, Harroy worked to create a network of conservationists, numbered first in hundreds and then in thousands, with the Union as their central information exchange. With the support of Julian Huxley and UNESCO, he also sought to convene conferences that would reinforce those exchanges.[2]

Writing in 1988, Harroy recalled that the first programme the Board drew up in 1948 and asked him to implement had three main objectives.[3] The first and most important was '*to make the Union known, accepted, esteemed, and officially recognized*'. Second, they sought:

> '*to weld the tiny embryonic nucleus of European and American naturalists already converted to conservation into a powerful, constantly expanding, worldwide...network of "conservationists" (which was already a catchword in English) from all walks of life: politicians, economists, civil servants, pioneer ecologists, field workers, lawyers, directors of NGOs, and so on, who knew one another personally, who corresponded with one another, who exchanged documents and who helped one another*'.

The third objective '*in so far as the Union's meagre resources permitted, and while striving constantly to increase them*' was to start promoting, at national level and particularly in the developing world, information and education of the public and authorities; local actions on behalf of conservation; and coordinated ecological research of every kind. The Union sought to participate voluntarily in every major international action on behalf of 'the protection of nature'[3]

The Union was clearly seen as the centre of a network, and as a facilitator and catalyst. It was, moreover, to facilitate a certain group of people – scientists, administrators, naturalists, politicians and so on – *who knew one another personally, who corresponded with one another, who exchanged documents*. The corresponding network is a system well known in science – Linneus, Gilbert White of Selborne and Charles Darwin all used it – but by adopting it IUPN set out to work with and through an elite. They were – at least initially – those committed people who had dominated the process of its creation. Almost all were 'Northern' establishment figures, although many – like Harroy and Coolidge – had worked in the developing world, knew some of its problems and had many contacts there.

The surprising thing about Harroy's manifesto is that it spoke of a 'tiny embryonic nucleus' when so many powerful organizations actually existed in parts of Europe and North America even in 1948. The Sierra Club, the Wilderness Society, the National Wildlife Federation, the Boone and Crockett Club, the Izaac Walton League, the New York Zoological Society (with the Conservation Foundation), the American Museum of Natural History, the American Wildlife Institute, the Smithsonian Institution, the National Audubon Society and many others were active in the United States and their collective membership was in the hundreds of thousands.[4] Britain probably had the greatest variety of naturalist's socicties of any country,[5]) but there were many also in France, the Netherlands, Belgium and Switzerland (these four nations contributed 27 founder members of IUCN).[6] The European bodies included many people interested in the wildlife of their colonial, or ex-colonial territories. Surely the challenge was to convince them of the need for the international dimension, and to see IUPN as a body that would give them what we now call 'value added'?

The IUPN approach was totally different from that which later moved the World Wildlife Fund, Friends of the Earth and Greenpeace – all of which were also built around a small group of committed professionals, but reached out to and stimulated the wider public. These bodies have worked by creating popular momentum to raise funds for conservation, or to demand action, or both. Although IUPN talked about informing and educating the public, when it urged action on governments it did so from within the constitutional system, and with due respect. It was not an activist pressure-group, and perhaps it did not press its potential members and supporters hard enough.

The Union relied on ecology and ecologists. This too is a radically different approach from that of the later activist international organizations. It had its strengths and its risks. Strengths in that it meant that IUPN's proposals were founded on respectable scientific logic. Risks, because academic ecologists had shown themselves prone to be dismissive of human needs and to value most highly those ecosystems that were not disturbed by people. Yet if the Union was really to promote action in the developing world, it would have to understand the needs of people – especially poor people – and sympathize with the reasons why at times they destroyed nature. Here the process became as important as the substance, and there was worry about the way Europeans seemed '*to be trying from the outside to propose (or impose) themselves or their techniques*' on the '*autonomous peoples of the tropics*'.[7] The expeditions, surveys and advice might be good, and accelerate the formation of plans, but Jean-Paul Harroy argued that they would be valued and implemented better if they were '*obtained the hard way, by initiative from within...*'.[7] A further problem was the reverential attitude that affected parts of the early IUPN and saw nature protection as a moral duty, based on respect for '*this world whose intricacies transcend human imagination and whose forms surpass in beauty all the works of humanity*'.[1] This was not an easy notion to transfer to countries experiencing poverty and hunger.

The First Challenge: Success at Lake Success

There were two major environmental conferences in 1949, both held at the temporary UN Headquarters at Lake Success in the United States. The first was UNSCCUR, which brought together some 4000 scientists, economists, engineers, resource technicians and other specialists from all regions of the world to discuss how to apply the techniques of resource conservation and utilization to the development that was so essential in the post-war world.[8,9] The second, held in parallel, was the IUPN–UNESCO Conference on the Protection of Nature. It was charged by Julian Huxley with examining '*means of educating the public to a better understanding of man's relationship to his environment,*' making '*recommendations concerning legislative measures which might be taken on a national and international scale for the maintenance of nature's equilibrium*' and undertaking '*a preliminary study of a World Convention for the Protection of Nature*'.[10] Under a contract signed on 4 November 1948, UNESCO assigned to the new Union the main scientific responsibility for preparing it.[10]

Not everyone was keen on these events. The British, in particular, were very negative, giving substance to Miriam Rothschild's impression that the Americans were the positive ones.[11] Max Nicholson wrote bluntly that in the British view '*so far as the protection of nature is concerned, neither of the Conferences need ever have been held*'.[12] The UK refused to send a special delegation to the Protection of Nature Conference, instead naming Professor Solly Zuckerman (later Chief Scientific Adviser to the British Government) and Dr W A Macfarlane, head of the UK Scientific Mission in Washington, who were to be there for UNSCCUR anyway. Max Nicholson's brief for them rehearsed the history of IUPN, making it clear that in his view (and that of his colleagues) the whole exercise had been premature. He then criticized the Conference itself saying that:

> '*not only has the UNSCCUR conference against our advice been extended, quite unnecessarily, to cover nature protection, about which the UN knows nothing, but also this special Technical Conference on the Protection of Nature has been organised by UNESCO at the same time, and participation in it has been made the price of any UNESCO financial support for the IUPN*'.[12]

Julian Huxley, in contrast, saw the Conference as important vindication of his efforts in creating IUPN. For him it was the new Union's 'moment of truth' – a proof that it really could make a difference to the world scene. He assigned Eleen Sam to work with IUPN on preparations, and also enlisted the help of the celebrated American conservationist, Fred M Packard, the Field Secretary of the National Parks

Association,[13] and a young Frenchman, Alain Gille.[15,16] The IUPN Executive Board drew up a list of experts whose participation should be supported.[14] Some 130 people attended, those from the IUPN establishment including Ira Gabrielson, Director of the US Fish and Wildlife Service (who chaired the Conference), Charles Bernard, Hal Coolidge, Frank Fraser Darling, Roger Heim, Jean-Paul Harroy and Theodore Monod. By today's standards, perhaps, the programme was a little incoherent – raising, as it did, topics any one of which would now be the subject of a conference in its own right. But equally, it is astonishing (and perhaps depressing) how many of the topics chosen would be topical today. Between the opening and closing plenary sessions, five themes were considered in a total of 12 sessions.[18]

The first theme (allocated three sessions) was the worldwide education of the public in nature protection, using the most suitable information media and schooling at various educational levels. The role of national parks and protected areas in the cultural and aesthetic education of the general public was also debated.

The theme to be given greatest emphasis, with a total of six sessions, was international cooperation to promote ecological research. There was particular emphasis on the effects of development enterprises on the 'balance of nature'; the impact of DDT and other pesticides (this was, let it be remembered, 15 years before Rachel Carson published *Silent Spring*); the possible ecological impacts of the use of the drug antrycide against sleeping sickness in cattle; the consequences of the uncontrolled introduction of exotic species; the problem of vanishing large mammals in Asia and Africa; and the emergency action needed for preserving vanishing species of flora and fauna.

The remaining three themes received more summary treatment, with only one session each. They were the possibility of a World Convention on Nature Protection; the role of the IUPN central office in coordinating activities and facilitating the exchange of information on the protection of nature; and the special problems arising from national parks bordering a frontier.

The Lake Success Conference was the first landmark in IUPN's history, and it was important in building world action for nature protection, as Max Nicholson admitted afterwards.[17,18] The emphasis on ecological analysis was deliberate and it shows how the leaders of the Union saw its role. They wanted to build nature protection on modern ecological principles, and clearly saw the strong representation of scientific research centres and natural history societies in IUPN as a unique asset to this end. One reason why the Conference was judged a success was that it struck a new balance between the traditional focus on national parks and nature reserves, fish and game laws and forest exploitation and the new recognition of '*the necessity of developing ecological studies in all domains in order to base modern standards of nature protection on a less experimental foundation than had been done in the past*'.[19] A resolution dealing with the need to promote studies on human ecology was very well received by the delegates to the UN Economic and Social Council:

> '*another proof, if more proof is needed, of the urgent significance of ecology in the methods humanity must resort to, and that to the utmost, if it is to maintain for future generations the natural resources indispensable to their subsistence*'.[19]

The Lake Success Conference also proved that an independent and professional non-UN body could, by working in partnership with a UN agency such as UNESCO, deliver results of real value.[2] It caused the Executive Board to organize a series of technical conferences, some linked to sessions of the General Assembly at Brussels in 1950, Caracas in 1952, and Copenhagen in 1954 and others at The Hague and Salzburg in the intervening years. In the first six years these conferences considered rural landscape as a habitat for fauna and flora in densely populated countries, the management of nature reserves, the consequences for agriculture of the use of fire, the protection of endemic species on small islands, tourism and the protection of nature, the protection of fauna and flora at high altitudes, the Arctic fauna and the noxious effects of insecticides and herbicides on mammals and birds.[20]

Developing the Union

But after the euphoria of Lake Success, Harroy and his Board faced the mundane challenge of making IUPN into an organization effective enough to achieve the prizes that seemed to lie just beyond its grasp. They wanted to do as much as possible as quickly as possible. Yet the activities of the infant Union were constrained by circumstances. It needed more members and more money.

The membership in 1949 had, in a sense, passed through three sieves. The first of these selected, from the totality of world governments, international agencies and national nature protection bodies, those with sufficient interest to come to Fontainebleau at all. They were drawn from only 32 nations and nine international organizations.[21] The second sieve – the willingness to sign the Final Act – thinned the ranks further. Eighteen governments put their names down, eight from Western Europe, one (Poland) from Eastern Europe, five from Latin America (Argentina, Brazil, the Dominican Republic, Panama and Venezuela), one only from Africa (Egypt), two from South and East Asia (India and Siam (now Thailand)), and one from West Asia (Syria). No North American or Oceanian government was represented or signed. The non-governmental signatories were dominated by the 77 from Western Europe, followed by 17 from North America and seven from South America. Although the delegates' list records representatives from Greece, Iran, Mexico, Monaco, Nicaragua, New Zealand and Peru, none of these signed; nor did the Pan-American Union among the international organizations.

Moreover some of this 'representation' was of a kind we would consider doubtful today. Dr G F Herbert Smith of the United Kingdom is also listed as the sole New Zealand delegate, and he and Dr J H Westermann of the Netherlands were also the only 'Australian' representatives.[21] There was clearly a good deal of economical cross-representation, which also confirms that many governments were cool about the conference: Paris, after all, was awash with diplomats who *could* have been briefed to attend had their masters back home felt it appropriate. The gathering, in fact, was a meeting of the converted, especially from non-governmental societies.

The toughest sieve came after Fontainebleau. It was the test of confirmation of membership – backed by money. Not surprisingly, governments were the most backward at coming forward. By 1 July 1949 only two had confirmed their membership – Switzerland and Luxembourg – although Belgium, the host country for the new organization, had announced that it was taking the necessary formal steps.[13] In total IUPN had 65 confirmed members, of whom 36 had paid some kind of subscription. Of these 40 came from Western Europe, two from Eastern Europe, 17 from North America, four from Central and South America and two from Australasia and Oceania. There was none from Africa or Asia.[6,22]

It is slightly surprising that IUPN is said to have been seen in the United States as primarily a European show because the United States contributed the largest total of founding members, including most of the 'big names' in national conservation. But in this period many American organizations were largely concerned with action at home.[4] The Europeans, perhaps because they lived in small countries on a crowded continent, and had numerous colonial links, were more international. One early challenge was to convince the North Americans that they should take a wider view and make use of the new Union and its networks.

Looking at subject areas, the non-governmental members comprised 17 nature protection bodies, 15 scientific research organizations (including museums and universities), 13 natural history societies, five organizations especially concerned with national parks and nature reserves, four bodies strongly interested in landscape and scenery, four 'natural resource' bodies concerned with agriculture, forestry and wildlife management, two hunting organizations and four 'miscellaneous' clubs – the Alpine Clubs of France and Switzerland and the Touring Clubs of France and Italy.[13]

The finances were:

> '*one of the most difficult and delicate problems the Fontainebleau Conference had to face. Two equally pressing necessities led to an obvious deadlock. On the one hand it was essential to vote an immediate budget for the year 1948–9 so that the Union could begin working.*'[21]

That budget would have two elements, administrative and operative – the former being the sum essential for the work of the central Secretariat, and the latter the sum available for outside activities. But before a budget could be set, income had to be calculated and this was impossible:

> '*because the number of members paying contributions to the Union was unknown and because none of the delegates present could or would pledge his government or organization to pay a contribution which had not been previously fixed.*'[21]

It was an absurd situation, and that was not the end of it.

> '*There remains the question naturally put by every government or institution asked to join the Union: "what will be my membership fee?" The answer is simple: each member is free to fix his own subscription. The Union relies on the goodwill of those who have created it.*'[21]

The Financial Committee did lay down some guidelines. Governments were to be asked to pay according to population, the figure rising from US$250 a year for those with under five million inhabitants to $2000 a year for nations with over 20 million people. There was no adjustment for state of development, so the USA, China, India, Brazil and most of the larger South American states, and many European nations would have been on the same level. International organizations (whether governmental or non-governmental), 'public services' (ie government agencies) and national non-governmental bodies were all asked for $50 a year, again with no discrimination between states or between bodies of differing wealth. But of course these figures were not binding – it was hoped that members who could afford more would pay more, while others would pay less:

*'either because their country suffered from the war or because their
existing commitments make heavy demands on their budget. That need
be no obstacle. The manner of giving is worth more than the amount
contributed. A draft for a few dollars with a letter of encouragement
will be welcomed with gratitude if it comes from an association limited
in its resources but heartily devoted to the work of the Union.'*[21]

The people who met at Fontainebleau were realists. They must have understood the
administrative fatuity of such an approach. But they were in a dilemma. Either they
could create a new Union without any obligatory financial rules, and risk recurrent
crises, or they could have aborted the whole exercise. They were people of faith, and
chose to go ahead. But they were well aware that the non-governmental organizations had very little spare money,[23] while governments had almost universally refused
to incur any financial obligations (the concerns of the French, American and British
Governments, described in Chapter 2, were certainly shared by others, and the British
Treasury maintained almost identical arguments in 1956 when Max Nicholson tried
to secure agreement to UK membership at the time of the Edinburgh General
Assembly).[24] Returning from Fontainebleau, Henry G Maurice, President of the
Zoological Society of London, who had led the British contingent, noted that money
was likely to be the key to success.[25] But there was no way to secure even the most
modest operative or administrative budget.

IUPN began with one great strength – its relationship with UNESCO. It was the
only international environmental body to be created by a UN agency which then
stood back and encouraged it to pursue actions that could conceivably have been part
of the mandate of that agency. And it is unique that an agency of the United Nations
– which has generally been very wary of giving any semblance of authority to non-
governmental bodies – should have helped in the creation of a hybrid organization
that brought governments, government agencies, international governmental and
non-governmental organizations and national non-governmental organizations into
the same debating chamber.

As Chapter 2 demonstrates, Julian Huxley deserves much of the personal credit
for that act of creation, working at times against the doubts of his own Government
and Executive Board. He clearly delighted in it, for in 1970, when receiving a WWF
Gold Medal, he said *'my greatest source of pride is to have helped create IUCN – in
the teeth of considerable opposition I must say – when I was Director of UNESCO'*.[26]
Some say that the opposition never forgave him, and that their criticism was one
reason why he did not get a second term of office in 1949.[15] He clearly saw IUPN as
an important vehicle for associating nature protection experts with the wider scientific community, already tied to UNESCO through the latter's agreements with the
International Council of Scientific Unions, ICSU.

In its early years, UNESCO's subventions were IUPN's life-line. Some people
clearly expected that they would continue, so that IUPN would, in effect, be a permanent agent of the organization. Max Nicholson has commented that *'it was at least
partly through misunderstanding concerning UNESCO's initial support that the
Union was launched without any funding base and was forced for years to struggle
along in penury'*.[27] But Huxley himself had made it clear from the beginning that its
policy was not to provide long-term unrestricted funding to external organizations,
even those started with its encouragement.[28] Balked of substantial governmental
support, IUPN would have to look to its richer non-governmental members, most of
whom were in the United States.

At Fontainebleau, Fairfield Osborn had asked '*Who is going to pay for it?*' and received the answer '*You are, Fair!*'[17,29] Max Nicholson recalls that in 1947 Ira Gabrielson and Hal Coolidge (who was, of all the Americans, the one with most international experience) Americans called on him and asked blunt questions about the new body, which some felt was being wished on them by the Europeans. The financial difficulties may well have been aggravated by the fact that the Union was dominated by conservationists who were not money-raisers, and did not build bridges to potential money-raisers who were not respected as conservationists.[11] This, of course, was the problem Nicholson and others tried to resolve a decade later when they created the World Wildlife Fund.

An Organization on a Shoe-string

Throughout the period between 1948 and 1956, the IUPN Secretariat remained almost constant in size, and very small. Jean-Paul Harroy, as Secretary-General, provided the leadership, but Marguerite Caram, the head of the Secretariat, was clearly the anchor.[2] Her commitment, judgement and international sensitivity won wide acclaim.[7,30] Through the good offices of Hal Coolidge, three Americans – Sue Coolidge, Nancy Thacher and Richard Purser – came in succession to serve as general assistants at no cost to IUPN.[2] There were two Belgian secretaries. The accounts were placed under the eye of the accountant of the National Scientific Research Funds in Brussels. A librarian–typist was engaged early in 1949 and put at the disposal of the International Office for the Protection of Nature. Another grant from UNESCO made it possible to begin work on unpacking the voluminous documentation collected by that Office, which had been boxed for security during the war.[13] The tightness of the funds can be judged by the fact that three members of the Secretariat paid their own way to the third General Assembly in Caracas, Venezuela.[31]

Jean-Paul Harroy did not have an easy time. To start with, he had two jobs – that at IUPN and that as General Secretary of the Belgian Institute for Scientific Research in Central Africa, IRSAC. Most of his salary came from the latter, and life was complicated by the fact that he and Louis van den Berghe, the head of IRSAC, did not get on very well. Van den Berghe had not been at all pleased when Harroy was appointed to IUPN, and interpreted the 'gentleman's agreement' under which he could not devote 'official' IRSAC time to IUPN strictly. Harroy therefore had to work for IRSAC until 5.30 pm each day, and for IUPN in the evenings, at weekends, and frequently during his holidays. Fortunately, his wife, Mady, not only accepted the situation but herself gave a lot of support to IUPN. Jean-Paul, says Alain Gille,[15] who knew him well, '*was a real bulldozer*', adding '*if IUPN was able to operate, and operate efficiently, immediately after the Fontainebleau Conference it was mainly due to Jean-Paul Harroy and his strong personality*'. He was also a man of immense charm, warmth and commitment, as the many appreciations following his death in 1995 at the age of 86 testify.[30]

Widening the membership was important. All those who had signed up at Fontainebleau were approached and asked to confirm their membership (and to pay as much as they could afford). Ten thousand copies of a brochure (5000 of them in French and 5000 in English) were printed. The Government of Belgium was asked to approach all other governments and urge their adherence. Meanwhile the Board allowed some bodies who had not signed the Fontainebleau Final Act to join as temporary members, and three – the American Museum of Natural History, the Biological Service of the United Kingdom (later transformed into the UK Nature Conservancy) and the Forest and Bird Protection Society of New Zealand – did so.[13]

The Programme of IUPN

Despite all these impediments, IUPN began an ambitious programme. Following Article I of the Statutes, it had six themes:

1 To participate in safeguarding those parts of nature, habitats or species which are in danger of being destroyed.
2 To spread the knowledge that is already available on the art and science of nature protection.
3 To educate adults and children to realize the danger which lies in the alteration of natural resources and the necessity of action against such a danger.
4 To instigate international agreements on the protection of nature.
5 To encourage and increase knowledge on the art and science of nature protection.
6 To disseminate information about the protection of nature which is likely to promote conservation throughout the world when made known either to the public or to persons or bodies concerned with conserving natural communities.

Quite evidently, this called for an interdisciplinary approach which, even if ecology was at its heart, must embrace economics, law, education, communications and an understanding of public administration.[1] Given the tiny Secretariat it is also clear it could only work if national organizations and societies pressed forward vigorously in these fields, using the IUPN as a network through which to exchange experience, pool information and reinforce one another. As Max Nicholson put it:

> '*International protection, in our view, is not a separate subject on its own, but the natural outcome of a number of effective national protection movements and organizations co-operating with each other. Little, if anything, can be done in international protection, except on the basis of practical measures of education, legislation and organization in at least some of the leading countries concerned. Experience and information so gathered can readily be made available to all interested countries, and we are very willing to do this through IUPN, but we do not regard the Union, or any other international initiative in this field, as capable of very great development, except on the basis of properly organized national support which it is still premature to expect. What the Union needs most is two or three years of looking around, gathering information and support, encouraging suitable education and propaganda, and winning the confidence of the experts and administrations in the interested countries, with a minimum of international conferences and grandiose or expensive projects.*'[12]

One way forward was through partnership with other international bodies, and especially UN agencies. In 1950–52, the Union was involved in many international conferences, and especially in the Advisory Committee on Arid Zones created by UNESCO in 1951 at a meeting in Algiers.[32,33] There was significant input to a symposium on the conservation of nature in the Near East, organized by UNESCO in Beirut in June 1954. There were contacts with a string of UNESCO technical missions, and the beginning of partnership with FAO (on vegetable species threatened with extinction), with the International Whaling Commission and with the International Hunting Council (particularly on the protection of African anthropoid apes).

Saving Species and Habitats

The Lake Success Conference called for action to promote the conservation of animals threatened with extinction. In response, Hal Coolidge devised the Survival Service, which started in 1950 under the leadership of J-M Vrydagh, thanks to a special grant of US$2500 from UNESCO.[34]. Coolidge modelled it on the panels and Commissions of the United States National Academy of Sciences, where he was Director of the Pacific Science Board.[35] This structure drew in outstanding volunteer experts (who did not have to come only from IUPN member organizations). It allowed for a great deal of flexibility in the topics addressed. It also cost the Union very little (since Commission members bore their own costs and worked largely through correspondence). It was also more attractive to donors of funds than support for a central bureaucracy would have been. But what the infant IUPN lacked – and world conservation largely lacked until the creation of WWF – was the funding to send experts into the field to investigate the real nature of alleged problems, or to set up projects in partnership with conservationists on the ground in developing countries.

The Survival Service was the forerunner of the Species Survival Commission, which has unquestionably been one of IUCN's greatest successes, and the 'Coolidge model' was later applied with equal effect to national parks and protected areas. By 1954 the Service was reporting to the Beirut meeting on such things as the status of the Syrian and Nubian wild asses and the Arabian oryx, and supporting an expert symposium held at Ambuklao in the Philippines after the Pacific Science Congress in November 1953 (with Julian Huxley, now an honorary member of IUPN, in the Chair).

Having gathered as much information as it could, IUPN raised a number of issues directly with governments. The Board meeting on 18 March 1949 decided '*with all the necessary caution...to commence immediately to intervene directly with certain Governments in order to stimulate, support or facilitate important initiatives taken in favour of the protection of nature*'.[14] It wrote to the newly independent Government of Indonesia urging protection of the orang-utan and the Javan and Sumatran rhinoceros. It pressed the new Government of India to conserve the great one-horned Asian rhinoceros. Jakarta and Delhi returned comforting words. It addressed Belgium, the Netherlands, Switzerland, the UK and the Military High Commission in occupied Germany about disturbance of their limited surviving wild areas by military manoeuvres. All except the last returned favourable answers. In Italy, it urged the promotion of science teaching in schools, action to control the hunting of quails, the protection of the Valley of Aosta and the protection of the European brown bear in two regions where it was threatened. The Italians were encouraging about bears, but less precise about quails, Aosta and schoolchildren. Algeria and Morocco (still under French rule) were harangued about the status of the North African hartebeest (bubal), and both made favourable answers. Action was also being prepared over the introduction of the axis deer into Hawaii, a dam at Esneux in Belgium, 'game' control in Rhodesia (now Zambia and Zimbabwe), and possible frontier national parks between Switzerland, France, Italy and Spain.

Much the same pattern of activity continued through the period of the General Assembly held in Brussels in 1950, that in Caracas, Venezuela in 1952, and the Fourth Assembly in Copenhagen in 1954. The creation of an International Commission for the Protection of Nature in the Alps, with Charles Bernard as President, brought a young German, Wolfgang Burhenne, then Secretary-General of the Schutzgemeinschaft Deutsches Wild of Munich, into contact with IUPN for the first time. Approaches were made to the Governments of Austria, Belgium, Chile, the French Pacific Union, Germany, Indonesia, Italy, Japan, Nepal, Turkey and Venezuela – but once again the Board repeated its policy never to intervene with governments unless there had been a serious study of all aspects of the problem because '*all would be lost by a badly-advised approach which might bring a negative response from a State, pointing out some pertinent factors unknown to the Union*'.[36] This caution and professionalism was, undoubtedly, what the members wanted and did much to confirm the role of the Union as a scientific body – but it again points to the contrast with the activist campaigners of the late 20th century, who would scarcely give a button for '*a negative response from a State.*'

Not all the early judgements about conservation issues have stood the hard test of hindsight. In September 1952, for example, the Executive Board discussed the protection of the whale and concluded that

> '*this protection being assured – and successfully – by a specialist inter-national organization, it is decided that the Union will not undertake any separate action in favour of this mammal, but that it will contact the International Whaling Board with the aim of possibly lending it support in case of need*'.[37]

Applying Existing Knowledge

The second theme was '*to spread the knowledge that is already available on the art and science of nature protection*'. Publications were of great concern to the infant Union. Indeed an entire meeting of the Executive Board, on 19 March 1949, was dedicated to the topic.[38] It proved impossible for IUPN to continue the excellent, but expensive, journal *Pro Natura*, which the Swiss League had started on behalf of the Provisional Union, and the Union was without a journal for some years, relying instead on biennial reports from the Secretary-General while recognizing that these could not do what was needed.[19,34]

But there were important publications none the less. For example, in February 1949 the Secretariat issued a 100-page set of preparatory documents for the Lake Success Conference.[19,36] In 1950 the 583-page volume of proceedings of that Conference and a major volume on *The Position of Nature Protection Throughout the World* appeared.[39] By the time of the Fourth General Assembly, held in

Copenhagen in 1954, five volumes arising from technical meetings and several other major works had been published or were in preparation.[40],[41] The Union was conspicuously acknowledged in the report of the Third International Conference for the Protection of the Fauna and Flora of Africa held in Bukavu (in the then Belgian Congo) in 1953, of which Jean-Paul Harroy was rapporteur general and editor. The point was clearly established: IUPN was beginning to make a difference by creating a library shelf of conservation volumes of many kinds, and it was bringing the expertise of the world together to focus on contemporary themes.[40]

Advancing Education

Theme 3 was '*to educate adults and children to realize the danger which lies in the alteration of natural resources and the necessity of action against such a danger*'. It was pursued in two ways – through the Secretariat, working closely with UNESCO, and through an Education Commission. Alain Gille, appointed to UNESCO in January 1948 to prepare a report on '*Education for the conservation and more efficient use of natural resources*', became the first Secretary of the Commission, holding the post for over six years.[42] As he recalls:

> '*the symbiosis with UNESCO in this period was close. With UNESCO support, the Union produced film strips, exhibitions, manuals and other material to disseminate the concept of nature protection among UN member states. UNESCO was interested directly both in science and education and established a number of Regional Offices of science and technology in order to build communication between local scientists and intellectuals.*'[15]

In 1950 Jean-Paul Harroy reported to the Brussels General Assembly that, thanks to a special grant of US$1500 from UNESCO, IUPN had produced 39,000 booklets and 130,000 illustrated pamphlets for use by teachers and children in Italy, which became '*the first country in which an active campaign for making known the concept of nature protection was launched*' with at least one compulsory lesson a year on the theme in intermediate-level classes. After the Brussels General Assembly even more weight was put on education, because UNESCO indicated that '*it was particularly disposed to underwrite such enterprises*'.[36] The school programme was greatly amplified.[43] And UNESCO wanted to broaden the programme to include adult information, so a 'universal document' was to be published, initially in English, French and Spanish. FAO also contributed to these efforts.[42] An exhibition, a film strip, posters for youth hostels, postage stamps, nature protection slogans for government use – the programme had burgeoned.[43] On the UNESCO side, its energetic promoter was Eleen Sam, now Mme Jean Thierry-Mieg.

The logical assumption was that the Commission on Education would serve as a voluntary network drawing in experts to back the Secretariat and make IUPN indispensable to UNESCO as its right hand in this specialized field. Sadly, the Commission did not start very well. Although it had been established at Fontainebleau, under the chairmanship of William Vogt of the United States, and with Jean Baer, George Brewer and Frank Fraser Darling among the eight members, it had done little more than prepare the agenda for three meetings at the Lake

Success Conference, '*devoted to the study of how the general public can be educated in problems of nature protection*'.[13] Indeed, Harroy told the Brussels General Assembly bluntly that it '*had failed to function*', and saw this as '*one of the handicaps which have hampered the Union from the start*'. But the Commission was revitalized between 1952 and 1954 under a new Chair, Dr Ira Gabrielson of the USA, with Alain Gille as Secretary. It took the lead in producing material for the film strip called for by UNESCO. Dr Gabrielson brought to Caracas the draft of the *Handbook of Conservation* prepared in Washington by Laurence Palmer, who was a Gabrielson associate.[36] This may have been the first publication in the history of the Union attributable to a voluntary Commission: in the report to the 1954 Assembly it was described by Jean-Paul Harroy as '*the best and most important contribution to the work of IUPN achieved by someone not belonging to the Board or Secretariat*'.[40]

UNESCO and IUPN worked closely together in their relationships with youth, and IUPN took part in a meeting in November 1950 with representatives of international youth organizations. International youth nature study camps were held in 1952 and 1953 and planned for 1955, although IUPN was only able to help support the first. These camps were seen as important because many of those attending them went on to pursue education as a career. They led to the creation by IUCN of a new International Youth Federation which, by 1958, was becoming active in Europe and with which the Union was to have an uneasy relationship down the years.[44]

Promoting International Agreements

The fourth theme was '*to instigate international agreements on the protection of nature*'. Lake Success resolutions requested IUPN to press the competent authorities to convene conferences to review the effectiveness of two major regional conventions – that adopted in London in 1933 on the protection of species in Africa, and the Washington Convention of 1940 which did the same for Latin America. But the British (once again!) said '*not yet – it's premature*' and the Americans also hedged. However, things changed, and the Committee for Technical Coordination in Africa did agree to convene the conference in Bukavu in October 1953 which (among other things) reviewed the workings of the 1933 London Convention. On the other hand the notion of getting Venezuela to convene a western hemisphere group at the time of the Caracas General Assembly fell flat.[36]

One of the sessions at Lake Success had considered the case for a World Convention for the Protection of Nature. Instead IUPN chose '*to substitute a World Charter inspired by the Universal Declaration on the Rights of Man*'.[36] The French and English Vice-Presidents, Roger Heim and G F Herbert Smith, set to work on texts, in partnership with the UNESCO legal service. It was not until 20 years later, however, that the World Charter for Nature was endorsed by the UN General Assembly – and there was no link between the two initiatives.[45] There was also little progress on the vexed issue of overlapping nomenclature, especially on national parks and nature reserves – '*where an effort on the part of the Union might have thrown some light on a subject which needs clarification to avoid confusion*'. Again, writing in 1950, Jean-Paul Harroy was blunt: '*the difficulty of launching the Commission appointed at Fontainebleau is again the reason why so little has been done*'. Nothing happened to change the situation, and the Commission (and subject) sank from sight in the drifting sands of time, to be exhumed by the Commission on National Parks and Protected Areas in the 1970s.

Increasing Scientific Knowledge

Theme 5 was '*to encourage and increase knowledge of the art and science of nature protection*'. Setting up the Survival Service was seen as a positive step in this direction, but IUPN also favoured getting ecological experts onto the ground. It was suggested that it might send independent specialists to look at the problems encountered by the massive (and disastrous) ground-nut growing scheme in what was then Tanganyika: the British authorities and the developers agreed but the venture failed because UNESCO was unable to provide finance for work in a colony.[46] Another proposed ecological study was to be on the effects of bush fires in Africa, and here the Marshall Plan was asked for money. This did not get going either, but in 1952–54 there was an input to the UNESCO arid zone project, and the Union encouraged a pioneer study, by Dr Enrique Beltran of Mexico, of wildlife along the Pan-American Highway.[36]

Yet other early projects concerned '*the repercussions – harmful or not, apparent or not, desired or not – of the generalized use of powerful modern agricultural chemicals*' including insecticides and herbicides based on plant hormones.[34] Between the Brussels and Caracas General Assemblies, there were technical meetings on the management of nature reserves and '*rural landscape as a habitat for flora and fauna in densely populated countries*'.[36]

Promoting Conservation

The sixth theme was '*to disseminate information about the protection of nature which is likely to promote conservation throughout the world when made known either to the public or to persons or bodies concerned with conserving natural communities*'. The many publications were seen as important here, although so far as wider dissemination went, in 1950 '*the Union has been almost completely blocked by not having a mouthpiece such as Pro Natura*'.[34] The situation did not change until January 1952, when a simple four-page IUPN bulletin commenced publication, appearing every second month thereafter.

Collaboration with the International Office for the Protection of Nature was another element. In 1950–52, the IOPN, then led by Mlle Renee Houba, began to pull together its information base and compile a book on the '*Position of Nature Protection throughout the world in 1950*'.[36,39] The project was linked to another – the *Atlas of Nature Reserves of the World* – and led directly to the continuing IUPN/IUCN role as the producer of what was first termed the *World List of National Parks and Equivalent Reserves* and is now the *United Nations List of National Parks and Protected Areas*.[47]

Information was also disseminated by representational and promotional visits. Vice-Presidents Hal Coolidge and Roger Heim flew the flag with great success at the Seventh Pacific Science Congress – so much so that the Committee agreed to seek membership. Hal Coolidge went to Japan and made '*extraordinarily fruitful contacts*'. Jean-Paul Harroy visited the UK and also South Africa, on other missions of liaison and promotion. And a UNESCO contract allowed IUPN to establish a Conservation Service whose task was continuing liaison between the members of the Union and other organizations and individuals '*concerned with the conservation and protection of nature and resources in general*'.[36]

Visions and Limitations

There is no doubt that in its formative years IUPN brought together leading scientists and conservationists who were full of ideas and who correctly identified issues that were to vex the world for many decades to come. The tragedy is that very few were followed up with vigour, and for this a lack of money was certainly one cause. Even so, there is a puzzle. There were powerful and well-endowed national organizations in many countries, even then. A number were members of IUPN. Others must have known of it, and seen its publications. For some reason the messages did not get through. Had they done so, and been acted on, billions of dollars might have been saved. But that is hindsight.

Jean-Paul Harroy's report to the Brussels General Assembly in 1950 made an almost breathtaking plea for higher status.[19,34] He argued that '*it is not unreasonable to claim that the United Nations should place the Union on a level with its principal specialized agencies*' and fund it accordingly. He thought there would be no risk of conflict with FAO or other agencies – the tasks were more than enough for all – and (echoing Franklin Roosevelt and UNSCCUR) asserted that the IUPN,

> '*given the means to act on a scale commensurable with its objectives could play a major part in securing world peace. If the unbridled devastation of natural resources, which is permitted in the 20th century throughout the world were curbed...by consolidating the basis of world economy a greater contribution would be made towards averting the risks of war than that resulting from political meetings and military coalitions.*'

The visions were there. The ecologists were there. The machinery was there – or could have been developed. But Harroy was critical of his own members. '*If we want it to be a success, the organization has the right to expect more concrete support from its members*', he wrote. '*Only with the active participation of the members in the life of the Union...will the organization derive the necessary vigour to face the gigantic task which it has been given*'.[34]

He went on to urge them to take some practical steps: to obtain the adherence of their governments, as state members, paying a substantial fee; to obtain new members; to participate actively in the technical Commissions and make them work; to make space available in their own publications so that IUPN's work could be highlighted; to alert the Union to issues it might publicize; and to help the Union obtain consultative status with other UN agencies besides UNESCO (consultative status with ECOSOC was obtained on 19 March 1951).[48] On the other hand, given the inclusion of governments among the Union's members, the Executive Board rejected the idea that it might become a member of the International Council of

Scientific Unions (probably a wise decision also because of the arguments Joseph Needham had adduced at the beginning).[49]

Relations with the membership were obviously crucial, for they had to be the channels for applying the Union's syntheses of knowledge. In recent years National Committees have played an increasingly important part in the liaison process. But in the early years some Committees were created as a device to save money.[50] These countries,

> '*instead of leaving the Union in direct contact with its members, as provided by the constitution, have grouped all the services and institutions into one committee which pays a higher fee than that demanded of each member but not as high as the sum that would be received if the members had adhered separately to the Union*'.

The British were particular offenders, and the report to the Second Session of the General Assembly[34] made it clear that their conduct was unacceptable. The Secretary-General was sent to London '*in order to clarify the relations between the Union and the British Coordinating Committee*'.

A different problem arose in Italy. In January 1954 the Board was astonished to learn that a body called the Union Italienne pour la Protection de la Nature had adopted the initials 'UIPN' as its letter head and called its periodical *Pro Natura*. The President was asked to jump on those concerned from the greatest achievable height.[51] Six months later the Board was told that the organization in question had actually applied to join the *International* UIPN, and minuted testily '*that the International Union for the Protection of Nature was little inclined to welcome to its bosom an institution which had deliberately chosen a title which gave rise through its initials to a confusion with the acronym of the IUPN*'.[52]

Yet other members complained because they thought actions lagged behind words. The American Society of Mammalogists resigned from membership in 1954 on the grounds that IUPN had not brought about sufficient results in the field of conservation of mammals.[40] The Survival Service had made recommendations and the letters sent to the authorities concerned had been politely acknowledged but very little action had followed. The resignation was, perhaps, the Union's first failure.

But financial worries run like a thread through the minutes of the early sessions of the Executive Board. As late as March 1949 the IUPN had still not repaid the Swiss League the costs the latter had incurred on behalf of the Provisional IUPN, and the League was pressing.[53] The problem was that membership grew slowly, and many members did not pay up. At the time of the Second Session of the General Assembly in Brussels in 1950 there were still only four state members (Belgium and the Netherlands were the two accessions). As to the rest, the 72 'founder members' were augmented by 15 who had been admitted to temporary membership by the Executive Board and there were another 18 applicants, making the tally 109.[34] Although IUPN did not cost very much, by the end of 1949 it was in deficit [19,54] and a number of American and British member institutions made supplementary contributions in 1950; so did France, through the Académie des Sciences.[42]

Subscriptions were wholly inadequate to support the central office, which depended heavily on the partnership with UNESCO.[32,55] In the early years (up to 1953) there was a special line in the UNESCO biennial programme and budget assigning US$3000 a year to IUPN, which was grouped with ICSU as a 'scientific NGO'.[56] There were also numerous special payments for activities such as publications and brochures [48] and work with youth clubs. But these contracts skewed the programme, pushing topics the Board thought important, but which did not attract money, into the background (another problem that has dogged the Union for 50 years).[57]

Julian Huxley had warned in the beginning that UNESCO could not give open-ended support to outside bodies – even those it had helped to create.[28] In 1953, the prophecy came true. There was no special line for IUPN in the biennial budget.[56] Early in 1954 Jean-Paul Harroy reported '*a decision from UNESCO to cease the financial help which had been granted to the Union until then*'. That decision seems to have been taken at the organization's General Conference, about which Alain Gille (Eleen Sam's replacement as UNESCO observer) briefed the IUPN Board on 15 January 1954.[58]

It is not quite clear why the regular small grant stopped. It may have been no more than a reflection of established policy. But Michel Batisse [56]suggests that it may also have been because IUPN did not lobby effectively enough – in contrast to ICSU, which argued its case constantly in the UNESCO Executive Board. A third factor may have been a change in the make-up of that Board. In the beginning it had been composed of 'wise men' '*chosen for their international repute and qualities (mostly intellectual)*', but as time passed the members:

> '*became Government representatives. Instead of being an independent, intellectual body, the Executive Board became a political body (that was the beginning of the Cold War period). It was also decided to establish a classification of NGOs which were put in three categories, A, B and C by the General Conference.*'[15]

It appears that IUPN may have been placed in category B, although it was elevated to category A in 1971.[42]

The result was to undermine efforts that had been made, in the shape of appeals, to improve the Union's funds. Consequently, in August 1954, the Secretariat of IUPN was smaller than it had been two years before, while the work was considerably greater.[40] The result was some cuts in the programme. Documents for the Executive Board had not all been processed as fast as was needed (fortunately the Board had now dropped to two meetings a year). It was decided not to organize technical meetings between General Assemblies. While the tempo of publication, including the *Bulletin*, was maintained some other work suffered.[2]

The situation was rescued by Hal Coolidge, then Vice-President, who secured a donation of US$25,000, to be paid at a rate of $5000 per annum over five years from the Old Dominion Foundation of New York (later merged into the Andrew Mellon Foundation). This was on top of other American donations: in the two years 1954 and 1955 United States sources were in fact paying just under half of the total budget of the Union (which stood at around $33,000 a year). The 1954 payment allowed IUPN to wipe out the deficit carried forward from 1953, to meet the increased costs caused by the Copenhagen Assembly, and to carry a modest surplus forward to 1955.[59]

While Hal Coolidge was winning support in the USA, it is clear that the Government of Belgium, as IUPN's host, was making representations to UNESCO. Alain Gille made some suggestions about how to win backing for certain programme elements, and how to present the IUPN case to the next UNESCO Conference.[60]

*'I encouraged IUPN to collaborate more closely in the execution of
UNESCO's programme, and to obtain contracts for the execution of
specific activities such as publication of books, pamphlets for schools,
preparation and organization of exhibitions, production of films and
filmstrips for schools and so on'.*[15]

Special grants began to appear again, and UNESCO's financial assistance is acknowledged in most of IUPN's (and IUCN's) early publications. By January 1955 three
new contracts with UNESCO, worth US$2500, were agreed and the Board was told
that the UNESCO Director-General wanted IUPN to collaborate with other bodies to
prepare a programme of study on the damaging impacts of hydroelectric schemes on
natural resources.[9]

A Symbol for the Union

The year 1950 saw another issue raised for the first time – insignia for the Union (or
what we would now call a logo or badge). The need had been recognized at the
Brussels General Assembly, and Hal Coolidge had proposed the use of a device
adopted for a 1948 conference in Denver. In 1951 the Board rejected a proposal by a
German artist, [61] and desultory discussions dragged on until 1953, when a competition was launched through the Commission on Public Information, with a prize of
US$250. A jury was set up, chaired by the artist Foujita.[62] It met on 18 January 1954
and chose the device later known throughout IUCN as 'the Brussels Sprout' (and
even later, 'the Flaming Artichoke'). At the time, however, it was greeted with almost
hushed respect:

*'The Emblem displayed on the first page of this Bulletin has been
selected from among 171 designs...Should a symbol be sought?...A
bud perhaps blossoming into the IUPN? Or perhaps a torch, deriving
its light from the Union...the essential thing is that henceforth the
simple evocative power of this clever drawing will proclaim the
existence of the IUPN to the four corners of the earth.'*[63]

A First Step to the South

The third General Assembly of IUPN, held in Caracas, Venezuela, in 1952 was also
the first major international conservation conference to be held in Latin America. The
invitation had come from the Government via the Venezuelan member of the
Executive Board, William H Phelps, in 1951 – and when, after a change of government, promised resources ceased to be available, Phelps took personal responsibility
for the costs of organizing the Assembly.[2] It attracted 193 delegates from 29 countries,
and they had good reason to feel that 'Things were Happening'.

The themes discussed in Caracas have a fascinating topicality even 40 years
later:

Figure 3.1 *The three logos of IUCN. On the left the 'Brussels Sprout' or 'Flaming Artichoke', adopted in 1954; in the centre the letter block agreed in 1977; and on the right the present logo, dating from May 1992.*

1   Whether to adopt a resolution on human population questions. The argument made everyone late for an official Foreign Office reception to which they were convoyed at speed, police sirens shrieking.[45]
2   Hydroelectricity and its impact on the protection of nature (a topic dear to the heart of the Executive Board at this time, and of recurrent interest to IUCN ever since).[64]
3   The preservation of wild fauna in semi-arid regions, especially in Central and South America.
4   The apparent conflicts between the requirements of agriculture and of conservation – including the problems of fire.
5   The preservation of plant and animal species endemic to small islands, particularly in the Caribbean.
6   The raising of wild animals in semi-captivity outside their natural habitats (with special emphasis on the need for such captive breeding for the great wild ox (the kouprey) of the Cambodian forests).[65]

But not all the talk was quite so down to earth. UNESCO refused to help secure the adherence of governments to the Caracas Manifesto for Nature Protection on the grounds that the text '*was of a purely idealistic character. No practical measure was proposed.*' While the ideas expressed in the draft manifesto were accepted, the Union was asked to prepare '*a more concrete text giving indications of the measures which should be taken. UNESCO could then forward this to the member states.*'[66]

Bill Phelps of Venezuela (and the USA) was one of the first citizens of a developing country to make a mark on IUPN. Another was Enrique Beltran of Mexico. The challenge to IUPN was to secure more of their kind. For although the South was a major focus of concern, and most of the conservation issues debated in the Union concerned the developing world, the knowledge and action came from the North. The Union itself was led by a man who, however sincere and broad his personal outlook, was bound to be seen as a Belgian colonial official. And this was a time of sudden change in the world's political landscape. The era of colonies was over. It was obvious that Asia and Africa would speedily be occupied by new, independent, nations. But 'Northern' conservationists showed a rather paternalistic concern about the consequences of those changes, especially in Africa. The British colonial governments had established national parks from which native Africans were excluded, and game reserves where only white safari hunters could shoot. They condemned native people who lived on wildlife as 'poachers'.[67] One entire tribal unit in Kenya – the Waliangulu, who occupied an area inland from Mombasa – fell victim as a consequence. It had lived by hunting elephants for meat, but elephant hunting was forbidden under the game laws. The men were imprisoned and the women dispersed: the tribe was destroyed.[67]

Clearly, independence would and should bring changes. But conservationists worried that the demands of economic development would become paramount, and that national parks and wild animal protection would be rejected as a legacy of colonialism. The title of Bernhard Grzimek's famous book *Serengeti Shall Not Die*[68] is one manifestation of this dilemma: to many it, and the work of Grzimek and his son Michael, tragically killed when his aircraft collided with a vulture over the Serengeti plains, are manifestations of the deepest and most laudable commitment to conservation, but as a political statement it can be read as a foreigner's determination to direct how Tanganyika, after independence, would use a vast tract of its territory. The issues were serious and posed a major challenge to the new Union and to the newly independent nations.

The structure of the Executive Board did not help move the Union southwards. It was not constituted on a basis of 'equitable geographical distribution' with parity of members from the various regions. Throughout the period from 1948 to 1956, Europeans dominated, with between eight and ten members, France and the UK usually having two, and one, Walery Goetel, coming from the East (Poland). There were two North Americans, and three or four from 'the rest of the world' – the countries actually represented being Argentina, Canada, Mexico, New Zealand, Peru and Venezuela. But when it came to attendance, the European dominance was even more obvious.

The Board normally had two meetings a year, each lasting two days, and Brussels was the principal venue (with Caracas, Copenhagen, Paris, The Hague, London, New York and Salzburg as alternates, usually because General Assemblies or Technical Conferences were being held there). Attendance was normally between four and eight members out of 15, rising to peaks at times of Assemblies or Conferences. Between 1948 and 1958, the proportion of voting members from developing countries present at meetings of the Board never rose above 10 per cent and was often below 5 per cent.[69] Enrique Beltran of Mexico served on the Board for five years without attending a meeting in Europe: Jose Yepes of Argentina and Jehan Vellard of Peru came only to a session at Fontainebleau. Even distant developed country representatives were at a huge disadvantage: R A Falla of New Zealand, for example, served for six years but never attended. The problems were obvious – cost and time, in a period when worldwide air travel was novel and expensive. But without a solution, how could IUPN be accepted in the developing world as belonging there, too?

Challenges for the Future

The Fourth General Assembly, held in Copenhagen from 25 August to 3 September 1954, listened to a record of substantial activities. Great emphasis was placed on the publications and on the educational work. The report from Jean-Paul Harroy was distinctly up-beat. '*The present situation*', he wrote in August 1954,

> '*is extremely encouraging and has been especially so in the last few months. The volume of mail is increasing and the name of the IUPN is quoted more and more often in various publications and in the press.*

> *The Union's opinions and advice are sought by international meetings of biologists and conservation specialists and in many other cases. The Secretariat is literally swamped with work, which is always a sign that the life of an organization is sound. The Union may owe this progress to the fact that, since 1948, people have become more receptive to the idea of Nature Protection, but it is surely also due to the Union's existence and action that these ideas have progressed. If one is not careful, success may become self-destructive for the Union. It may create a general impression that it is a powerful international organization and positive action may be expected from it in all countries, representation requested at numerous international gatherings as well as coordination with the United Nations and their specialized agencies. But such action would be out of proportion with the means at our disposal...'*[40]

One problem was getting governments to act. '*The implementation of the resolutions of technical meetings is...a disappointment*' wrote Jean-Paul Harroy.[40] '*Most of the time the letters written by the Union are officially acknowledged with a polite note to the effect that they would be "forwarded to the competent departments".*' It was noted that Wolfgang Burhenne had proposed a way of addressing this last problem. He cannot have succeeded, for it remains in 1998. Another unanswered question was how much difference was membership making to the members? It seems unlikely that it was much help to well-established national bodies in their own national campaigns (and this is probably why it attracted little recognition in the United States, where only a handful of bodies and people were seeking to develop an international perspective at this time). It had more to offer smaller organizations in the newly emerging nations of the post-colonial era, but these built up their conservation capacities slowly. There was a great deal of space to be watched!

A final uncertain issue was how widely the Union's mandate should go. For example, should it involve itself in human population issues? The Caracas debate led to a committee to consider what position IUPN should take regarding '*the problem of overpopulation*'. It was to report to the following session of the Assembly.[70] As that event approached, the Board decided to appoint a group of six or eight people to meet and prepare a paper which could be circulated. The issues were detailed in a note appended to the Board's minutes. '*The problem is as follows*', it said:

> '*The increase in numbers of human beings is weighing unquestionably on natural resources exploited for food and other purposes... Demographic growth is, therefore, a menace to the future of humanity if no solution is found which will tend to increase production without it being detrimental to the natural resources exploited. As there seems to be no immediate hope of seeing such a solution materialize, the answer seems to be found in birth control, and this, in turn, gives rise to numerous and often violent controversies...*'[70]

A Preparatory Commission considered the IUPN position a few days before the 1954 General Assembly in Copenhagen, but concluded that while population issues were of immense importance, it would not make sense for IUPN to take them on board. The World Population Congress was then in session, and IUPN sent a message of support, with best wishes for success.

The General Assembly in Copenhagen in 1954 was the beginning of a new phase in the history of IUPN – the Stage of Science. In Edinburgh, in 1956, the title and stated mission of the Union were transformed. It entered upon a new phase of activity, which was to last until 1966 and is the subject of Chapter 4.

4 A Time for Science

Challenges and Changes

The years between 1954 and 1961 saw rapid political change. Europe emerged from the trauma of post-war reconstruction, and embarked on a period of increasing prosperity. Former colonies were gaining their independence rapidly. New nations grappled with daunting needs – for development, for economic growth, for land management, for social change.

Julian Huxley and the other founders of IUPN had foreseen the challenges such reconstruction would pose to those concerned with nature. IUPN had been created to help the world's governments and the world's ecologists to build new partnerships, so that development was based on conservation. In the first phase of its existence it had demonstrated its ability to convene the world's leading conservationists and focus on key issues, but the challenges always outstripped the resources.

Max Nicholson has commented that the early history of IUPN/IUCN went through four stages.

> '*The first began even before Fontainebleau, with all the arguments about the creation of IUPN, and went on to Lake Success, where there were surprising achievements largely through UNESCO support. That meeting got IUPN on the map. It was remarkably prescient: the first time the threat from pesticides was seriously debated, 15 years before Silent Spring. But in the 1950s, we realized that more had to be done. One need was to link the protection of nature to the development of the environment – which was started at the Hague at the Technical Meeting on rural landscape as a habitat, and grew later into the Committee on Landscape Conservation, chaired by R J Benthem.*'[1]

Nicholson's second stage began at the Fourth General Assembly in Copenhagen in 1954, when the founding President of IUPN, Charles Bernard, was succeeded by Roger Heim, Member of the French Academy of Sciences and Director of the great Muséum National d'Histoire Naturelle in Paris. Heim had Jewish ancestry, and had ended the war in a concentration camp with friends dying all around him and leaving messages for him to pass on. Miriam Rothschild found him deeply impressive:

> '*His experiences made him seem aloof, but he was a super man. He came straight back from Buchenwald to his desk and threw himself into his science as if it had never happened. Fontainebleau must have*

*seemed very unreal to him, but he did a wonderful job leading the
scientific meeting. I remember going into the forest with him looking
for fungi. He was a good naturalist and deeply respected.*'[2]

The election of Roger Heim was hailed as a great coup, and it was symbolically
important.[1] Now IUPN was a science-based body. Under his leadership and that of
his successors, the Swiss biologist Jean Baer and the French physiologist and ecologist, François Bourlière, close links were built with ICSU and other scientific
organizations.

There was another important change in 1955. Jean-Paul Harroy was appointed
Vice-Governor-General of the Belgian Congo and Governor (subsequently Resident
General) of '*the important, but eroded and overgrazed Belgian Trust Territory of
Ruanda-Urundi*'.[3,4] Marguerite Caram took over as Head of the Secretariat, and the
Board invited one of the Vice-Presidents, M C Bloemers of the Netherlands, to
oversee the work of the Secretariat until the next General Assembly, held in
Edinburgh in 1956.[5] There, Mr Tracy Philipps of the UK took his place, while
Marguerite Caram was appointed Deputy Secretary-General.[6] The Board expressed
deep appreciation to Philipps for helping the Union's precarious finances by giving
his services without salary, simply receiving payment of his expenses.[7] Writing in his
autobiography, Jean-Paul Harroy noted with satisfaction that in 1955 he handed to
his successor a treasury that had always been in balance – and noted sadly that things
were different after he had gone.[8]

A Mission to Asia

The year 1954 brought another landmark – the first field mission that IUPN had
mounted. The fate of threatened species had been recognized at Fontainebleau as a
principal interest of the Union.[9] At Lake Success a first official list of gravely endangered species had been drawn up (it was, of course, the forerunner of the Red Lists
that were to become IUCN's most famous product). But effective conservation action
clearly depended on knowledge of the status of these species and of their ecology.
For many months the Executive Board debated the need to attach a staff ecologist to
the Secretariat.[10] In November 1954 Hal Coolidge came to the rescue. He secured a
grant of US$7000 from Russell M Arundel to support a young ecologist who would
undertake a mission to collect information on various large mammals.[11,12] The ecologist was Lee Merriam Talbot, and he came to Europe in early December 1954, settled
in Brussels, made contact with Roger Heim and explained his plans to the Board on
7 January.[5]

The Talbot mission had three specific objectives: first, to survey the status of a
series of threatened species; second, to work out how IUPN could cooperate most
effectively with authorities, institutions or people concerned with conservation in the
countries concerned; and third, to collect other information about threatened species
in particular or conservation in general.[5] He was to spend three months in Western
Europe (Brussels, Paris, London, Copenhagen) and then travel for four or five months
in India, Indonesia, Syria and perhaps Egypt. On his return in August 1955 he would
prepare a report. His mission might be extended into 1956, and might take him to
Africa. The Board grilled him hard. They noted that he would not be presenting
himself as 'the IUPN Ecologist' but as an ecologist attached to the Secretariat of the

Union. He would not be speaking in the name of the Union, or making proposals to the authorities in the countries he visited. His mandate was to collect information, and any proposals for action would come afterwards. He appeared sensitive to the political delicacies he would inevitably encounter.

Interview over, the Board went into a huddle. Some were obviously concerned that they were being confronted with a different kind of ecologist, with a different mandate, from the one they had started with. But they liked what they saw of Lee Talbot (Jean-Paul Harroy commented that '*we wanted bread, and have been given cake!*'.[13] The mission went ahead – but the Board still hankered after getting a different ecologist to tackle their own pet topics (including 'hydroelectricity and nature protection').[11]

Talbot reported back in December 1955. He had traversed the eastern desert of Egypt, north-west Syria, the Gir Forest of India, the Kashmiri Himalaya, Lower Assam, Nepal, south-west Sumatra and Udjung Kulon in Java. He had travelled 42,000 miles, and visited 30 countries. He had talked to Prime Minister Nehru in India, to many other ministers, to officials at many levels of government, to scientists, IUPN members, forest guards and media correspondents. He had examined the status of numerous species, most notably the three Asian rhinoceroses, the Asian lion, the Arabian oryx, and the Syrian wild ass (which was judged to be extinct in the wild).[12–14] The mission led to a book and a host of magazine articles which brought both the conservation message and IUPN to a wide audience in Europe and America.[13] It also provided the foundation for conservation action plans for several prominent species. Two months after the mission, Prime Minister Nehru visited the Gir Forest and declared it a National Park.[13]

A Change of Name in Edinburgh

The General Assembly in Edinburgh was a landmark. It was organized by John Berry, as director in Scotland of the Nature Conservancy, of which Max Nicholson was then Director-General.[15] Nicholson was by this time so convinced of the value of IUPN that he pressed ministers and a reluctant Treasury to agree to the UK becoming a State member. He told them that '*the IUPN functions very much as an international ecological Conference and...is the only international body competent to deal with this important field of science*'.[16] The bid failed (UK state membership did not arrive for another ten years), but an extra voluntary contribution through the Nature Conservancy was authorized).[17] The Nature Conservancy also persuaded other UK agencies concerned with resource management, like the Forestry Commission and the National Coal Board, to become involved in the Assembly, and arranged what may have been the first Nature Film Festival, in which a young zoologist turned filmmaker, David Attenborough, walked the international conservation stage for the first time.[18]

The Edinburgh Assembly included technical meetings on three topics – the management of nature reserves, the rehabilitation of areas devastated by human disturbance, and the relationship of ecology to landscape planning. But it is best remembered because it saw the change of name from IUPN to IUCN – International Union for Conservation of Nature and Natural Resources.

By the time of the meeting,

> *'it had become apparent to the Union's leadership and members that the name "International Union for the Protection of Nature" had come to project a much more limited and perhaps more defensive or sentimental image than was warranted by the vitally important work to which it was devoted'.*[19]

The members of the Ecology Commission were unanimous in wanting change – and John Berry, as local organizer, prepared the ground for action by inviting the 'top brass' to a discussion at the Royal Society of Edinburgh just before the Assembly opened.[15]

Lee Talbot recalls that he had encountered the problem continually during his travels in Africa and Asia, and this led him to prepare a paper on the subject which served as a lightning rod for many strongly-held opinions.[13,20]

The paper hit hard:

> *' "Protection of nature" in English often carries the connotation of a sentimental, impractical, negative objective...The common reaction I have met is that an organization bearing this name cannot be taken seriously...In the United States, I have been told that the government departments generally dare not even bring up the name before appropriations groups asking for funds...because of the adverse effect it has...I have found the reaction against the name in England, Germany, Denmark, English-speaking Africa, English-speaking portions of the Middle East, India, Burma, Malaya, Japan, Canada and the United States...Overworked game and parks departments in Africa have no time for something which sounds to them so basically impractical and disassociated from their pressing everyday problems...'.*[20]

Talbot therefore argued strongly for a change to a short, comprehensive, name such as 'International Conservation Union', saying that although there were translation problems in both German and French, the English word 'conservation' was understood the world over. Frank Fraser Darling, the best-known ecologist in Scotland, agreed and no doubt inflamed the debate by saying that the word 'nature' had been so debased that it, too, should be dropped from the title![13]

The title was changed – despite a good deal of opposition. *'The debate – or power struggle – presaged the division between the proponents of preservation and utilization which continues to the present'.*[13] The inclusion of the word 'resources' reflected a considerable change in the orientation of the Union's activities.[21] Some members wanted to go even further and adopt the language of UNSCCUR – inserting 'and Utilization' after 'Conservation', but this was a leap too far and was rejected.[22]

The change of name was welcomed by the Executive Board because it would *'help them to make the Union's aims clearer when approaching governments and members of the public'.*[23] It was supported by the Americans, led by Fairfield Osborn, most British, most Scandinavians, all international organization representatives, most of the few people from the developing countries, and some – but by no means all – mainland Europeans.[13] The change marked the adoption of the US–UK view of conservation – the view of Leopold and of Huxley – in place of the more sentimental protectionism that survived in some parts of Europe. Max Nicholson saw it as the third stage in the maturation of the Union, and crucial in bringing the Americans *'who apart from Hal Coolidge had been rather on the fringe before that, properly on board*.[1] The formula 'conservation of nature and natural resources' was adopted partly to get round the problem of translating 'conservation', and partly because some Europeans believed passionately that the moral and ethical values which should be addressed by the Union demanded reference to 'nature'. '*The debate also brought out the anti-American views of some Europeans which have always lurked just under the surface at IUCN*'.[13] It was at Edinburgh that the 'two chamber' system of voting in the General Assembly, which made it impossible for governmental members to carry a resolution against the NGOs and vice versa, was adopted.[22]

Alain Gille, who was centrally involved at the time, also saw the change as important:

> '*The Union has evolved a great deal and the initial idea of nature protection was to some degree modified to incorporate concepts of economics and of the protection of the environment and its resources. The purists of the first period often reacted against this idea of "economics", which has considerably altered the actions of the Secretariat of the Union. Little by little, a balance has been sought between the role of the Union as protector of nature and as the applier of a brake to the irrational exploitation of the natural resources which represent a capital to be preserved for future years...*'.[21]

This concern for natural resources led to Max Nicholson's 'stage four', when pasture and range management became a major topic, increasing the relevance of IUCN to countries for whom resource management was a major preoccupation.

After Edinburgh, the 'Stage of Science' was marked, first, by the increasing role of the Commission on Ecology, then by the outstanding contribution of the Africa Special Project (ASP) (which showed what IUCN could do to assist governments in the developing world to address the problems of conservation and natural resource management), and later by the more peripheral role of the Union in the International Biological Programme (Chapter 5).

Maintaining Solvency

The Edinburgh General Assembly may have marked a change in culture, but it was not matched by new economics. The chronic financial weakness of the Union had again been highlighted in 1954, and this may have stimulated the first ideas about a new fund for world wildlife. Jean-Paul Harroy recalled that '*even before my departure in 1955 we were discussing the idea mooted by Peter Scott and others of setting up a partner organization to IUPN, a semi-governmental organization which would be better equipped to raise private funds and finance projects*'.[24]

In January 1956, before the Edinburgh Assembly, the Executive Board criticized the Secretary-General for responding to the mounting work-load by taking on more staff, when there had not been any corresponding growth in funds.[5] Life was made more difficult by the fact that the contracts from the two UN agencies with which the Union worked most closely – UNESCO and FAO – did not cover the associated administrative costs.[26] Roger Heim had approached UNESCO for support in the form of a block grant, but their decision would not be known for some time.[27,28]

At what was obviously a crucial meeting on 20 June 1956, immediately before the Edinburgh Assembly opened, Fairfield Osborn and Hal Coolidge announced that the USA would find one third of the total budget if the remaining two-thirds could be secured elsewhere.[23] Max Nicholson reported the prospect of an increased British contribution.[17] Enrique Beltran offered to set up a Caribbean Committee to promote the Union in his region and (hopefully) secure more members. The Board also appointed M C Bloemers, Head of the Nature Protection Bureau in the Netherlands, as financial adviser and agreed to propose the creation of a permanent Finance Committee.[29] But there was no instant magic. Opening the Assembly, Roger Heim emphasized the financial crisis. '*The Union was in debt. We were faced with a dilemma, either to reduce our programme and activities or find new financial means at once.*'[30]

In February 1957 M C Bloemers reported a US$9000 deficit carried forward from 1956, while US$14,000 had to be raised to balance the books for 1957. The Finance Committee proposed three options – closing down, curtailing the Secretariat, and seeking new money. Not for the last time, Hal Coolidge telegraphed from the United States the good news of an additional US$10,000 to eliminate the deficit and pay sums owing to the Union's printer. The third option was chosen, thereby setting a precedent that has been followed repeatedly in the ensuing 40 years.[31] Happily, it worked, for in 1958 Tracy Philipps was able to report that financial solvency had been achieved.[26] Not for the last time, IUCN had lurched towards bankruptcy and back again.

The time-honoured long-term solution was more state members, and these arrived slowly. Four joined between 1956 and 1958, along with 20 national organizations. Another device in which great hope was placed was the creation in 1956 of a body of 'Friends of IUCN' in Belgium, the Netherlands, France, Great Britain and the United States. It started well – taking in over 100,000 Belgian francs in the first few months and leaving a healthy credit balance even after the start-up costs had been deducted.[7] It was agreed the income should fund the *Bulletin*.[29] But somehow IUCN never tapped public imagination, and it had too few 'Friends'. The problem, then as now, was that its enormous range of activities never got across to the public. It was becoming obvious that conservation needed a new marketing strategy.

IUCN's Approach and Priorities

The Secretary-General, Tracy Philipps, responded by analysing priorities. Reporting to the Sixth General Assembly, held in Athens and Delphi in 1958,[26] he listed the Union's primary international tasks as approaching governments and other appropriate bodies; promoting conservation based on scientific research; supporting international conservation education and maintaining the Union's role as a clearing house, receiving and disseminating knowledge. '*The Union must assume its proper coordinating position at the intersection of kindred specialized scientific organizations*' he went on, '*and offer information and material from which governments and societies could draw inspiration and advantage.*'

Given the chronic limitation of resources, IUCN had to be selective. Two years later, when he had become Secretary-General, M C Bloemers suggested that when the programme was constructed, the test questions should be whether the Union was better placed than any other organization to tackle the problem, whether it could afford the investment required, what would be the return, and whether the proposed operation was so urgent that every effort should be made to give it priority.[32]

Bloemers affirmed that the primary function of the Union was '*collecting and classifying information*'. This was the foundation for providing advice to those who needed it. The voluntary Commissions were seen as a unique asset, especially for producing processed information. Technical meetings and symposia were likewise valuable means of synthesis. '*Building up documentation, disseminating information, and providing the standing Commissions with sufficient assistance are first priorities*'.[32] IUCN was clearly still seen as a supportive body, facilitating the activities of its members, advising governments, but rarely doing work on the ground itself.

The international concerns between 1956 and 1960 stand out from the minutes of the Executive Board.[33] Threatened species and habitats – whether in green zones around cities, national parks or areas that might become parks – came high on the list. Species of concern included Asiatic lion, Asian greater one-horned rhinoceros and Sumatran rhinos (and especially their capture by traders). There was discussion of the Indian rosy-headed duck, African weaver-birds (*Quelea*) and their role as a pest of agriculture, the medicinal plant *Dioscorea sylvatica*, important as a base for cortisone manufacture, Madagascan lemurs, Angolan giraffes and giant sable antelope, mountain gorillas in the Albert National Park of the then Belgian Congo, the poaching of white rhinoceros and the management of Ugandan hippopotamus. But there was also concern over the Arctic fauna, rare and threatened animals of the Mediterranean basin, the netting of birds in the Mediterranean, trade in protected animals and the unique endemic life of the Galapagos islands. With ICBP, IUCN backed action for a network of European reserves that would safeguard migratory birds.

As early as 1956–58 there were the first echoes of what was to become a major argument about national parks policy. Tracy Philipps wrote that IUCN was being accused of protecting nature *against* people rather than for people.[26] The accusation arose from the Union's support for the 'Yellowstone model' of national park, which was held to require the removal of damaging human occupation, in African locations like the Serengeti. Although it was rebutted at the time, the attack probably had justification: it took some years for IUCN to change its position and see that the 'Yellowstone model' did not fit in Africa, and that local people must be willing partners in national park management.[34]

Education, information and publication remained priorities. Much of IUCN's educational work was done at the request of UNESCO and FAO. One goal was to include teaching about the inter-relationship between people and their physical and cultural surroundings in the curriculum of senior primary schools.[26] Universities and centres of adult education were also targeted. The Union produced educational source books and visual aids for use in Asia, pamphlets and manuals for Africa, and an Arabic-language handbook on conservation for use in schools throughout the Middle East. UNESCO later contracted it to prepare a manual for teachers on the conservation of natural resources.[32] By 1958 the *Bulletin* circulated in every continent and was increasingly quoted in the press.[26] The old IOPN Library – renamed the 'Van Tienhoven Library' – was the Union's information nerve centre.[35]

The Programme and the Commissions

The Commissions remained the best – almost the only – way of getting a lot done with a tiny Secretariat and budget. The growing prominence of the Commission on

Ecology was a clear manifestation of the new emphasis on science. It had been established in 1954, with John Berry as one of the architects and the interim Chairman. '*I thought we, as ecologists, should try to steer the absolute protectionists into a more positive approach, and for that we needed to study what was actually going on. Mörzer-Bruyns* (later to be Secretary of the Commission) '*as an ecologist, was very keen and we met in Denmark in 1954 and then in London in 1955, and started the action*'.[15] Berry's idea was that Frank Fraser Darling should be the first Chairman of the Commission. But Darling refused, arguing that '*we know enough about ecology, and don't want any more Bureaucratic Commissions: let's get on with it!*'

Max Nicholson, who as Director-General of the British Nature Conservancy was Berry's boss, gave powerful backing to the new Commission. Its members had an energetic tour in East Anglia and Scotland in 1955.[15] Even so, it began slowly – hampered by the usual financial constraints and by the fact that the Chairman who took over from Berry, Dr Victor Westhoff, fell ill almost at once.[6] However, it took on new momentum when Edward H Graham, a well-known American soil scientist, succeeded to the Chair; Fraser Darling was persuaded to become Vice-Chair and J Derrick Ovington, Head of the Nature Conservancy's Forest and Woodland Management Section, became Secretary. An initial worry over overlap with the ICSU Union of Biological Sciences was soon overcome. A French ecologist, Roger Balleydier, was appointed to the Secretariat in January 1956, chiefly to support the Commission.[37,38]

The early programme of the Commission was remarkably broad. It covered the promotion of ecological research, the protection of natural areas and landscapes, and associated education and information.[39] In the period between 1956 and 1958 it advised the Secretariat on such diverse matters as the control of hippopotamus populations in Uganda, the evaluation of a large tract of land in British Columbia, the status of the Serengeti National Park in Tanganyika and the creation in Karachi of a centre concerned with agricultural machinery and soil conservation.[39] It circularized its members on the shortage of taxonomists, the use of aerial photography for the study and management of nature reserves, and a proposed cooperative project on national parks with a Commission member, Professor Szafer of Poland.

It is clear that the infant Commission on Ecology (COE) worked in fields which overlapped with the Commission for the Survival Service and were later to fall to the National Parks Commission and what became first the Committee and then the Commission on Landscape Planning. The breadth of its activities worried the Executive Board, who questioned the practicability of Derrick Ovington's service as Secretary of both the Commission and Committees.[40] There was even more worry over a proposed initiative on the Arctic fauna, which ran into trouble for lack of resources.[41] This very breadth of COE may help to explain why it went into decline when its most conservation-oriented spearheads became attached to the lances of other voluntary networks as IUCN evolved.

The mid-1950s also saw major evolutionary changes in those networks. The Survival Service had been driven forward by the immense energy of Hal Coolidge. It had broken new ground through the pioneering missions of Lee Talbot in Asia and then in Africa. Much of the Service's work was also strongly ecological. In 1956, for example, the Executive Board endorsed new proposals for ecological and behavioural studies of the Asian greater one-horned rhinoceros and the Asiatic lion, and an analysis of the position of threatened animals – particularly lemurs – in Madagascar by Jean-Jacques Petter.[7] The same meeting agreed that a permanent Commission with 'correspondents' throughout the world should be created: members would be selected by the Chairman but endorsed by the Board. The Commission on the Survival Service was approved at the Edinburgh General Assembly in 1956.[37] Hal Coolidge continued as Chairman, and Lee Talbot and Jean-Jacques Petter were appointed as Assistant Secretaries.[40]

The Board wanted to make sure that the Commissions worked effectively. Jean Baer, speaking for several others, proposed in 1957 that '*the composition of the IUCN Commissions should be entirely reconsidered at the next General Assembly. Such Commissions should always in future be submitted for approval by the Assembly*'. It was agreed that such a requirement should be incorporated in the Statutes of the Union which were then being revised,[36] and this task was taken on board at the Athens General Assembly in 1958 where Baer succeeded Roger Heim as President.

Unusually for IUCN, a Commission – on Information – was dissolved in 1958 at its own request. But in September of that year, after Athens, three still remained: Ecology, by then chaired by Ed Graham (with John Berry as deputy); Education, led by Ira Gabrielson of the USA; and the Commission for the Survival Service which Hal Coolidge had handed over to Lt Col C L Boyle, head of the UK Fauna Preservation Society. The Ecology Commission had set up two sub-committees, one for landscape management and the other on ecological aspects of soil and water conservation.[42,43]

This focus on the practical application of ecology led naturally to an emphasis on the management of ecosystems used by people, and especially 'rangeland' – pasture for wild and domestic animals, or mixtures of them. A technical meeting held in association with the General Assembly in Warsaw in 1960 produced an important book, *Ecology and the Management of Wild Grazing Mammals in Temperate Zones* edited by a future President of IUCN, François Bourlière.[44] It was this practical approach that brought Russian scientists into the Union, especially at the Warsaw General Assembly in 1960.[1] It was strongly supported in the United States. Because it placed conservation in the wider context of land management, it was also especially attractive to the United Nations: IUCN's work in Africa was partly funded by the UN Special Fund (predecessor of the UN Development Programme) which channelled its money through FAO. Another consequence was that FAO itself became more interested in nature conservation, establishing a 'Wildlife and Forest Recreation Section' within its Forestry and Forest Industries Division[45] and promoting protected area systems in South and Central America as well as in Uganda, Ethiopia, Nepal, India and Indonesia.[46] The original protectionist flavour was changing, and the IUCN programme was becoming more oriented towards the needs of the developing countries – and this was clearly a challenge to be faced in future growth.

The General Assembly at Athens and Delphi in 1958 was charged, in particular, with action on national parks. A group was to be convened '*composed of persons responsible for the management of national parks in their own countries and capable of lending the weight of their authority and experience to the development of the proposed machinery*'.[42] A number of people (including Hal Coolidge and Jean-Paul Harroy) wanted to create a full Commission.[47,48] But to start with, a Provisional Committee on National Parks was established under Coolidge's chairmanship with five members representing Africa, three for Asia, and one each for North America, Latin America and Europe – a clear demonstration of the importance of bringing in the South. The mandate was safely 'IUCN mainstream' – to support the Board and Secretariat in providing advice and stimulating international cooperation, to amass information, to encourage the publication of the atlas entitled *Last Refuges* in a range of languages, to encourage research (especially in ecology) that would help in the management of national parks, and to aid scientific exchanges and expert cooperation.

Meanwhile, Hal Coolidge, who was often in New York, lobbied hard at UN headquarters for a special mandate from the United Nations, under which IUCN would take responsibility for preparing a world list of national parks. His manoeuvres upset UNESCO and FAO, the Union's normal contacts and sponsors in the UN.[28,48] But in 1959 the Economic and Social Council duly adopted a resolution requesting the Secretary-General to organize the preparation and publication of a United Nations list of national parks and equivalent reserves. The Secretary-General asked IUCN to do the job, and the task fell very largely to what became the Commission on National Parks in 1960. The Commission tackled the issue of definitions, preparing a classification of types of protected area that, developed down the years (and revised significantly in 1978 and 1994), has remained the accepted international taxonomy of the subject. The first world list of parks was submitted to ECOSOC and published in 1961, and IUCN has continued to produce revisions ever since.[37,49]

IUCN's catalytic role in this period was considerable. The missions of Lee Talbot, E P Gee, Oliver Milton and Jean-Jacques Petter to various parts of Asia and Africa were a stimulus to action by national governments. Talbot's visits to Uganda, for example, led the Government to encourage research by American Fulbright scholars: George Schaller began work on mountain gorillas, and the laboratory established in the Queen Elizabeth National Park evolved into the Nuffield Institute for Tropical Animal Ecology.[13] Joint ventures with UN agencies also broke new ground – for example a dialogue in 1957 between IUCN and ICOMOS, the International Committee on Monuments, Artistic Sites and Archaeological Excavations, led to a suggestion that UNESCO might '*take action with a view to protecting the character and beauty of the countryside of Member States*' – a process which led to the Convention on the Protection of the World Cultural and Natural Heritage (known as the World Heritage Convention) adopted by the UNESCO General Conference in 1972 (see Chapter 6).[26,37] In 1959–60 contacts with FAO strengthened considerably, and the first links were forged with the Council of Europe.[32]

One outstanding initiative of the period was a major programme of action, undertaken in collaboration with UNESCO, to save the unique fauna of the Galapagos Islands of Ecuador, made famous by Charles Darwin in *The Voyage of the Beagle*. Following a mission by the Austrian zoologist, Dr Irenäus Eibl-Eibesfelt, this culminated in 1959 (the centenary year of the publication of Darwin and Wallace's first paper on evolution by natural selection) in the creation of the Charles Darwin Foundation. It was chaired at first by Victor van Straelen, but he died suddenly about a fortnight after the formal inauguration and was succeeded by the French ornithologist, Jean Dorst. The Government of Ecuador gave warm support, and designated the islands as a national park.[26,50]

Ecology, species conservation and protected areas, together with education thus emerged as central themes of IUCN. They were closely interlinked, and were developed in a common and effective pattern. It was recognized that each should have somebody in the small central Secretariat to support the initiatives and relate the work done by the volunteer networks to the overall administration of the Union. Law – to become a major area of IUCN achievement, thanks especially to the efforts of Wolfgang Burhenne – came late on the scene: it was only at the Warsaw General Assembly in 1960 that a Committee on Legislation was created, very much as a trial, and although raised to Commission status after a few years, it did not evolve into the

Commission on Environmental Policy, Law and Administration until the New Delhi meeting eight years afterwards.[22]

Despite the effort to build developing-region representation into the new Committee on National Parks, the IUCN Commissions were, at the outset, very much 'Northern' institutions (nobody from a developing country became Chair of any of them until 1984, when Dr Jose Furtado of Singapore was elected to head the Commission on Ecology). Most of the members were likewise from the developed world. Success, however, depended on linkage with the specialists that did exist in developing countries. The new Committee on Legislation faced up to this problem. There were few lawyers in the South interested in nature and natural resources, but one of its earliest goals was to assist developing countries, and it built a network of contacts in such countries as rapidly as possible. It was partly because of these contacts that the Commission was welcomed by the Organization of African Unity as the drafter of the African Convention for the Conservation of Nature and Natural Resources, adopted in Algiers in 1968.[51,52]

Action in Africa

This period was, in many ways, the Era of Africa. The decolonization process brought concern that the efforts made for conservation of the continent's outstanding wildlife might be jeopardized. IUCN had become involved as early as 1955. The focus was the Serengeti National Park in Tanganyika – a vast tract, reaching from the shores of Lake Victoria to the Ngorongoro caldera, and taking in the Olduvai gorge with its fossil records of early hominids on the way. The park was (and is) the home of the greatest assemblage of large mammals left on earth – elephants, antelopes, buffalo, giraffes, lions, leopards, cheetah, rhinoceros. The seasonal migrations of hundreds of thousands of wildebeest northwards towards the Masai Mara plains in Kenya and back again are perhaps the world's greatest wildlife spectacle. But, as independence neared, there were questions over whether the country could and would maintain this whole vast tract as a national park. There were treaties between the colonial powers and the Masai whose traditional homeland it was, but these did not work very well, and there was tension because although the Masai coexisted with wildlife, they hunted – and the game laws forbade this.[34]

In 1955 conservationists in the UK and the USA heard rumours that the Government of Tanganyika was proposing to cut the Ngorongoro highlands and central plain out of the Park, leaving only the western corridor. Lee Talbot, who was based in East Africa for three months, went to investigate – thanks to funds from Russell Arundel, again obtained through Hal Coolidge's good offices. In Dar es Salaam he got hold of a draft of the Government's White Paper: he went up-country and confirmed that the plans would bring ecological disaster, and wrote a report to the Colonial Secretary urging that no decisions be taken until an ecological expert had done a thorough study on the ground.[13] The Fauna Preservation Society agreed to fund the investigation, and Frank Fraser Darling was asked to do it, but family illness made him unavailable and Professor W H Pearsall went instead. His report caused the government to modify its plans'.[13,53] IUCN decided to urge governments not to reach decisions in cases like this until *they had had the chance to study a report prepared by a qualified ecologist or other scientific specialist*.[36]

The changing situation in Africa also had an important impact on the work of the

United Nations, and especially UNESCO and FAO. UNESCO's Arid Lands Major Project had come under the charge of an energetic French physicist, Michel Batisse, and in 1958 an outstanding Russian soil scientist, Victor Kovda, became Head of the Science Sector. Both strongly supported research on natural resources. They pressed for an increase in UNESCO's support for IUCN, which was raised to US$10,000 a year by 1966.[28]

Julian Huxley undertook a major mission for UNESCO between July and September 1960.[54] Writing afterwards, he summed up the debate about land use and wildlife management in Africa cogently:[55] *'Wildlife, of course, includes the entire ecological community and natural habitats include forests. Game and wildlife, forests, and also the areas of wild land in general, have been much reduced in the last 100 years, and there are still many serious threats to them.'* He listed organized poaching, the spread of cultivation, the spread of pastoralism and the increase of cattle and other stock, resulting in over-grazing and destruction of forest habitat, and the alarming increase in human population as the principal threats. He noted that *'there is also widespread African resentment against game as destroying crops or competing with native cattle, and resentment against National Parks and Game Reserves as European inventions and relics of "colonialism" which occupy land coveted by Africans'.[55]*

Huxley stressed that *'the whole question boils down to one of optimum land use'* and noted a number of factors favourable to conservation.[56] He went on to urge various practical actions in research, training, adoption of wildlife and conservation policies by African governments, education and publicity including using wildlife films. He proposed that IUCN sponsor a joint conference with CCTA, the Commission for Technical Cooperation in Africa South of the Sahara, in September 1961, and urged support for it by UNESCO and FAO.[55]

IUCN agreed, and at the Warsaw General Assembly in 1960 it set up the Africa Special Project. This was chaired by Barton Worthington, one-time leader of the Cambridge Expedition to the African Lakes and Deputy Director of the UK Nature Conservancy, who was elected to the IUCN Executive Board at Warsaw. He gathered a galaxy of ecological talent around him.[57] Sir Hugh Elliott of the UK, a keen ornithologist and former Permanent Secretary of the Ministry of Agriculture and Natural Resources in Tanganyika, served as Secretary.[37]

The idea of the project was not to do ecological research on the ground but to convince African leaders and African public opinion of the importance to their new countries of *'conservation practices based on ecological knowledge'*. The first stage was a kind of promotional tour to discuss the issues with African leaders and officials, and Gerald Watterson, lent to IUCN by FAO, spent nearly a year doing this and checking the situation on the ground. The second stage was a Conference, sponsored jointly by IUCN and CCTA, with FAO and UNESCO support, held in Arusha in 1961. Why Arusha? Because Tanganyika was the next African state to become independent, had spectacular wildlife that was the foundation of highly profitable tourism, was already the focus of scientific expertise and at the same time lacked local people with wildlife management skills.[58]

Bernhard Grzimek, well-known as the author of *Serengeti Shall not Die*, had two interviews with Dr Julius Nyerere, then Chief Minister of Tanganyika, shortly before the Conference. *'Your country, Tanganyika'*, he said, *'is not so beautiful that it could compete with Switzerland or the Rocky Mountains. If tourists come here, then it is because they can watch, easily and safely, elephants, lions, giraffes and rhinos – animals not to be found elsewhere. And they will keep on coming – if the elephants are still there.'*[59] Nyerere admitted that he himself did not care greatly for wild animals. He could not imagine himself spending a holiday looking at crocodiles. *'But I know that Europeans and Americans enjoy this. I shall see to it that they are able to see big game in our country. It is my view that wild animals will be Tanganyika's third most important source of revenue after sisal and diamonds.'*[59] The message that wildlife was of immense potential economic importance was just the one to get across at a time when the newly independent countries had to plan how they would support their development.

The conference was attended by some 150 representatives of 21 African states, six non-African countries and five international organizations.[37] Julian Huxley, fresh from his 1960 mission, was there. Julius Nyerere presented a keynote statement later known as the Arusha Declaration, which set the tone for conservation in Africa for years to come. It echoed the message that Grzimek and others had been pressing on him:

> *'The survival of our wildlife is a matter of grave concern to all of us in Africa. These wild creatures, amid the wild places they inhabit, are not only important as a source of wonder and inspiration but are an integral part of our natural resources and of our future livelihood and well-being.*
>
> *In accepting the trusteeship of our wildlife we solemnly declare that we will do everything in our power to make sure that our children's grandchildren will be able to enjoy this rich and precious inheritance.*
>
> *The conservation of wildlife and wild places calls for specialist knowledge, trained manpower and money, and we look to other nations to cooperate in this important task – the success or failure of which not only affects the Continent of Africa but the rest of the world as well.'*[60]

The ASP and the conference were the stimulus for the African Convention on the Conservation of Nature and Natural Resources. The text was prepared by the IUCN Committee on Environmental Law (and in particular by Wolfgang Burhenne), but matters were complicated when FAO prepared its own draft – and relations became somewhat sour when CCTA and then OAU backed the IUCN version.[51] This preference *'was due to the perception that the Law Commission was indeed working with Africans for Africa'.*[52] A text was adopted by OAU member states at Algiers on 15 September 1968. The Convention was important for two reasons: as a framework for international cooperation and because the countries concerned took pride in having their own, uniquely African, legal instrument.[34]

The Arusha Conference was also followed by Stage Three of the African Special Project, lasting until 1963 and involving visits of weeks or months to 19 African countries to provide advice and help with the development of their wildlife resources. Thane Riney, an ecologist, and Peter Hill, an educationalist, undertook this work and many of their reports became blueprints for national policy. Another concrete outcome, meeting the need for local expertise, was the establishment of the College of African Wildlife Management at Mweka in Tanzania, where generations of African parks' directors and wardens have been trained. Its first brochure makes it clear that most of the money to establish it came from the US Government through USAID, with other support from the British and German Governments, and from the Rockefeller Brothers Fund, the Old Dominion Foundation and WWF.[37,61] A second centre for French-speaking staff was established at Garoua in Cameroun.[62]

There is no doubt that the ASP had substantial achievements. But it can be argued that it was still rooted in 'Northern' concepts, and was inherently antagonistic to local people.[63] It is true that Bernhard Grzimek commented with approval on actions that moved local people out of national parks in the former Belgian Congo.[59] Lee Talbot, writing in 1957, also condemned Masai overgrazing with *'herds of economically worthless cattle... which 'have already overgrazed and laid waste too much of the 23,000 square miles of Tanganyika they control, and as they move into the Serengeti...bring the desert with them, and the wilderness and wildlife must bow before their heads'.*[64] It was not until the late 1980s that IUCN, working in partnership with the Frankfurt Zoological Society in the Serengeti and the Tanzanian Ngorongoro Conservation Area Authority in the Ngorongoro caldera, began to apply scientific knowledge in strategies for coexistence between local African people and wild species, to their mutual benefit.[65]

The World Conservation Agenda

The issues IUCN considered were in the dominant environmental concerns of their day. They were developed by groups of people who were among the world leaders in their field. The voluntary networks – the Commissions and Committees – were progressively broadened to provide very wide international coverage. The test in admitting Commission members was their professional standing, and the Union gained an increasing reputation as *the* expert body on the status of wildlife and wild habitats around the world, and the source of advice on their conservation. This was demonstrated a few years later, in January 1963, when the United Nations General Assembly adopted a Resolution on Development and the Conservation of Nature, which urged early action towards preserving, restoring and making rational use of natural resources and increasing their productivity, noted with satisfaction the work of UNESCO in this field and urged assistance to IUCN.[66]

Ecology of both species and habitats, ecologically sound environmental management and the promotion of national parks and other protected areas dominated the agenda in the late 1950s and early 1960s, and the ASP was its first major intervention in the developing world. But other issues – including some that were soon to become popular concerns – were not ignored. Technical meetings addressed such issues as soil and water conservation, the use of vegetation in erosion control, the effects of dams and barrages on flora, fauna, landscape and habitats, *'the conservation of marine resources and the measures to be taken against methods of exploitation that risk their exhaustion or depletion'*, oil pollution of the sea following the deaths of thousands of seabirds in the Baltic in January 1957 and *'the impact of the present scientific and industrial revolution in the form of "biological hazards arising from the pollution of man's environment with atomic waste" '*.[26,33] In 1958, the need to create a new organization to regulate antiparasitic products was debated, and the Union agreed to cooperate with FAO in an enquiry into *'the varied effects of pesticides on soils, crop quality, and on man and animals'*, with emphasis on *'the repercussions of the large-scale application of such chemical products on birds, and on bees and other pollinating insects'*.[26] There was occasional mention of the problem of human population increase – and the need to treat *'this delicate and complex problem'* sensitively.[33]

The people who led the Commissions and served on the IUCN Board had standing on the world scene, and many of them played a prominent part in member organizations. But they had one other thing in common beyond their professional qualifications: they were 'establishment' figures. None of them was likely to back strident populist campaigns, or tangle with governments, for many of them were of the government world, and a lot of them were paid from government funds, as academics or officials. They undoubtedly believed that the way forward was to work with and through governments, influencing them to support conservation and showing them that IUCN was just the kind of professional body that could help them. The fact that this would – it was hoped – encourage more governments to become state members of IUCN and strengthen the woefully shaky financial base was another pertinent consideration.

The point was well put by M C Bloemers when he reported as Secretary-General to the Seventh Session of the General Assembly held in Warsaw in 1960.[32] He pointed out that:

> '*when the Union was set up in 1948 its only starting capital was its prestige as the first and only world organization for nature protection, and the goodwill of a great number of eminent scientists and devoted champions. Any international organization which is neither invested with autonomous legislative and executive powers nor limited in its objectives merely to establishing contacts, has essentially one aim only: to provoke action by those whom human society has entrusted with effective power, such as the government in its country, the local or specialized authority in its district or field of activity or the individual in the performance of...daily work and civic duties.*'[32]

The Secretary-General argued that this must mean making people aware of the values nature represents, and helping them to use those values without exhausting them. But it was also important to make people aware of how far humanity had already gone in destroying forms of life. People should be told how their actions affected both the wildlife they valued and the resources on which society depended. Some of that knowledge was available, but some had to be sought by research. The scientific basis for action must be sound. A publication on pesticides by the Conservation Foundation – a new body, founded by an IUCN member, the New York Zoological Society – was quoted with approval – '*no one can defend as reasonable current practices of use about whose effects we are quite ignorant*'.[67]

These aspects of IUCN explain two important things. First, why it did not become the spearhead of the new environmentalism that emerged in the mid-1960s. Second, why the Union became increasingly side-lined when campaigning 'green' lobbies began to hit the headlines. For the new environmentalism was essentially urban in its popular base and alarmist in its tone. It tried to get people agitated about their environment – and it succeeded. But it was not concerned with nature conservation so much as with the problems generated by urban and industrial activities – notably chemical pollution derived from industry and its products, radioactive contamination of the biosphere, initially through nuclear weapons and their testing but later also from the emissions and wastes of civil nuclear power, and activities such as the dumping of wastes in the oceans. IUCN was concerned with these things – but wildlife, protected areas and ecosystems were its main focus. And IUCN's emphasis on science made it cautious, or even antagonistic, when it came to media campaigns based on the selective, and often highly dramatized, presentation of data that most responsible scientists regarded as highly inadequate as a basis for decisions that could affect many lives and immense resources. It opted out of 'popularization', and as a result it never became 'popular'.

The Move to Morges

In 1958, at the Athens General Assembly (when the tenth anniversary of the creation of the Union was duly celebrated),[68] Roger Heim bowed out as President, handing over to the Swiss biologist, Jean Baer, with an eloquent speech in the ancient amphitheatre at Delphi.[62] But despite Tracy Philipps' optimism, the following period was again haunted by financial crisis. It was also a traumatic one for individuals. Philipps himself fell ill soon after the Assembly and retired at the end of the year. M C Bloemers, formerly Finance Adviser, took over in January 1959, and Philipps died in July. The Assistant Secretary-General, Marguerite ('Gogo') Caram, a stalwart from the very earliest days, was also taken ill and never fully regained her health: she retired in 1960 and died on 31 August 1961. The Secretariat team was almost completely new as 1960 drew to its close.

There were other problems. Bloemers complained of a lack of staff and money.[32] The offices were proving inadequate. There was also some dissatisfaction with the Secretary-General (Victor van Straelen complained that Bloemers played the violin in the office!).[62] The new President, Jean Baer, complained that he could not control things from a distance.[69] Doubts were also raised about the appropriateness of Brussels as a base because of Belgium's colonial past.

Ed Graham, Max Nicholson and Hal Coolidge (the Executive Board members from the principal funding countries) clearly presented some kind of ultimatum at the Board meeting in June 1960, although their comments are discreetly minuted as '*it would be difficult to count on further financial support unless steps were taken to improve the efficiency of the Secretariat*'.[70] Jean Baer argued that international political sensitivities, and the Union's expanding role in Africa, combined to suggest that it would be better to move the headquarters to a neutral country which had never had colonies, and Ed Graham and Hal Coolidge suggested Geneva. The Board resolved unanimously to propose to the General Assembly '*that the Executive Board be given authority to transfer the seat of the Union before the end of the year to Geneva or to some other place in Switzerland*'.[70]

When this became known, however, there was a Dutch reaction recalling the Bernard–van Tienhoven fracas in 1947, and foreshadowing events in 1988.[71,72] The Dutch wanted other State members to be asked what facilities they could offer, and insisted that a transfer should only be made if funds were available to increase the activities of the Union. The decision was postponed until the Assembly re-convened in Cracow after the mid-session tour customary at that time. By then, a number of African members had rallied behind the proposal that the headquarters should be in a non-colonial country. The Board revised its resolution, dropping any specific mention of Geneva and thus gaining flexibility in the choice of a Swiss location, and it went through.[37,72]

These proposals clearly put the Dutch Secretary-General, M C Bloemers, on the spot. It was not surprising that on 24 June 1960, just before the Warsaw General Assembly, he told the Board of his impending resignation. The formal minutes conceal what was undoubtedly an emotional occasion:

'the Secretary General stated his views. The lack of sufficient staff meant that the Secretary General had to see to all the details in the Secretariat. In addition the transfer involved starting again from scratch and without backing, and for this a younger man would be preferable. He also felt that the confidence so necessary between the Board and the Secretary General was lacking on both sides. He proposed to announce his wish to resign in the future but to say that he would accept re-election as no other nominations would be forthcoming in the Assembly.'[72]

After a good deal of frank debate, this was what happened. The General Assembly accepted the resignation of the Secretary-General with regret, expressed gratitude for his willingness to remain in office for a limited period, and gave the Board authority to appoint his successor (necessary, because at that time the Secretary-General was elected by the General Assembly). All fell into place. Bloemers resigned as Secretary-General on 1 December 1960 and Gerald Watterson came on secondment from FAO to take over in March 1961.[37]

The move from Brussels to Switzerland did not go smoothly. The President, Jean Baer, who was clearly expecting to play a leading part, was seriously injured in a road accident, and put out of action for some time. He asked Barton Worthington, who was steering the Africa Special Project, to take on a number of tasks relating to the move.[73] The first need was obviously to find inexpensive accommodation, and the task was remitted to the staff ecologist, G Treichel, because Watterson was about to leave for the next stage of the ASP. He was helped by a close friend of the President, Erico Nicola, a meteorologist and wartime aviator, who lived at Buchillon on the shore of Lake Geneva.[74] After the first formal meeting of the Executive Board in Switzerland, in April 1961, at the Musée Alexis Forel at Morges near Lausanne, Nicola invited everyone to dinner at his home and agreed to *'take over the Friends of the Union'*.[75] At the meeting it was reported that office premises had been secured in a former small hotel called 'Les Uttins' in the town of Morges. The building itself had no particular architectural merit, and was noisily close to the railway tracks, but the town itself was pleasant enough, with its lakeside walks, mediaeval chateau and ancient streets. The rent was SFr1000 per month, rising to SFr1500 in September, when the whole building would be available. It was for sale at a price of SFr330,000, and the Board hoped to raise the money to buy it (it was actually acquired by a fund established by IUCN on behalf of its staff in 1965).[75,76] Action was taken to register the Union as a legal entity in Switzerland, while Charles van der Elst, the Union's financial adviser, took steps to dissolve it as a Belgian institution.

The transfer had other traumas. Perhaps the most serious was the burning of many of the archives, by Baer personally. His motives are unclear – but Mady Harroy has written that he seemed determined to *'bury the Belgian past of the Union'*.[69] As a result, the archives now in Gland contain little from the earlier period apart from the *Bulletins*, records of Board and Commission meetings, and a small amount of correspondence handed over by people who had worked with the young Union. That Morges marked a new start is clear from the fact that the minutes of the Executive Board were re-numbered, the 'first meeting' being that held in Morges in April 1961 (it would have been the 87th meeting, old style). The *Bulletin* and publications were also re-launched as 'New Series' and a brochure 'What is IUCN?' followed in 1962.[77]

A number of friends and members provided generous help. The Dutch, in particular, despite their initial resistance to the move, paid SFr4000 for furnishing a 'Van

Figure 4.1 *The move to Morges. Gerald Watterson's sketches of the town and of 'Les Uttins' adorn the Union's Visitors Book.*

Tienhoven Reading Room' in the new headquarters. This was the first significant gift for the headquarters from outside the United States, and the Netherlands Commission for International Nature Conservation were warmly thanked for it.[78] But this generosity did not solve the chronic financial malaise. In April 1961, Gerald Watterson told the Executive Board that '*less than SFr 2000 remained in hand for 1st May, if debts or commitments already incurred in Switzerland were to be met with funds actually available for such purposes*'. Erico Nicola reported that the Benefactors, Donors and Friends had together contributed a total of only SFr31,000 since the scheme was started, and only SFr4000 remained in the account.[75] Peter Scott elicited the fact that 25 per cent of the members paid no subscription, while others paid less than US$50! The Board told the Secretary-General to request all members who owed subscriptions either to pay up or resign. Mr de Roover, the Honorary Treasurer of the Union, who was a Belgian financier, resigned on the grounds that since the transfer to Switzerland he could no longer provide the services even of one of his accountants. The Board appointed Charles van der Elst, Wolfgang Burhenne and Peter Scott as a working group '*to discuss ways of raising money to meet the Brussels debts and the SFr 65,000 deficit on the previous year's working*'.

So – IUCN had arrived in its new home, with important action in hand, especially in Africa. It was clear that new opportunities awaited it, not least in Asia. The application of science to resource management was emerging as a key theme for the future. But the old problem – resources – remained crippling. What could be done?

5 The New Ark Puts to Sea

Overwhelming Challenge

In the period between 1961 and 1966 the conservation movement was gripped by a sense of failure. Habitat destruction and threats to species were visibly accelerating. Environmental pollution had become an issue and the publication in 1963 of Rachel Carson's *Silent Spring* jarred many consciences (as Chapter 6 describes in greater depth). At the same time, many national organizations were gaining strength. In the United Kingdom the Nature Conservancy, led by Max Nicholson, was busily establishing and managing nature reserves and undertaking the research needed to underpin national conservation. In the United States, Canada and many other developed countries, national programmes were also advancing.

Global scientific cooperation had received an immense boost in the International Geophysical Year of 1956–57. This, among other things, had laid the foundation for international harmony in Antarctica, formalized in the Antarctic Treaty, which opened the whole region to peaceful scientific endeavour. The International Union of Biological Sciences determined that an International Biological Programme should follow. It took as its theme 'biological productivity and human welfare' and included a substantial conservation component.

All these developments posed a new challenge to IUCN and its members. There was clearly an even greater need for a body that would get to grips with the deepening global environmental crisis. But the chronic financial problems that had plagued most of the Union's 15 years of existence seemed certain to stop it meeting that need.

A New Fund for Nature

In April 1961 the IUCN Executive Board – still struggling for financial survival – saw a bright gleam in the sky.

> '*The Secretary General outlined the plan devised by Mr Nicholson for raising large sums of money through an International Wildlife Trust. Dr Worthington asked Mr Scott to read out a short appeal by Mr Nicholson introducing the scheme, which he requested Board members to sign. Mr Scott then presented a parallel project of his own, namely to try to persuade some multi-millionaire to set up a $30 million foundation of his own specifically for nature conservation. He asked the Board for assistance in suggesting names...*'[25]

The rationale was obvious. It:

> '*had become increasingly evident that the impact of human progress and development on the natural world had produced what amounted to a state of emergency for wildlife. Powerful arguments – ethical, aesthetic, scientific and economic – seemed to place a direct moral responsibility on mankind to take a long-term view and to conserve the natural heritage wisely. Clearly, the time was ripe for a massive attempt to raise money professionally on a world-wide scale, and to feed it into conservation channels under the best scientific advice available and working wherever possible through existing organizations.*'[1]

Such an idea had been around for some time – indeed Jean-Paul Harroy, writing in 1988, recalled that the idea had been discussed even before he left IUPN in 1955.[2] But the real trigger seems to have been a letter from Victor Stolan to Sir Julian Huxley in 1960.[1] After his African mission for UNESCO, Huxley had written a series of articles on the plight of African wildlife for *The Observer*.[3] Referring to these, Stolan argued that:

> '*however excellent your suggestions…without a vigorous and immediate action to raise the great funds needed the irreparable detriment will not be prevented from becoming a fact. However, there must be a way to the conscience and the heart and pride and vanity of the very rich people to persuade them to sink their hands deeply in their pockets and thus serve a cause which is greater and nobler than any other…*'

Stolan concluded by arguing that a '*single and uninhibited mind must take charge of such a world-embracing situation*', and while he did not claim that role for himself he said he had '*some ideas as to how to collect substantial donations, but nobody of sufficient importance to speak to*'. He asked Huxley to make the contact with a Person of Importance.

Huxley sent the letter to Max Nicholson for advice. It was positive. Yes, there was a case for a large-scale international effort to raise money for conservation. And Max Nicholson and Peter Scott had already discussed such a proposal.[4] The two of them were fed up with the slow and impoverished pace of action in IUCN. Nicholson complained at the Warsaw General Assembly in June 1960 that the IUCN agenda never changed, and that '*what we need is better fund-raising. When we have it, the agenda can change*'. He and Scott became determined to kick-start a new effort.

Peter Scott was unique among members of the IUCN Executive Board at the time. He was another hunter – wildfowler – turned conservationist, and a well-known painter of ducks, geese and their watery haunts. He had been an Olympic yachtsman, had a distinguished war record as commander of small Naval patrol gunships, and had been national glider champion.[5] A keen collector of live waterfowl, his home on the edge of the Severn marshes at Slimbridge in western England became a centre where rare species were bred in captivity and research on waterfowl and their ecology was conducted. He had led expeditions to the Arctic breeding grounds of various geese. A practical conservationist, the restoration of the Hawaiian nene goose to the wild, using Slimbridge stock, was one of the first such achievements in the world. Scott was also an outstanding communicator and broadcaster, and his *Look* television series was one of the first to bring animals and birds into the living rooms of middle-class Britain. He thus had the practical knowledge of how to appeal to the public that the academic scientists on the IUCN Board lacked.

Early in March 1961, Max Nicholson visited the United States and discussed the notion with colleagues, including Ira Gabrielson.[1] With that behind him, he prepared the memorandum that was read to the IUCN Executive Board in April. He also spoke to Guy Mountfort, UK businessman and an old friend and fellow-ornithologist. In May he invited a small group of key people to meet with him in his office at the Nature Conservancy in Belgrave Square.[6] The purpose was simply to '*conduct the first probes for Jean Baer, to whom I reported constantly to keep IUCN in the picture*'.[7]

The group did not include academic ecologists or people from overseas because IUCN was thought of as providing those linkages.[7] It included people from the world of business and the media because it was clear that their expertise would be crucial. Nicholson, Scott and others had run repeatedly against negative brick walls of officialdom in trying to get money from governmental sources, and the UK lacked the large charitable foundations that Hal Coolidge had been able to tap in the United States. They therefore wanted, in a sense, to create a new world foundation for conservation, funded outside government. They wanted '*a world fund-raising organization which would work in collaboration with existing bodies to bring massive financial support to the conservation movement*'. They called it the World Wildlife Fund, and Peter Scott drew the Panda symbol, based on a sketch by Gerald Watterson.[1]

They had to launch a new campaign, targeted at the public and at the business community. For this they needed professional fund-raising advice. At around this time, Guy Mountfort met Ian MacPhail, a professional PR consultant, and told him that:

> '*many leading international conservationists...realized that the growing pressures on the natural world needed to be urgently dealt with...At the same time it had also become clear that the work of conserving nature was constantly hampered for lack of money. Fund-raising, it was recognized, was a highly specialized activity with which scientists and conservationists were not necessarily familiar.*'

MacPhail was asked to produce a blue-print for a brand new organization which he likened to '*a kind of international Red Cross for wildlife*'. In due course he became International Campaigns Director for the new venture.[8] Start-up money came from two anonymous loans, which together provided £3000, and a gift of £10,000 from the British impresario Jack Cotton. Ian McPhail began work, and attended the Arusha Conference, where the creation of WWF was announced.[8,9]

The Morges Manifesto was adopted at about the same time. It was a short statement of needs and aims, and the initial cry of near-despair seems sadly topical 35 years later.

> '*All over the world today, vast numbers of fine and harmless wild creatures are losing their lives or their homes as the result of thoughtless and needless destruction. In the name of advancing civilization they are being shot or trapped out of existence on land taken to be exploited, or drowned by new dams, poisoned by toxic chemicals, killed by poachers for gain, or destroyed in the course of political upheaval.*'

Recalling that the 1960s seemed likely to beat all records for this destruction, the Manifesto predicted that '*feelings of guilt and shame will follow and will haunt our children, deprived of nature's rich inheritance by ignorance, greed and folly*'. But then came the call for action:

> '*Although the eleventh hour has struck, it is not yet quite too late to think again. Skilful and admirable men, and admirable organizations, are struggling to save the world's wildlife. They have the ability and the will to do it, but they tragically lack the support and resources. They are battling at this moment on many fronts and against many daily changing and growing threats. They need, above all, money to carry out mercy missions and meet conservation emergencies by acquiring land where wildlife treasures are threatened, and in many other ways. Money, for example, to pay guardians of wildlife refuges, money for education and propaganda among those who would care to help if only they understood; money to send out experts to danger spots and to train more local wardens and helpers, in Africa and elsewhere.*
>
> *The emergency must be tackled with vigour and efficiency on the much enlarged scale which it demands, but success will depend not only on the devoted efforts of enthusiasts for wildlife, but on winning the respect and backing of many other interests which must not be overlooked or antagonized.*
>
> *Mankind's self-respect, and mankind's inheritance on this earth will not be preserved by narrow or short-sighted means!*'[1,10,11]

The Manifesto was signed by 16 people. Eleven – including Jean Baer, François Bourlière, Wolfgang Burhenne, Peter Scott, Ed Graham, Kai Curry-Lindahl, Eugen Gerstenmaier (then President of the Bundestag, the German parliament) and Barton Worthington – were serving members of the IUCN Executive Board. They were joined by Charles Bernard as President Emeritus, Julian Huxley, Max Nicholson and Erico Nicola.[11]

The Manifesto is important because it was the point of departure for WWF, and it makes it clear that from the very outset the Fund was to be a different kind of body from IUCN. It appeals unashamedly to sentiment – to revulsion over the destruction of wildlife, and to guilt that short-term human interests would deprive future generations of the rich heritage of nature. It calls for 'mercy missions'. It asserts that there is an army of capable and dedicated professionals standing by, and able to save wildlife – if they are given the money. The implication is clear – that people upset by the destruction of nature can stop it, because the expert defenders are ready and waiting, held back by the sole barrier of financial lack. The slogan – '*We* can save nature – we only need *your* money', rings out. Little has changed in 36 years. Although a great deal of money has been raised, the need is undiminished and the message continues to be marketed.

Even before WWF became a legal entity, a lot of thought was given to its relationship with other conservation bodies. A paper setting out 'Heads for a Contract' between WWF and IUCN was drawn up on 16 August 1961.[12] It states that WWF recognized IUCN '*as the representative and authoritative world conservation organization responsible for the study and conservation of wildlife and wildlife habitat*'. WWF would respect IUCN's status in this field and its ties with international bodies such as UNESCO and FAO. Accordingly the WWF would '*at all times consult and cooperate with IUCN in all such matters as are within IUCN's sphere of responsibility, and will look to IUCN for advice and guidance on such matters as and where appropriate*'. Because WWF recognized the need for a strong and effective IUCN, the new body would '*make regular contributions towards the overheads and administrative expenditures of IUCN on an agreed basis*'. The special role of ICBP in the ornithological field was similarly recognized.

For its part IUCN was to establish and maintain (with WWF support) an 'operations room' where information about the status of current conservation problems and projects would be centred, and an operations group that brought in the President and Secretary-General of the Union, the Secretary of ICBP, the Chairs of Commissions, and representatives of Africa, Asia, Europe, North America and the Pacific (including Australasia). IUCN agreed to provide advice to WWF, to submit an annual budget, to do all in its power to maintain the confidence of the worldwide supporters of WWF, and to acknowledge WWF support in its publications and in other ways.

The World Wildlife Fund was formed under Swiss law at Zurich on 11 September 1961, and on 16 October that year it was registered as a tax-exempt charitable foundation.[1] The deed of foundation states the objective of the new body was:

> '*to collect, manage and disburse funds through suitable international or national bodies or individuals for the conservation of world fauna, flora, forests, landscapes, water, soils and other natural resources by the acquisition and management of land, research and investigation, education at all levels, information and publicity, coordination of efforts, cooperation with other interested parties and all other appropriate means...*'.

It was to review the long-term financial needs of world conservation, support education and exhibitions, finance specialist and student exchanges, especially from less developed countries, and acquire property and establish branches, especially with the support of other organizations. Operating expenses having been deducted, one third of the sums raised would go to the central account in Switzerland and be distributed by the International Board, one third would be deployed at the discretion of national trustees, and one third would go to whichever could make a case for needing it most.

The World Wildlife Fund was launched in London on 26 September 1961 under the allegorical panels of the Great Room of the Royal Society for the Encouragement of Arts, Manufactures and Commerce.[1,10] Julian Huxley, Jean Baer (who, as President of IUCN was also the acting President of the Fund) and Peter Scott (soon elected Chairman of WWF) were the speakers. Ian MacPhail was in attendance. A World Wildlife Charter [13] was read and adopted, and IUCN announced that it would take the steps necessary to secure its endorsement by the UN. The Charter committed its signatories to take seven key steps:

1   To prevent any further extermination of wildlife.
2   To make sure that room shall be left for wildlife.
3   To protect all wildlife from unintentional or wanton cruelty.
4   To encourage children to develop a love and understanding of wildlife.
5   To make certain that all those whose work has an impact on nature should recognize their responsibility to wildlife.
6   To arrange to help those nations in need of it in order to preserve their wildlife.
7   To work together to save the world's wildlife.

The target was to raise £1.5 million (or US$4.2 million at the rate of exchange then prevailing). The Press coverage was good, and on 9 October 1961 the *Daily Mirror* brought out a 'shock issue' devoting seven pages to the wildlife emergency. It was edited by Ian MacPhail (who was friendly with the then Editor of the *Mirror*, Hugh Cudlipp).[8] The front cover had the form of a poster. A female black rhinoceros and calf appeared beneath a caption:

> '*DOOMED – to disappear from the face of the earth due to Man's FOLLY, GREED, NEGLECT.*'

It was soon clear that public interest had been stirred, and money came flowing in – some £50,000 of it in direct response to the *Mirror*'s shock treatment.

The United Kingdom appeal began on 23 November 1961 with HRH Prince Philip, Duke of Edinburgh in the lead (the start of 35 years of close personal involvement with WWF). The United States followed on 1 December. Ex-President Eisenhower was the nominal President of the appeal. The moving energies included Ira Gabrielson, ex-Head of US Fish and Wildlife Service and ex-Chair of the IUCN Commission on Education, C R 'Pink' Gutermuth (former Director of Education of the Indiana Department of Conservation, creator of over 500 conservation clubs in that State, and erstwhile President of the Wildlife Management Institute), Hal Coolidge (who was the principal bridge to IUCN) and a former judge of the US Tax Court, Russell Train (like so many other distinguished conservationists, an ex-hunter who had made two safaris to East Africa). Train had been involved with Coolidge and Russell Arundel in establishing the African Wildlife Leadership Foundation, and was to be drawn ever more closely into the conservation network, especially after 1965 when he left the Tax Court and became head of the Conservation Foundation in New York and transferred its office to Washington DC.[14]

The Swiss, Dutch, German and Austrian ventures were all up and running by February 1964. The German venture was launched by two members of the IUCN Board, Wolfgang Burhenne and Eugen Gerstenmeier.[15] Prince Philip approached HRH Prince Bernhard of the Netherlands, who became Patron, and later President, of WWF International.[10] In December 1961 a young Swiss businessman named Fritz Vollmar was engaged as Secretary-General to the World Wildlife Fund (International) and in March 1962 he set up his office in the IUCN building in Morges.[9,10] The first highly-professional illustrated brochure (with a foreword by Prince Bernhard and many drawings by Peter Scott) soon appeared.[13]

WWF and IUCN

Many people in IUCN have clung to the belief that WWF was really founded to support the Union. But those who planned WWF decided it had to be a new body rather than a fund-raising arm of IUCN. '*WWF was not set up as part of IUCN but as a leading financial supporter. There was much discussion about this*'.[16] None the less, '*the impetus and primary rationale for such an organization was the need to support IUCN and elevate it well above its historically finance-limited activities*'.[17] While the Deed of Foundation made it clear that WWF was legally required to disburse its funds through '*suitable international or national bodies or individuals*' the founders accepted that '*in order to be a successful fund-raising mechanism, it would have to have a broader mandate than the support of one organization'.*[17] As Prince Philip has put it: *'it was like the Cancer Research Fund – it raised money, and gave it to the experts to get on with'.*[18]

The crucial point is that WWF and IUCN needed to be *complementary.* IUCN had shown it could convene the world's leading professional conservationists. It could produce books, lists, manuals and technical advice. It was great at meetings. But it was dominated by scientists and government administrators who excelled in cautious judgement, but had no skill whatever in publicity and fund-raising. WWF set out to change all that. But both bodies were expected to be *enabling*, supporting the societies and organizations on the ground – IUCN with scientific knowledge, and WWF with money. Both would build capacity in the developing world. What nobody probably recognized at that time was that if it succeeded, WWF would be seen by the public as the leader of world conservation. IUCN staff would have to accept the status of 'back room boys' (and girls). Time was to show that they found it hard to do this gracefully.

In its first five years, 1961–64, WWF raised US$1.9 million. It spent most of it on small grants for protected areas, species protection, education and research. About half the grants went to Africa, but the biggest single payment went to buy 65 square kilometres of wonderful bird-rich marshland on the Coto Doñana, at the mouth of the Guadalquivir River in Spain.[7,19] But it stood by its promise to support global conservation bodies, and IUCN, ICBP, the International Waterfowl Research Bureau which ICBP had founded in the 1950s, the Charles Darwin Foundation on the Galapagos Islands and the International Youth Foundation (regarded at the time as the 'junior arm' of IUCN) were beneficiaries of the first five WWF projects.[20]

From the beginning the working partnership between WWF and IUCN was very close. The Secretary-General of the new Fund, Fritz Vollmar, was given an office in the IUCN headquarters building at Morges, although the International Campaigns Director (Ian MacPhail) stayed in Britain. The Coordinating Committee for the Fund was joint with IUCN and ICBP. Its task was *'to draw up and put into operation a Grand Strategic Plan for world conservation'.*[1]

The new WWF Trustees did not see the amount of voluntary money available for conservation as finite. They sought *'to deepen the well, and dig more wells'.* They thought that conservation was operating in an expanding market, and that it was essential that there was coordination among the operators. *'The more cooperation that can be obtained, and the more conservation organizations that can be seen to be working harmoniously within an accepted pattern, the better the prospect of success towards our common goals'.*[1] WWF sought *'to avoid coming into competition with any other conservation organizations'.* Peter Scott repeatedly emphasized in later years that there was never any intention that WWF would compete with, or seek to control, IUCN.[17]

When it started operating, WWF referred all project proposals to two independent referees and to the HQ staff of IUCN or the liaison office of the ICBP (which led on all ornithological matters). Their comments went to all members of the IUCN Executive Board and to the WWF Trustees. A Green Book of project proposals and comments was compiled, and twice a year a special Screening Committee of IUCN considered all the items, and assigned each a priority rating, putting the 'category A' proposals in ranking order from a scientific standpoint. The WWF Trustees took the final decision in allocating available funds, but they only altered the priority order if there were overriding non-scientific considerations or a particular need related to the campaigns and appeals.

The categories on which attention focussed were also common ground between WWF and IUCN. In the short term, there were to be rescue operations '*to save the most threatened species at the eleventh hour*'. A second goal was the safeguarding of habitats, which meant more national parks and nature reserves. For the long term, changing attitudes through education was seen as all-important, and here funds were needed to teach people, especially young people, the fundamental principles of conservation. Research and education were therefore integral to most projects, building understanding and effectiveness in the field, and stimulating more general public support. As WWF stated: '*Our task, impossible though it may seem, is to change the attitude of the great mass of human beings to the natural world, and we have at most one generation span in which to do it. We are satisfied that it can be done*'.[1]

One consequence of the creation of WWF was the clearer articulation of IUCN's own policy. In a paper presented to the Executive Board in November 1962, Noel Simon emphasized that the policy must embrace a statement of principles and objectives, a working programme, a budget, machinery for obtaining expert advice where needed and facilities for programme planning.[21] He considered the aim of the Union to be '*at national level to encourage each country to formulate and implement a sound policy designed to conserve wildlife and natural resources*'. At the continental level it should ensure that provision was made for the effective protection of habitats and to ensure that each species of indigenous wild animal was accorded proper sanctuary in perpetuity in at least part of each continent. IUCN's goal '*must be the betterment of mankind through wise use of organic nature*'. The strategy was to influence the adoption of conservation policies in those countries which lacked the money and expertise to create their own. The tactics must include the accumulation of fundamental data and the drawing up of conceptual conservation schemes wherever the need was greatest. In 1963, the Union's general policy was restated in a paper drafted originally by Ed Graham, and polished by Peter Scott.[22]

WWF succeeded because it caught the tide of public awareness and concern – something Peter Scott and Aubrey Buxton had done much to foster through television. Writing to Hugh Elliott in March 1963, Max Nicholson quoted some British statistics – seven or eight million viewers for the wildlife programmes of Armand and Michaela Denis, five to seven million for Scott's *Look*, and six million for Buxton's Anglia series. Eleven million people had watched a special Christmas presentation of *The New Ark*. Yet despite this popular interest, newspaper and TV news coverage of environmental issues remained inadequate in quality and quantity.[23] Another concern was that programmes like those of Scott in the UK and Jacques Cousteau in France brought nature, in gift-wrapped form, to people's armchairs and might foster escapism rather than activism. Nicholson saw clearly that the hostility to the environment and to nature that characterized much of industry at that period needed tough confrontation which the people on the Boards of IUCN and similar organizations would not and could not provide. From the beginning, WWF had to consider vigorous, independent action.[24]

WWF also worked because it had a simple structure and a clear goal. It was run by businessmen and communicators. It had national Boards whose members – themselves influential figures – chose others of the same kind without the complications of periodic election in General Assemblies. Its programme was decided by the governing Councils, and was not subject to amendment by resolutions from members pursuing their own pet topics. It had goals the public could identify with – like 'saving the tiger', where IUCN was far more esoteric and indeed proved almost impossible to market as an attraction to WWF subscribers.[8] And WWF was finance-led: that is,

Figure 5.1 *Biological diversity in action. Théodore Monod's sketch of the IUCN Executive Board in 1965. It is not clear what malicious outside force is represented by the diabolical fisherman!*

it got the money first and allocated only the resources it had. It was a businesslike outfit.

Success may have come also because WWF had a strong ethical basis, summarized by Peter Scott in *The Launching of the New Ark*.[1] Extinction, he wrote, was due to human ignorance. There was a clear human moral responsibility *'to keep "a place in the sun" for the animal species which share the Earth with us'*. Eradicating other species was morally wrong, and only justified by all-compelling reasons. Another ethical principle, that of responsibility to future generations, was enunciated 20 years before the World Commission on Environment and Development emphasized it as the touchstone of 'sustainable development'. Scott also drew on aesthetic and economic arguments that were to become familiar 15 years later in the World Conservation Strategy. He urged that science be heeded, pointing out (as Huxley, Fraser Darling, Ray Dasmann and the Talbots, among others, had done) that recent ecological research had showed that wildlife harvesting could yield more food for human consumption than the raising of domestic livestock on the same range. Finally, he emphasized the importance of a reverence for life – and (as a bow in the direction of the hunting interests that were among the supporters of conservation) he noted that the ethics of taking life were separate from the ethics of exterminating species – hunters and non-hunters sharing a condemnation of extinction even if they differed on the former matter.

Conservation in Action

In 1961, WWF was no more than an unproven new initiative. IUCN had to get on with as much active conservation as it could. The agenda was still dominated by Africa – not only the ASP, but the dire situation in the Congo, where war and administrative collapse threatened the Albert and Garamba National Parks.[25] The situation was reported personally by Jacques Verschuren, who had just returned from the stricken areas. Charles van der Elst told the Executive Board that Belgium, the former colonial power, might assist in funding conservation on the ground, but that for presentational reasons it was essential that other nations contributed, and Wolfgang Burhenne, Chairman of the Legislation Committee, said that German funds would be available (they came, especially, from the Frankfurt Zoological Society, which has since that time been active in African conservation, especially in Garamba and in the Serengeti).[26]

The ASP demonstrated that IUCN could be a spearhead of conservation in the developing world. It worked – as it was intended to do – in partnership with (and supported by) national and international bodies. FAO and UNESCO had funded field activities and meetings. The Fauna Preservation Society, the New York Zoological Society, Deutsche Afrika Gesellschaft, UNESCO and sources in Belgium, South Africa and the UK were all making positive noises about contributing towards the US$20,000 needed for African fellowships in Stage II. FAO, UNESCO and American sources were all being mildly encouraging about Stage III even though the main call on American funds for conservation had been the 1962 National Parks Conference in Seattle.[25,26]

By the time the General Assembly met in Nairobi in September 1963, Phase III of the ASP (the tours by Thane Riney and Peter Hill) was up and running, the College of African Wildlife Management at Mweka had opened its doors and educational campaigns supported by UNESCO were in progress in three countries. A Phase IV was contemplated, which UNESCO and FAO would finance through regional and country programmes, while IUCN planned an *African Wildlife Management Field Book*, to be published in partnership with the Fauna Preservation Society.[27] The whole conservation initiative in Africa, building on the Arusha Declaration, was burgeoning.[28] A technical meeting organized by the Commission on Ecology discussed 'the ecology of man in the tropical environment', with five sub-themes: pre-industrial man and the tropical environment; type habitats and biological productivity in the tropics; the impact of man on the tropical environment; ecological research and development in the tropics; and the role of international organizations.[27,29]

No doubt East Africa was the preferred venue for the eighth session of the General Assembly in 1963 because of the prominence of the Africa Special Project. There were, however, some dissident voices. Some thought it was time to move on, and that Asia would be better, thereby paving the way for a successor special project in that continent.[25] Another concern was security, because of the guerilla war which was to accelerate the move towards Kenyan independence, and it was suggested that Uganda or South Africa might provide alternative sites.[25] In the event, both the Government of Kenya and that of Uganda issued invitations, and the proposal was made to hold Commission meetings and workshops in Kampala, and the Assembly in Nairobi.

The model of the ASP clearly might be useful elsewhere. In 1961 there had been interest in flanking the IUCN 'African desk' with a 'European desk'. The Council of Europe was considering enlisting IUCN as its lead partner in coordinating conservation throughout Europe.[26] There was also discussion of an Asian Project and Asian desk, building on a Nature Conservation Symposium to be held in Indonesia early in 1962 under the auspices of the South East Asia Science Cooperation Office of UNESCO. A small regional working group was already active under Dr Boonsong Lekagul of Thailand, himself a distinguished physician and amateur zoologist and member of the IUCN Executive Board.[27] The project was developed under the banner of the National Parks Commission (with Hal Coolidge again securing funding) and was approved at the Nairobi General Assembly.[17]

The project was directed by Lee Talbot, and he and his wife, Marty, were the staff team. There was close cooperation with FAO, UNESCO, the UN Technical Assistance Board and the Conservation Section of the International Biological Programme. Ten countries were visited, and in each the government was consulted, there were discussions with conservationists, field reconnaissance covered as much of the country as possible and the recommendations were then evaluated with those involved. National reports were produced and the whole effort was pulled together at a major Conference on Conservation of Nature and Natural Resources in Tropical South-east Asia, held at Bangkok from 29 November to 4 December 1965 and attended by 192 participants from 23 countries.[31] This was the first truly international conference on conservation in the region, and it raised the profile of the subject and built new links between regional conservation bodies. UNESCO, FAO and a number of Asian governments followed up the recommendations. The project generated more than 20 publications, and led to action to safeguard threatened species, new or reconstituted national parks, new national laws and institutions for conservation and education programmes.[17]

The Charles Darwin Research Station in the Galapagos also forged ahead. It received considerable support from UNESCO, while IUCN's scientific input was overseen by a Steering Committee of François Bourlière, Hal Coolidge, Jean Dorst and Peter Scott. In the farthest south, Antarctic conservation had begun to attract attention: the first Antarctic Treaty Consultative Meeting in 1961 received proposals (not from IUCN) for what became the Agreed Measures for the Conservation of Antarctic Fauna and Flora, and François Bourlière acted as local host to the first Symposium on Antarctic Biology held in Paris in 1962 at which the need for more extensive conservation measures encompassing the sub-Antarctic islands was discussed.[32]

Project MAR – a joint venture with ICBP and the International Wildfowl Research Bureau (IWRB) to study and assess the conservation priorities for marshes, bogs and other wetlands – was the Union's second structured project activity. It was proposed at the 1960 Warsaw General Assembly by Lukas (Luc) Hoffmann, a member of the Swiss business family that started the pharmaceutical company Hoffmann LaRoche and himself creator of the research centre at the Tour du Valat in the Camargue. In 1962 (the year in which he also became Honorary Director of the IWRB), Hoffmann organized a MAR conference on the conservation and management of temperate wetlands.[30,33] This not only produced a major volume of proceedings[33] and an educational booklet entitled *Liquid Assets*, but inspired a joint IUCN–WWF campaign for wetland conservation called 'Life at the Water's Edge'. Over the following nine years, discussions in a series of meetings in the UK, the Netherlands and the USSR led to the elaboration of an international agreement which became the Ramsar Convention on Wetlands of International Importance especially as Waterfowl Habitat.[30]

The Commissions also marched forward strongly. The Commission on Ecology encouraged several scientific symposia, including the MAR Conference on Wetlands and another on the coordination of Ecological Research in National Parks which fed directly into the International Biological Programme (IBP).[34] The Commission also embarked on a study of natural communities, and in addition to the Committees on Ecological Aspects of Soil and Water Conservation and Ecological Aspects of Landscape Planning, created a new group on Ecological Effects of Chemical Controls under Dr Donald Kuenen, himself an insect physiologist of distinction, '*to advise the Union on pesticides and toxic chemicals*'. There was also a Committee on Ecological Research in IBP, led by Professor Ellenberg of Germany.[25,27,29]

The Commission on National Parks gained great credit through the publication of the first 300-page volume of the *United Nations List of National Parks*. Hal Coolidge, as Chairman, also played a central part in setting up the first World Conference on National Parks, held in Seattle in 1962. This landmark event was organized by IUCN, with the National Park Service of the US Department of the Interior as host and UNESCO, FAO, the National Park Service and the Natural Resources Council of America as co-sponsors.[28,35] Jean Baer was Honorary Chairman, Hal Coolidge General Chairman, and IUCN activists were prominent among the 250 participants. It raised IUCN's profile in North America (it was the first major IUCN event attended by the Sierra Club).[36] The steady growth of conservation in the developing world was demonstrated by the presence of people from 15 countries in Latin America as well as many from Africa, Australia, New Zealand, North America and Europe.[28,35] It was at this time that IUCN and WWF people – including Jean-Paul Harroy, Luc Hoffmann and Ian Grimwood – first came to the notice of Peruvian 'parks people' and WWF began to fund projects in South America.[37]

The Conference set a target for the future. It opined that each species of plant or animal threatened with extinction should be safeguarded by including an area of natural habitat sufficient to maintain an adequate reproductive population in a national park or nature reserve. An early WWF project also appeared at Seattle, in the shape of the proposed World Wildlife Charter, which was endorsed and transmitted to the IUCN General Assembly in Nairobi. Later in 1962 Jean-Paul Harroy, on his retirement from his post in Africa, renewed his active involvement in IUCN as Vice-Chairman of the Commission on National Parks with special responsibility for revising and reorganizing the UN List.[28]

The Survival Service Commission remained the focus of many actions on behalf of threatened species, and the advent of WWF made its work infinitely easier. In 1961, Lt Col Boyle threw the Commission behind a project that was to hit world headlines – 'Operation Oryx'. Lee Talbot had reported on the dire plight of the Arabian oryx in 1956, and suggested that it could only be saved by a captive breeding project, which he and Ian Grimwood planned from Kenya.[17] Funds for action became available in 1960, thanks largely to the Fauna Preservation Society and WWF. Political tensions in Kenya blocked the original plan to establish the 'survival herd' there. Instead, the group of captured wild animals plus others gathered from zoos was built up in the United States (Arizona, and later also California). The eventual reintroduction, especially in Oman, was a resounding success – the first time a large mammal has been saved in captivity and reintroduced to its former range.[17,26,28]

The SSC was closely involved in the establishment of the 'Operations Intelligence Centre' at IUCN headquarters in 1960 – with accelerated growth after WWF arrived in October 1961, although a Secretariat crisis in 1962 (see below) imposed delays and created some friction.[28,38] It housed dossiers, with maps, diagrams, graphs, indices and check lists, supplemented by the best available photographs, on topics such as '*the status of threatened species, critical habitats, existing and projected conservation measures (with special reference to those with which the World Wildlife Fund is concerned), productivity and land use or misuse*'.[28] The 'Red Data Books', which came to fruition after Peter Scott had taken over the Chair of SSC from Lt Col Boyle in 1963 and were his most enduring legacy to IUCN, were devised:

> '*to provide more detailed biographies of all endangered species under the headings: present and former distribution (with map), status and estimated numbers, breeding rate, reasons for decline, protective measures already taken and proposed, numbers in zoos, breeding potential in captivity, and references*'.[28]

The Red Data Books were themselves based on the SSC list of '*Animals and Plants Threatened with Extinction*', which was in turn backed up by a card index created by Lt Col Boyle in about 1959.[27] Boyle had also established a small unit in London to gather information on species of threatened mammals and their geographical distribution.[39] The SSC derived further information from van Tienhoven's International Office for the Protection of Nature, and from major published sources.[39] The first Red Data Books (which date from 1962) appear to have been compilations for internal use by Commission members and IUCN staff: about 50 copies were produced, in loose-leaf format held in red plastic binders.[40] The volume on mammals was compiled by Noel Simon and that on birds by Col Jack Vincent, who was posted by ICBP to IUCN headquarters;[28] plants were to be considered by a botanical subcommittee established in 1962 under the Chairmanship of Sir George Taylor, Director of Kew Gardens in Britain.[27,28] The format allowed entries to be revised easily – a need appreciated from the beginning, not least because of a recognized initial bias towards large mammals, reptiles and birds.

Another burning issue that emerged in this period was the threat to some species posed by trade – not least for zoological gardens, which seemed inclined to collect species regardless of their status in the wild. Barton Worthington raised the issue at the Board meeting in April 1961, and urged legal controls.[25] At the Arusha Conference in September, many government officials in charge of wildlife in African countries complained that their efforts at controlling poaching were being undermined by the high prices on offer.[17] In November, the Board was stirred to stronger action by reports of the illegal capture and export of ten mountain gorillas from Kivu to East Africa.[26] The Board agreed to establish closer ties with the International Union of Directors of Zoological Gardens (a founder member of IUCN), and there were also discussions at the XIIIth International Conference of the ICBP in June 1962.

Wolfgang Burhenne, Chairman of the newly-constituted IUCN Committee on Legislation and Administration which held its first meeting in 1962, secured Board support for an examination of the existing Convention on International Transport of Animals to see how it might be amended to cope with such problems: the Council of Europe was mentioned as a possible backer.[27] By the time of the Nairobi General Assembly in September 1963 Burhenne had approached 125 governments, while the SSC, in partnership with the Fauna Preservation Society, had been involved in drafting proposed new laws for the UK on the control of importation of rare animals.[28] The General Assembly passed a resolution encouraging further action.[15] These various moves, carried forward nearly a decade later in a fringe meeting at the Banff General Assembly, were the genesis of CITES, the Convention on International Trade in Endangered Species of Wild Fauna and Flora, adopted in Washington in 1973.

The Committee on Legislation and Administration also began to accumulate legal and administrative information: by May 1962, 110 countries had been contacted, and 84 had replied.[27] Wolfgang Burhenne emphasized the need to assess this documentation, organize it so that it would be a serviceable tool, and draw up a check-list of basic items that should feature in conservation legislation.[27] The result, in the end, was the Environmental Law Centre in Bonn. Wolfgang Burhenne also reported on plans to publish a new edition of the IUCN Statutes in English, French, German, Russian and Spanish (though it took nearly 30 years for Spanish to join English and French as an official language of the Union).

Restoring the Secretariat

Although WWF grew rapidly, IUCN still grappled with financial turmoil during 1961. Only 100 out of the 196 full members of the Union had paid their membership fees in whole or part: '*there was some indication of 52 others contributing*', 33 were several years in arrears and had not answered the demand to pay up and 11 had said they could not pay. Debts of about US$21,000 had been left behind in Brussels, and the Board agreed to use the cash in hand to pay the most important of these.[27] This left the money required to run the office for the remainder of 1961 to be found from 'other sources'. As for 1962, the budget was set at US$122,000, of which only a fifth would come from membership dues: UNESCO would grant $6000; gifts from the USA would total $20,000; other gifts would provide $2000 and WWF would provide the balancing sum of $73,000. The New Ark was clearly alongside and providing buoyancy without which the ship would have sunk.[27,42]

These events brought pressure on both the Secretariat and the Presidency.[26] The Board had to find a new Secretary-General to take over when Gerald Watterson's secondment from FAO ended in August 1962. Noel Simon was working almost single-handed on Red Data Books and other species conservation projects. George Treichel, the staff ecologist, was heavily committed to a book on the parks of Africa and could give only one or two hours a day to IUCN: he also planned to return to the United States in June 1962. Despite the financial problems, the staff had to be strengthened and the Board authorized the recruitment of an education/information officer, a library assistant, an administrative assistant and two bilingual secretaries. Watterson also pointed out that the staff had no proper contracts and no pension arrangements beyond the compulsory Swiss national retirement, medical and family allowance schemes.[26]

The preparation of the Operations Room that was to be the nerve centre for IUCN and WWF projects, was delayed. WWF got restive. Peter Scott wrote sharply in August 1962 saying that the supply of data had '*been part of IUCN's undertaking for WWF for a great many months now, and the Trustees are liable to explode about them unless something begins to take concrete shape pretty quickly*'.[38] His irritation may well have been the greater because at the time IUCN was the source of the essential data WWF needed in order to raise money for conservation – including lifelines for IUCN.[41]

The succession to Watterson was dealt with in a circuitous manner. In November 1961, Barton Worthington asked for, and obtained, authority to engage Sir Hugh Elliott, then based in the UK and serving as Secretary to the Africa Special Project, for 18 months in order to build close relations with Commonwealth countries: there would be no cost to IUCN. At that stage, it does not seem that he was thought of as a successor to Watterson, but that is how it turned out. Hugh Elliott became Acting Secretary-General in December 1962, was confirmed in office when the General Assembly met in Nairobi in September 1963, and served until 1966.

Elliott did not find an easy situation in Morges. According to a visiting colleague and confidante, Jack Lipscomb, '*the basic trouble is the situation of the offices. A staff of mixed nationalities has been placed in a town which has no social amenities for foreigners and insufficient other foreign nationals to form a community*'.[43] Lipscomb advocated moving the office to Geneva. He also emphasized that IUCN simply must have enough funds of its own to meet its core costs, writing that he could not see '*how the Union can ever really call its soul its own as long as it depends on WWF to balance its budget for administration*'.[44] He urged the Secretary-General to devote his whole time to policy and to contact with the Commissions and partner organizations, with an Assistant Secretary-General to manage the office. That person should be an administrator, not a scientist, for '*you are already overburdened with scientists all chasing their pet hares*'.[44] This appointment was the more necessary because Hugh Elliott lived in the United Kingdom and felt unable to move to Switzerland: he visited Morges regularly, but conceded that the Secretariat could not be run from London.[45]

By August 1963, with the General Assembly not far away, there was also a crisis of confidence in the IUCN President and Board. Peter Scott (who was to take over the Chair of SSC from Lt Col C L Boyle that year) wrote pungently on the matter to Luc Hoffmann, and it is clear that both were sharing their concerns with Hal Coolidge. They were worried that Jean Baer's judgement could not be relied on and that he was not helping IUCN's image. The Board was ineffectual. '*By far the best solution*' Scott wrote, '*would be for Baer to make way for Bourlière at once, though I think it is essential that this should be done without a "row" and the subsequent bitterness...*'.[46] It happened. François Bourlière indeed succeeded to the Presidency in Nairobi. The new President was a man who blended charm with steel. Originally qualified in medicine and expert on the biochemistry of ageing in birds and mammals (including humans), he always described himself as an amateur ecologist, yet he was to play a leading role in that science. Perhaps more to the point, he had a strong personality, was a brilliant teacher and communicator, and '*a certain taste for domination led him to play a leading role at international level in IUCN*'.[47] When he visited the United States in 1964 '*everyone was most impressed with his ability and brilliance*'.[48]

Biology and Human Welfare: the International Biological Programme

The International Geophysical Year of 1957–58 had been a great success, showing how a coordinated global research programme could yield new insights into how planetary systems worked. Now some members of the biological community wanted to do likewise.[49] The newly-elected President of the International Union of Biological Sciences, C H (Hal) Waddington, was cool about the notion when he first learned of it, but decided that if it was to proceed it must focus on '*something which was indubitably of major social and economic concern for mankind as a whole*'.[50] His choice was a coordinated, world-wide, study of '*the way in which man can modify the natural environment so that it produces with maximum efficiency on a long-term basis the kind of products he can use*'.[50] Today, we would call the concept 'the ecological basis for sustainable development'.

This was – or should have been – 'right up IUCN's street'. It should have allowed the Union, and especially the Commission on Ecology, to build the worldwide linkage between ecology and conservation of which Julian Huxley had dreamed. Waddington visited Morges in May 1962, at Jean Baer's invitation. Professor H Ellenberg of the Ecology Commission, Max Nicholson and Ed Graham were all there. The discussions were held, not surprisingly, in a rather 'conservation oriented' atmosphere.[50]

The Commission on Ecology had been developing their proposals since May 1961, when a committee on ecological research in the IBP under Professor Ellenberg's Chairmanship and with Ed Graham as a member had begun to digest the results of a symposium on ecological methods held in Zurich and to debate what ecological studies would be appropriate in the IBP.[51] They had worked out proposals for measuring productivity in woodlands[52] and Ellenberg, by June 1962, was suggesting three committees concerned respectively with the general survey of terrestrial biological communities (to be convened by himself), the metabolism of terrestrial biological communities (to be led by H Florkin of Belgium) and the conservation of terrestrial communities (to be convened by Max Nicholson).[53]

In the end, the subject of IBP was defined as '*The Biological Basis of Productivity and Human Welfare*',[54] and it was divided into seven sections concerned respectively with production processes, the fundamental biological machinery by which organisms fix and transfer energy (PP); productivity in terrestrial, freshwater and marine ecosystems (PT, PF and PM respectively); human adaptability (largely from a medical standpoint) (HA); the conservation of terrestrial ecosystems (CT); and the use and management of natural resources (UM). An early proposal for a section on education and training came to nothing.[55] Very late in the game, the Americans proposed two other sections – systematics and biogeography (SB) and comparative physiology (CP) – to meet with heated opposition in the Scientific Committee for the IBP (SCIBP), on the grounds that everything they wanted was already included in the CT and HA sections.[56] This hostile treatment – which made the leading American delegate, Roger Revelle, turn red and splutter with rage – probably put the final stop to any prospect of significant American finance for the IBP.[41,56]

The basic aim of the CT programme was to document the extent to which the national parks, nature reserves and other protected areas in the world included a scientifically adequate sample of all major ecosystems, both for the protection of species and communities and as a basis for research.[55,57] This clearly required some kind of global classification – which could be biogeographical (dividing the world into realms and regions based on the distinctiveness of their floras and faunas), phytosociological (based on the species composition of vegetation) or physiognomic (where the physical structure of the dominant vegetation provided the main units).

The CT section spent a long time agonizing over which of the available, imperfect, systems to use. In the end it chose a physiognomic system devised by a member, Raymond Fosberg. People around the world were asked to complete a check sheet for 'IBP areas' – which might be existing protected areas or places that deserved conservation. The sheets recorded climatic, geological and other physical characteristics, together with the composition and structure of the vegetation and what was known about the associated fauna.[58] Various field trials tested the system, and some 3000 check sheets were returned. The drawback was that the results *'told one very little of importance about the conservation value of the units in question, for this importance depended on other features, especially floristics'*.[59]

Max Nicholson expounded the CT programme during the Eighth General Assembly in Nairobi and it was agreed that IBP presented a great opportunity for ecologists and conservationists *'which it is essential not to miss'*.[60] By 1964 the Executive Board was ready to set up an IUCN IBP Committee drawn from all parts of the Union, and the Ecology Commission was proposing an 'ecological unit' in the Secretariat to coordinate action. Jean Baer was nominated as IUCN representative to the SCIBP, which was to hold its first General Meeting at UNESCO in July. His successor as President, François Bourlière, was worried that IBP might *'look a little too much like an IUCN offshoot'*.[61] *'Jean Baer has been appointed President of the SCIBP'*, he wrote to Hugh Elliott in July 1964, *'Barton Worthington becomes Scientific Director of the IBP, and of the five Convenors, Max Nicholson is in charge of Section CT (Conservation) and myself of Section PT (Biological Productivity)'*.[61]

But despite these overlaps in personnel, the institutional links between IUCN and IBP remained slender. Although IUCN was one of the two non-UN and non-ICSU international bodies represented on the SCIBP, there was no *ex officio* IUCN representative on any of the sectional committees – not even CT – and the Secretariat for the latter was provided in the UK, with a base at the Nature Conservancy's Monks Wood Experimental Station. Financial stringency within the Union blocked the creation of the unit at Morges. The result was that there was no focus in the Secretariat to tie the contributions of IUCN's leading individuals together and relate them to the Commissions and the membership.

The separation of CT from IUCN caused surprise and concern during 1965, not least over *'the apparent diminution of support for IUCN at a time when IBP Section CT is canvassing for support both financially and scientifically for work which it might appear could be done equally well by IUCN'*.[62] A statement defining the *'complementary and mutually supportive'* roles of the two bodies was prepared after a meeting on 25 September of Jean Baer, François Bourlière, Ed Graham, Hugh Elliott, Max Nicholson and Barton Worthington. It argued that IUCN's business was to promote or support *'the perpetuation of wild nature and nature reserves in as many parts of the world as possible not only for their intrinsic cultural or scientific values but also for the long-term economic and social welfare of mankind'*. The purpose of IBP/CT was *'the establishment of the necessary scientific basis for a comprehensive world programme of preservation and safeguarding of areas of biological and physiographic importance for future scientists'*.[63]

This ducked the issue, for the Commission on Ecology had, in its initial years, been closely concerned with the ecological basis for the protection of habitats, the management of national parks and nature reserves, and *'the creation of an international network of parks for the study of certain major ecological problems'*.[64,65] But the Commission did endeavour to tie things together. In 1969 it reported that a major aim of its Secretary in preparing the English text of the second edition of the UN List of National Parks and Equivalent Reserves had been *'to bring this into line with the IBP/CT survey of terrestrial habitats of scientific importance and, for this purpose, as much use as possible was made of all completed CT check-sheets for such reserved areas'*.[66] It was agreed that after IBP ended in 1972, the check-sheet survey would continue under an agreement between the British Nature Conservancy and IUCN, and the database would be transferred to IUCN as essential documentation of key sites for conservation and research.[67]

The Commission on Ecology did take responsibility for continuing the check-sheet survey,[68] and the check sheets are said to have been used in compiling the loose-leaf *World Data Book of National Parks and Protected Areas*.[69,70] But in the early 1970s, the Commission on Ecology was adviser to Secretariat projects (led by Ray Dasmann) on the development of both a 'Working System for the Classification of World Vegetation' and the elaboration of a series of Biotic Provinces of the World by Professor Miklos Udvardy of the California State University at Sacramento.[71] In the mid-1970s the National Parks Commission of IUCN adopted a biogeographical classification system based on Udvardy's work, and the emphasis switched to identifying gaps in coverage. These developments combined to make the check sheets of limited relevance,[59] and they went into limbo in the archive at the British Museum (Natural History).

As IBP proceeded, the IUCN Executive Board also became interested in working with IBP field conservation projects such as that in the Coto Donana in Spain (initially developed, and largely supported, by WWF). But for this to happen they had to secure resources for the 'ecology unit' that had been talked about for years, and in 1965 they urged Ed Graham, still Chairman of the Commission on Ecology, to get on with the necessary action.[72] For its part, IBP/CT provided some support for international stations such as that in the Galapagos, at Seronera in the Serengeti and planned for Azraq in Jordan (where a mission by Julian Huxley and Guy Mountfort led directly to the founding of the Jordanian Royal Society for the Conservation of Nature).[73]

With hindsight, it remains extraordinary that IUCN and the world conservation community got so little out of the conservation section of IBP. The stated objectives of CT fitted squarely within the sphere of interest of the Union and its Commissions on Ecology and National Parks. The First World Parks Conference had emphasized the enormous value of protected areas in safeguarding species and ecosystems and as a basis for public information and research. IBP could have been used as a means of developing and testing an agreed methodology for classifying protected areas, such as the biogeographical system later developed by Udvardy; for evaluating how a global protected area system could safeguard the full diversity of the planet's ecosystems; for developing a database on such areas, and as a means of identifying priorities and gaps. It could have advanced the work of the Commission by several years. As it was, it went down a blind alley.

The Biosphere Conference

The 1963 General Assembly in Nairobi discussed the idea of an international conference that would build on UNSCCUR and address cooperation for conservation.[3] In January 1965, Peter Scott wrote to the US Secretary of the Interior, Stewart Udall, and suggested holding such a meeting in the USA.[74] On 25 June Congressman Henry S Reuss presented a House Concurrent Resolution stating:

> '*that it is in the sense of the Congress that the United States shall promote the worldwide conservation of wildlife, particularly of species that are rare, and that the United States shall convene an International Conference on the Conservation of Wildlife under the sponsorship of the United Nations*'.

---

* Ed Graham died in 1966. Until his final illness he was strongly favoured to succeed François Boulière as President of IUCN.

On 11 August Phyllis Barclay-Smith of the International Council for Bird Preservation, acting also for IUCN, invited UNESCO, FAO, WWF and the US Government to a meeting held at the British Museum (Natural History) in London to prepare an agenda for such a conference (retitled Intergovernmental World Conference on the Conservation of Living Natural Resources) to be held in the United States in 1967 or early 1968, and designed to lead to a ten-year plan for world conservation.[72]

At the same time, UNESCO had been strengthening its programme. A new Division for Natural Resources had been established in 1961, with Michel Batisse in charge. By 1965 it had merged its former Arid Zone Committee and Humid Tropics Committee into a Natural Resources Research Committee which included such eminent scientists as Gilbert F White of the USA, Victor Kovda of Russia, Georges Aubert of France and David Wasawo of Kenya. In the same year it launched a major world programme on water – the International Hydrological Decade. Alain Gille was appointed to direct a new UNESCO Science Office for Africa in Nairobi. And in 1966 UNESCO and FAO were invited by ECOSOC to prepare a report on 'Conservation and Rational Use of the Environment'. Michel Batisse asked Gilbert White and Luna Leopold to suggest a consultant, and they proposed Raymond F Dasmann, then Director of International Programs at the Conservation Foundation in Washington DC, and later to be senior ecologist at IUCN. His report in which François Bourlière, Hal Coolidge, Jean-Paul Harroy, Lee Talbot and Barton Worthington were all involved, was adopted by ECOSOC in 1968.[75–77]

At its first session in September 1965, the UNESCO Committee suggested a world conference as a way of stimulating a '*larger undertaking of international scientific cooperation which could be launched...in close association with FAO and in collaboration with IUCN...*'[75,76] This became, in due course, the 'Intergovernmental Conference of Experts on the Scientific Basis for the Rational Use and Conservation of the Resources of the Biosphere' which, not surprisingly, was shortened to 'the Biosphere Conference'.[75] This, incidentally, led to a much increased use in world literature of the term 'biosphere', originally coined by V I Vernadsky but little used outside the USSR until championed in the debates of the UNESCO Committee by Victor Kovda.[76]

It must have been obvious that the world did not need two Conferences. On 17 May 1966 Michel Batisse lunched in Paris with Peter Scott, François Bourlière and Phyllis Barclay-Smith, and briefed them on the plans for the Biosphere Conference and on IUCN's possible role in it.[76] The proposals for the conference in the USA were soon dropped.[17] The result was to replace a conference that was to address world problems and define social policies with one that emphasized science as the foundation for action. IUCN was strongly represented at the Biosphere Conference, which was presided over by François Bourlière and attended by 14 members of the Commission on Ecology and its committees.[66]

The Biosphere Conference looked at the conclusions emerging from IBP (which, however, was to continue until 1974) and suggested '*that IBP might usefully be followed by*' a new programme, in which some governments (including the United States) saw a major role for IUCN on the conservation side.[17,78] This was the genesis of the UNESCO Man and Biosphere programme (MAB),[75] which was launched in 1970 and covered the whole spectrum of land, freshwater and coastal ecosystems from the polar to the tropical zones.[79,80] It was a much broader programme than IBP and dealt with all manner of human interactions with ecosystems, with worldwide processes and impacts like the effects of pollutants, biocides and engineering works and with the significance of attitudes to and perceptions of the environment. It was based on academic science but it was expected to generate practical applications.

Programme Eight of MAB was about ecosystems and the genetic resources they contained. It proposed the selection of samples of natural systems as 'controls', which could be used to monitor changes in adjacent areas. The result was one of the most important and durable products of MAB – the concept of biosphere reserves.[81] Such sites are zoned, with a strict core area managed for nature and used only for non-destructive research and monitoring, surrounding buffer zones which isolate the core from external influences and may be used for experimental research, and transition areas for regulated and sustainable human activities beyond that.[81,82] The concept was first developed in Paris at a meeting in 1971 held in association with the MAB International Coordinating Committee, and elaborated at a UNESCO/IUCN meeting in Morges in 1973.[76,83] MAB sought to establish a biosphere reserve in each of the world's main types of ecosystem.

The biosphere reserve concept was important in stressing the need to harmonize nature conservation with human interests.[81,84–86] But its adoption did not lead to an immediate surge in the designation of new protected areas. In some parts of the world (including Latin America and southern Africa) the approach of designating strongly protected core areas surrounded by buffer zones was already established. Biosphere reserves, as such, were favoured particularly in countries where little wild land remained (as in Mexico) or where protected areas were managed by bodies with a strong research flavour, as in the then USSR.[87] The value of the concept came through the changes it prompted in the management of protected areas, and this was progressively taken on board in IUCN, notably at the Third World Congress on National Parks at Bali in Indonesia in 1982 and in resolutions at successive General Assemblies.[86,87]

By taking the lead in MAB, UNESCO effectively grasped from both IUCN and the International Council of Scientific Unions (ICSU), lead responsibility for placing the academic approach of IBP in a socially relevant context. But IUCN Commission members played an active role.[66] François Bourlière was the first Chairman of the International Coordinating Committee, of which IUCN was a statutory member.[75] IUCN also contributed a critical analysis of the status of biosphere reserves around the world, and the trends in their establishment, for the first conference on biosphere reserves organized by UNESCO and UNEP, in partnership with IUCN and FAO, and held in Minsk (Belarus) in 1983.[76,87,88] That conference gave birth to a ten-year action plan which was endorsed by the IUCN Council in 1985. But IUCN's participation in the actual programme was less than had originally been expected,[75] perhaps because the Commission on National Parks preferred to do things its own way.

A Time of Transition

Looking back over 30 years, the period between 1960 and 1966 appears a time both of strengthening and incipient fragmentation in the international conservation movement. After 1961, IUCN and ICBP were no longer alone on the world's conservation stage, and as the WWF grew in strength so the power of its purse began to alter the work of IUCN – and to reinforce the efforts of a steadily widening circle of other groups including many IUCN members. Thirty-five years later, WWF had launched or implemented more than 11,000 projects in 149 countries,[19] and by 1988 it had injected over SFr43 million into IUCN core and programme activities.[42]

The expansion of project activities – partly supported by WWF, but also by the UN – also brought a transformation in IUCN's relationships. It helped demonstrate its relevance to its members, especially those struggling to cope with the massive problems on the ground in the developing world. But it undermined the old partnership with UNESCO and FAO. When the United Nations Special Fund for Development (later to become the UN Development Programme, UNDP) was established in 1959, with a mandate to finance pre-investment projects in developing countries, UNESCO and FAO were designated as 'executing agencies'. They were therefore able to strengthen their field activities. Both looked to IUCN as a professional adviser on conservation. But,

> *'with the progressive development of operational activities in IUCN, originally with WWF support and later with funding from the UN Environment Programme, UNEP, this complementarity was blurred and transformed radically its relationships with both FAO and UNESCO in the late 1970s'.*[75]

At the same time, IUCN lost some of its scientific standing. Whereas in 1956 the Commission on Ecology really was a main focus for ecologists concerned with the conservation of nature and natural resources and the management of species and ecosystems, by 1970 the Union's position was severely eroded. In 1969, partly so as to establish its status as a major scientific partner in the preparations for the forthcoming Stockholm Conference,[75] ICSU established a Scientific Committee on Problems of the Environment (SCOPE), '*to report on global trends in the biosphere and environmental issues most urgently requiring international and interdisciplinary scientific effort*'. A little later it set up INTECOL, the International Association of Ecology, partly because of '*a feeling that no one was speaking for the ecological community*' (which implies that a significant part of that community did not feel that either UNESCO or IUCN was their natural home).[89] INTECOL was designed to bring together the world's ecologists and address a number of practical issues, especially the working of tropical and agricultural systems.[89,90] With IBP and MAB, it undoubtedly provided a stimulus to the evolution of environmental science and ecological research in the developing world.

These changes had an impact on IUCN. The Commission on Ecology, led in succession by François Bourlière, Jim Cragg and Donald Kuenen, retained a broad programme which, between 1966 and 1973, encompassed ecological aspects of soil and water conservation, the ecological effects of pesticides, ecosystems of international importance (especially wetlands), aspects of marine, coastal and island conservation, the conservation of fragile ecosystems, the ecological effects of environmental disturbance and the effects of introductions of flora and fauna. But it did not succeed in pulling the world's top ecologists together to provide intellectual or practical products that the member organizations needed and could use. As both ICSU and UNESCO developed new activities which attracted many ecologists, the Commission on Ecology withered, while the Species Survival Commission, the National Parks Commission and the Commission on Environmental Policy, Law and Administration gained strength.

This period thus saw the beginning of the separation of the conservation movement from scientific ecology – a separation which weakened conservation until the mid-1980s, when the Society for Conservation Biology began in the United States and the concepts both of sustainable development and of biodiversity began to bring the two together again, and to draw in economists, social scientists and political figures as well.

6 The Environmental Explosion

The New Environmentalism

The period between 1966 and 1975 was a time of immense change on the world environmental scene. New, energetic, bodies began campaigning for action. Governments began to establish departments of environment. There was a flurry of environmental law-making. The first intergovernmental 'summit' on global environmental policy – the Stockholm Conference – was followed by the creation of UNEP, the UN Environment Programme. IUCN, ICBP and WWF, with UNESCO and FAO, no longer had the global environmental scene to themselves.

The 'new environmentalism' had several roots:

> '*First, as affluent nations grew more affluent, interest in a cleaner environment rose... Secondly, there were sharp reminders – the 1952 smog in London, the mercury poisoning from fish in Japan – that pollution can kill. Thirdly there was the evidence that DDT doesn't just vanish when sprayed on the crops: it accumulates in alarmingly unexpected places. And fourthly there was the shock wave from the Middle East when OPEC reminded the industrial nations that they were parasitic upon the Moslem world for the bulk of their oil supplies.*'[1]

And fifthly (or some would say, first of all), there was public alarm over the environmental impact of nuclear weapons testing in the atmosphere, especially in the Pacific.[2]

The popular environmental movement was influenced by, and to a degree grew out of, the peace movement. People switched from '*Ban the Bomb*' to '*Save the Planet*'. '*As the Campaign for Nuclear Disarmament went down in the 1960s, the environmental movement came up*'.[3] The first Greenpeace campaigns, for example, were against nuclear testing (in 1971–73) and it was not until 1974 that they turned their attention to the plight of whales.[4]

Three books had a particular influence on the new movement. The first – and perhaps the most influential – was Rachel Carson's *Silent Spring*, published in 1962, which portrayed the insidious side-effects of the new pesticides, until then uncritically hailed as 'wonder chemicals' because of their contribution to the control of malaria and the safeguarding of crops from insect pests.[5,6] In 1968, Paul Ehrlich published *The Population Bomb*, which argued that burgeoning human numbers were on a course of catastrophic collision with the planetary life-support system.[7] In 1971

Barry Commoner's *The Closing Circle* argued that industrial society had broken out of the 'circle of life' – the natural cycles of the biosphere – and must find a way to close that circle if catastrophe was to be averted.[8]

Widely-publicized disasters came thick and fast. In 1967 the *Torrey Canyon* ran on to the Seven Stones reef east of the Isles of Scilly (UK) and gave the world its first supertanker disaster. Two years later there was an oil and gas blowout in the Santa Barbara Channel in California. Mercury poisoning – caused by a quite unexpected bacterial transformation of metallic mercury to the highly toxic methyl form – crippled hundreds of fish-eating people at Minamata Bay in Japan. Air pollution, oil pollution, acid rain, cadmium and zinc pollution, and the ever-present nuclear contamination of the biosphere all hit the headlines and made people demand action.[2,9]

The concerns went deeper than that. They amounted to a challenge to fundamental social assumptions. Since the end of the Second World War, new towns and cities, new factories, new farming methods, new gadgets and chemicals and new approaches to education and health care had all been welcomed as the benefits of a science-based new world. Now the environmentalists were arguing that the other side of the gleaming coin of post-war reconstruction was the destruction of the world of nature, on which humanity ultimately depended. By the mid-1970s, professional ecologists were proclaiming ever more loudly that '*Man continues to simplify the natural environment drastically and at an ever increasing rate*', that '*at the present rate of destruction the tropical rain forests of the world would disappear in 85 years*' while '*of the 891 threatened species or sub-species of vertebrate animals, all are endangered by habitat destruction and/or overconsumption*' and '*a large proportion of the world's genetic diversity has already been lost*'.[10] Despite the efforts of IUCN and its member organizations, the world was losing ground. The debate was '*no longer about the future of affluence and abundance…it is now about the future of scarcity*'.[1] Garret Hardin's influential essay on 'the tragedy of the commons' opened up new debate on how to manage and control humanity's destructive impacts. And criticisms of the much-vaunted development process led by the World Bank, UNDP, FAO and national development aid organizations were becoming more strident – such bodies, it was said '*designed most of their projects in an ecologically unwise way*' making such ill-judged development '*one of the currently most important global conservation problems*'.[10]

Concern provoked action, and organizations mushroomed in response. Nuclear contamination not only spawned the Ban the Bomb movement, but was one of the major concerns that led a group of students at the University of British Columbia to found Greenpeace – a body dedicated to the promotion of action for peace, nuclear disarmament and the protection of the world environment from pollution and misuse.[11] Some established conservation bodies tried to redevelop themselves, adding programmes on the fashionable new issues like population, resources, pollution and energy.[12] The Sierra Club in the United States – long regarded as an archetypal and rather conservative body – was taken over by a group of 'young Turks' led by the photographer, Ansel Adams and by David Brower, and became a powerful lobbyist for wilderness and for national parks. In 1969 – after internal wrangling – Brower left to found an even more militant group, Friends of the Earth.[13] It grew rapidly, on several continents, with action against pollution and the wasteful over-consumption of natural resources at the top of its agenda, recruited some highly articulate and committed publicists, and built close links with the Press.[14]

New environmentalism burgeoned in the USA, with the largest environmental demonstration in history on 'Earth Day' in 1970.[2,13] It was a diffuse, diverse, mass of demonstrations and events, all sparked by concern over environmental degradation.[13] Although Earth Day was largely a North American phenomenon, it was the crest of a world-wide wave. In Britain, Edward Goldsmith started *The Ecologist* in 1970, and in 1972 he and others (including Robert Prescott-Allen, soon to work in IUCN)* produced the *Blueprint for Survival* which diagnosed that '*the principal defect of the industrial way of life with its ethos of expansion is that it is not sustainable*'.[15] Barbara Ward's concept of 'spaceship earth' was taken up by Adlai Stevenson in an address to the UN Economic and Social Council in Geneva. An apparently irrefutable mathematical link between exploding human populations, all-pervasive pollution, escalating resource depletion and a collapsing environment was published by the Club of Rome.[16]

The surge of spontaneity that marked Earth Day bypassed (and rather surprised) many established environmental bodies.[13] But these bodies – and nature conservation – did not lose their appeal. Indeed they increased in number and scope.[10] New international organizations like the Foundation for Environmental Conservation appeared, while national bodies like the New York Zoological Society, the National Audubon Society (New York), the National Wildlife Federation (Washington DC), the Sierra Club (San Francisco), the Fauna Preservation Society (London) and the Zoologische Gesellschaft (Frankfurt) took on a widening international role. In the United States, Hal Coolidge's old American Committee for International Wildlife Protection (by now under Lee Talbot's Chairmanship) transformed itself into ACIC, the American Committee for International Conservation, as a forum for the coordination of the new international interests which so many national conservation organizations were developing.[6] Nor were such bodies confined to the developed North: the East African Wildlife Society, based in Nairobi, grew in strength and activity alongside the African Wildlife Leadership Foundation, the American body set up by Hal Coolidge and Russell Train which later became the African Wildlife Foundation. IUCN was a natural forum for '*moderate left-of-centre bodies like the Sierra Club or the Australian Wilderness Society that sought international links*'.[12] IUCN membership grew steadily, passing 200 in 1961 and surging to 300 in 1973 and 400 in 1975 – doubtless as a reflection of widening worldwide activity.[17] WWF's income also grew dramatically and its support for IUCN leaped from SFr519,000 in 1970 to over SFr2 million in 1974.[18]

There was a major change in style. The older voluntary organizations concerned with nature had worked largely within the established political system – and had been frustrated by its frequent hostility.[19] IUCN inevitably followed this route because of its State and government agency members – and because national parks, fish, wildlife and 'game management' departments were the oldest (and in some countries the only) official environmental bodies. The founders of the new organizations saw IUCN as impossibly 'establishment' and largely irrelevant to their concerns.

> '*We thought it was marginal, out-of-date, not concerned with natural resource issues, and had got the population issue quite wrong. It evaded issues like Ehrlich's Population Bomb. IUCN didn't appeal to 1960s kids dealing with what they saw as the real world. We were quite willing to use the Red Data Books and other useful products but we didn't want to know about the organization...*'[20]

---

* Robert Allen became Robert Prescott-Allen following his marriage to Christine Prescott in 1980, and after he had left IUCN. For clarity, at his request, his later name is used throughout this book.

Public interest was reflected in the great and growing market for 'glossy' 'coffee table' books, which deployed masterly new skills in colour printing. The National Geographic 'special productions' and many others brought the beauties of nature – and the threats to it – to lie in the living rooms of millions. Many such books were launched in parallel with wonderful television series, where the pioneers like Scott, Buxton and Cousteau were joined by such presenters as David Attenborough, David Suzuki and David Bellamy. But the surge of social concern about the impact of the industrial society on the biosphere did push nature conservation somewhat aside in the Northern, developed world. The sense of urgency also tended to sweep the careful scientific analysis IUCN stood for aside – and any supposed conservationist who argued that the scientific evidence was insufficient to justify a loudly-trumpeted call for action was liable to attack as a traitor to the cause. At the same time there were symptoms of a new militancy and strength among animal welfare groups, partly linked to revulsion against the perceived cruelty of 'factory farming', hunting and scientific experimentation on animals, and evolving into increasingly confrontational hunt – and laboratory – saboteur movements.

Reconstruction in IUCN

IUCN did not change its fundamental style in response to the 'new environmentalism'. It stood by its commitment to science-based conservation, advanced by providing governments and other users with the best analysis of the problems and the best available means for response.[12] But it was clear – at least to Hal Coolidge when he assumed the Presidency in 1966 – that unless the Union could secure new resources and employ a professional Secretariat that would give the members the support they needed, the tide of events would sweep past it (as they had largely done in IBP and threatened to do in MAB).

The need to strengthen the Secretariat had become increasingly evident. Although Hugh Elliott had shrugged off the problems of location in Morges in his reporting to the Nairobi General Assembly in 1963,[21] limitations were evident. In 1966, the President and Executive Board worried about the lack of 'critical mass', and the isolation from other scientific units. The professional staff were largely Anglophone and did not forge links with local universities or research teams.[22] The University of Geneva might not have existed so far as IUCN was concerned. Although Elliott consulted Eleen Thierry-Mieg of UNESCO about a new formula for dues which might bring in more income,[23] it was clear that the members would never pay enough to fund the services they wanted. An approach to secure US state membership had failed.[24] Despite the success of the Africa Special Project (ASP) and its follow-up in Asia, IUCN simply lacked the resources to keep the momentum going. Despite IUCN's deep involvement in the genesis of the IBP, its operational participation as an organization had been slight and IUCN members had got little out of it. Despite WWF finances, the organization remained weak.

A telling insight into the situation is provided by a forthright memorandum to Hugh Elliott written in July 1965 by Max Newman, who was leaving following a spell of attachment to the Secretariat. He criticized two key leaders of IUCN, Hal Coolidge and Peter Scott, for fund raising '*primarily for the greater glory of the NPC (National Parks Commission) or the SSC (Species Survival Commission)*' rather than '*greasing the hub of IUCN*'.[25] He may have missed the point that Coolidge and Scott were trying to build IUCN up via the Commissions as the cheapest way of getting things done.[6] But he was clear that:

> '*the root of the rot, which will inevitably and rapidly reduce IUCN to the state of impotency under which it suffered before moving to Switzerland, is that the Executive Board cannot or will not face up to what must be its immediate and main purpose, which is to provide the Union with an adequate, competent and contented Secretariat, proud and eager to work for an organization which, potentially, can do in its small way as much for humanity as any international organization in existence*'.[25]

Outside observers might have thought the answer simple – wasn't that why WWF had been established? Newman wrote rudely of the latter, suggesting that a chronic disease that infected IUCN–WWF relationships almost from the start had already erupted. It may have arisen partly from the fundamental differences between the organizations. Prince Philip noted this from the instant he became involved.

> '*What struck me from the beginning was how different the cultures were. People in IUCN were academics, or from technical research laboratories. The people in WWF were from a business culture: the Trustees were business and finance-oriented. This became more and more evident as the WWF evolved and perhaps most obvious in the 1980s when we did merge accounting, information and administration for a while*'[26](see Chapters 7–9).

The difference was deliberate. WWF was purposely designed to bring in business leadership as a complement to the academics in IUCN.[19] But this fuelled jealousy. IUCN saw itself as the world's expert conservation body, was dismissive of WWF's technical understanding, and resented the Union's financial dependence on the Fund. There was also suspicion about first Fritz Vollmar, and then his co-Director-General and eventual successor (Charles de Haes wanted to make WWF not only a separate power but the dominant one).[27] On WWF's side there was respect for IUCN's scientific expertise, acceptance of its leadership with governments and international organizations, but irritation over the slowness with which it dealt with issues and a feeling that its management was unbusinesslike For its part, the Fund was determined to maintain its leadership in the public eye, because this was essential for successful fund-raising.[28] The differences rarely erupted into open dispute – indeed the records of Board and Council meetings are full of warm statements about the closeness of the relationship. But personal comments, especially from IUCN staff in the period, tell another story.

Relations cannot have been helped by a reduction in WWF support for the Union, from a peak of SFr205,000 in 1963 to only SFr70,000 in 1965. Fortunately some reserves had been built up, but the casualties of retrenchment were serious.[29] It proved impossible to build up the intelligence centre as an operations room rather than an archive. The follow-up to the ASP was hampered, and several technical units needed to support the Commissions fell victim.[29] The only Commission to be backed by a fully established unit at Morges in 1965 was the SSC, where Noel Simon was already at work on the Red Data Books.[29,30] Although 20 publications appeared in the 1963–66 triennium and the Union had participated in 37 international conferences and meetings, this lack of support was a disaster.

Why did WWF cut back on its funding? One reason was simple: money had not been coming in at the expected rate and the Fund itself was struggling. In July 1965 '*it was common knowledge in Morges that IUCN and the WWF were in financial difficulties*'.[25] Fritz Vollmar wrote frankly about the problems to Hugh Elliott admitting that '*due to a considerable shortage of funds the World Wildlife Fund has not come up to the expectation of the various applicants for annual grant for 1965*'.[31] Elliott had obviously written sharply to Peter Scott who found his comments provocative and said:

> '*I am not sure that I will allow that WWF has "forgotten about the good and specific purpose for which it was created"...But of course it has failed to provide the massive financial support which we all hoped it would. I still believe it can be got, but it is going to be increasingly difficult in the current world economic situation...*'[32]

Another problem that may well have confronted the Trustees of WWF even at this early stage was the difficulty of persuading donors to give money to a fund that did not itself use it directly on the 'good causes' it appealed for. '*It wasn't a criticism of IUCN – it was just hard to say to people "give us the money and IUCN will spend it"* '.[26] WWF had to be seen to be responding to the wishes of its supporters.

The result was that when, at the Lucerne General Assembly, Sir Hugh Elliott stepped down as Secretary-General to be succeeded by another Briton, E J H ('Joe') Berwick, formerly a '*British Civil Servant with many years service as an agronomist in South-East Asia*',[30,33] IUCN could fairly have been said to have missed several important opportunities for want of money. From the moment of his election as President in 1966, in succession to François Bourlière, Hal Coolidge grappled with the widening gap between the growing global need for conservation and the limited capacity of the Union to respond.

The Coolidge Solution

Whether or not Coolidge ever saw Max Newman's blunt message, he responded to its essence. In a lengthy harangue to the Board which amounted to a personal manifesto, he noted the small number of dedicated staff on whom so much depended.[34] To complete even the modest agreed programme for 1967–69, a total of SFr1,518,000 would be needed – and only SFr387,000 was currently available. Russell Train, a new member of the Board, urged the need for each Commission to maintain a Secretary at Morges. There was also a clear need to address even bigger issues. The Board wanted to launch a new plan for world conservation, and an international conservation Quinquennium from 1967 to 1972, perhaps as an initiative that could be related to the UNESCO Biosphere Conference, and certainly to be seen as a joint effort with WWF and ICBP.[35]

Another proposal (of which Russell Train was principal architect)[36] was for a Trust for the World Heritage which might safeguard sites in developing countries such as Angkor Wat in Cambodia and the Congolese (=Zairois) national parks. The idea emerged from a White House Conference on International Cooperation, launched by President Lyndon Johnson and chaired by Professor Joe Fisher. Fisher and Train thought it would be a good topic for 1972, the centenary year of

Yellowstone and the year of the Second World Conference on National Parks, because it would seek to establish the 'Yellowstone values' worldwide. (The proposers, both Americans, were clearly unaware that the Yellowstone values were coming under sharp attack, for example in Africa.)[37] Lyndon Johnson was encouraging, and in the Northern autumn of 1965 Train addressed a WWF meeting in Amsterdam, chaired by Prince Bernhard, suggesting that the scheme be expanded to take in historic monuments.[36] Joe Fisher gave the keynote address to the IUCN General Assembly in 1966, in which he floated another idea – the compilation of a world audit of environmental damage. This would be a kind of Black Book containing examples of the worst kind of environmental destruction. The Commission on Ecology suggested that a White Book of good practice would have greater value.

These ideas were debated and questioned. UNESCO (speaking through its representative, Sven Evteev, the Russian ex-Antarcticist who was later to be Assistant Executive Director of the United Nations Environment Programme) asked whether the Quinquennium was to be '*propaganda, as the Council of Europe's Conservation Year, or...a coordinated programme such as those of the IBP...?*'.[35] Fritz Vollmar, Secretary-General of WWF, agreed with the idea of the Quinquennium but had reservations about the finances. Peter Scott wanted a five-year propaganda Quinquennium followed by a ten-year conservation programme in the field. Luc Hoffmann thought the first five years should include planning as well as propaganda, and Russell Train wanted the first phase to include recommendations for international and national action, with priorities and goals. Similarly the notion of a Black Book was challenged by Wolfgang Burhenne, who thought environmental damage covered so vast a range that it was too big a subject for IUCN, while Donald Kuenen asked sharply '*if there was any point in discussing it if we could not raise funds for the fundamental functioning of IUCN?*'

This, of course, was the key point. Ideas are easy, but there had to be realism. It was obvious that without a quantum leap in resources none of these notions would get very far.[38] Hal Coolidge took up the challenge, probably recognizing that make-or-break time was near. He arranged to work full-time in Europe for two months in 1967.[34] Russell Train helped to raise funds for his Presidency, securing US$20,000 to cover the costs of the visits to Morges.36 While there, he was very much in command, taking over the Secretary-General's office and relegating Joe Berwick to a small room in the basement.[39]

Such an approach reflected his personality. Coolidge was a man of immense commitment and energy, and the record shows that without him IUCN might well have gone under several times. Even when he did not hold formal office '*he was a kind of President in Exile, organizing things while the Board and Secretariat fiddled. He travelled widely and kept popping up in places where he'd started projects.*'[6] He had immense dedication and a strong tradition of public service (as befitted a kinsman and namesake of two American Presidents). He was unquestionably one of the great men of world conservation.

But this did not mean that he was easy to work with. He had a manner that some found difficult. A short, deep-chested man with a loud, gravelly voice, he had that assertive and at times effusive American style that makes some Europeans curl up. He was dedicated and energetic, but he was not a good listener.[40] He was also a demanding taskmaster: writing in January 1966 to Noel Simon, Coolidge's assistant Lenore Smith commented tellingly '*there either aren't enough hours, or we don't put our hours to best use, to do all that HJC promises people he will do*'.[41]

Finance, and the role of the organization in a time of great change, were no doubt uppermost in Hal Coolidge's mind. Many opportunities were being missed, and it was clear by now that WWF was not going to be the financial gravy-train that some had naively expected. But suddenly, it all came right. He negotiated a major financial package with the Ford Foundation. After some probing questions, dealt with at a special meeting of the Executive Board at UNESCO in Paris,[42] Ford agreed a grant of US$650,000 for the almost three-year period from 1 April 1970 to 31 December 1972.[43]

A New Mandate, and a Director-General

The Tenth General Assembly in New Delhi in November 1969 was a turning point for IUCN. It adopted a paper drafted by the Chair of the Programme and Budget Committee, Lee Talbot, together with Duncan Poore and Kai Curry-Lindahl, which argued that:

> '*the time had come for a new strategic approach; one emphasizing attack on basic causes, toward prevention in addition to cure, toward providing a world-wide overview of conservation and towards focusing available resources within and without the Union on major environmental problems*'.[6,44,45]

The General Assembly affirmed that IUCN was

> '*concerned with the quality of life, with the physical, educational, social and aesthetic values which add richness, meaning and satisfaction to human experience. To this end, IUCN initiates and promotes scientifically-based action that will ensure perpetuation and enhancement of the living world – man's natural environment – and the natural resources on which all living things depend. Conservation was defined as management (which term includes survey, research, administration, preservation, utilization, and implies education and training) of air, water, soil, minerals and living species including man, so as to achieve the highest sustainable quality of life.*'[44]

New Delhi adopted five revised formal objectives for the Union:[44]

1   To provide a continuing review and assessment of world environmental problems.
2   To formulate and promulgate statements of policy on topics of importance for the conservation of natural resources based on the best scientific evidence.
3   To promote research and new techniques relating to the conservation of nature and natural resources.
4   To provide advice to governments and organizations concerning the conservation of nature and natural resources.
5   To assist governments, on request, in developing national policies of conservation and to assist in their execution by providing advice and establishing cooperative programmes with other international agencies.

This was immensely significant. IUCN was setting out its stall as a world body, contributing to the solution of world environmental problems and applying the best available science to the conservation of nature and natural resources for human welfare. It adopted 'sustainable quality of life' as a goal 11 years ahead of the elaboration of 'sustainable development' in the World Conservation Strategy and its later popularization by the World Commission on Environment and Development (the Brundtland Commission).[46] The Union was clearly seeking to move with the rising tide of popular environmental concern – but in a way that would carry support in the developing countries. While it was clearly not seeking to become the forum for the whole expanding environment movement of the 1960s, it did present itself as a bridge between governmental and non-governmental sectors, and a link between national bodies and international agencies concerned with the conservation and sustainable use of nature and natural resources.

IUCN's ambitious new approach would have been laughable had not the Ford Foundation money allowed the Secretariat to be strengthened. One condition of the grant was that IUCN should appoint a professional scientist as head of its strengthened Secretariat. Joe Berwick did not qualify, and agreed to leave at the end of March 1970. François Bourlière and Jean Baer, no doubt with Hal Coolidge's encouragement, approached a young agronomist and tropical forester, Dr Gerardo Budowski, who was a member of the IBP CT Sectional Committee and had been working at UNESCO as a member of Michel Batisse's scientific team preparing the Biosphere Conference. He knew IUCN well, having represented UNESCO at meetings of the Board.

Budowski's qualifications were excellent. A dedicated scientist, who had found the administrative and political preoccupations of UNESCO increasingly confining, he saw in IUCN the chance to place '*science in the service of future generations*'.[39] His own background qualified him to build bridges between 'Northern' and 'Southern' regions. Born in Berlin in 1925 to a father who was a distinguished Russian chemist of Jewish extraction and a German mother, he had become a French citizen in 1938, moved to Venezuela following the German occupation of France, completed his scientific studies there, married a Panamanian teacher and won appointment to a senior scientific post.[39,47] He had led the forestry programme of the Tropical Research and Training Centre of the Inter-American Institute for Agricultural Sciences in Turrialba, Costa Rica – and his graduate students spread from there to key posts throughout Latin America.[48] His command of Spanish, English, French and German, his wide network of scientific contacts, and his own high professional standing were great assets to IUCN. So, maybe, was the fact that he had been for several years the chess champion of Venezuela.

The Ford Foundation had also demanded the appointment of a seasoned administrator, and Hal Coolidge offered the post to Frank Nicholls, then in Thailand on a UNDP assignment to establish a new institute applying science to development. Nicholls was an all-rounder: a physical scientist with an early career in atmospheric science who had moved into administration as a Research Secretary of the Australian Commonwealth Scientific and Industrial Research Organization (CSIRO). He had been trained in legal drafting and was also interested in entomology and a keen aqualung diver. While in Thailand he had participated in surveys of ecological resources and had studied coral reefs.[49] Hal Coolidge originally proposed that he come to IUCN as Secretary-General, while Gerardo Budowski was styled Director-General, but Nicholls felt that a division of responsibilities like that would not work and preferred to come as Deputy DG.[49] He proved a tough, organized manager, well able to keep tabs on the programme.[50]

Gerardo Budowski was elected IUCN's first Director-General at the General Assembly in New Delhi, took up his post on 1 April 1970, and was re-elected in

Banff in September 1972. He and Frank Nicholls shared the goal of establishing IUCN '*as the international body providing the scientific basis for conservation, and with conservation for development (management of renewable resources) as a major goal*'.[49] Their efforts were greatly strengthened by the arrival in 1970 of Dr Raymond F Dasmann as Senior Ecologist and head of the research and planning group, to form a managing 'troika' with Budowski and Nicholls.[50] Dasmann was a great 'catch' for IUCN – a ranking American ecologist with important books to his name, including a classic tome on *Environmental Conservation* published in 1959.[51] He had been the main author of the 1968 UNESCO/FAO report to ECOSOC on 'Conservation and Rational Use of the Environment', and he was very much a link between the 'new environmentalism' and conservation, believing strongly that the latter existed to serve humanity as well as safeguard nature. Not long afterwards he was joined by another distinguished ecologist, Dr Duncan Poore, former Director of the UK Nature Conservancy (and former IUCN Executive Board member).

The new IUCN Secretariat was a far cry from the old-style, informal, 'family' concern. From the beginning, there was a change of procedure of some symbolic importance: when Hal Coolidge came to Morges he did not take over the Director-General's office, but had a smaller one in the basement assigned for his use![36,39] Ford had insisted that competitive salaries should be paid, and Frank Nicholls adapted the UN system, using the same terms of employment but with the posts graded below comparable UN ones and salaries around 75 per cent of those received by comparable UN officers.[49,52] Even so, this linkage was a cause of some jealousy and suspicion among non-governmental IUCN member organizations. An attempt was also made to maintain 'equitable geographical distribution' in appointments. Frank Nicholls introduced a new, formal, procedure for project design and approval.[44] The growth in staff caused pressure on space, eased when the WWF Secretariat moved in April to a second building in Morges, named 'La Gracieuse'.[53]

The Stockholm Conference

As these changes were rolling forward, the governmental world was bursting with environmental activity. All round the world, environment departments, environmental laws and national State of the Environment Reports sprang up like seedlings after rain. Whereas only four major environmental laws were passed by OECD countries in the five years between 1956 and 1960, ten followed in the next five years, 18 in 1966–70, and 31 between 1971 and 1975.[9] Government Departments of the Environment proliferated. The United States set up the President's Council on Environmental Quality in 1970 (the Environment Protection Agency dates from the same year), and this allowed its first Chairman, Russell Train, to put the idea of action to safeguard the world heritage into President Nixon's Message to Congress.[36] At intergovernmental level, many UN agencies added environmental elements to their programmes. ECE, the UN Economic Commission for Europe (which was important in bringing 'East' and 'West' together), established a Committee of Senior Advisers on Environmental Problems. OECD created an Environment Committee in 1970, which was also designated European Conservation Year. The global scene, however, was dominated by preparations for the United Nations Conference on the Human Environment, held in Stockholm in 1972.

The Stockholm Conference was the direct consequence of a proposal put forward at ECOSOC in July 1968 by the Swedish Ambassador to the UN, Sverker Astrom, and endorsed at the end of that year by the UN General Assembly. It was prompted by growing concern in the Nordic countries over environmental degradation. The Biosphere Conference, which took place between the ECOSOC and General Assembly meetings, reinforced by the rising tide of active environmentalism, no doubt made the Assembly more favourable towards the Swedish proposal. The Conference was to '*provide a framework within which the UN could comprehensively assess the problems of the human environment and focus the attention of governments and public opinion*'.[2]

The process moved slowly until early 1970, when a dynamic 41-year-old Canadian, Maurice Strong, then serving as Deputy Minister and first head of his country's International Development Agency, was appointed Secretary-General of the Conference. He was not in any sense a scientist – indeed his formal education had been limited: he had left school at 14, had never attended university, and after various jobs at sea and in the Canadian Arctic had joined the United Nations ancillary staff at the age of 18. But he was an entrepreneur, a self-made millionaire in the energy sector, a committed environmentalist, a superb stimulator of groups and people – and he understood the UN system.[54,55] The Preparatory Committee began to hum, and the Conference roared down the runway to take-off. Strong began to pay visits to governments around the world, and his enthusiasm and commitment became infectious. He proposed that all countries should prepare national reports to Stockholm detailing what they were doing about their environment, and this was one of the prompts to a clamour of national activity.[9] And as a way of reaching the thoughtful public, he commissioned a 'background book' from the American microbiologist, René Dubos, and the British writer and economist, Barbara Ward. *Only One Earth: the Care and Maintenance of a Small Planet* was an outstanding survey of the world's problems and their solutions, and became a best-seller.[56]

The Stockholm Conference did not win a universal welcome. Although Maurice Strong himself was clear that it should *not* be dominated by pollution abatement and other 'Northern' problems, it took some time to convince the developing countries that there was something important in it for them. For they were unmoved by all the breast-beating and green hysteria in the North. They did not want the UN discussions diverted from the pressing problems posed by 'the pollution of poverty' (a concept developed to telling effect by Indira Gandhi in the most memorable of the speeches at the Conference itself). While they saw lessons to be learned from the mistakes in the rich countries, their imperative was for development and economic growth. They were particularly hostile to the rather extreme proposition in *The Limits to Growth* that economic development might have to be halted because of the threats of environmental dislocation and resource depletion. In 1971 several developing countries, led by Brazil, promoted a UN General Assembly resolution that said (among other things) that '*no environmental policy should adversely affect the present or future development possibilities of developing countries...*'.[57] What Maurice Strong had to do was convince them that their natural environmental resources were the essential assets on which economic growth would be based – and hence that conservation and development were inseparable. His experience as head of the international aid agency of a country untainted by a colonial past, coupled with his evident personal sincerity, helped him to convert the doubters.

As a bridge-building exercise, Strong convened a pre-Conference conference at Founex near Geneva in 1971. That meeting had enduring impact. It:

*'began to clarify the links between environment and development,
destroyed the false idea that they were necessarily incompatible, and
began to convince the representatives of the developing countries that
environmental concerns were both more widespread and more relevant
to their situation than they had appreciated.'*[9]

Partly as a result, the Conference agenda was broadened to take in topics such as
human settlements, desertification, agriculture and forestry, water supply and tropical
ecosystem management.[2] After Stockholm, the thinking was further developed at a
meeting in Cocoyoc in Mexico, where Maurice Strong introduced the term 'ecodevelopment' – a forerunner of 'sustainable development'.[51,58]

The Stockholm Conference, despite Maurice Strong's efforts at Founex, still
spent a lot of time on pollution issues and 'Northern' interests. The Eastern European
bloc of socialist countries (except Romania) did not attend because they resented the
exclusion of what was then the German Democratic Republic. The developing
country participation was limited and often challenging: Brazil and China were
outspoken critics of many statements. Some commentators argued that the
Conference generated very few new ideas, and that for the most part it elaborated the
themes of the UNESCO Biosphere Conference of 1968.[2] But *'while Paris addressed
the scientific aspects of environmental problems, Stockholm looked at the wider political, social and economic questions'*. That, in turn, made for easier press publicity
and for a more energetic involvement of the 'activist' non-governmental organizations which held a parallel 'Environment Forum' alongside the intergovernmental
debates. Moreover, Stockholm did stimulate a review of the role and effectiveness of
the various official and governmental bodies dealing with environment – and found
many wanting.[10] The Conference led directly to the creation of UNEP, the United
Nations Environment Programme. This was *'conceived of as drawing together and
giving added strength to the environmental activities of the whole United Nations
system'*, with a small Secretariat, a 58-nation Governing Council, a voluntary fund
(with a target of US$100 million over the first five years) and an Environment
Coordination Board to bring the UN agencies together.[9]

Thanks to Hal Coolidge, Ford, and the revitalization of the Secretariat, IUCN
was far better placed to contribute to the Stockholm process than it had been for IBP
or MAB. And it responded. Maurice Strong visited Morges in September 1971, and
close links were built with his Secretariat. IUCN staff contributed to papers and acted
as consultants. Gerardo Budowski was asked to chair a three-day conference in
Geneva in February 1972 designed to *'provide an opportunity for non-governmental
organizations to air their expectations and hopes towards the forthcoming Stockholm
Conference'*.[59] Over 100 NGOs attended.[52] Around the world, people who had been
involved in IUCN meetings and activities found themselves contributing to national
reports and policy analyses: they were the backbone of the environmental capacity of
many developing countries. The worldwide network of 'IUCN people' was drawn to
Stockholm in many national delegations, making liaison and negotiation easier.[6]

Maurice Strong wrote subsequently of IUCN's valuable contribution to the
preparatory process and to the Stockholm Conference itself.[60] But the records suggest
a considerable streak of scepticism. The 1971 Annual Report stated that *'few who
had worked closely with the Preparatory Committee held out hope that Stockholm
would produce any basically new approach to the problems of the environment'*.[53]
The 1972 Annual Report placed more emphasis on the Second World Conference on
National Parks and the World Heritage Convention than on the outcome of

Stockholm.[61] Gerardo Budowski, speaking to the Conference itself, conceded only that '*the time and place were favourable*'[62] although the 1972 Annual Report states that '*his remarks on the subject of conservation and development were received with enthusiasm*'.[61] Part of the problem may have been that Stockholm was a conference centred upon human uses of the environment, while many IUCN members still gave high priority to nature protection. Some scientists were also suspicious of the inter-governmental political process, and resented the idea that governments were taking over.[63]

IUCN's position at Stockholm, repeated 20 years later at the UN Conference on Environment and Development at Rio, was markedly different from that of most non-governmental environmental organizations. In both instances, it participated in the preparatory process, and worked with the Secretariat to prepare documents. In both instances, the Director-General addressed the plenary session of the Conference. This status and recognition reflected IUCN's legitimacy as an established and respected international body representing a 'major group' of interests, with a number of state members as well as a substantial NGO constituency, even though as a 'hybrid' GONGO it was outside the UN and treated by that body as an NGO. On the other hand almost all the environmental NGOs – including IUCN members – were not admitted to the main Conference. Many resented this exclusion, and some may have worried that the Union was getting too absorbed in the UN system'.[3] IUCN did organize a panel discussion at the Forum, but it was an argumentative occasion that may have further emphasized the gulf between it and the more strident campaigning NGOs, and convinced the latter that IUCN belonged irredeemably to the 'establish-ment' camp.[58]

Three New Conservation Treaties

The Stockholm Conference gave powerful impetus to the adoption of new interna-tional environmental laws. IUCN suggested that the Conference might back four particular Conventions – on the conservation of certain islands as islands for science (a notion that Max Nicholson had launched at the Eleventh Pacific Science Congress in 1966);[64] on the export, import and transit of certain species of wild animals and plants; on the conservation of wetlands of international importance especially as waterfowl habitat; and on the conservation of the world heritage.[61] A meeting to review all the Conventions which might be advanced within the Stockholm envelope was held in New York under the chairmanship of Eskandar Firouz, Deputy Prime Minister and minister responsible for environment in Iran (and an IUCN Councillor and Vice-President).[65] Twenty-seven countries were represented. In the end only the 'islands for science' proposal failed to win support (and even here the situation was not wholly negative, for a number of outstanding islands have been designated as 'natural sites' under the World Heritage Convention).

IUCN had already taken action in three of these areas. The Convention on Wetlands of International Importance especially as Waterfowl Habitat grew out of Project MAR,[65] and had been adopted at a conference supported by IUCN, IWRB, UNESCO and WWF at Ramsar in Iran, in 1971. The first draft text had been prepared in the Netherlands in 1966, an alternative Russian version appeared '*rather unexpect-edly*' in 1969, and the final document was developed by IWRB, ICBP and IUCN and adopted at Ramsar, where Frank Nicholls and Geoffrey Matthews, who had succeeded Luc Hoffmann as director of IWRB, played a central part.[49,65] The Ramsar Conference was the initiative of Eskandar Firouz, who saw it as Iran's particular contribution to world conservation.[66] But in 1972 it needed more signatures and IUCN – which had been given responsibility for the Secretariat – saw the Stockholm process as a means of attracting these.

The World Heritage Convention had a complicated history. There were two separate, and ultimately convergent, processes. The decision to build the Aswan High Dam in Egypt, and the campaign led by UNESCO to rescue the great monuments of Nubia from inundation, sparked ideas of wider cooperation to save the great cultural monuments of the past. A draft convention on the protection of cultural and historical properties – 'Monuments, Groups of Buildings and Sites' – was prepared in the cultural section of UNESCO, with the help of the newly established International Council on Monuments and Sites (ICOMOS), and a draft was circulated in the middle of 1971.[67–69]

Meanwhile, IUCN had been following up Russell Train's initiative for a convention on the world heritage, and a draft was also ready early in 1971. Reflecting the fact that in the USA both natural and cultural monuments come under the same administration, the IUCN draft embraced both.[67–70] The US Government supported the proposal, and President Nixon urged that it be adopted on the occasion of the celebration of the centenary of Yellowstone National Park in 1972.[69] The problem of overlap between the IUCN and UNESCO initiatives came to light in the Stockholm Preparatory Committee in 1971, and it was agreed that something had to be done to reconcile them. The United States, led by Russell Train, pressed strongly for merging the two.

A working group was established, chaired by Eskandar Firouz and with UNESCO, FAO and Stockholm Secretariat participation.[66] The negotiations were delicate and tortuous, and it became clear that a final text could not be made ready for adoption in Stockholm, but could be agreed at the UNESCO General Conference in November 1972 (which would have taken the draft on cultural monuments anyway).[69,70] In the end IUCN articles on the natural heritage were incorporated in manuscript on the UNESCO draft tabled on the very brink of the final negotiating session.[27] IUCN was established as the expert body advising on the strength of proposals for natural sites nominated by governments for inclusion under the Convention, while ICOMOS had this responsibility for built monuments. Gerardo Budowski, Frank Nicholls and Eskandar Firouz wanted IUCN to administer the Secretariat, but Maurice Strong felt that it was more appropriate for UNESCO, which has had the responsibility ever since.[66,69]

The story of what became the Convention on International Trade in Endangered Species (CITES) is an even longer one. The call for action was first heard at Nairobi in 1963, in a recommendation demanding '*an international Convention on regulations of export, transit and import of rare or threatened wildlife species or their skins or trophies*'.[27] A draft Convention on Trade in Threatened Species of Wildlife was prepared by the IUCN Committee on Law in 1964, and after discussion at the 1966 General Assembly in Lucerne it was circulated to about 90 governments and international organizations. Later drafts were prepared by the Commission on Environmental Law, Policy and Administration and circulated in 1969 and 1971.[67]

Things were not altogether smooth, however. The US Department of the Interior found the original IUCN text:

'a very European document, influenced by European industry and Customs. The United States decided not to support it. The Audubon Society sent an expert to Kenya to work with UNEP and a "Kenya version" was produced: the USA then got it adopted as the working text of the Washington Conference. It was more sensitive to developing countries and to conservation.'

At long last (see Note 71 for a suggestion about the cause of this delay), the formal intergovernmental negotiating conference was convened by the United States, in Washington DC, in 1973. Duncan Poore chaired the drafting committee (wearing the hat of a member of the UK delegation),[45] while Frank Nicholls and Françoise Burhenne-Guilmin, together with a Spanish-speaking lawyer, prepared, edited and harmonized the texts in the three working languages.[49]

The assumption had been that IUCN would provide and manage the Secretariat for CITES, but since it was not a formal intergovernmental organization it was thought inappropriate to mention it in the Convention.[72] Maurice Strong, by now Executive Director of United Nations Environment Programme, wanted the latter to gain prominence by being named. Wolfgang Burhenne asked him, in the presence of Christian Herter Jr (the Chair of the meeting), whether he had a mandate to incur the financial obligations of a Secretariat. He confirmed a few days later by telex that he had.[71] The offer was doubly welcome, for it meant that the delegates did not have to discuss the financing of a Secretariat – and the US delegation, led by Curtis 'Buff' Bohlen, were distrustful of IUCN and backed UNEP *'largely to keep IUCN at bay!'*[72,73] Although IUCN did provide the Secretariat from 1973 until mid-1984, it therefore did this as an agent for the Executive Director of UNEP.[67]

A New Programme in IUCN

By the end of 1973 the IUCN Secretariat at Morges numbered 18. The ecological team headed by Ray Dasmann and Duncan Poore included Colin Holloway (whose original research had been on the ecology of roe deer). There were full-time Executive Officers to support the work of the Survival Service Commission (Tony Mence) and Ecology Commission (Mona Bjorklund). Ray Dasmann himself guided the Executive Officer for National Parks, while Alfred Hoffmann handled environmental planning. Jan Čeřovský of Czechoslovakia (later to be an IUCN Vice-President), serviced the education programme and supported the Commission under Dr Shaposhnikov of the USSR: this Commission had a major influence in Eastern Europe.[74] Frank Nicholls oversaw policy, law and administration with a Legal Officer, Françoise Burhenne-Guilmin, based in Bonn, in support.[27] There was an External Relations Officer, an Information Officer (Bob Standish, seconded by the US Forest Service), an Administrative Officer, a Librarian, a Finance Officer, a Translator, an Administrative Aide and a Special Assistant (Membership) (Estelle Buckley, later better known in IUCN as Estelle Viguet, mentor to several successive Director-Generals). For the first time, IUCN had what amounted to an adequate professional team to back the work of the voluntary networks and a clear programme, involving Secretariat operations as well as Commission activities.[33,75] The result was *'more effective use of the Commission structure embracing several hundred scientists and experts from all over the world'.*[43]

And the budget – US$1.5 million for the three-year period from 1970 to 1972 – was vast by previous standards.[43] In addition to the Ford Foundation grant, and a continuing welcome subvention of US$10,000 from UNESCO, WWF had become an increasingly close partner providing well over SFr500,000 a year to core and programme costs.[18] The time of chronic suspicion and mutual criticism seemed past – perhaps because both bodies were now so much stronger and WWF respected IUCN's new professionalism. As Peter Jackson, then Reuters' Chief Correspondent in India, who joined WWF as Director of Information soon after New Delhi, recalls, *'there was a great feeling that the future was rosy...there was close cooperation between the Secretariats of IUCN and WWF and I had no sense of conflict and jealousy...'.*[76]

One illustration of that cooperation was one of WWF's most celebrated and highest-profile projects – Operation Tiger.[76] As Peter Jackson recalls, *'this was a time of despair for Indian conservationists, with rapid deterioration in the natural environment'*. Kalish Sankhala of the Indian Forest Service told a shocked IUCN General Assembly in New Delhi that only 2500 tigers survived in the whole of India, where there had been 40,000 at the turn of the century. The General Assembly voted to include the Bengal tiger in the list of endangered species, and called for a ban on hunting. Guy Mountfort, an international trustee of WWF, took the matter up. In 1972 he announced that he would raise US$1 million for 'Operation Tiger'. He and Charles de Haes, by then seconded to WWF staff, found themselves in India and went together to see the Prime Minister, Indira Gandhi (to whom Mountfort repeated his pledge).[8]

Mrs Gandhi set up an Indian task force led by Kalish Sankhala to plan the action on the ground.[76] She herself took the chair of the Project Tiger Steering Committee, and put one of her most dynamic ministers, Karan Singh, in charge. The latter promised that WWF's $1 million should be kept for those things that needed foreign exchange: India would find the rupees for internal costs.[28] Peter Jackson, as *'the only WWF staffer who had seen a tiger'* worked with Sankhala as Programme Manager, while Colin Holloway of IUCN screened the tiger reserve management plans. In all, about $1.8 million was raised for tiger conservation in India, Bangladesh, Nepal and Thailand. *'Project Tiger turned things around in India. Conservationists began to hope. This was because of Indira Gandhi's open commitment to nature conservation, and active involvement such as chairing the Committee.'*[76]

This was a period of such close bonding between the two organizations that it almost looked as if a merger was on the cards. At the end of 1971 arrangements were made for joint management of all IUCN and WWF projects – costing over a million dollars a year. WWF had decided to seek endowment funds, not least through its '1001' scheme,[28*] to provide enough revenue to support the Fund's core costs[77] – and a number of contributors including Hal Coolidge clearly believed the endowment would support IUCN also.[78] In 1972 *'WWF, in the light of its greatly strengthened association with IUCN, has made a clear commitment that the income from the endowment funds that are presently being accumulated should provide for IUCN's hard core expenditure by 1976'.*[43] Plans were well advanced for a joint headquarters in Geneva. The WWF Treasurer, Samuel Schweizer, had obtained a pledged donation of SFr10 million and a new Foundation for the Conservation of Nature and Environment had been set up (at IUCN's request) to hold this money.[28] A site had

---

* Formally entitled 'The 1001: A Nature Trust'. Charles de Haes points out that from the beginning the letter-heading declared it to be 'A Trust for the World Wildlife Fund': its possible use to endow IUCN as well as WWF was never raised with him.[28]

been selected on the Lake of Geneva and next to the botanical gardens and the UN complex.

But there were clouds on IUCN's financial horizon. Even before the Stockholm Conference, Maurice Strong had been approached by Gerardo Budowski with an appeal for help because the Ford Foundation grant was coming to its end. Strong persuaded Ford to extend its support until UNEP was in a position to take over,[79] and some members of that Foundation's staff also used their good offices to promote a new tranche of support from the Rockefeller Brothers Fund.[39] The result was that Budowski and Nicholls were able to present a confident report to the eleventh session of the General Assembly at Banff in Canada in 1972 (where Hal Coolidge retired as President, to be replaced by the Chairman of the Commission on Ecology, the Dutch Professor and entomologist, Donald Kuenen). There had been a major restructuring of the programme, reflecting the new priorities agreed in New Delhi. '*The proper management of the world's renewable resources*' was recorded as:

> '*a major concern of the Union, absorbing a considerable part of senior staff time. Emphasis is on the impact of man on his environment and the importance of ensuring that development programmes are planned in accordance with ecological principles. This concern is reflected in the theme of "Conservation for Development" selected for the Union's 11th General Assembly and associated Technical Meeting at Banff*'[43]

At the same time it was emphasized that:

> '*the Union continues its major interest in conservation of the natural environment, the field that gave it the central role in conservation matters. Here, too, there has been a change in emphasis with greater concern for the conservation of biotic communities, the promotion of effective assistance for a world network of national parks and other protected areas, and the social and long-term economic values of wildlife and wild places...*'.

And the continued attachment to ecology is evident in the statement that '*although its overall emphasis is on applied aspects of conservation, the Union has continued its pioneering work on the basic scientific and philosophical concepts on which conservation depends.*'

What had been done in detail? One striking feature of the report is that its very first section is headed 'Conservation for Development'. Here the major event was the publication, following an expert workshop convened by IUCN and the Conservation Foundation in Rome in September 1970, of the book *Ecological Principles for Economic Development* by Raymond Dasmann, John Milton and Peter Freeman and edited by Sir Hugh Elliott.[80] It was written from the point of view of an ecologist for the use of those more concerned with development – whether at national level or in connection with the aid programmes of international agencies. It set out the goals of development, and how they might be attained. It reviewed the ecological context and the particular problems of development in the humid tropics and in arid and sub-humid regions. It considered agriculture, pastoral systems, river basin development and the management of tourism. Two of its most resounding general statements are well worth quotation:

> *'Conservation and economic development should ideally be directed towards a common goal – the rational use of the earth's resources to achieve the highest quality of living for mankind.*
>
> *With both conservation and economic development it is essential to consider the physical and biological rules within which all life on earth must operate. These are the subject of the science of ecology, which is the study of the relationships of organisms with their environment. Proper consideration of ecological principles will assist those concerned with development or conservation to achieve their aims with the minimum of undesirable side-effects, reducing the likelihood of major environmental disturbance which could be harmful to all life within a region or throughout the world. Lack of consideration for the ecological realities of an environment can doom development efforts, with consequent waste of money and impairment of the conditions of life just as surely as if the technological, economic, political or social factors were to be ignored...'.*[80]

This is the philosophy of Haeckel and of Huxley, of the World Conservation Strategy of 1980 and of *Caring for the Earth*, launched in 1991. It is the central message that IUCN has been enunciating since its foundation. And it was only one element in a greatly strengthened scientific programme, in which for the first time the Secretariat figured as prominently as most of the Commissions.

One major thrust was the development of ecological guidelines for the conservation of tropical forests, mountains, arid lands, coastal regions and islands. These were Secretariat initiatives: Duncan Poore led the first three (with FAO support for the work on tropical forests, which included special meetings in Latin America and South-east Asia) while Ray Dasmann handled coasts and islands.[45] Meanwhile, the Commission on Ecology, headed by Derrick Ovington, pursued a different agenda. *'Up to around 1969, the Commission's chief role was to put over ecology as the basis for the management of ecosystems and National Parks. But by the 1970s, ecology was part of everyone's thinking. The advocacy role of the Commission on Ecology was past'.*[45] With MAB and INTECOL providing a focus for many academic ecologists, and with an IUCN Secretariat applying ecology in a steadily widening programme, the Commission never regained its former position as *the* scientific 'think tank' of IUCN.

The other Commissions remained active and worked closely with the Secretariat. The Environmental Law Centre in Bonn, led by the Burhennes, had developed a system for indexing and analysing legal and administrative documents, and demonstrated it to delegates at the Stockholm Conference. The educational work had also flowed forward on a wide front. The *Bulletin* had become a monthly production. A second edition of the *UN List of National Parks and Equivalent Reserves* had been prepared by Sir Hugh Elliott under the leadership of Jean-Paul Harroy, now retired from Africa and serving as Chair of the Commission on National Parks. A classification had been developed, although at this stage it was relatively narrow, with three categories – national parks, scientific reserves and natural monuments.[81] A study had been begun on the conservation status of areas around the Mediterranean. A joint meeting with the South Pacific Commission had led to the first marine reserve covering coral reef formations in New Caledonia. A vast amount of 'fire brigade action' for threatened species had continued under the SSC. Five volumes of the Red Data Book had been published – for mammals, birds, amphibia and reptiles, fish and flowering plants – and an extensive revision of the whole series was in hand. The International Fur Trade Federation had been persuaded by IUCN and WWF to place a moratorium on the use of skins of threatened cats – especially spotted ones.

The Banff General Assembly was a landmark: a turning point. It was the time when IUCN became truly operational, as a professional organization. It must have seemed amazing to the participants, used to a recurrent diet of financial disaster, staff inadequacies and initiatives glimpsed but out of reach. The money, the staff, the programme were all there: the partnership with WWF was at a new and all-time high. The Stockholm Conference had come, gone, and left the environment higher on the governmental world agenda than ever before, and IUCN was deeply involved in the action. Maurice Strong had attended the General Assembly and made his support for IUCN clear.[59] Immediately after the meetings in Banff, the Second World Congress on National Parks, held in Yellowstone and Grand Teton, was chaired jointly by the Director of US National Parks and the Director-General of IUCN and attracted numerous conservationists from developing countries – paid for most generously by the United States.[59] Gerardo Budowski had reason to take pride in the fact that when he took over as Director-General the IUCN budget was US$350,000, and when he left in 1976 it had risen to $3.5 million and was supporting outstanding professional staff, who were paid good salaries.[39]

This was a time when IUCN's reputation in the developing world grew fast. For Latin Americans, the presence of one of their number as Director-General was an important factor.[82] The increased prominence of people from the South in Commissions – for example with Judge Nagendra Singh, later Chief Justice of India, as Vice-Chairman of CEPLA – was another factor. '*It wasn't so much the number of members but the fact that the Commission had the reputation of being on the side of developing nations, and supportive of the efforts of developing country environmental lawyers that made the difference.*'[83] And IUCN's name carried weight. In 1972 Eskandar Firouz was presenting a new Bill on Environment to the Iranian Parliament. '*I persuaded the Government and Parliament that our reputation and standing vis-à-vis the international community would suffer if we did not conform to the major criteria set forth by IUCN...*'.[4] Iran itself became seen as a model and IUCN advised other developing countries, including Mongolia, Ethiopia and Afghanistan, to send teams to see what was being done.[84] IUCN was itself seeking good projects in the South – the limitation was in national infrastructure, and as awareness was built, especially after Stockholm, so this tended to develop.[85]

One key to success was the development of close ties with UNEP.[39] Those links were in part the result of an excellent personal relationship between Maurice Strong and Gerardo Budowski, but even more because of the institutional attractions of the alliance.[79,86] IUCN was a professional organization employing a team of expert conservation scientists, and had the merit of spanning the governmental and non-governmental sectors, thus bringing in some of the bodies that had attended the NGO Forum in Stockholm, with whom Strong had cultivated a good personal relationship, and through whom he wished UNEP to work. Through the Commissions, the Union could draw on a worldwide network of experts. It made good sense for UNEP (which was conceived as a small, central, catalytic body rather than a self-contained agency) to use IUCN as its nature conservation arm. The men at the top of UNEP – Maurice Strong, Peter Thacher and Bob Frosch – saw clearly that unless money was pushed into IUCN it could well founder: if they were to use it they had to sustain it.[87]

It was therefore agreed that IUCN would work for UNEP on a regular review of the state of world conservation. The contract (negotiated largely by Frank Nicholls) was worth US$1.5 million. It recognized IUCN as the leading agency for addressing the conservation element of the global environmental agenda, and linked it to the new spearhead of world environmental action.[39] The idea of a world conservation strategy first arose in dialogue with UNEP, partly because it would be the kind of tangible entity that would justify the funding.[45,87] And the relationship helped Gerardo Budowski towards his goal of creating a small, specialized, professional agency modelled on the UN bodies.[48,49]

By 1975, life at the headquarters in Morges had settled down. The original headquarters building, 'Les Uttins', became too small and a large house to the south named 'Floreal', set in a spacious and lovely garden, was rented.[45] The atmosphere was warm, even if it struck some visitors as *'a rather quaint selection of eccentrics in an odd building'*.[14] The impression of oddity was reinforced by some of the offices: *'Robert Prescott-Allen's office had been a bathroom. Some of the plumbing was still there.'*[14] Ursula Hiltbrunner, who joined WWF in 1975 to assist the Dutch Rear Admiral, Rudolf Idzerda, to set up a National Coordination Office, has similar memories of IUCN (to which she transferred soon afterwards):

> *'There were lots of nice people, but we were never quite clear what they were doing. WWF had much more sharply focussed objectives. The IUCN Desk Officers were supposed to review projects, but they handled them very slowly. We felt that although IUCN was strong on science, it was a bit sleepy, unrealistic and bad on deadlines.'*[88]

Tony Mence, then the Executive Officer responsible for the SSC, suggests that this comment reflects a lack of understanding:

> *'The project screening delay had nothing to do with "sleepiness", rather with the constitutional difference between WWF HQ and the IUCN Secretariat. Whereas the former was an operational centre under the direct command of its Director General, IUCN's Secretariat obtained and coordinated input from its constituent parts, particularly the Commissions...Project screening was not within Secretariat competence but with the appropriate Commissions, where the expertise lay. Since Commissions were outside direct control of the Secretariat, delay was inevitable and often lengthy...The screening delay thus incurred was just as exasperating to the Secretariat as to WWF.'*[75]

For its part, WWF wondered why, having identified the problem, the IUCN management did not do something about it.[28]

These comments suggest that despite the smiling public face of the WWF–IUCN partnership, there was still a touch of neuralgia under the skin. Ray Dasmann also recalls that while Morges was *'an idyllic setting in which idealism should thrive...it did not'*.[50] He felt that the IUCN programme was slanted too much:

> *'toward the areas of interest to its Board and leaders, or folks with money, rather than the areas of greatest need. There were or had been numbers of projects in East Africa, because the British VIPs liked to go there. There were few in West Africa. There were many projects in India, another favourite hang-out of wealthy British, but few in the rest of Asia except for Indonesia, which the Dutch VIPs favoured.'*[50]

And he was increasingly aware of a growing antagonism to Frank Nicholls among staff who were left under his direction for perhaps 30 per cent of the time while Gerardo Budowski attended meetings and visited IUCN member organizations and Commission members around the world.[50,52]

Meanwhile, the financial affairs of WWF had been put in much better order. The improvement was largely due to an energetic Belgian businessman with degrees in both law and economics, Charles de Haes, who was seconded to WWF in 1971 by his employer, the South African tycoon Anton Rupert.[89] His goal was to raise US$10 million for the WWF.[28]

De Haes made two conditions: that he had a free hand, and that he reported only to Rupert. He came up with a simple idea: the '1001 project' under which that number of wealthy people would be persuaded each to pay US$10,000 into a WWF Trust Fund. Prince Bernhard of the Netherlands, the President of WWF International, agreed to be leader of the venture. It must have looked daunting at the time (when $10,000 was a considerable sum), but de Haes did the job in dramatically effective style, using his considerable skills of persuasion, presentation and charm, and taking less than three years to complete the tally.[77,89]

With his mission accomplished, Charles de Haes expected to go back to Rupert International or resume a career in law,[89] but Prince Bernhard, Peter Scott and Luc Hoffmann had other ideas. They urged him to stay on, to continue promotion and fund-raising. Again, de Haes insisted on having one boss only – and Luc Hoffmann acted in that capacity (and took over sponsorship of his salary). Prince Bernhard and Charles de Haes became the 'mobile wing' of WWF, travelling so extensively that the former became known as '*the Flying Prince of Conservation*'.

Fritz Vollmar remained in charge of the headquarters. He has been described as:

> '*a gentle, well-educated German-Swiss, dedicated to the cause, whose terms of reference may not have been as clear as they should have been, and who was having to find his own way through a mass of ideas from many sources*'.[90]

He had done an excellent job in getting WWF going, but as the funds rolled in and the work expanded it became clear that he needed support, especially in management and finance. These were Charles de Haes' skills, but it was obvious that he could not be made subordinate to Fritz Vollmar – or vice versa. In August 1975 Luc Hoffmann was made Executive Vice-President of WWF, and Vollmar and de Haes became joint Directors-General under him, with mandates that did not overlap. One dealt with conservation, education and projects and the other handled money-raising, publicity, information and business management.[28,91] This arrangement was in operation when IUCN gathered for its next General Assembly in Kinshasa in the following month. Luc Hoffmann and Fritz Vollmar represented WWF, since the relationship with IUCN was part of the latter's responsibilities.

Any reader of the report by Gerardo Budowski and Frank Nicholls prepared for that General Assembly on the theme of 'conservation for decision-makers' would have had good grounds for satisfaction.[92] The central concern had continued to be the proper management of the world's renewable resources. The theme of 'conservation for development' had been pursued – and led naturally to the theme for the Twelfth Assembly. IUCN was building links between organizations, scientists and government officials around the world, and especially in developing countries, and the UN and other international organizations with which it had close relations. A world conservation strategy was to be formulated, and a broad programme for action developed: IUCN had the support of UNEP and would work in partnership with WWF and other collaborators. An impressive range of detailed activities was reviewed.[92]

The organization looked in good shape. The Environmental Law Centre had developed ELIS, the Environmental Law Information System, and provided a lot of advice. ELIS had been designated a special sectoral source within INFOTERRA, the International Referral System on sources of environmental information which was one of UNEP's major post-Stockholm initiatives.[27,93] A task force was looking at the conservation implications of the growing demand for energy. A system of classification of vegetation and ecological communities was being developed in association with MAB. Environmental education remained a priority and the appointment of a full-time Executive Officer in 1968 had been the springboard for an expanded programme in many regions, with an input to Stockholm and a major contribution to the preparations for a world conference which UNESCO and UNEP were organizing at Tbilisi in the USSR in 1976.[74]

Public awareness was being boosted by science writing and media promotions (Robert Prescott-Allen joined as science writer in 1975), and a number of publications had rolled off the press: participation in meetings and conferences remained a daunting demand on staff time. The six Commissions were active (though they take up only a tiny fraction of the lengthy Director-General's report). The number of State members had risen from 29 to 39, agency members from 88 to 111, national NGO members from 194 to 230, and international NGO members from 18 to 20 – and the membership spanned 97 countries. Cooperation with other organizations was excellent – especially UNEP: an ecosystem conservation group had been established to help coordination between UNEP, FAO, UNESCO and IUCN. Progress had been made with almost all the resolutions adopted by the General Assembly in Banff.[92]

On the face of it, the finances looked good. Banff had approved a budget of US$3,170,000 to cover core costs in the triennium, and expenditure was expected to total $3,130,000. Thanks to Maurice Strong, the Ford Foundation had made a further grant of $300,000, taking their total support to nearly $1 million. Another SFr1 million had come from the Emil Barell-Stiftung in Germany. Rockefeller Brothers Fund had provided over $100,000. UNESCO was maintaining close ties, and Michel Batisse, who since 1973 had been the Director of a new Department of Environmental Sciences and Natural Resources Research, had been able to raise their yearly subvention to $18,000 and place a contract to allow the publication of the magazine *Parks* in time for the Kinshasa General Assembly.[63] WWF had made a gift of $100,000 as a kind of 'birthday present' to mark IUCN's 25th anniversary, as well as paying about $1 million a year to support projects, which continued to be managed jointly.

Another fund-raising device was the Conservation Coin Collection, sponsored jointly by IUCN and WWF, in which 24 nations were issuing limited editions of their legal coinage bearing wildlife designs: net proceeds were to go to the two sponsor organizations. McKinsey's examined the scheme and were optimistic: it was hoped to raise US$10 million, though rough calculations suggested that if all went perfectly the maximum sales might total US$167 million of which IUCN and WWF might receive $70 million after costs had been covered.[28] The well-known firm of numismatists, Spink & Son, were to administer the scheme, doing '*all the work apart from making the initial contact with countries and the subsequent negotiations up to and including contract*'.[89,94]

The only faint hints of clouded horizons were the admission that financial limitations had blocked some of the actions agreed at Banff, that not all the projected staff recruitment had been possible, and that construction of the new headquarters had not yet started – largely because the Foundation holding the funds had instructed the architect to prepare over-ambitious plans which were impossibly costly.[28] But it was still expected that work would start soon, with the building ready for occupation in 1977.

The Board was evidently content with its Director-General, for on 5 May 1975, at its last session before Kinshasa, it resolved to nominate Gerardo Budowski for another term of three years.[95] In the same session it decided that '*the main foci of the IUCN programme should be the conservation by wise management of plant and animal species and of areas (including both natural areas and cultivated landscapes, and including marine areas)*'. It also stated:

> '*that the programme so formulated would continue to involve the promotion of environmental policies, legislation and administrative structures, land use planning, education and public awareness, and its success would depend on the application of ecological knowledge and on public opinion which was sensitive to conservation issues. IUCN should engage in these activities in so far as they related to the main focus.*'[95]

Some people have suggested that this redefinition – which, when compared with the New Delhi statement seems to imply a return to more traditional nature conservation – was the outcome of yet another debate between 'conservationists' and 'protectionists'.[3] This was not just an internal argument: in the 1970s there were many battles between preservationists and wildlife managers. '*It was not yet fashionable to speak of wildlife management to feed and to raise the incomes of poor peasants; it was not accepted to sustain that forest management for profit was a good option outside protected areas.*'[82] Robert Prescott-Allen[72] was conscious of a great complexity of views about both the environment to be considered and the weight to be given to social concern among both staff and IUCN members.

In the IUCN of 1975, some people focused on the parts of the 'environmental axis' relating to nature and wildlife and others on the whole ecosystem (including air and water quality, resource depletion, land use and energy). On the 'social axis' some put the ecosystem first while others argued that at least as much attention had to be given to people as to the ecosystem.[72] Delmar Blasco, soon to start work for UNEP as head of the newly-created Environment Liaison Centre International in Nairobi, had the impression that while IUCN spoke the rhetoric of development, its actions were dominated by the 'Old Masters' of nature conservation.[96] In practice, it was almost inevitable that both would be pursued in parallel: the sustainable use and development aspects of conservation were being promoted in a whole series of ecological guidelines and had the strong backing of FAO, but nature protection loomed large in the Commission programmes and in WWF-supported projects.[97]

'*The problem was that it wanted to sell conservation to the development constituency, but it did not understand what the development constituency was like. The conservationists didn't see that development was the driving force in human affairs.*'[3] In Robert Prescott-Allen's view this was where the new environmental movement diverged from the older conservation bodies. The new movement was a social movement, concerned with peace, pollution and resources:

> *'IUCN was, and always has been, a conservation body and has never figured out how to get into the social, urban or environmental area: it did not become even the "environmentalist" focus for non-urban areas, with emphasis on sustainable agriculture and forestry. This was partly due to opposition from bodies including FAO and UNEP who wanted to keep IUCN focussed on wildlife.'[3]*

In some ways, UNESCO was part of that opposition. Michel Batisse had told the Banff General Assembly in 1972 that:

> *'IUCN should continue to defend the very cause for which it was created...Nobody expects IUCN to limit itself to the narrow role of species and landscape conservation. But everybody expects IUCN, faithful to the cause of conservation which is its specific responsibility, to pursue and develop the scientific work, technical studies, campaigns and interventions which in the few years of its existence have brought it the prestige which it has today.'[98]*

In fact, UNESCO looked on IUCN in much the same way as it regarded ICSU and was not convinced that its mission would benefit if it became an operational agency, undertaking projects on the ground in parallel with the UN agencies.[70] And the relationship may not have been helped by the fact that IUCN was competing with UNESCO and to a lesser extent with FAO in its search for UN funds.[49]

It was not until the time of the World Conservation Strategy and the era of 'sustainable development' that the two streams began to flow together. There was, however, an effort to get together with at least one of the new 'development' institutions. In 1972 the International Institute for Environmental Affairs had been set up in the United States, especially through the efforts of Robert O Anderson, then Chairman of the oil company Atlantic Richfield. It was especially concerned with the social and institutional aspects of environmental change, and it gained an early supporter in Barbara Ward, co-author with René Dubos of the 'background' book for the Stockholm Conference, *Only One Earth*.[56] Early in 1973, Barbara Ward became President of the Institute, brokered a new name 'International Institute for Environment and Development', and established an office in London to parallel the original base in Washington DC and give the whole a less American flavour.[2,14] David Runnalls (who headed IIED in Washington DC at this period) recalls contacts between IUCN and IIED and internal divisions over how far IUCN should walk down the development road.[14] IIED was clear that its role was to study the long-term relationship between the environment and social development. Gerardo Budowski and Frank Nicholls suggested that IUCN might clarify the ecological constraints on development. But then came the events of Kinshasa.

Upheaval in Kinshasa: the 'Night of the Long Knives'

The General Assembly in Kinshasa in September 1975 is remembered in IUCN especially because of a dramatic (and quite unexpected) upheaval within the Secretariat. But it was an important meeting in other ways. It brought many African wildlife departments into IUCN as members, attracted by the change in the Union's central philosophy towards 'conservation for development'. The Assembly adopted Recommendation 12/05, promoted by Ray Dasmann, that stressed the need to retain indigenous peoples and cater for their traditional rights in national parks and protected areas. The resolution had an immense impact in places as far apart as Canada (where current policy was to eject such people) and East Africa (where a hunting ban had failed to curb rampant poaching, and where WWF had supported the exclusion of people from the parks).[37,99]

The minutes of the Executive Board and its Executive Committee contain no clues about why the Kinshasa General Assembly was the scene of a major upheaval. Gerardo Budowski recollects that disagreement over programme objectives may have played a part. Given the recurrent eruption of tension between 'protectionists' and 'conservationists' in successive General Assemblies, it is virtually certain that both camps had their followers among the membership. But Ray Dasmann does not believe that these differences of opinion were the reason for the '*discontent and even desperation voiced in Zaire*',[58] and Lee Talbot agrees.[6]

Gerardo Budowski recalls more serious criticisms over the alliance that he had forged with UNEP.[39] On the face of it, this link should have been enormously welcome, for while the funding from the Ford Foundation, later supplemented by the Rockefeller Brothers Fund, had allowed the reconstruction of the Secretariat, such finance was not intended to turn into a long-term commitment. UNEP, on the other hand, was in a position to maintain continuing support for IUCN, provided that the latter went on providing worthwhile expert knowledge in its specialized field. But some US non-governmental members of IUCN accused the Board and the Director-General of 'surrendering to the United Nations', and were deeply suspicious of the broadening of IUCN's agenda.[39,48] Gerardo Budowski considers that some at least of their unhappiness arose because they were themselves intent on expanding in other continents and found that IUCN was already there.[59]

There was also criticism of the way in which IUCN was being developed as an operational agency, modelled on UN bodies and paid on UN salary scales. The Sierra Club and others took the view that IUCN was basically an NGO, and opposed its conversion into an institution with a governmental character. They saw that as disempowering the NGOs.[100] Many members did not want IUCN to become a bureaucracy, favouring the catalytic role that UNEP was also being pressed by governments to adopt.[40] The American Committee on International Wildlife (the forum for the NGO members in the United States) met before Kinshasa and decided that these problems had to be addressed there.[99]

But no signs of stress are evident in the record of the opening meeting the Executive Board held in Zaire on 7 September 1975.[101] Indeed there were two optimistic financial statements. Luc Hoffmann reported that the Conservation Coin Collection was expected to provide '*at least £100,000 a month from now on*', and the President announced a contribution of £50,000 a year from the Government of Saudi Arabia, and thanked Sir Peter Scott warmly for negotiating it (Peter Scott's knighthood had been awarded in recognition especially of his services to conservation). The only slight hint of trouble was the warning that the UNEP and UNESCO payments could not be counted on for 1977–78, and that WWF could not guarantee its payments at that stage either, though it expected to maintain its level of support. But these concerns appear to have been swept aside with the comment that the Programme and Budget Committee of the Assembly would examine all these issues thoroughly and revise the draft budget where necessary.

Minutes of meetings do not, of course, tell the whole story. Clearly the problems went deeper than policy. Staff had begun to murmur uneasily, well before they left for Kinshasa, and a committee with Alfred Hoffmann, then Secretary of the Landscape Planning Commission, as spokesman was pressing for change.[102] One major concern was that the Executive Board and the General Assembly were not being given essential information about the real financial health of the organization.[3,6] Duncan Poore noted at the time that there was *'strong criticism of the programme and budget at the Executive Board Meeting on Saturday 6th, and questioning especially of the Conservation Coin Collection figures given by Frank Nicholls and Luc Hoffmann'*.[103] Lee Talbot (who was at the time a Vice-President of IUCN and Chair of the General Assembly Programme and Budget Committee) comments that the underlying problem had been that in the years before Kinshasa, Frank Nicholls had had to keep the organization going by hunting contracts that provided core funds as overheads.

> *'The result was that the immediate source of funds determined the Union's activity instead of the agreed-upon programme. This often zig-zag course was not presented very explicitly to the Board, and the programme prepared by Nicholls for the coming triennium appeared to be designed for more of the same, rather than for...advancing global conservation and development making maximum use of the Union's unique character and human resources.'*[6]

In fact, no proper programme document had been prepared (Duncan Poore wrote a back-up document in case it was needed, as it was).[45]

The Commissions were another area of discontent. In the National Parks Commission meeting that discontent was largely directed at its Chair, Jack Nicol, the director of Parks Canada, who had been elected in Banff, but had not been able to give enough time.[99] He was replaced, initially, by the Deputy Director of the US Parks Service, Ted Swem, as Acting Chair, with Fred Packard as Secretary of CNPPA. Somewhat later Kenton Miller of the University of Michigan became substantive Chairman.[81] But the Director-General was believed to be seeking to down-grade the 'junior' Commissions – Ecology, Education and Planning – and this rankled. The outline programme tabled by Frank Nicholls upset the Commissions because it contained minimal provision for them.[3] Grenville Lucas of Kew and Morton Boyd of the Nature Conservancy in Scotland spoke privately of possible opposition to the reappointment of the Director-General.

During the following week Lee Talbot raised his concerns on the floor of the Assembly and elicited sympathetic murmurs – and threw some of the meetings of the Programme and Budget Committee open to delegates, providing an opportunity for participation that had been lacking in previous General Assemblies.[48] This meant that delegates saw for the first time the levels of salary and the high costs of operating in Switzerland, and the proportion of funds reaching conservation projects on the ground.[48] Dr Wayne King of SSC was an outspoken critic of the draft programme, calling for more *'real conservation work'*. There was a further demand to allocate more funds to the work of the Commissions.[48] The alternative programme prepared by Duncan Poore was adopted and circulated by the Programme and Budget Committee: it was amended in discussion to place more emphasis on what was then called 'ecodevelopment'.[103]

This kind of debate has recurred in a number of sessions of the General Assembly, is entirely legitimate, and on its own it should not have led to crisis. But there was another issue. Many senior staff members and some Councillors were critical of the top management.[48] The hostility was not to Gerardo Budowski personally – he was widely liked, and respected as a scientist – but to his style of management (including his lengthy absences from headquarters). The Director-General, who had charm, an engaging presentational style and a broad scientific knowledge, acted as a kind of roving ambassador for conservation, and made a real contribution to international debates. Most of the serious scientific work at headquarters was done by Ray Dasmann and Duncan Poore. The management was done by Frank Nicholls, and his style aroused hostility although his ability was unquestioned.[3,75]

Dissatisfaction was, in fact, rife before the General Assembly, and it was exacerbated by the conditions under which the Assembly was held. It was very hot and humid. The auditorium and meeting rooms were excellent but much of the accommodation was primitive.[50,75] '*The food was terrible and drinks, with the exception of Zairean beer, were very expensive.*'[50] The staff were accommodated in one of President Mobutu's palace compounds by the river, and the place was crawling with the President's special troops, wielding automatic weapons. The atmosphere was highly uncomfortable, and a number of delegates began to voice dissatisfaction. The staff were adamant that the Director-General should 'come clean' with the Programme and Budget Committee about the financial situation.[3] Ray Dasmann was summoned to a meeting with the American delegates, who said bluntly that the USA would pull out of IUCN unless there was a change of top management.[50] '*This was all that was needed to blow the lid off*' and emergency staff meetings went on all night.

Negotiations might have been easier had not the programme of the Assembly been disrupted by the mid-session excursion usual at that period – this time to the Virunga National Park. This event had been carefully planned and Donald Kuenen and Gerardo Budowski had flown up in a light aircraft to reconnoitre – having a hair-raising and highly dangerous encounter with the interior of a tropical storm full of hailstones on the way.[39] But just before the main party was due to depart, the Zairois military announced that only two aircraft could be made available, and one of them was rather small.[27] They therefore restricted the excursion to heads of delegation, accompanied by the President, Vice-Presidents, Commission Chairs, Director-General and some invited VIPs.

This last-minute decision caused fury. Peter Scott refused to go because his wife was excluded. There were representations to President Mobutu, who refused to overrule his military (on whom he depended, and of whom, even then, he appeared to be scared).[39] Hal Eidsvik got into hot water with Donald Kuenen for buying a boarding card for his wife from a member of the Organizing Committee (it cost him US$100).[104] Mrs Kuenen, the other wives, and all the Secretariat except the Director-General remained behind. Matters were not helped by a delay to the return flight from Virunga.[71] While the captain and officers were away, the mutineers seized the ship. Robert Prescott-Allen recalls that they determined to tell the Director-General that they would place their concerns over finance before the Assembly if he didn't.[3] Ray Dasmann records that some were prepared to strike, halting the Assembly, unless the Director-General agreed not to run for re-election.[50] Duncan Poore was asked whether he would be willing to act as Director, and said he would, if essential, for one year in the first instance.[103] Meanwhile Ray Dasmann took on the unpleasant job of confronting Gerardo Budowski, who was an old friend, on his return. He was '*genuinely shattered*',[50] having told Luc Hoffmann during the excursion that he did not think his reappointment was in danger.[102]

There was a long and unhappy discussion. Factions formed, and the helpful Zairois offered to throw the mutineers into jail – which would certainly have brought IUCN greater worldwide publicity than it had ever had before.[50] Donald Kuenen took Duncan Poore aside and asked about the causes of dissatisfaction, and specifically about the role of Frank Nicholls (who had been excluded from the 'mutinous assemblies' although he did not go on the excursion to Virunga).[45,103] The 'ringleaders' were called to an emergency meeting of the Executive Board. Kenton Miller, who had worked under Gerardo Budowski early in his career at Turrialba, acted as a go-between and tried to persuade him to continue as Director-General but change his deputy. Budowski stood firmly by Frank Nicholls, who had indeed been very loyal to him. From then on it became clear that both men might depart.[48] In the end, Gerardo Budowski decided to withdraw his candidacy for re-election. On 16 September the Board, accepting the Director-General's decision, none the less resolved to ask the Assembly to approve his continuation for another six months while a replacement was recruited.[105] At the same time they recognized the need to take a hard look at the whole governance of the Union and the relationship between the Director-General, the Board, the Commissions and the membership.

The President took this proposition to the senior staff.[103,105,106] The Board agreed to appoint a task force on organization and structure, chaired by Lee Talbot. Don McMichael of Australia was asked to lead a group to prepare guidelines for changes in the statutes, by-laws and rules of procedure, and an Extraordinary General Assembly was to be called in January 1977 to consider the proposals. The package was accepted. The revised programme and budget were approved (albeit by a narrow margin), Donald Kuenen announced the retirements of Budowski and Nicholls (with what struck Duncan Poore as less than justice to their achievements), and the Assembly broke up after a bad-tempered session of the Executive Board which revealed the tensions between the President and senior staff. WWF, in the persons of Luc Hoffmann and Fritz Vollmar '*looked bleak*'.[103] Hoffmann afterwards described the whole incident as '*very sad*'.[89] Robert Prescott-Allen comments that '*everybody was scarred. Most of the delegates went home thoroughly confused.*'[3]

It is clear that this was a nasty interlude – not least because it broke out so suddenly and was conducted in such a 'back-stairs' manner. With hindsight it is easy to see that there were failures all round. The Executive Board had failed to ensure that a properly detailed programme and budget had been put before the General Assembly. The Director-General and his deputy had failed to discuss the matter with the senior staff and build agreement in their team before the Assembly. The senior staff had failed to press their concerns while there was yet time. And the President had failed to give firm yet sensitive leadership. It is interesting to speculate how Hal Coolidge would have dealt with it had he been President at the time. Donald Kuenen was not the best man for such a situation: although a distinguished scientist, he could be aloof and tended to stand on his dignity as Rector Magnificus of an ancient University. He was clearly very angry at the way the staff had left him and the Board members out of the action, and had confronted Gerardo Budowski directly. He was certainly not at his best in the final session of the Executive Board ('*dictatorial and dogmatic, but also very unclear*').[103] But the deed was done.

And so a quite extraordinary reversal of fortunes was played out. Once again, IUCN had fallen to the ground just when it appeared to be well and truly airborne.

And whether or not it was a factor in the dissension, one immediate victim was cooperation with the IIED. '*Then came Kinshasa, and Budowski and Nicholls were ejected, and IIED realized there was no future in association with IUCN at that time.*'[14] By 1979, when a United Nations Conference on Human Settlements was held in Vancouver and a UN Centre for Human Settlements (Habitat) was established separate from, but alongside, UNEP in Nairobi, the unity of environment and development was looking frayed.

7 A Strategy for World Conservation

The Rough Road from Kinshasa

The upheavals in IUCN in 1975 went almost unnoticed in the wider environmental community. For the centre of international action had shifted to UNEP. In the five years following the Stockholm Conference, the UNEP Governing Council established itself as the global forum in which governments debated world environmental issues and coordinated action. More and more ministers began to attend the annual (and later biennial) sessions of the Council. UNEP also established a series of global services – GEMS, the Global Environmental Monitoring System; IRPTC, the International Register of Potentially Toxic Chemicals; INFOTERRA, the International Environmental Information System; and (as a joint venture with UNESCO) IEEP, the International Environmental Education Programme. UNEP also began to establish itself as a major promoter of new international environmental law.[1]

Several of these fields – notably education and law – remained a concern of IUCN, which did participate in IEEP. But the effect of the rise of UNEP was to alter the status of the IUCN General Assembly. It was no longer the unique global forum for environmental discussions. Equally, UNEP did not seek to involve itself directly in nature conservation, and it was here that IUCN was seen as the focus of international expertise and the source of information and guidance. As the specialist agency in this field the Union gained new opportunities through the rise of UNEP – especially while the latter remained a close partner and supporter.

Despite the internal upheavals with which the IUCN began 1976, the *Bulletin* issued at the start of the year looked forward with clear vision:

> '*The next 25 years, 1976–2000 may justly be regarded as conservation's critical quarter century. During this period, the tasks facing IUCN and its member organizations will grow progressively more difficult. They will involve unpleasant choices and demand a tactical flexibility and clarity of thought that the conservation movement has not always shown.*'

The *Bulletin* sets out the challenges in two prophetic paragraphs which clearly try to bridge the 'protectionist' and 'conservationist' divide:

> '*During this period, the pressure of world population on the environment will grow much more severe. The trend towards greater urbanization, unless it is deliberately reversed, could result in still*

*greater environmental disruption. Pressure on living resources will
mount enormously.*

*As a result the prospects for conservation will be much the poorer.
Species diversity will be further reduced and ecosystem integrity most
severely undermined. The most pressing economic needs will be shared
by still greater numbers of people; and in the face of their just demand
for food and jobs, governments will weaken further in their defence of
their people's biological heritage.'*[2]

The response? There must be a much more rigorous definition of priorities. There
must be a much more rigorous assessment of feasibility. Action would succeed only
if it took full account of the needs, attitudes and knowledge of the local people. A
much more flexible approach was essential. *'Conservationists can increase their
prospects of success by devoting at least some of their efforts to cooperating with
others in devising forms of development that are sensitive to ecological and social
diversity.'* And while:

*'it may be repugnant for conservationists to divert their precious
energies from conservation proper, or to be involved in development at
all...unless we are involved much (if not all) that we have achieved in
the past, and hope to achieve during the coming years, will be destroyed
by the efforts to survive of millions of poor and hungry – helped only by
biologically prodigal development on the one hand and socially naive
conservation on the other, and therefore not helped at all'.*[2]

That is the message of the World Conservation Strategy, which was not to appear for
another four years. It was the message that IUCN and its members needed to launch
like a shooting star in the political firmament. But before IUCN could play its proper
part in that action, it had to sort out its internal problems, and this proved extraordinarily traumatic.

Like the radiation from the 'big bang' at the beginning of the universe, the turmoil
that followed Kinshasa is still faintly discernible at the outer limits of IUCN folk-
memory. It was not only that the first Director-General, still widely liked and
respected as a scientist, had left with scant acknowledgement for his role in the
creation of a modern, professional organization, but also that the Executive Board
was also seen to have *'fallen down on the job of keeping IUCN on an even keel'.*[3]
There was a need to restore confidence and leadership, stabilize the financial position,
maintain continuity in the programme, make a proper input to meetings like the
Habitat Conference and pave the way for a new beginning at the Special Session of
the General Assembly to be held in 1977.

Donald Kuenen visited Morges three times in the Northern autumn of 1975 –
*'the first time intensely suspicious, but by the second time...convinced that what
happened in Zaire was not a plot but a completely spontaneous series of events'.*[4,5]
The leadership of the Secretariat was strengthened by making Ray Dasmann Acting
Director-General when Gerardo Budowski was away – a muddled arrangement, since
Frank Nicholls was nominally Deputy Director-General and continued to run the
administration, while when he was at Morges the outgoing Director-General kept his
hands on much of the action.[4]

Balancing the books was an immediate challenge. It was soon evident that the
concerns expressed at the General Assembly were right – and at the end of 1975

IUCN was SFr700,000 in the red, with a similar deficit in prospect for 1976. Somebody had to find nearly a million Swiss francs from somewhere, and quickly.[6,7] Ray Dasmann and Duncan Poore went to UNESCO, met with clear expressions of goodwill, and brought back a contract for work on the World Heritage Convention, but when Duncan Poore and Tony Mence went to see FAO in Rome they sensed '*a great deal of reserve behind our welcome*'.[4] UNEP (from which Maurice Strong had, by this time, departed) had '*tightened up on the release of funds and obviously a great deal of spade work had to be done there to restore confidence*'.[4] They therefore '*had to beg funds from WWF to meet the next payroll*'.[8] Charles de Haes commented that any organization that was in financial trouble and spent 80 per cent of its budget on staff had no option but to cut salaries or reduce the number of employees.[4,9]

A new Management and Finance Committee chaired by Bob Boote of the UK, with Donald Kuenen, Luc Hoffmann and Dietrich von Hegel (the head of the Nature Conservation Department in the German Ministry of Environment) as members and Michael Hervey of McKinsey as an adviser plumbed the depths of the financial situation.[10] They found that all cash except for SFr50,000 on deposit would be exhausted by mid-February 1976 '*and as IUCN would no longer be liquid, difficult legal issues could arise*'. Yet any reduction in staffing below the current total of 35 could impair IUCN's ability to undertake the agreed programme.[10]

If costs were to be reduced but staff numbers maintained, the only option was to cut pay. Staff, while not accepting that they were overpaid, had agreed to give or loan part of their salaries (this agreement was in written form and carried the proviso that the sum so loaned was repayable should financial improvement so allow).[4,11] A more formal squeeze was now imposed. On 30 January 1976, immediately before the meeting of the Executive Committee, Donald Kuenen and Luc Hoffmann (invited by Kuenen because he felt it vital to show WWF support)[12] '*settled themselves downstairs like a couple of gentlemen of the Inquisition and started...seeing people*'.[4] They started with Gerardo Budowski, Frank Nicholls, Duncan Poore and Ray Dasmann.

Whatever the depth of financial crisis, Kuenen's handling of the situation was felt by the staff to be inexcusably traumatic. They had no prior warning. They were called in separately, '*and told that their employment was now terminated unless they were prepared to sign the new contracts then presented. Coming so abruptly after making an already substantial voluntary reduction, and seeing the WWF presence, this was shocking*'.[11] The new contract included acceptance of a 'voluntary' 25 per cent reduction in salary: Alan Pike, who was on secondment from the UK as Administrative Officer, negotiated a lower rate for junior staff and those with dependants.[4] The result was that '*the atmosphere in the office was one of severe resentment...There is total distrust of the President and the Executive Board*'.[13] A Staff Committee was formed to prevent such arbitrary action against individual staff members happening in future. But in Ray Dasmann's view '*much more than anything that happened in Zaire, the actions of last weekend have made it difficult for IUCN to function as an effective organization...*'.[13] He refused to sign the new contract, and announced that he would serve no longer as Acting DG and would leave as soon as he had finished the projects he was working on (he actually left in July 1976, to become Professor of Ecology at the University of California, Santa Cruz).[8,13] IUCN and WWF hardly did themselves good by treating one of the world's leading ecologists in this way.

The Executive Committee met next day, with only Gerardo Budowski and Frank Nicholls in attendance. Budowski made it clear that he wanted to hand over his main responsibilities by the end of February, and would return in April to the Tropical Centre for Research and Training at Turrialba in Costa Rica as head of the Department of Forest Sciences.[14] Frank Nicholls also wished to leave in April.[5] There would clearly be no time to recruit a new Director-General in two months, and a full-time acting appointment was inevitable: the Committee appointed Duncan Poore with effect from 1 March 1976.[15] They hoped that the full Executive Board might make its choice in May 1976, but in fact the 'temporary' appointment lasted for a whole year longer.[6,7]

Organization and structure were also back in the melting-pot. McKinsey's had undertaken a study, arranged by WWF, in August 1975 but their interim report had not been put before the General Assembly in Kinshasa and it was now dismissed out of hand as '*more applicable to a commercial enterprise than to a scientific organization like IUCN*'.[4,7] A task force led by Lee Talbot had concluded that the key internal issue was the relationship between the Director-General and Secretariat (who were the Union's executive) on the one hand, and the Commissions (who were not executive) on the other.[7,6] The Executive Board considered and rejected amalgamation with WWF. Luc Hoffmann considered that this would not work. IUCN linked governmental and non-governmental bodies: WWF had a quite different structure, and a different accountability. The structural changes a merger would demand would probably be unacceptable to both. It would take away more than it added, since (when IUCN was working properly) the two bodies complemented each other. Cooperation would achieve the most effective operating results, and common services in a joint headquarters should enhance efficiency further. The proposition was shelved, if not buried.[7]

Even though the need for cooperation was clear, the relationship between IUCN and WWF was one short-term casualty of the upheaval. WWF could not be blamed for the deficit that had brought IUCN close to disaster. But IUCN staff did blame WWF for the conditions imposed as the price of rescue.[11] They had a journalistic ally. '*IUCN today*' wrote Jon Tinker of the *New Scientist*,

> '*has an irreplaceable role on the world environmental stage, providing a vital network of links between the scientific community, UN agencies, national governments and the voluntary conservation movement. In this spectrum the World Wildlife Fund plays an important but in the last resort a peripheral part. It is neither appropriate nor acceptable that an alliance of European princes and businessmen should seek in any way to dictate the personnel of a global scientific institution*'.[17]

But, according to Tinker (who no doubt echoed briefings from Morges), that was just what they were doing. He reported that Donald Kuenen had attended the WWF Executive Committee meeting under Prince Bernhard's Chairmanship at Soestdijk Palace, and consulted it over the candidates for appointment as IUCN Director-General. Tinker attacked WWF, '*originally established to finance IUCN*', for '*not paying the piper*'. In 1976–77 only 18 per cent of the funds raised by WWF were due to go to IUCN, most being deployed on projects on the ground which were not envisaged in the Fund's original trust deed. WWF was accused of starving IUCN, and making dictation the price of resuscitation. '*The ideal solution from IUCN's point of view – more WWF money and less WWF interference – clearly involves such an improbable degree of self-restraint on the part of WWF as to be inherently impracticable*'.[17] It can also be argued that it would have been improper: the WWF Board was accountable for the use of its funds. Peter Scott, then the WWF Chairman, protested that he was only interested in seeing that IUCN restored effective leadership.

This was also a time of reconstruction in WWF. The 'power sharing' arrangement between Fritz Vollmar and Charles de Haes was to last for two years, after which the latter expected to return to industry.[9] But as the first year came to an end, in the summer of 1976, Vollmar decided to step down, giving the Executive Committee the opportunity to retain de Haes as sole Director-General. One Executive Committee member proposed, however, that Vollmar be retained as a 'roving ambassador', visiting ministers and other key contacts and photographing WWF projects (he was an expert with a camera). Charles de Haes opposed this plan and it was rejected – causing some bitterness between the two men.[9]

As sole Director-General of WWF, de Haes' entrepreneurial skill and personal drive became more and more apparent, and some people sensed that he soon became impatient with IUCN. '*Charles saw the value of IUCN, but was critical of its management*', one noted.[18] For his part, he wanted results. He respected IUCN's scientific expertise and was happy to work through it, for example in executing projects, so long as the work was done well, the expenditure was properly audited, and the results were reported.[9] But his manner, reflecting the business world he had come from, gave some IUCN staff the impression that he wanted WWF to be the dominant partner, supporting IUCN but not encouraging it to be too strong or independent.

Despite the turmoil, IUCN business had to be carried on as normally as possible. It is a tribute to the dedication and professionalism of the staff that despite all the upheavals, and despite cuts in pay that would have made many people profoundly disaffected, they and the Commission Chairs made an effective job of implementing the programme adopted in Kinshasa. Preparations were made for the Special Session of the General Assembly to be held in Geneva in April 1977. There was the usual round of Committee and other meetings. The Canadian Committee for IUCN was launched in December. The Commission on Environmental Law and the Environmental Law Centre were asked by the German Government to prepare a draft text of what became the Convention on Migratory Species.[19]

Debates over finances and staff pay continued'.[20] It was eventually agreed that salary scales should be linked to those of the Swiss Federal Civil Service rather than the United Nations.[21] A more or less balanced budget was adopted in February 1977, thanks to UNEP support and to WWF's decision to pay SFr1,350,000 for a specified series of services.[22] The financial constraints made both IUCN and WWF re-think the proposal for a new joint headquarters in Geneva.[22] The Staff Liaison Committee argued that it would increase costs and bring no evident advantages.[23] Some IUCN members said they did not want to pay larger subscriptions simply because the administration became more costly.[24] The situation became complicated when the Canton of Geneva made it clear that they did not welcome the proposed building on the prestige site near the Botanical Garden, while the Canton of Vaud, in which Morges is located, made a bid to keep IUCN and WWF in its territory.[25] WWF said rather tartly that it had always wanted to stay in Morges and that it was IUCN that had forced the decision to move to Geneva.[24] The *coup de grâce* appears to have been given when an IUCN staff member infuriated the principal donor by questioning his business ethics (he had taken advantage of a perfectly legal tax avoidance opportunity by moving to Switzerland, but had been criticized in the German press for so doing).[9] Thereafter he would deal only with WWF.

The Conservation Coin Collection was another headache. Despite the optimism in Kinshasa, very little money was coming in and a dispute had arisen with the firm who administered the scheme.[22,26] Sir Frank Figgures, a towering presence on the UK financial scene, was called in to arbitrate.[26] A new high-powered group, including Prince Bernhard of the Netherlands, Luc Hoffmann, Donald Kuenen, Peter Scott and Bob Boote, together with the Director-General of WWF, Charles de Haes, and the acting DG of IUCN, Duncan Poore, were empowered to sign contracts with countries entering the scheme.[6,7] At the end of 1976, new income allowed the book deficit to be reduced by SFr75,000 but there were still major problems, and it was noted that in 1977 '*any income from the scheme would be balanced by expenditure*'.[22] Although it did eventually produce some funds, these were used primarily to support WWF projects in the countries where the revenue was generated, with the last remaining income used to pay for the travel of participants from those countries to the Third World Congress on National Parks in Bali in 1982).[27] Thus it never generated much funding for headquarters expenditure, and certainly offered no prospects of easing the 1976 crisis.

Early 1977 saw a further unhappy twist in the long saga of the appointment of a new Director-General. The hope at the start of 1976 had been that a successor to Gerardo Budowski would be secured in a very few months.[7] It seems clear that the President (with Kinshasa well behind him) wanted the job to go to Duncan Poore, and Mohamed Kassas supported him.[5, 28] But the Executive Committee demurred and wanted to consider a wider range of candidates.[29] Mohamed Kassas suggested that three qualities were essential in an IUCN Director-General: scientific merit, international experience and managerial ability.[30] By November 1976, the President noted a field of some 30 suggested candidates, among whom seven (including Duncan Poore and the man eventually appointed, David Munro) were 'serious'. One of them, Lee Talbot, was pushed strongly by Executive Board members, but declined consideration.[31] Duncan Poore was asked to soldier on, it being understood that he would be on the short list for the final interviews, whenever these were held. In February 1977 the Board got as far as appointing a selection panel, chaired by the President.[22] Interviews were held on 30 March 1977. Duncan Poore was not selected, but no appointment was made: he was left to get on with preparations for the Extraordinary Session of the General Assembly, to be held in Geneva in April. The World Health Organization generously agreed to provide the meeting rooms and interpretation facilities free of charge.[24]

The Extraordinary General Assembly: New Statutes and a New Bureau

The Assembly had been assigned three tasks: to revise the Statutes; to review progress in implementing the programme adopted in Kinshasa; and to confirm the appointment of a new Director-General.

A drafting panel consisting of a Vice-President, Don McMichael of Australia, the Vice-Chairman of the Commission on Environmental Policy, Law and Administration, Wolfgang Burhenne and the outgoing Deputy Director-General, Frank Nicholls, with Françoise Burhenne-Guilmin and Robert Prescott-Allen in support, was given the task of preparing proposed new Statutes. These were to be circulated to members for comments well before finalization. The Extraordinary General Assembly was to negotiate, but not adopt, a text which was to be submitted to a postal ballot of members.[7]

The proposed changes included the replacement of the Executive Board by a Council (which, however, would still have an Executive Committee, made up of members *'specifically competent in finance, management, public awareness etc'*). Two-thirds of the Councillors should represent regions, and they should be elected by the *whole* membership, not just those in their regions. A series of eight regions was defined, in a conscious attempt *'both to reflect the biodiversity regions and groupings of states which were politically compatible'.*[32] The President should be elected directly by the General Assembly but the Council should appoint the Chairs of Commissions (although the membership should be able to nominate candidates).[6] Officers (such as a Treasurer) should be elected.[22] The Director-General should be appointed by the Council, not elected by the General Assembly (a way of preventing another debacle like that at Kinshasa).

The new Statutes were affected by an important event late in 1976. Maurice Strong, architect of Stockholm and first Executive Director of UNEP, who had left the latter to attend to his business concerns as head of Petro-Canada, wrote to offer his services as a special consultant for IUCN.[22] It is rumoured that he said he would have no difficulty in raising US$1 million as a contribution to the chronic financial situation. Be that as it may, his offer was accepted with the enthusiasm of those who, looking into the teeth of dragons, hear the trumpet of the next shining knight in the hills.

The Executive Board indeed wondered whether Maurice Strong would be the next Director-General, but that was clearly unrealistic. The next idea was to make him Special Adviser to the President. But then came inspiration – turn the proposed Executive Committee of the reconstituted Council into a Bureau and make Maurice Strong its Chairman. It was so proposed, and so agreed. The drafting panel succeeded in getting all its main proposals adopted – except that on the election of Commission Chairs. The General Assembly insisted on retaining its right to elect them directly. The revised Statutes were adopted unanimously[25] and stood until a complete new version was agreed in 1996.

On 21 April 1977, immediately after the Extraordinary General Assembly, Maurice Strong was coopted to the Council with acclamation, and immediately elected Chairman of the Bureau. Accepting the job, he said that *'he saw his role as one of adding a dimension of support to the scientific qualities of IUCN and its professional excellence'.* That may, perhaps, be translated as: *'contributing his experience and expertise as a businessman to sort out the organization's chronically incompetent management'.* He was also still interested in developing IUCN as an operational agency, undertaking field projects that spanned conservation and development.[33] Lee Talbot, who had looked financial dragons as closely in the teeth as anyone, *'expressed his gratitude to Mr Strong for his important contribution to the cause of worldwide conservation. These remarks were received with acclamation.'*[25] Everybody must have felt lovely.

The Programme since Kinshasa

The programme had been the subject of a good deal of debate since Kinshasa. The General Assembly had decided that *'the role of IUCN should be to design strategies for action and to act as a stimulus and catalyst'.* It had also demanded a critical approach, based on a study of regional priorities for conservation, the choice of topics of greatest global importance, and a pragmatic evaluation of what was practicable and who should take the lead in doing it.[34] This implied pulling back from field operations, and acting rather more as a 'think tank' – something closer to the original vision and warmly supported by many members.[35] The Extraordinary Session in Geneva was now urged to accept a 'programme for the 1980s', with a build-up commencing in 1977.[24] The Commissions were to be used to the full, with IUCN acting as a catalyst to accelerate action through others. The culmination was to be a World Conservation Strategy.

Duncan Poore summed up the new approach in his report, which defined what the strategy would be about. His message was that conservation was about people.

> '*The Union is concerned with values more, I would say, even than with science. For science should be the servant not the master of mankind. Our strategy must be firmly based in realism but it must move ahead with vision. We should be the architects of guided change (call it development if you will) – guided change in the direction of increasing the well-being of mankind – not only the standard of living but the good life – but (and the but is all important) in such a way that the potential of the biosphere to support this good life is not diminished.*'[34]

Cooperation was clearly crucial, for any grandiose idea that IUCN could become a free-standing conservation agency running major programmes of its own must surely have been blown away by the chill winds from the Virunga volcanoes. The Ecosystems Conservation Group, set up by UNEP, was to bring UNESCO, FAO, IUCN and UNEP itself together to discuss which organization should do what, so making the whole programme more efficient and cohesive. The partnership with WWF meant that the latter also used the strategic analyses to spend its funds to the very best advantage.[34] Relations with WWF were clearly central, and a joint review committee was set up in 1976, involving one Vice-President from each organization (Don McMichael and Luc Hoffmann) and the two Director-Generals (Duncan Poore and Charles de Haes).[22] Known to some as the 'Grey Areas' Committee, '*its purpose was to look at real or potential areas of overlap between WWF and IUCN, and try to find sensible ways of dealing with them*'.[32] There was also to be one meeting a year between the Executive Committees, while WWF proposed to establish a Conservation Committee at Board level, to which IUCN was invited to send two members.

In the United Nations system, cooperation with UNEP remained crucial. The Government of Kenya agreed to allow IUCN to establish formal representation in Nairobi, with privileges including duty-free import of IUCN/WWF equipment.[7] Major Ian Grimwood was appointed IUCN representative to UNEP. A very high-level meeting in January 1977, involving Dr Mostafa Tolba, who had succeeded Maurice Strong as UNEP Executive Director, and other UNEP 'top brass', heard that '*UNEP wished to strengthen IUCN's capacity to act as a non-governmental organization in the ecosystem field...while no commitment could be given, IUCN could plan in the expectation of substantial financial support for a further four years. The parties concurred in the view that such support should be less than 50% of the total IUCN budget (probably of the order of one third)*'. There were to be regular meetings. The new contract would be negotiated in June or July. The Executive Committee congratulated Duncan Poore and the staff on their part in preparing such a successful outcome.

The Search for a New Director-General

The third task of the Extraordinary Session – confirming the appointment of a new Director-General – could not be done because nobody had been selected. But the item was on the agenda, and when it came the President, Donald Kuenen, made a speech[36] in which he said time and time again that Duncan Poore (who had not been told about what was coming) was not considered up to the job. It was acutely embarrassing. Judy Poore, Duncan's wife, was so incensed that she asked for an opportunity to address the Executive Board – and told them in no uncertain terms what she thought of their conduct (she was the daughter of a general, and sounded like one).[4]

Duncan Poore made it clear that if he was not to be confirmed as Director-General, he did not want to continue in an acting capacity.[37] The Council therefore resolved that '*until a Director General is appointed...the Chairman of the Bureau shall exercise the powers of the Director General as provided for in the Statutes*'.[25] Maurice Strong wrote to Duncan Poore on 2 May 1977 making it quite clear that the latter continued '*as Scientific Director and the most senior member of the staff at present with IUCN. You will retain...responsibility for the programme and any other responsibilities that I may delegate to you from time to time...You will become officer in charge during my absences from Morges...*'.[38] Duncan Poore remained as Scientific Director of IUCN until February 1978 when he returned to the United Kingdom, becoming Professor of Forest Science at Oxford University in 1980. The Council and Bureau, who may well have felt a bit sheepish over the way they had treated him, agreed to find a 'suitable means' of recognition. A presentation was eventually authorized in February 1978:[39,40] it took the form of Swiss pewter beer mugs.[4] He was elected a Member of Honour at the Ashkhabad Assembly.

The Bureau was given the job of serving as selection panel for a substantive DG, and at its meeting at Morges on 31 May 1977, it decided to offer the post to Dr David A Munro '*for an initial period to 31 December 1978 on agreed conditions*'. David Munro was a wildlife biologist who had served for five years as the Director of the Canadian Wildlife Service, and had been Assistant Deputy Minister in the Department of Northern Territories and Indian Affairs. After a variety of other posts in Canada, including the Directorship of International Affairs in Environment, Canada, he went to UNEP in 1976 as Special Adviser to the Executive Director. The hand of Maurice Strong can be seen here, for he had been behind the UNEP appointment, and knew that Munro was finding the work frustrating because Mostafa Tolba, Strong's successor, kept a tight personal control on things. It was not difficult to lure him to IUCN, which offered '*an attractive opportunity to broaden experience and knowledge*'.[41] There was no interview: Maurice Strong persuaded the Bureau that they had the right man at last, and David Munro arrived in Morges in the summer of 1977.

Duncan Poore passed on a tidy administration, with rigorous accounting procedures, an agreed salary structure, a contractual agreement with WWF, renewed good relations with UNESCO, and three regional desk officers for Africa, Asia and Latin America.[42] John Kundaeli (who had been on the staff at Mweka College) came for Africa, Chew Wee Lek for Asia, and Felipe Matos for Latin America. They were the first staff members from the developing world to handle the affairs of their regions directly in IUCN headquarters, and their appointment marked an important small step in adjusting the North–South balance.[11,41] There was an agreed strategy and programme. The World Conservation Strategy was being prepared, albeit with some doubts over just what was really needed. During the six months that they worked together, Munro and Poore convened the first-ever meeting of Commission Chairs to discuss a joint approach to programming. Calm seemed to have succeeded chaos.

Achievement at Ashkhabad

The General Assembly held in Ashkhabad in 1978 was seen to '*mark a radical change in the world conservation movement. And remarkably for an organization which in recent years has delighted in acerbic and* ad hominem *public disputation, IUCN's 30th anniversary meeting was extraordinarily harmonious.*'[43] The journalist who wrote those words was the same Jon Tinker of *New Scientist* who had written so rudely about WWF's role two years before. He went on to highlight three decisions – to back the World Charter for Nature, to support the World Conservation Strategy and '*to switch its emphasis decidedly towards the needs of the Third World.*' Summing up, Tinker commented that '*the fate of wildlife and natural resources will increasingly be decided in political arenas in Africa, Asia and Latin America*'. IUCN '*has taken some important steps towards arming itself for these future battles*'.[43] As Reuben Olembo of Kenya (and UNEP) commented, '*the "old school" publicly realized that a new conservation tide had begun to flow. That of course encouraged us to proceed along the path we had chosen for the World Conservation Strategy*'.[44]

David Munro reported in Ashkhabad that relations between IUCN and WWF had never been better. WWF had raised the level of its financial support – perhaps because its confidence in the management of IUCN had been restored. In fact, in both 1978 and 1979 the WWF contribution to IUCN central and programme costs was just below SFr2 million, and in the two following years it rose well above that figure.[45] The respective roles of the two organizations had been redefined, and there was a great deal of cross-representation on committees and in meetings. IUCN continued to advise WWF on programmes and to screen project proposals, and David Munro told the General Assembly that Charles de Haes had decided to transfer the WWF Project Management Department to IUCN and give the Union's Secretariat responsibility for managing all field projects.[9,6]

The operational role of IUCN was thus strengthened. In Asia and the Pacific there were over 50 active, WWF-funded, projects; in Latin America the number was 35, and in Africa, 27 (with 11 more under development). WWF was also funding 25 projects in Europe. The work-load in parts of South-East Asia was such that the first country programme with a joint WWF/IUCN Field Officer – a young American named Jeffrey McNeely – had been established in 1977.[47] With this, and the formal agreement in Kenya, IUCN was taking its first steps towards presence on the ground in the developing world.

Since 1972, the developing world had been much more strongly represented on the IUCN Executive Board/Council than in the early years of the Union. In 1975–77 the North–South ratio had moved from about 90:10 to about 60:40. The developing world seemed to do less well after the 1977 Extraordinary General Assembly simply because the new Statutes made Commission Chairs voting members of Council.[48] But it is clear that the Union was now positively committed to strengthening its links with the South, and it voted funds to help its Councillors to attend meetings. The change in balance was also advanced in Ashkhabad by the election of the first IUCN President from a developing country.

Two outstanding candidates had been considered for nomination as Donald Kuenen's successor. The Board's first choice was Eskandar Firouz of Iran, Deputy Prime Minister of his country, Vice-President of IUCN, architect of the Ramsar Convention and Chair of the 1977 Special Session (where his selection had been announced). But things went wrong for him. The Shah's brother, Prince Abdurreza, who was a hunting devotee, had become President of CIC, the Conseil International de la Chasse, and the election of Firouz to a much more important post would have caused political difficulties. As it was, Firouz left his government post during 1977 and ceased to be in contention for IUCN.[49]

Fortunately another outstanding developing country scientist was available. Mohamed Kassas, Professor of Botany at the University of Cairo, had a worldwide reputation as a specialist in desert ecology, and as a committed conservationist. He had been closely associated with the arid zone and MAB programmes of UNESCO.[50] He wrote and spoke well, and at times with passion. He was on excellent terms with his fellow Egyptian, Mostafa Tolba, the Executive Director of UNEP, and advised him on many technical matters. It was a popular choice. '*After his five European and one American predecessors, the gentle wisdom of this distinguished and internationally experienced ecologist will prove a major asset to the International Union*', wrote Jon Tinker.[43] The team of an Egyptian President and a Canadian Director-General worked well, and had a 'correct' ring to it in a world that was becoming increasingly sensitive over the North–South divide. The pattern then established – that so far as practicable, if the Director-General came from the North, the President should come from the South – has endured.

The Ashkhabad Assembly had its bizarre features. The location, on the southern edge of the plains of Turkmenia, under the Kopet Dag mountains that form the frontier with Iran, was not easy of access. There were problems with the host country over the issue of visas for Israeli, South African and South Korean members. It is an IUCN rule that any country offering to host a General Assembly must allow the entry of accredited delegates – provided that the individuals do not have criminal or other records that make them personally inadmissible. The USSR insisted that while they would not bar these nationalities, they would choose for themselves which individuals to let in. The Israelis and South Africans were told to come to Geneva and get their visas there, helped by Robert Prescott-Allen and Richard Herring (the new Director of Finance, on secondment from the Government of Canada, who had arrived soon after David Munro took up his post). The decision was delayed, and David Munro told the Russians that unless they acted he and the Secretariat would not travel and the General Assembly would not open. The visas were delivered to Geneva airport at the last possible moment, while the Director-General, staff and delegates waited.[41,51] The delegates were still banned from post-conference tours,[52] but after talks with the Russian Liaison Officer Donald Kuenen reported that protests would be unreasonable as the Organizing Committee for the Assembly was not responsible for the ban, which came from 'higher up'.

More alarming was a running battle between participants from South Korea and North Korea – with the latter as the aggressors. Lee Talbot recalls that he:

> '*was asked to intervene by the South Koreans, whom I knew, because the North Koreans were physically assaulting them in the lodging halls and threatening various types of mayhem. Donald Kuenen did not wish to get involved so I took the matter up with our Russian hosts who assured me that things would be taken care of. Apparently they were,*

and the problem seemed to go away until the end of the Assembly... Many of the delegates, South Koreans and some Americans among them, flew to Moscow to get flights to their respective homes. After the delegates de-planed at the Moscow airport a gang of North Koreans tried to attack the southerners while they were getting their luggage. The Americans, several of whom were quite large, surrounded the South Koreans and literally pushed off the North Korean thugs who continued to shout and threaten the southerners and try to get them. The South Koreans had to go into Moscow, so to help protect them from the North Koreans a car from the US Embassy, which was there to pick up some of the American officials, took the South Koreans instead. A car with North Koreans chased them, ramming the American car and repeatedly trying to run it off the road. The skilful driver of the US Embassy car (who was a Russian) evaded them, and stopped at a Police post on the outskirts of Moscow, and the North Korean thugs drove away...'[53]

These events did not mar the achievements of a reassuring Assembly. David Munro reported action to implement the agreements of Kinshasa and Geneva under four headings: monitoring of the status of species, ecosystems and protected areas; planning of programmes and projects; promotion of action by governments, inter-governmental organizations and other bodies; and the provision of assistance and advice.[46] The finances were much improved, but while WWF and UNEP each contributed about one-third of the total IUCN budget, membership dues only supplied 16 per cent. The Bureau wanted a 60 per cent increase, which would still leave the members supporting only a quarter of the budget.[40]

A lot had been done to monitor the status of species and ecosystems. The SSC had benefited from the support of Earl Baysinger, seconded from the US Fish and Wildlife Service as Executive Officer. All four volumes of the Red Data Book were being revised: the work on fishes was finished, that on birds half done, that on amphibians and reptiles was under way and that on mammals just starting. A list of rare and threatened European plants had been published by the Council of Europe. A plant Red Data Book was being compiled. Cooperation with botanic gardens was becoming ever closer. There had been interventions in support of the last sizeable forest habitat for Sumatran rhinoceros in Peninsular Malaysia, for the Kagera River basin in East Africa, for coastal ecosystems in Indonesia, and for whales in Chile and Panama. The scientific basis for regulating the annual harvest of harp seals in Canada had been questioned, and studies commissioned of the implications of krill fishery and other resource use in Antarctica. The Secretariat managed a large amount of project work: the marine programme alone had 40 fully operational projects and 30 under development. Some were species-oriented, and of these a study of the Mediterranean monk seal and how to conserve it was regarded as most urgent, because of its highly threatened status. There were also projects on threatened marine areas (notably the European Wadden Sea). On land, conservation reviews of the tropical rain forests of South-east Asia and Latin America were beginning.[46]

The protected areas programme had also made strides, thanks in part to the arrival in October 1977 of Hal Eidsvik on secondment from Parks Canada to serve as Executive Officer. He was also the Deputy Chair of CNPPA (he was appointed at the Special Session in Geneva when Kenton Miller became Chairman), but stepped down after a year because of possible conflicts between his roles at the Council.[54] Miller and Eidsvik set about rebuilding the Commission after its own upheavals in Kinshasa, and by 1978 the agenda was a long one and the membership was passing the hundred mark. A completely new edition of the UN List was being planned; a two-volume *World Directory of National Parks* and other protected areas was completed; a *Directory of Outstanding Landscapes* in nine European countries was also out and work was beginning on a *Directory of Wetlands in the Western Palaearctic*. A working group reviewed the confused diversity of categories of protected area found in national and international legislation, discovering that over 140 were in use. With the help of Zane Smith from the US Forest Service, these were analysed and rationalized – and the final framework included forest reserves with multiple resource management objectives which none the less contributed importantly to the conservation of nature and natural resources. The proposals for new IUCN categories were published in 1978.[55,56]

Following Kinshasa, there was continuing debate about parks policy. The collapse of African elephant populations, especially in Kenya, had been documented by Iain Douglas-Hamilton and his colleagues: it was estimated that in 1976 the ivory trade, much of it illegal, accounted for between 100,000 and 400,000 elephants a year. Walter Lusigi predicted that the problem would remain until wildlife conservation was made meaningful to African citizens and local people were involved in it.[57] He urged Hal Eidsvik to try the MAB biosphere reserves model, and found a welcome for his ideas – no doubt partly because of the change in attitude begun in Kinshasa. But 'hardliners' who argued that parks should be free from resident people, with access only for car-borne sightseers, were in the majority at this period.[57]

There was another nasty battle over the utilization of wild vicuña in Peru during the same period. The government policy – supported by cooperating overseas development agencies and international conservation organizations including IUCN and WWF – was that once populations of vicuña had built up to levels defined in part by the carrying capacity of the rangeland, old indigenous techniques for harvesting animals would be restored. The benefits would be shared between the indigenous communities, the management agency and central government.[56] Marc Dourojeanni, as IUCN Regional Councillor and Vice-President, strongly supported this plan. Felipe Benavides, a passionately outspoken advocate of wildlife preservation, bitterly disputed it . There was a flurry of argument and counter-argument, press articles and even lawsuits. The President of WWF International, John Loudon, invited Benavides to a meeting in New York attended by Luc Hoffmann, Peter Scott, Russell Train, Ian Grimwood, J MacLain Stewart of McKinsey's and Charles de Haes and persuaded him not to oppose limited culling.[9] Grimwood and de Haes travelled on to Peru to make the terms of the agreement known – but Benavides reneged on it, and after further argument was asked to resign from the WWF International Board while WWF Peru was disenfranchised.[9] The row also ended Marc Dourojeanni's period as an elected Regional Councillor and IUCN Vice-President.[58]

Promoting national and international action was clearly seen as very important. IUCN had criticized the draft text for the new UN Convention on the Law of the Sea, expressing '*disappointment at the lack of a systematic and coherent approach to the environmental management of the world's oceans*' and spelling out possible improvements, which the US delegation had received with enthusiasm and which other IUCN members were urged to press.[59] The UN Conference on Desertification, held in Nairobi, had expanded its agreed action plan to take in IUCN points. Ecological guidelines for development in arid and semi-arid lands and high mountain regions had been produced. There had been significant input to the UNESCO/UNEP

Intergovernmental Conference on Environmental Education, held at Tbilisi. Thailand was being advised on a National Conservation Plan, and Indonesia, Jordan, Malawi and Panama on legislation. CITES, the Ramsar Convention, the Migratory Species Convention, the World Heritage Convention and the European Convention for the Conservation of Wildlife and Natural Habitats had all been supported. The Environmental Law Centre had continued to monitor developments in international and national law and extended its database.[46]

As the Assembly concluded, the membership had every reason for confidence that the Union was once again in good heart, under a Director-General with a calm, collegiate style and a grasp on organization, programme and budget.[54]

The Commissions Reviewed

The Commission programmes remained at the heart of IUCN's endeavours. The first meeting of Chairs with the Director-General had been held in January 1978.[41,60] David Munro recalls that he was impressed by the vision of those who created such voluntary networks as a means of bringing informed opinion into a body with slender means and an over-stretched Secretariat.[41] However, he noted at the same time that the Commissions could easily be seized by centrifugal force. The SSC, and its specialist groups, operated very much on their own, and '*you only needed to attend an SSC meeting to step into another world*'. The SSC could have become an independent body, but both it and IUCN (and WWF, to whom it was particularly important because saving endangered and appealing species was the soundest basis for fundraising) would have lost in the process. The Commissions gained semi-autonomy because the Chairs were elected by the General Assembly (the move to transfer this power to Council had failed at the 1977 Special Session). They therefore felt that they had direct authority to execute their programmes.[54] The Commissions seemed particularly attractive to Americans, who used the machinery to set up and run their chosen groups – and with the rising tide of US prosperity there were funds to support such initiatives.[41]

The meeting between the Director-General and Chairs had identified two keys to success: adequate coordination of Commission activities, and adequate support of them by the Secretariat.[60] Hal Eidsvik's view was that a good Chair and a good Executive Officer, working together properly, guaranteed success: a Commission could survive when one only of the two was able and energetic, but weakness on both sides was fatal.[54] As it was, only the Survival Service Commission and the Commission on National Parks and Protected Areas had full-time Executive Officers.

There was particular concern over the Commission on Education. It had lost the services of Jan Čeřovský in January 1973, when he was recalled by his Government and accused of being too 'pro-imperialist': part of his difficulties may have arisen because of his strong Christian faith.[61] Its mandate was not clear, especially with the advent of the new International Environmental Education Programme (IEEP), and in March 1979 Vice-President Bob Boote pointed to the danger of duplicating the activities of UNESCO, UNEP or WWF.[62] Argumentation over rival candidates had blocked the appointment of Don Aldridge, Council's nominee for the Chair at Ashkhabad. Professor Pierre Goeldlin of Lausanne, the Acting Chair, wanted to hand over as soon as possible. He was frank about the problems, notably '*the difficulties presented by the abstract nature of educational concepts and the wide scope of the subject*'.[63]

The review '*recommended concentration on out-of-school education aimed at priority target groups, and had identified projects so that the new Commission work could start right away*'. The situation was not resolved until November 1979, when two former UNESCO staff members, Dr Al Baez of the United States, a physicist who had worked in science education (and was, incidentally, the father of the well-known singer, Joan Baez) and Julia Marton-Lefevre (who held a senior staff post in ICSU) were appointed Chair and Deputy.[64] Under their leadership, the Commission produced an information booklet on the WCS for decision-makers, a multi-media pack and illustrated glossary for teachers, an environmental education activities handbook, and a guidebook to assist young leaders in the formation of wildlife clubs.[65]

The Commission on Environmental Planning was expected to be a spearhead for thought about the nature of the sustainable development process. It also addressed problems in urban fringes, devastated landscapes, the links between cultural values and beliefs and conservation, and resource management tools for indigenous Arctic communities.[65] In contrast, the Commission on Ecology was clearly at a crossroads. As its Chair, Professor Derrick Ovington, had told the General Assembly, it '*had a leading, innovative, role in the early development of IUCN. Initially its activities were wide-ranging but as new Commissions have been established and ecologists appointed to the staff of IUCN there has been a progressive change in emphasis*'. It was now to focus on the theory and practice of conservation, on major ecological changes and their consequences, on methods for evaluating the status of resources and environment, and on providing advice on management issues. There were 16 projects, five of them led by scientists from the developing world, and most of the studies were in the South.[66] A Council member from Kenya, Professor Tom Odhiambo, suggested the management of savannas should also be addressed.[63]

There was little need to tamper with the three Commissions for which IUCN was most famous – SSC, CNPPA and CEPLA. There was no counterpart to the SSC in the whole world. It had no difficulty in attracting experts to serve on its specialist groups. Its Red Data Books and Action Plans were universally respected. In 1974 it had set up a Threatened Plants Committee, and in 1978 it had produced the first Red Data Book on Plants, compiled at Kew by Dr Ronald Melville and Hugh Synge. The List covered 89 countries.[65,67]

In Peter Scott SSC had an outstanding communicator as leader. In 1979 it had strengthened its central capacity through the establishment of a data unit – the Species Conservation Monitoring Unit (SCMU). This brought together three hitherto separate activities – the preparation of Red Data Books, the collection of data on trade in species listed under CITES, and the operation of the Threatened Plants Committee. A Protected Areas Data Unit was added to the group soon afterwards. By June 1980 SCMU (incorporated as part of the IUCN Secretariat) had seven staff and was fully operational under the supervision of Gren Lucas, Director of the Herbarium at the Royal Botanic Gardens, Kew, England and SSC Vice-Chairman for Plant Matters.[68] By 1981 it had become the Conservation Monitoring Centre, with four component units divided between Kew and Cambridge: it was computerized and was deep into the production of new Red Data Books.[65] It was also linked into, and worked as part of, the UNEP Global Environment Monitoring System (GEMS). The SSC, coming to the end of an era with Sir Peter Scott's impending retirement from the Chair, proposed in November 1980 that it be renamed 'Species Survival Commission': Council approved, and the familiar modern name came into use.

Very similarly, the Commission on National Parks and Protected Areas was the world network linking 'parks people'. It led in the production of the UN List, which was the global reference work. Kenton Miller and Hal Eidsvik worked together as a highly effective team, from 1977 until Eidsvik's return to Canada in 1980. It was Miller who picked up the work done by Ray Dasmann on the classification of protected areas, and elaborated the list of ten categories that passed into worldwide use in 1979.[54] The period also saw the adoption of the generic term 'protected area' in place of the more restricted (and ambiguous) 'national park'.[69] From 1979 onwards, with UNESCO's backing, the Commission produced *Parks* magazine, which was at least potentially the 'house journal' of the national parks movement. In 1981 the establishment of the Protected Areas Data Unit allowed the mass of information on the 2000 national parks and other major protected areas around the world (with a total area of over 3 million square kilometres) to be computerized. Between 1978 and 1981 it also produced major volumes on *Conserving Africa's Natural Heritage* and *Conserving the Natural Heritage of Latin America and the Caribbean*.[65]

One evident need was for some kind of systematic basis for analysing how far the world protected area system included all the main ecosystems of the globe. Professor Miklos Udvardy had defined a series of 198 biogeographical provinces, and Hal Eidsvik seized on these as a framework.[54] The 1980 edition of the UN List was the first to be structured by biomes, and to emphasize that Categories I to V would have priority so far as the Commission's work was concerned. The major realms of Udvardy's classification also provided a non-political organizational structure for the Commission, which appointed a Vice-Chair for each realm: it thus became the first Commission to become regionalized, albeit with different units from those used for IUCN Council elections.[54,56]

And the Commission on Environmental Policy, Law and Administration was for its part a unique network of the top experts on environmental law, including High Court judges as well as leading academics, while in the Environmental Law Centre there was a unique computerized law library, database and reference system. In 1980 it started work on Islamic law in relation to conservation.[70] The Commission, centre and database provided the foundation for much of IUCN's support to international conventions, for weighty publications including a multi-volume series of *Multilateral Treaties–International Environmental Law*, and for responses to many requests for information.[65] They were flanked by ICEL (International Council for Environmental Law) founded in 1969 in New Delhi with the aim of promoting exchanges of information on legal, administrative and policy matters: it had two regional governors from each of ten regions, and since 1975 had published the well-known journal *Environmental Policy and Law*. Wolfgang and Françoise Burhenne played a key role in it – as in all the other elements of IUCN's legal nexus.[71]

One important outcome of the 1979 review was the much fuller and more regular reports to Council on the work of the Commissions which characterized 1980 and the years that followed, and allowed much closer integration with other elements of the programme. As in earlier years, catalysing that work by providing adequate support appeared highly cost-effective and in November 1980 the Council resolved that each should, as a minimum, have an Executive Officer with Secretary and travel support SFr20,000 to support the volunteer network, and SFr20,000 for programme development. These two latter figures are the origin of the 'Chairman's Fund' later placed at the disposal of the Commissions.[70]

Managing the Union

As Director-General, David Munro found himself concentrating on three particular issues.[41] The World Conservation Strategy was one – and its preparation, launch and follow-up took a great deal of time. Even more effort went into securing the money to keep the programme going. Here UNEP presented the main challenge, for it was itself in financial difficulties due to a situation not wholly unlike that which had threatened the infant IUPN 30 years before. At Stockholm, governments had agreed to set up the new organization, but they refused to make any major and binding new financial commitments. They demanded a small, coordinating Secretariat, with only a handful of posts borne on the regular budget of the UN. They insisted that the new programmes UNEP was to catalyse should be paid for by a *voluntary* fund, and as the glamour of Stockholm waned and new preoccupations emerged, the pledges to that voluntary fund dropped. It was inevitable that IUCN faced a struggle in winning continuing support from UNEP.

David Munro built a harmonious team, noting that '*he had never before encountered a staff that gave so willingly of its time*'. The need for effective programme coordination was evident, and soon after the Ashkhabad Assembly he appointed Adrian Phillips (with whom he had worked at UNEP in Nairobi), as Director of Programme. Phillips created a Programme Planning Advisory Group (PPAG), designed to advise the Director-General on the development of the IUCN programme (including the programme of the Commissions) and its relation to the programme of WWF.[72] The Munro–Phillips partnership gave IUCN, for the first time, a mechanism for preparing a systematic programme that reflected the needs of IUCN members around the world. The Commissions were centrally involved, and the Chairs devoted weeks of effort each year to consulting their members, and summarizing their proposals.[70] From autumn 1979 onwards the Council regularly reviewed the whole programme of the Secretariat and Commissions and had available to them full details also of the work supported by WWF.[64]

The UNEP-led Ecosystems Conservation Group (ECG) also began, in 1979, to undertake 'thematic joint planning' and to align the programmes of IUCN, UNEP, UNESCO and FAO.[46, 63] ECG was unique in linking three United Nations organizations with a non-UN body, and its existence was recognition of IUCN's standing as the focus of the conservation world. It was the stranger, because the UN system was in this period distinctly stand-offish when it came to recognizing outside bodies. NGOs – even those granted consultative status with ECOSOC – were treated as poor relations, admitted to only some meetings and then generally, like children in a past era, to be 'seen but not heard'. In meetings like the UNEP Governing Council, NGOs were permitted to speak only by the consent of the governments, and then only after all the governments had spoken – which made it almost impossible to comment meaningfully on a specific topic under consideration. But in ECG, IUCN was treated as a full partner. Its programme was also, at a slightly later date, noted in SWMTEP (the System Wide Medium Term Environmental Programme of the United Nations).[41] The mechanism was never developed to full potential (and ECG did become a dreadful talking shop), but there were important principles here.

David Munro's third challenge was to work with Charles de Haes to find a new joint headquarters, for Morges was impossibly confined.[41,72,73] WWF was empowered to purchase the best place they could find, on behalf of both organizations,[9] and Charles de Haes discovered a building near Geneva airport which was big enough and affordable (it was offered at a concessionary price) – but in a most unattractive location. He made an oral agreement to purchase – and only a few days later, a much more suitable empty modern building at Gland, near Nyon, between Geneva and Lausanne, came to light. With equal good fortune it was discovered that the Geneva building was scheduled to have an autoroute extension built past it at window height – and this gave de Haes the material grounds needed for withdrawing his offer! The old site near the Geneva Botanical Garden was sold; Louis Franck, Treasurer of WWF, raised the additional money needed – and the building in Gland was purchased for SFr2.8 million, leaving SFr200,000 for fitting it out.[9,74] The Vaudois authorities helped the purchase by agreeing to waive certain financial claims on the building.[9]

Neither Gland nor the new headquarters was beautiful. Gland may once have been a sleepy Swiss village centred on a cluster of old farms, but by 1980 it was a fast-growing community set about with commercial buildings and apartment blocks. It had a go-ahead Syndic (Chief Officer) who wanted to make it rival the nearby towns of Nyon and Rolle and doubtless welcomed the advent of two world-famous organizations. The building itself was constructed in the modular form common at the time: it was practical, offered enough accommodation on four floors, and had ample car parking. It did lack a conference room, but Louis Franck donated SFr200,000 to convert the basement garage and was persuaded to let it be named after him. Other Trustees gave money to convert parts of the basement into the library and photolibrary, and the former company Chairman's office into a boardroom: their names were commemorated in the Kleinwort Library, the Richard and Beryl Ivey Photolibrary and the Audrey Mars Room.[9] A written agreement between the partners specified that the ownership of the building was vested in WWF, but that IUCN had a right to occupy half of it: there was to be a sharing of common costs and were it sold, the proceeds would be shared.

The process of moving in began in July 1979, and the building was opened formally by HRH Prince Philip, Duke of Edinburgh, newly elected President of WWF International, in June 1980.[62–64,75] In November 1980 Charles de Haes told the Council that '*the last 15 months had brought a great step forward in cooperation*', identifying three special achievements – the move into shared headquarters, the launch of the World Conservation Strategy, and the China project.[70] There was joint programme planning, and IUCN provided all scientific services for WWF, very much as had been intended in the beginning. There was close cooperation in many specialist activities including the monitoring of wildlife trade, where IUCN maintained a special unit in the Conservation Monitoring Centre and WWF and IUCN were joint partners in TRAFFIC, the Trade Records Analysis of Fauna and Flora in Commerce, which relied on WWF-supported trade data centres in Washington, Frankfurt, Nairobi and Tokyo.[65] In 1978 Charles de Haes had appointed Lee Talbot, former IUCN Vice-President, as his Director of Conservation and Special Scientific Adviser as a further means of improving relations with IUCN.[9,26]

The move to the new headquarters in Gland brought with it a further linkage between the two organizations. IUCN had already been given responsibility for running the field projects on behalf of both partners, and it was now agreed that it did not make sense for the organizations to retain separate financial, personnel and administrative services. '*Because WWF was more "business" oriented, as opposed to IUCN's more scientific activity, we agreed that WWF should carry out the bulk of these services on our behalf*' while IUCN handled project management and the library.[76] Dr Stephan Suwald, Director of Administration for WWF, therefore became

IUCN's head of finance, and IUCN's accounting staff transferred to his unit. The shared units were, of course, responsible for servicing the two organizations and their Director-Generals as the latter required.[9]

The World Charter for Nature

One document before the General Assembly in Ashkhabad was a direct product of Kinshasa – the draft text of what later became the World Charter for Nature.[77] It had started with the inaugural address in Kinshasa by the then President of Zaire, Mobutu Sese Seko. In it he asserted that *'the seas, the oceans, the upper atmosphere belong to the human community. One cannot freely over-use such international resources...If I had any advice for you, I would suggest the establishment of a Charter for Nature.'*

Or was that the start? The concept of a World Convention on the Protection of Nature had been around since Fontainebleau and Lake Success (see Chapters 2 and 3). The Caracas General Assembly had *'chosen to substitute a World Charter inspired by the Universal Declaration of the Rights of Man'*. Soon after its foundation, the infant World Wildlife Fund had drawn up a 'World Wildlife Charter' *'for ultimate presentation to the United Nations'*.[78] That document, recorded in Peter Scott's book *The Launching of the New Ark*, is very different from the World Charter which reached the UN nearly 20 years later. But the strands of consciousness may well have extended down the years, given the fact that some of the same people were involved.

President Mobutu's proposal in Kinshasa was written into his speech by David Matuka Kabala, then Director of Zaire's national parks, who later joined UNESCO and died tragically in Paris.[50] It was taken up by IUCN, which set up a task force from the Commission on Environmental Policy, Law and Administration led by Wolfgang Burhenne. The task force, which included Nicholas Robinson (later to be Chair of the Commission on Environmental Law) and Mike McCloskey of the Sierra Club, met in Bonn with the staff of the Environmental Law Centre (notably Françoise Burhenne-Guilmin and Dan Navid) and prepared a text which was presented for discussion at the General Assembly in Ashkhabad in 1978.[79] The new President, Mohamed Kassas, flew with Burhenne and Munro to Zaire to present the final text to Mobutu on 26 November 1979. The Zairois sent them first-class tickets.[80]

There is a saying that *'it is better to travel hopefully than to arrive'*. They arrived – and Mobutu was nowhere to be seen. After two days of waiting, Wolfgang Burhenne and David Munro felt that they had to depart. *'You are developed country people'*, said Kassas. *'For you, two days is enough. I am an African. I remain until the President is ready to see me.'* Next day he was received for breakfast at Mobutu's country palace, where food was served on gold plates.[41,80] The ostentation in the midst of poverty shocked him.

President Mobutu offered Zaire's continuing assistance in promoting the text at the UN, and his Ambassador was the channel of communication when it was presented to the Secretary-General in 1980, in time for discussion at the 35th Session of the UN General Assembly.[77] In October, the Secretary-General asked member states for their views. There followed a not-unfamiliar round of criticism and revision, spread over two years so that the final text did not come to the vote until the 37th Session in 1982.

The final stage was bizarre. Most states had commented favourably, but the United States asked for further delay so that a small working group could sort out the

Paul Sarasin, whose vision inspired
the creators of IUPN. He is pictured
(standing) in the Swiss National Park

Pieter van Tienhoven, 1953

Lake Success, 1949. Roger Heim is seated on the left of the table, and Charles
Bernard (in shirtsleeves) and Hal Coolidge are on the right

Salzburg, 1953. Charles Bernard, Marguerite Caram,
Jean-Paul Harroy and Roger Heim

Wolfgang Burhenne and Marguerite Caram, *c.*1958

Ed Graham, Jean Baer, Julian Huxley and
L G Sagini (Kenyan Minister for Natural Resources), Nairobi, 1963

The Executive Board at Les Uttins, Morges, probably in May 1966.
Seated (from left): Luc Hoffmann, Donald Kuenen, Hal Coolidge, Frank Fraser Darling.
Standing: Colin Holloway, (unidentified), Jan Čeřovský, Kai Curry-Lindahl, Kay Williams,
Françoise Burhenne-Guilmin, (unidentified), (unidentified), Gerardo Budowski,
R. J. Benthem, (unidentified), Jean-Paul Harroy, (unidentified), Joe Berwick, John Corner,
Wolfgang Burhenne, Hugh Elliott, Peter Scott, (unidentified, possibly Hans Luther),
Thane Riney, Z. Futehally, David Wasawo, Barton Worthington, Johannes Goudswaard,
(unidentified).
NB Those present at the Board, not certainly identified, are: W A L Fuller, H E Luther
(FAO), A Dhondt (IYF), H J Angelo, J Petter, Fritz Vollmar, Noel Simon, M A J Warland,
M-J Dutoit

David Munro and Donald Kuenen, Director-General and President, 1978

Françoise Burhenne-Guilmin, Lee Talbot and Don McMichael, *c.*1980

Jean-Paul Harroy, Chair of CNPPA, presents Harold Coolidge
with a book on World National Parks, 1967

Mohamed Kassas,
June 1982

Peter Scott and Pierre Goeldlin, *c.*1980

David Munro, Charles de Haes and Lee Talbot, *c.*1979

Kenton Miller presents Rajiv Gandhi with the John C Phillips Memorial Medal awarded to his late mother, Indira Gandhi

Four DGs and two Acting DGs: from left, Gerardo Budowski, Kenton Miller, Ray Dasmann, David Munro, Lee Talbot and Duncan Poore, probably at the meeting to consider the management problems of IUCN in 1987

Prince Bernhard of the Netherlands greets Queen Noor of Jordan at the
IUCN 40th anniversary celebrations in 1988

Martin Holdgate, Brice Lalonde (French Minister for the Environment), Monkombu
Swaminathan and Frédéric Briand in Gland in 1988 to discuss arrangements for the
40th anniversary

Sir Shridath (Sonny) Ramphal and Martin Holdgate, 1991

Jay Hair presents Parvez Hassan with a certificate on his retirement as Councillor. Cath Wallace (retiring Councillor) and Ted Trzyna (retiring Commission Chair) look on. Montreal, 1996

Signing a UNEP–IUCN agreement at the Wasaa Centre, Nairobi, in 1994. From left: Perez Olindo, Elizabeth Dowdeswell (Executive Director, UNEP), David McDowell, Mersie Ejigu (IUCN representative, East Africa)

Maurice Strong (centre) and Jay Hair (right) discuss an IUCN/Harper MacRae Pty Ltd publication in Montreal

remaining difficulties. The US Ambassador nailed the Stars and Stripes to his mast, stating: '*If we act on this draft Charter today, my Government will reluctantly have to vote against it.*' Why? On the face of it, the objection was to the mandatory rather than exhortatory language the Charter uses at some points – with words like 'shall' rather than 'should'. But many observers thought that this was not the real reason, and some described the US action as '*a thinly veiled pressure tactic*' designed to mollify South American states that had been aggrieved by United States support for the United Kingdom in the Falklands war.[77]

It was true that the language of the Charter caused concern in quarters other than Washington DC. The Latin American states also disliked the quasi-mandatory language. India and Canada were among the countries who felt that the draft could be improved. The European countries were more positive, stressing that the Charter was complementary to the World Conservation Strategy (which, of course, had been published by then), and that its implementation needed to be closely tied to the programme of UNEP. But the mood was against further delay, and the motion for postponement was lost, by 73 votes to 36, so that the United States had no choice but to register the only vote of opposition. Resolution 37/7 was carried on 28 October 1982, with 111 states in favour, 18 abstentions and the United States against.[77] Two abstainers said afterwards that had they understood the proposal better, they would have voted in favour! Wolfgang Burhenne was overjoyed, and prompted the Elizabeth Haub Foundation to prepare bronze plaques bearing the text in several languages, for presentation and display in key buildings around the world.[81]

The Peak of Achievement – the World Conservation Strategy

The World Conservation Strategy (WCS) was not only IUCN's most important product in the late 1970s, but possibly its most important single contribution in the whole of its history. As Mohamed Kassas has put it:

> '*the process that produced this document, the launching of the document and the widespread acceptance of it, established the intellectual leadership of IUCN: other agencies rushed to cooperate with IUCN in the Ecosystems Conservation Group and set plans...to assist countries develop national conservation strategies. Here IUCN entered the business of technical assistance. Subsequent documents were good* (Caring for the Earth) *but did not add to the IUCN weight.*'[82]

There had been discussions about the need for a strategic approach to conservation as far back as 1969, but the project only got into the programme in about 1975 – some say as a result of prompting by UNEP, who saw it as a way of bringing the rather incoherent programme of IUCN to an ordered focus.[51] For the first two years not much happened – partly because of a lack of enthusiasm in the Secretariat and partly because neither UNEP nor WWF seemed to be clear about just what they wanted.[42,51] Duncan Poore asked Robert Prescott-Allen (who was by this time clear that there was no place for a 'science writer' in the IUCN of the day) to join him in preparing the first draft. This was very much a nature conservation document, addressing the conservation and sustainable management of major ecosystems and habitats for the

Figure 7.1 *The World Conservation Strategy takes Shape. Robert Prescott-Allen amid the drafts. Cartoon by Patrick Virolle.*

benefit of mankind.[42,51] Prescott-Allen had the task of organizing workshops and a diversity of committees, including a formal Advisory Committee led by IUCN but also involving the two funding sponsors, UNEP and WWF.

By 1977–78, the strategy had emerged as the Union's single most important task. With Duncan Poore's departure in February 1978, eight months before Ashkhabad, Prescott-Allen became responsible for its preparation. Reporting to the General Assembly in Ashkhabad, Director-General David Munro made it clear that it was meant to be an evolving document, continually revised and improved as knowledge advanced. The short text setting out the rationale and action points would be accompanied by a scientific sourcebook which went into greater detail about biomes and ecosystems, species, and issues and measures.[46] The Commission on Ecology was involved with texts on terrestrial, freshwater, coastal and marine ecosystems.[65]

The evolution of the strategy had two phases.[83] The first, in the period prior to and during the Ashkhabad Assembly, produced the first two formal drafts and several informal ones.[83] Each draft went for comment to all of IUCN's 400 members, to all Commission members, and to UNEP, FAO, UNESCO, WWF and many concerned organizations and individuals.[84] The drafts were also reviewed by special panels (named in David Munro's preface).[85] There was an all-day technical meeting at Ashkhabad which considered the second draft of the text, and a great deal of informal discussion in small groups and during the evenings.[69,86] It was in the technical meeting that the African members demanded a new approach. '*We know that the conservation of species and ecosystems is important*', they said. '*But we are in the midst of a crisis in the Sahel, and the Strategy must address water resources and agriculture. It can't just focus on nature!*'.[51]

After Ashkhabad, IUCN and WWF were agreed on the core ecosystem and conservation elements of the strategy, on the need to expand it to cover all living resources – including forests, agriculture and fisheries (which were within FAO's bailiwick) – and on the need to accommodate UNEP's increasing sensitivity to development concerns.[83] This was a major change in emphasis, going far beyond the traditional mandate of IUCN, and its acceptance '*meant that the prevailing definition of conservation (heavily oriented to nature and wildlife) no longer worked*'. In response Robert Prescott-Allen devised a new one with three elements: '*the mainte-nance of ecological processes, the preservation of genetic diversity and the sustainable utilization of species and ecosystems – all of which had been around separately in different sub-disciplines but not put together before*'.[51,83] The broadening of coverage had profound implications, for a strategy embracing such a wide field would inevitably be a blueprint for the work of many partners – including UNEP, FAO, UNESCO and WWF, but also embracing governments and the whole non-governmental environment movement, including all IUCN members.

After Ashkhabad, in the second phase of action, the emphasis was on reaching agreement with the three UN partners – and especially UNEP and FAO – and they became the dominant influence on the third and fourth drafts of the text although these were also reviewed by special panels.[46,51,83,87] The negotiations with the UN partners proved somewhat traumatic, partly because Prescott-Allen and the IUCN team had no means of knowing how the message they were trying to convey would be read by the development constituency.[83] In fact, neither UNESCO nor UNEP were happy when they saw the third draft. Duncan Poore, then working with Michel Batisse at UNESCO, drafted a critical commentary for Batisse to send to IUCN,[42] although in fact UNESCO were satisfied once the text gave adequate emphasis to world heritage, biosphere reserves and environmental education.[83] UNEP also came out forcefully, after having failed to respond to the first and second drafts. The text had been passed by Mona Bjorklund, a former IUCN staff member and now in charge of ecology and conservation at UNEP, to colleagues working on what was then termed 'ecodevelopment'. The response? '*This thing stinks! It is dyed-in-the-wool preservationism*'.[51] Reporting to Reuben Olembo, the Director responsible in this area, after Thomas Power and Jorge Morello had refereed the third draft, the staff member concerned, O M El Tayeb, wrote that '*change is necessary to*:

1   *resolve the fundamental differences in approach between UNEP and IUCN;*
2   *eliminate naive and emotional promotion of conservation for conservation's sake, and unnecessary references to controversial areas such as family planning, the warden-farmer concept...and...arguments which designate developing countries as eternal banks of genetic diversity at the expense of...people's welfare;*
3   *transform cosmetic references to ecologically and environmentally-sound development into concrete guidelines'.*[88]

Michael Gwynne, head of GEMS, himself an ecologist, was even ruder. He wrote to Mona Bjorklund that he was:

> '*amazed at the banal condescending approach used by the authors and the abundance of jargon employed. Decision makers are usually intel-ligent people and a presentation such as this, I fear, can only irritate them – though it might amuse some. Surely it is possible to write clearly, simply, factually and concisely without talking down to the reader?*'[89]

There was consternation in Morges. Robert Prescott-Allen flew to Nairobi. He was *'surprised at how unsympathetic many people in UNEP were to conservation (a symptom, I suspect, of UNEP's delegation of nature to IUCN)'*.[83] He concluded that *'the strategy HAD to be put in the context of development for it to be taken seriously. It HAD to cover what development was, and how conservation furthered it'*.[51] But he was worried that many UNEP staff thought that development should or would be at the expense of conservation.[83] He worked with Reuben Olembo to revise the document and make sure it spoke strongly for both conservation and development. He and David Munro then punched the document into its final successful shape. UNEP insisted that UNESCO and FAO confirmed formally that they were content with it.

The evolution of the WCS was also an evolution of thinking among the people and organizations that worked in its making. As Lee Talbot has put it:

> *'the first draft was essentially a wildlife conservation textbook, for at that time many conservationists regarded development as the enemy to be opposed, and many developers, for their part, regarded conservation as, at best, something to be ignored (or, at worst, as an obstacle to progress). However, each draft brought the two sides closer, and involved a process of education. The final draft represents a consensus between the practitioners of conservation and development...'*[87]

The printed Strategy[85] has just 40 pages of text, as 20 double-page spreads each covering a main theme. It starts with the central message: that living resource conservation is essential for sustainable development. The opening paragraph of the Foreword, signed by Mohamed Kassas as President of IUCN, Mostafa Tolba as Executive Director of UNEP, and John Loudon, Prince Philip's predecessor as President of WWF, sets out a message that is, in essence, the same as that which the World Commission for Environment and Development was to elaborate seven years later:

> *'Human beings, in their quest for economic development and enjoyment of the riches of nature, must come to terms with the reality of resource limitation and the carrying capacity of ecosystems, and must take account of the needs of future generations. This is the message of conservation. For if the object of development is to provide for social and economic welfare, the object of conservation is to ensure Earth's capacity to sustain development and to support all life.'*[85]

The first five paragraphs of the Introduction set out the issues in such a masterly – and such a topical – way that they are worth quoting in full:

> *'1   Earth is the only place in the universe known to sustain life. Yet human activities are progressively reducing the planet's life-supporting capacity at a time when rising human numbers and consumption are making increasingly heavy demands on it. The combined destructive impacts of a poor majority struggling to stay alive and an affluent minority consuming most of the world's resources are undermining the very means by which all people can survive and flourish.*
>
> *2   Humanity's relationship with the biosphere (the thin covering of the planet that contains and sustains life) will continue to deteriorate until a new international economic order is achieved, a new*

environmental ethic adopted, human populations stabilize, and
sustainable modes of development become the rule rather than the
exception. Among the prerequisites for sustainable development is
the conservation of living resources.

3   *Development is defined here as: the modification of the biosphere*
   and the application of human, financial, living and non-living
   resources to satisfy human needs and improve the quality of human
   life. For development to be sustainable it must take account of
   social and ecological factors, as well as economic ones; of the
   living and non-living resource base; and of the long term as well
   as the short term advantages and disadvantages of alternative
   actions.

4   *Conservation is defined here as: the management of human use of*
   the biosphere so that it may yield the greatest sustainable benefit
   to present generations while maintaining its potential to meet the
   needs and aspirations of future generations. Thus conservation is
   positive, embracing preservation, maintenance, sustainable utiliza-
   tion, restoration and enhancement of the natural environment.
   Living resource conservation is specifically concerned with plants,
   animals and microorganisms, and with those non-living elements
   of the environment on which they depend. Living resources have
   two important properties the combination of which distinguishes
   them from non-living resources: they are renewable if conserved;
   and they are destructible if not.

5   *Conservation, like development, is for people: while development*
   aims to achieve human goals largely through use of the biosphere,
   conservation aims to achieve them by ensuring that such use can
   continue. Conservation's concern for maintenance and sustain-
   ability is a rational response to the nature of living things
   (renewability + destructibility) and also an ethical imperative,
   expressed in the belief that "we have not inherited the earth from
   our parents, we have borrowed it from our children".'[85]

'Sustainable development' actually appears in the sub-title of the WCS, refuting the notion that the term was invented by Mrs Gro Harlem Brundtland and her Commissioners, while the first sentence of paragraph 4 encapsulates the WCED's celebrated phrase '*meets the needs of the present without compromising the ability of future generations to meet their own needs*'.[90] Eighteen years after it was written, the WCS Introduction stands today as one of the clearest and briefest statements of the conservation and development rationale.

The WCS goes on to state the broad objectives of conservation, and the require-ments for their achievement. Three 'spreads' deal with broad goals – the maintenance of essential ecological processes and life-support systems, the preser-vation of genetic diversity, and the sustainable utilization of species and ecosystems. This leads to three further sections detailing priority requirements in each of these areas. Again, the check-lists could be written today. For example those in the first area specify:

1   reserve good cropland for crops
2   manage cropland to high ecological standards

3   ensure that the principal management goal for watershed forest and pastures is protection of the watershed
4   ensure that the principal goal for estuaries, mangrove swamps and other coastal wetlands and shallows critical for fisheries is the maintenance of the processes on which the fisheries depend
5   control the discharge of pollutants

And having stated the essential requirements for sustainable and rational management of the biosphere, the strategy devotes seven sections to the priorities for national action and six more for those at international level.

This does not mean that the strategy lacks flaws. It is, as the leaders of IUCN, WWF and UNEP recognized a few years later, *'very weak on such issues as population, energy and agriculture'*[91] (although it does state the need for human populations to stabilize, and for every country to have a population policy).[51,83] It says next to nothing about environmental pollution, and largely ignores the growing number of international conventions and agreements that have sought to keep the planet clean. It devotes only three paragraphs to acid rain, ozone layer destruction and the possibility of climate change through the 'greenhouse effect'. And while it recognizes that conservation is for people, it is an ecosystem-centred rather than human community-centred document. It can be criticized as still echoing too much of what some have called the *'North Atlantic brand of anti-human environmentalism'*.[92] But for its time it was an outstanding statement.

The WCS was launched simultaneously in 35 countries around the world, on 5 March 1980. The 'media event' was largely organized by WWF, but prominent people from all the three sponsors were deployed. Among the locations were Amman, Bangkok, Beijing, Brasilia, Canberra, Caracas, Jakarta, London, Moscow, Nairobi, New Delhi, UN headquarters in New York, and Washington DC. They were chosen deliberately to span political systems and stages of economic development. Most of the events were presided over by heads of state or government, and many of them gave public endorsement to the message the strategy conveyed and announced national action programmes to implement it. The UN Secretary-General, Kurt Waldheim, described it as providing an *'agreement on what should be done to ensure the proper management and optimal use of the world's living resources, not only for ourselves but for future generations'*.[87,93] In all 17,500 copies – 12,000 in English, 2500 in French and 3000 in Spanish – were distributed through IUCN, UNEP, WWF, FAO, UNESCO and at the various launches.[94]

The WCS was the most ambitious effort undertaken so far in international conservation. It was certainly the first IUCN product to achieve worldwide acclaim, not only among the nature conservationists who made up the 'inner circle', but among governments and even in industry. It may have done something to correct the situation which Ray Dasmann encountered on his return to California – that *'IUCN was virtually unknown in the US and hence all the work I had been doing might just as well have happened on another planet'*.[8] It caught the mood of the times. It appeared at about the same time as the Brandt Commission published its report *North–South: a Programme for Survival*, analysing the need for a sweeping restructuring of the world's economic systems for the mutual benefit of developed and developing countries alike – and stressing the fact that *'the care of the natural environment is an essential aspect of development'*.[87,95] In the same year, the heads of the World Bank and eight regional development banks and development assistance agencies met in New York and signed a 'Declaration of Environmental Policies and Procedures Relating to Economic Development'.[87]

The WCS succeeded because it was so broadly based, both in preparation and in sponsorship and promotion. It was a truly participatory effort, involving individual scientists and other specialists, and both governmental and non-governmental organizations. It was the product of long and thorough discussion. It involved people from the developing as well as the developed world, and it clearly catered for the needs of the South far more than the formal conclusions of the Stockholm Conference had done. It was sponsored by the leading UN agencies concerned with environment, and by WWF as the best-known 'campaigning' conservation body of its time (though it did not involve other active bodies such as Friends of the Earth or Greenpeace, who were at that time focussing especially on the things the WCS played down, including global pollution and population). It also succeeded because it was brief, lucid and contained new ideas. For this Robert Prescott-Allen, who wrote it, and David Munro, who guided it, deserve especial credit. Many people would argue that it demonstrated the kind of thing IUCN did best, and should focus on – the drawing together of knowledge and insight and the production of strategies and draft laws, to stimulate and guide conservation efforts at the world level.

8 After the Strategy

A Time for New Dimensions

The completion and launch of the World Conservation strategy did '*more to put conservation on the world's agenda than any other event*'.[1] Whether they acknowledged it as the source of their inspiration or not, the world environmental movement from 1980 right up to 1992, when the United Nations Conference on Environment and Development met in Rio de Janeiro, was debating the central message of the WCS. The message? That development to ease human poverty and deprivation and give all people a decent quality of life is a dominant imperative, but that unless development cares for the renewable natural resources of the planet it will not endure.

The distinctive thing about the WCS is that it is development-oriented: as David Munro put it in a guest editorial in the journal *Environmental Conservation*,

> '*the foundation for the achievement of conservation is the popular will that it be achieved. It cannot be widely achieved while the everyday lives of hundreds of millions of people are shadowed by the threats of starvation, disease, and natural disasters. The concerns of these people are those of the moment, not of tomorrow. Unfortunately, conservation is most urgently needed in those parts of the world where poverty and under-development preclude any popular understanding of the need of it. Conservation will succeed in the Third World only when a sufficient number of its inhabitants can concern themselves with something more than simple survival. That is why conservation must espouse the principles of sustainable development for all*'.[2]

This message echoed the one that Maurice Strong had extracted from Stockholm and built into the foundations of UNEP. It is therefore not surprising that as early as 1976, long before the WCS was published, the IUCN Bureau under Strong's leadership was discussing a 'Conservation for Development' programme which would link IUCN's expertise to the programmes of the development assistance agencies '*in order to achieve more effective conservation and more sustainable development*'. In 1977, IUCN and WWF started a joint project entitled 'Conservation and Development Programme for Indonesia'.[3] In the same year WWF was asked to support a '*feasibility study for a Professional Services Organization (PSO) in the field of conservation*'. It was carried out by Adrian Phillips, on secondment from UNEP, and completed in April 1978.[4] The central idea was that the aid agencies would create a fund which would be drawn down by projects requested by developing countries and executed by the PSO.[5]

Maurice Strong wanted the PSO to have its own Board and to serve a wide range of users. The attractiveness of this idea was recognized by the Ford Foundation, to whom he turned for start-up finance. Marshall Robinson, Vice-President of the Foundation, wrote in April 1978 that:

> '*its collaboration with IUCN and UNEP will be vital, but so too will be its collaboration with the World Bank, various aid agencies, some foundations and a wide variety of government agencies. If it appears to be captured by any single outfit it may lose some of the others.*'[6]

The IUCN Council was not enthusiastic. They wanted to keep the venture – renamed the 'Conservation for Development Programme' – in-house and proposed that '*a unit would be established within IUCN to provide for project management, and the expertise required would be drawn primarily from IUCN's networks*'.[7] They were also '*preoccupied with the never-ending financial problems of the Union and saw the new facility as a means of financing the rest of the Secretariat and Commissions through the levy of a substantial tax on project turnover*'.[8,9] WWF themselves (in the person of Charles de Haes) also backed the proposal that the Conservation for Development Centre (CDC) should be an IUCN venture, seeing it as a way of helping to cure IUCN's financial difficulties.[10]

The effect of the decision, taken in 1979, was:

> '*to make the Secretariat truly operational for the first time in its history. In other words, in addition to the Commission work and the central policy development work of the Secretariat, IUCN was going to develop and implement field programmes in collaboration with its members. The ambition was ultimately to build a massive global force for conservation, turning the outputs of the Commissions into action on the ground.*'[9]

It was suggested that the Programme would make IUCN a logical adviser to the World Bank, and perhaps also to UNDP and regional development banks, on the conservation implications of their projects.[11]

The Ford Foundation approved a two-year start-up grant of US$245,000 in September 1979 – with the proviso that any money not spent by September 1981 would be reclaimed. At Russell Train's suggestion, various individual aid agencies were also approached.[12,13] But recruitment of a Director for the new CDC took a long time, partly because of Secretariat preoccupations with the WCS,[14] and partly due to internal wrangling in IUCN over the precise status of the CDC and its relationship with the Commissions, seen by the Council as its primary source of expertise. It was not until April 1981 that Michael J Cockerell, an English engineer who had worked for the Battelle Institute in Switzerland and was currently employed by the Environment Protection Agency of the Hong Kong Government, was appointed.[1,15]

These events were the beginning of a major change in world conservation, and a transformation in IUCN (and, to some extent, in WWF). The emphasis on the human dimension, on conservation for sustainable development, made IUCN far more relevant to those struggling to blend development and conservation in the developing world. It also made the Union attractive to bilateral government development assistance agencies, who saw it as a potential executor of their projects, especially through its members in developing countries. The early 1980s – after yet another appalling financial convulsion – saw IUCN poised for a stage of expansion which has continued ever since.

WWF faced more of a dilemma. It, too, was fully committed to implementing the World Conservation Strategy. It shared the conviction that conservation could only succeed by incorporating the human dimension (the case is argued eloquently in the book it published later to mark its 35th anniversary).[16] The principal objective of virtually every WWF/IUCN project (indeed of virtually every environmentalist campaign) was to change human behaviour. But saving species and wilderness remained the most potent money-winners. Sustainable development has little popular purse-appeal. So WWF continued to rely on traditional 'protectionist' themes in many of its campaigns, while increasingly tailoring its projects on the ground to incorporate the human dimension and enlist the local cooperation without which failure was certain.

A New Burst of Conservation Action

The 1970s and 1980s were decades of immense growth in intergovernmental and non-governmental environmental action. One consequent problem was that the burden of liaison increased enormously. It was at least theoretically possible for each body to spend all its time communicating with every other body, so that very little was really created or done! These problems bore especially heavily on IUCN, itself a widening web of organizations. How to collaborate with the UN agencies? How to relate to the European organizations such as the Council of Europe and the Communist bloc's Council for Mutual Economic Assistance? What about bodies in other regions, such as the Arab League Educational, Cultural and Scientific Organization? They could all be invited to General Assemblies – but these happened only once every three years. Only some 'cooperating organizations' could be asked to send representatives to report their work regularly to IUCN Council, though by 1980 the list had become a long one – UNEP, UNESCO, FAO, the Council of Europe, the International Council for Bird Preservation, the International Council of Scientific Unions, the International Geographical Union, the International Youth Federation and of course WWF.

As the tempo of international environmentalism increased, some NGOs formed coalitions, as the most economical way of combining resources and increasing their weight. This put IUCN in a dilemma. As Wolfgang Burhenne put it, '*as a coalition itself, it would be very difficult for IUCN to operate within another coalition*'.[17] Its obvious role was itself to '*initiate and be the ruling organization in a conservation coalition*' but this would demand resources – and also assumed that the member organizations were willing to have IUCN provide their umbrella, which many were not. On the other hand, it was often most effective for IUCN to work with coalitions and bring a collective influence to bear on governments – as was demonstrated in the conference that concluded the Convention on Migratory Species[17] and by a partnership with the Antarctica and Southern Oceans Coalition (ASOC), in the negotiation of the Convention on the Conservation of Antarctic Marine Living Resources (CCAMLR).[18] It was agreed that while IUCN should not as a rule join NGO coalitions, the Director-General could make exceptions where this was clearly the best way to advance its policy.

David Munro recalls that while relations with other bodies were important, and while he and others in IUCN were aware of the activities outside the IUCN–UNEP–WWF triangle, most of the active environmental organizations had a more narrowly defined role. *'They were pressure groups: IUCN was an advocate, but in a very disciplined way because it was accountable to a very broad constituency.'*[19] IUCN did not get involved in human population questions, or in pollution, and while it did argue vigorously against the depletion of natural resources it did not issue predictions of doom like the Club of Rome. Any links with the private sector of industry were left to WWF. One consequence was that IUCN's media visibility, never a strong point, decreased. Champions of the 'new environmentalism' like Greenpeace and Friends of the Earth grabbed public attention. WWF was equated with nature conservation, and nobody much in the North was interested in sustainable development in poor countries – except when famine struck and horrible pictures could be linked to banner headlines. IUCN was hemmed in by its own chosen limitations, and they were bound to hamper its ability to gain funds and recognition.

But the World Conservation Strategy did attract new members to IUCN. A special effort was made to establish links with the People's Republic of China, which had been taking a steadily more prominent role in international environmental affairs since its attendance at the 1972 Stockholm Conference. In 1979 a WWF team led by Peter Scott, and including Charles de Haes and Lee Talbot, had signed an agreement with the Chinese Association for Environmental Sciences. China had indicated that it would join IUCN and become a party to CITES,[17] and Kenton Miller, Chair of CNPPA, reported that a Chinese specialist had already attended one of his meetings. In June 1980 Li Chaobo, who was of ministerial rank as head of the Environment Protection Office and also led the Society for Environmental Sciences, the first Chinese member of IUCN, was coopted to the Council by acclamation, emphasized his country's commitment to conservation, and presented IUCN *'with a magnificent Chinese painting of cormorants'*.[20]

Expanding the membership was one thing. Linking, staying close to it, and supporting it from the Secretariat was another. The three Regional Officers at headquarters, John Kundaeli, Chew Wee Lek and Felipe Matos (replaced by Bernardo Zentilli in 1980), provided the essential liaison with members in Africa, Asia and Latin America and watched over conservation problems and projects on the ground.[21] In 1980 they were asked to compile short dossiers of information, country by country.[11] They were also asked to liaise with National Committees, which were being encouraged by the Council through the *Bulletin*,[22] and were becoming increasingly common.[15] And the Union encountered one of the recurrent problems in any GONGO – balancing the interests of the governmental and non-governmental members. As Bob Boote had pointed out to the Bureau in March 1979, as IUCN became more successful, and drew more funds from governments, it faced an increasing need also to maintain the confidence of the NGO community – and many NGO members in the North were far from happy about the sign that IUCN was becoming a development-related operational agency.[13,23]

This was also a period when international conventions on environmental topics multiplied. IUCN provided the Secretariat services for both the Ramsar Convention and CITES (the latter as agent of UNEP), and had a special role as adviser on World Heritage natural sites. The number of states party to Ramsar increased from 21 to 30 between 1978 and 1980, bringing the Convention into force: the first meeting of the contracting parties was held in Italy in November 1980.[1] There was debate over whether to base the permanent Bureau with the International Waterfowl Research

Bureau at Slimbridge in England or with IUCN in Switzerland, and in the end the latter was chosen. CITES almost doubled its membership between 1978 and 1981, and with 74 parties was the most widely accepted international conservation treaty.[1] A new wildlife trade monitoring unit which tabulated worldwide trade in wildlife and wildlife products, started in 1980 as part of the Conservation Monitoring Centre in Cambridge.[1] The Union also became concerned over oil pollution of the sea and acquired consultative status with the Intergovernmental Maritime Consultative Organization (IMCO), which administered the main international agreements on shipping,[11,17] but the Council refused to follow up a proposal of the Kinshasa Assembly for a legal measure to safeguard tropical rain forests because it felt that '*there was no likelihood of an effective convention being adopted*'.[24,25] It showed foresight, for this issue has rumbled inconsequentially on for 20 years.[26,27]

This was also the period when the conservation community first became involved in Antarctica, described in the World Conservation Strategy as one of the focal issues in world environmental management. Rival territorial claims had been set aside by the Antarctic Treaty, which decreed that the continent would be used for peaceful scientific purposes only, and a series of measures for the conservation of fauna and flora had been agreed.[28] But some governments and NGOs objected to the control of policy under the Treaty by the small group of nations that maintained bases in Antarctica, and argued that it was (or should be treated as) a 'global commons'. There was especial concern that the vast swarms of krill (the pelagic crustacean, *Euphausia superba*, which stood at the base of food chains leading to whales, seals and penguins) might be made the subject of a new fishery before the ecological implications had been worked out and proper control measures instituted.

A Convention on the Conservation of Antarctic Marine Living Resources was in preparation, and the draft text was unique among international laws in demanding that any exploitation of living resources should not impair the functioning of the ecosystems of the Antarctic Ocean. IUCN looked for a way to influence the negotiations at Canberra in May 1980.[12] It sent a statement to the governments involved, and to all IUCN members,[13] and requested a place at the negotiating table. It got it. The Union was invited as an observer, alongside FAO, the International Whaling Commission and two ICSU Scientific Committees (SCOR and SCAR), which were concerned with oceanic research and Antarctic research.[17] Bob Boote (IUCN Vice-President) and Don McMichael (Treasurer and Council member from Australia) represented the Union.

Although representatives of NGOs were not permitted to take part in the discussion of the Articles of the draft convention, Bob Boote was allowed to address the delegates in both the opening and concluding plenary sessions, and his statement was annexed to the report of the conference.[20,29] He noted that all the countries at the table were either State members of IUCN or had government agency members, and that '*six of the country representatives are, in fact, members of IUCN's Governing Council*'.[29] The implication was that they were expected to stand up for conservation, and support the IUCN line! As an accredited observer, IUCN was also able to introduce into the conference statements by ASOC, whose request for observer status had been rejected.[30]

IUCN's presence in Canberra was important in three ways. First, it paved the way for NGOs to participate in future meetings under the Convention. Second, it may well have been important in giving CCAMLR its unique ecological flavour. Third, it was the start of IUCN's serious interest in Antarctic conservation.[29,31] On his return, Bob Boote urged the Council '*to give Antarctica and the Southern Ocean and matters relating thereto high and continuing priority*'.[31] IUCN should press for the closure of the Indian Ocean sector of the Antarctic Ocean to krill fishery, so as to uphold its status as a whale sanctuary.

> '*In all work relating to Antarctica, IUCN needs to be an effective catalyst and communicator. It should not trespass on what the more specialized bodies are doing, or propose to do, but it should ensure that no significant part of the presently perceived total requirement is neglected.*'[31]

This meant a programme matrix which emphasized the scientific and professional basis for effective conservation, the development of practical operational measures (such as controls on krill harvests), and public affairs aspects (raising awareness of the issues and solutions). Bob Boote proposed that IUCN should press all its State members to ratify CCAMLR, and all Commissions should consider their role in Antarctica.[22]

Desertification was a 'hot issue' in the late 1970s and early 1980s. Mohamed Kassas was an architect of the plan of action which had been adopted in 1977 by a UN conference in Nairobi. The follow-up had been very disappointing, with virtually no money flowing into the special fund established by UNEP.[32] Adrian Phillips argued that IUCN could both include suitable items in its own programme and stimulate action among the members. Tropical forests were another biome of high prominence, but the start was slow until 1981 when the Commission on Ecology took up three issues that remain of central importance 30 years afterwards – the climatic implications of tropical forest clearance, the sustainability of traditional forest uses, and means of taking pressure off forests by using adjacent cultivated land better.[33] In 1981 a major IUCN/WWF campaign on forests and primates was also launched.[15]

As always, 'fire-fighting' actions in response to conservation emergencies featured prominently on the agenda. The deteriorating political situation in Uganda brought worries over the state of that country's outstanding national parks. Governments in Ethiopia, Zimbabwe, Mozambique and Oman were offered help on various aspects of conservation and law.[11,20] Poaching of elephants and rhinos in Malawi and Zambia was causing alarm, and a joint WWF/IUCN project was providing support for counteraction (which, it was emphasized, did not include the supply of weapons). SSC was deeply involved in the successful return of captive-bred Arabian oryx to the wild in Oman, in which WWF played a major part.[16,20] Hal Coolidge and CNPPA were worried by reports of looting at Angkor Wat, caught in the midst of war.[20] There was worry over the environmental impact of new oilfields in the Arctic.[11] Western Africa was another troubled region, where a project on conservation of addax and oryx in Chad had to be stopped because of war, but where a new project, supported by the German Technical Assistance Programme, on the protection and utilization of wild fauna and flora as a contribution to integrated rural development and desertification control was agreed as part of the 'new look' action on conservation for development.[1]

The Balloon Hits the Rocks on the Road to Christchurch

The Regional Councillor from New Zealand, PHC 'Bing' Lucas, suggested in 1979 that the 1981 Session of the General Assembly be held in Christchurch.[13] The invitation was accepted – but there was one concern. As Wolfgang Burhenne put it in June 1980, '*there would be no difficulties over visas, the accommodation was good, and the conference facilities excellent. The only major problem was that of getting participants to New Zealand*'.[20] President Kassas and others from the developing world seized on the issue. Bing Lucas commented that at least there was good access from the Asia–Pacific region, but this fell coolly on African and Latin American ears. UNEP, UNESCO and WWF were urged to help generously with funding.[20] The Vice-President from the USSR Alexander Borodin got the Soviet Ministry of Aviation to agree to lay on special charters half the costs of which would be payable in non-convertible currency, but this initiative ran into trouble over the grant of landing rights in New Zealand.[33]

But before anybody got near Christchurch the financial crisis of 1980 struck with a vengeance, and indeed for a while may have made people 'in the know' wonder whether there was going to be another General Assembly at all! Yet, like its predecessor in 1975, the storm came out of what appeared to be a cloudless sky. For the late 1970s had been a period of financial growth without deep disasters. The membership had agreed at Ashkhabad to a dues increase which meant that they paid a quarter of the costs of the organization.[12,25] Only a small deficit was carried forward from 1977 to 1978, and by November, thanks to an extra quarter of a million Swiss francs from WWF, the forecast deficit for that year had been pinned back to SFr70,000.[12] In March 1979 a new contract worth US$1.65 million was signed with UNEP for the two years 1979 and 1980.[13] In March 1980 the Bureau noted (over-confidently as it turned out) that '*the deficit had been almost eliminated*'.[11]

David Munro felt that the smooth relationship with WWF depended on skilled footwork by the Director-General. '*We were for ever the supplicant*', he recalls.

> '*I felt we always had to act in a way that would not cause WWF to lose trust in IUCN, and all this depended on the personal relationship I had with Charles de Haes. It wasn't bad – there was no hostility – but it was difficult. WWF had the financial reserves and total freedom. They handed projects to IUCN, and we carried any costs of failure to estimate properly. WWF had the primary power of the purse. It was quite a different world with John Loudon and Louis Franck accounting to a Board of aristocrats and businessmen. The Joint Financial Services seemed more sensible than having two organizations with similar aims doing this in parallel, but the situation got increasingly difficult. It had a cat-and-mouse dimension: we were never sure that WWF wouldn't turn and say "we're not sure that we can support this".*'[19]

In the midst of these problems and successes, personal tragedy intervened to compel another change of leadership. David Munro had been elected for a term of three years at the Ashkhabad Assembly in 1978,[33] and would, in all probability, have been reappointed at Christchurch. But early in 1980 his wife, Raye, became seriously ill.

The prognosis was bad, and the Munros decided that they must return to Canada, and to their family. The resignation of the Director-General was notified to the President in late February: the Bureau met in March 1980, and recruitment was set in hand at once.

There are rumours that around this time – possibly after David Munro's resignation and again after Lee Talbot left three years later – more than one person suggested that further recruitment was unnecessary, because Charles de Haes could be Director-General of both organizations.[19] If this was ever seriously considered, it was rejected and IUCN went on looking for its own Chief Executive. The three front-running external candidates were Bob Boote (a Vice-President, who had just retired from leading the United Kingdom Nature Conservancy Council), Don McMichael (the Treasurer, who was Secretary of the Australian Commonwealth Department of Home Affairs) and Lee Talbot, Director of Conservation and Senior Scientific Adviser to WWF International. Adrian Phillips, the Director of Programmes and architect of the Programme Planning Advisory Group, was the sole contender from among the Secretariat.

Bob Boote sensed that the Americans were determined that the job should go to Lee Talbot, and withdrew.[31] A number of US members indeed wrote expressing very strong support for Dr Talbot,[34] and Hal Coolidge and his wife Martha ('Muffy') canvassed openly as the Councillors arrived to take a decision.[5] Don McMichael, Lee Talbot and Adrian Phillips were all interviewed. They had quite different qualities. Adrian Phillips was a planner by profession, and had worked in the British Department of the Environment and for UNEP in Nairobi before moving to IUCN: he was obviously a 'flier', but was relatively junior, and it was soon evident that the choice lay between the other two.

Don McMichael offered outstanding experience as a senior administrator, blended with an extensive knowledge of conservation. He was articulate, outspoken, and tough – and was backed by Maurice Strong.[35] But some say that he was unwelcome to the Commissions because he had proposed the change in Statutes in 1977 which would have made the Council, not the General Assembly, responsible for appointing the Chairs,[35] and to WWF because he had criticized the joint financial management of the two organizations.[8] Hal Eidsvik also sensed that after Frank Nicholls, tough Australians were viewed with some caution![36]

Lee Talbot had been associated with IUCN from the very beginning, when as a young graduate he had been the Union's first staff ecologist and undertaken the first major missions to South-east Asia and Africa. He had served as a Regional Councillor and Vice-President and had been Senior Scientist of the United States Council on Environmental Quality and an adviser to the President of the USA. He could be expected to maintain a close link with WWF, who backed him strongly, as did the Commissions.

The Council chose Lee Talbot, and he was appointed on 27 June 1980, to take office on 1 August. WWF were visibly delighted: an enthusiastic Charles de Haes indeed burst into his part of the shared headquarters exulting that '*our man's got the job*' – only to apologize to Cassandra Phillips, Adrian's wife, who was present as a WWF staff member![37] Hal Coolidge paid a warm (and well-deserved) tribute to David Munro. The Talbot period began,[20] and the new incumbent walked right into deepening financial crisis.

The first signs of trouble were evident just as the changeover between Director-Generals was in progress. Despite all the nice things said about the WCS and the opportunities it presented, UNEP support was clearly going to decline. David Munro said that while IUCN could live with this '*the decline should follow at least two years notice and should be spread out over some years*'.[11] The paradox of praise and demolition was very evident in June 1980, when Peter Thacher, Assistant Executive Director of UNEP, addressed the Council. UNEP, he said, recognized IUCN as '*the primary international conservation organization outside the United Nations*'. They looked forward to continued collaboration, with especial emphasis on the promotion and implementation of the World Conservation Strategy. They would go on participating in PPAG and would use the Ecosystems Conservation Group to coordinate action. BUT instead of supporting the full package of 11 projects put to them, they would back seven in 1981, at a total value of US$575,000 – which was $225,000 less than the level of support in 1980.[20] They might support the four other projects, but could not guarantee this. Couldn't IUCN do something to use some of the $15 million of credit UNEP held in non-convertible currencies (mainly in Eastern Europe and the USSR)?

Lee Talbot knew, from his time in WWF, that the IUCN financial situation was graver than anyone was admitting, and as soon as he had taken up his new post he called for an audit. It was done in-house by Stephan Suwald, the Head of Accounting for both IUCN and WWF, with help from the professional auditors, Price Waterhouse of Geneva.[14] The figures were rough but indicated that IUCN had started 1980 with a deficit of some SFr2 million, and by July there was an additional operating deficit of about one million.

> '*I was warned by the accountant and by Bernard Gustin of McKinsey that if this should continue the organization would be dissolved under Swiss law. They said that to avoid this I would need to show real progress in reducing the deficit during the remainder of the year and eliminate the operating deficit (as opposed to the carry-over from pre-1980) entirely in 1981 or the accountants would have to cite IUCN as insolvent...I asked them to present the situation to the Council, which they did at the following meeting. I also telephoned Maurice Strong and Kassas to inform them of the situation. My impression was that neither of them believed it, since it was so far from what the Bureau and Council had been assured in the previous meetings.*'[14]

Addressing his first meeting of the Bureau in October 1980, Talbot reported these grave discoveries, and emphasized '*that consequently in 1981 there must be very substantial cuts in expenditure below present levels*'.[38] In closed session, the Council heard Dr Gustin advocate a 40 per cent cut in personnel. On 14 November he followed up with a presentation to the staff, and immediately afterwards Lee Talbot swung into action. A number of staff were asked to leave, or went of their own accord. Richard Herring and Hal Eidsvik returned to Canada,[36] Robert Prescott-Allen also departed voluntarily, and Tony Mence was re-located to run the Species Conservation Monitoring Unit in Cambridge.[39] Adrian Phillips stayed on until the end of May 1981, when he became Director of the Countryside Commission of England and Wales. On the positive side, new efforts were made to start the Conservation for Development Centre, get money from governments, UNEP and USAID, and negotiate tax-exempt status for IUCN in Switzerland.[14]

It is impossible after so many years to discover precisely how this near-disastrous state of affairs arose. Richard Herring, back in Ottawa in May 1981, set down his perspective in detail.[40] He addressed his paper to the Council, though there is no evidence in the minutes that they ever received it. He stated that when he joined

IUCN in 1978 he found that it had no system for financial planning or budgetary control. He therefore divided the operation into a number of clearly defined 'cost centres' so that the costs of activities could be related both to outputs and to budget. This allowed much better management, which was welcome to Council, to the membership at Ashkhabad, and to outside supporters including UNEP and WWF: indeed, it cleared the way for UNEP to place new contracts for 1979 and 1980.

Richard Herring placed the blame for the subsequent troubles squarely on the decision (for which IUCN was just as responsible as WWF[41]) to set up joint financial services in the new headquarters in Gland. He stated that the system of regular financial statements for each cost centre only continued until 30 September 1979: there was then a gap until April 1981. IUCN found themselves approximately SFr200,000 over budget following the close of 1979, but could not find out why because a year-end summary cost-centre budget comparison was not prepared.[40] Charles de Haes explained to the Bureau on 10 October 1980 *'that the services required by IUCN were being installed but that it would not be cost-effective to prepare a cost-centre report for the last half of 1979 or for 1980 since the period (being the period of the move to Gland) was exceptional'*.[38] Herring argued that IUCN's troubles stemmed directly from the fact that for well over a year they were running on the financial equivalent of a mariner's 'dead reckoning' at a time when they (and WWF, of course) had no experience of the cost of operating household services in the new building and when they were going through an unprecedented period of expense in launching the World Conservation Strategy.[40,42]

Whatever the rights and wrongs of it, the fact remained that IUCN was in a deep hole, and Lee Talbot's first round of cuts did not save enough money. Things still looked black in June 1981, when the auditors presented the accounts for 1980. They set them out in two forms, both conforming to sound audit practice, but presenting the Council with a choice of hooks to wriggle on.[15]

The Council accepted the version which minimized the visible deficit by allowing it to swallow up all available capital funds, but Mohamed Kassas asked the McKinsey representative, Dr Bernard Gustin, and the auditor, Mr Gravina, if they had further comments. They had. They emphasized that the financial situation was critical. Article 77 of the Swiss civil code provided for the automatic dissolution of an organization when insolvent, but the auditors concluded that IUCN was not insolvent at this time, largely because of the financial assistance that had been provided by WWF. *'Dr Gustin advised Council that IUCN was thus receiving a qualified financial opinion with the auditors making a statement to the public on the gravity of the situation. He remarked that should WWF decide that it wanted payment for its loans to IUCN, IUCN would be insolvent.'*[15]

The Council went into closed session. The simple fact was that IUCN now depended totally on WWF for its survival. Charles de Haes made it clear that they wanted IUCN to continue, and that they would therefore be supportive. But Lee Talbot noted that although the auditors had not cited the technical insolvency of IUCN in their report, *'because WWF is taking up the slack...if we had any operating deficit next year the organization would be dissolved as of 1 January 1982'*.[43]

Some lifelines snaked towards the troubled ship. Charles de Haes, commenting that despite the financial gloom the working relationship between the partner organizations had never been better, thought that WWF might make a loan of SFr400,000 at the time of the forthcoming General Assembly. Lee Talbot reported that IUCN had been awarded the Olympia Prize, worth US$100,000, by the Alexander S Onassis Foundation. Other pledges and contracts were coming in. The membership were paying their dues better, and one-third of the amount in arrears had been collected.[15] But several of these were windfalls, not the basis for a permanent balance in the budget. Talbot was still in a tight corner. He simply had to cut costs and find genuine new income. Immediately after the Council meeting – described by him as '*about the lowest point of my tenure here*'[43] – a second 'night of long knives' ensued.

Following McKinsey's recommendations, Talbot cut staff by 25 per cent.[15] The Bureau was assured '*that the decision as to which staff must leave had been made on the basis of function, not on the basis of the individuals involved*'[44] and, in a letter to Adrian Phillips, Talbot reported the endorsement of Mohamed Kassas as President and Pierre Goeldlin as Swiss (and Vaudois) Councillor.[43] There has, none the less, been a persistent IUCN belief that it was not entirely coincidental that most of the members of the Staff Liaison Committee were sacked![45] More seriously, the cuts removed most of the meagre developing country presence at headquarters – something that upset a Councillor from Africa, Dr E O A Asibey of Ghana. He argued that with the World Conservation Strategy, IUCN had committed itself to 'conservation for development' and needed to make a direct input to government action for environmental management. This could not be achieved by working through the Commissions, not least because so few specialist scientists were to be found in developing countries. There had to be capacity within IUCN – and preferably in the Secretariat:

> '*for properly evaluating scientific advice given against the full background picture of the area in which it is to be applied. Unless this can be achieved IUCN as an organization cannot be satisfied that its scientific work is going to be fully effective and its members in developing countries…will be given cause to question the value of such IUCN advice to them.*'[46]

There therefore needed to be a strong regional representation within the Secretariat '*and it appears to me that it should be a basic consideration for good management of IUCN as an impartial international organization*'.[46]

Lee Talbot did not retain the regional desks, but Asibey's plea was answered in another way when the Conservation for Development Centre was created soon afterwards and paved the way for the progressive regionalization and decentralization of the Secretariat (see Chapters 9–11). There was consolidation, with Peter Sand transferring from the Secretary-Generalship of CITES to become Assistant Director-General and Hartmut Jungius taking on an enlarged role as Director of Regional and Project Services.[15] Several programme budgets – including that for law, policy and administration – were cut hard. Travel expenses were no longer paid to those attending Council and Bureau. Members no longer got free copies of publications – though they still got a free *Bulletin* and Annual Report, and could buy other documents at cheap rates.[47] The staff cuts were estimated to deliver a saving of SFr500,000 a year.[48] Council decided to propose an increase of 30 per cent in membership dues with effect from 1982.[48] As presented to the Assembly, the budget would produce a surplus for the triennium.

The cuts undoubtedly weakened IUCN severely. They increased its professional as well as financial dependence on WWF. But they won the backing of Charles de Haes and the WWF Executive Committee.[48] At the Council meeting at the start of the Christchurch General Assembly de Haes announced additional support to the tune of SFr550,000, spread over the coming three years, in such a way that '*IUCN would not face a deficit in any one year in the coming triennium provided that all the other budgetary assumptions for the triennium were realized, including the planned increase in membership dues'.*[48] In fact, WWF's central support rose from SFr1.9 million in 1979 to SFr2.6 million in 1980 and SFr2.1 million in 1981, followed by an immense leap to SFr4.4 million in 1982/83.[49] The show stayed on the road. But its dependence on its partners was very evident.

The Balloon Relaunched

When Michael Cockerell arrived in April 1981, it was on the clear understanding that the CDC project was experimental, that the Ford grant was start-up money and would not continue, and that he had two years in which to secure the future of the centre (and his own job).[8] In fact it was worse than that, because Ford had included a cut-off date in the contract and less than six months remained before the unspent money would have to be returned. The new Director's first action was to rush to New York to negotiate an extension.[5,50] Another early action was to extend the dialogue that had already begun with the International Institute for Environment and Development (IIED) in Washington DC to its London headquarters. IIED was the leading non-governmental 'think tank' on many aspects of CDC's mandate and was talking of setting up its own *'Environmental Advisory Service'*.[4,48] It was envisaged that IIED and IUCN might merge their initiatives in a joint service, and a formal agreement was in fact signed in April 1981, very soon after Mike Cockerell's arrival.[4]

As established in 1981 the CDC had three main tasks. The first was *'the identification of problem areas in which substantial environmental degradation is being or will be caused by development (or lack of it) and the formulation of projects for the solution of the more significant of such problems'*. The second was *'the expansion of the IUCN expert/consultant roster system to ensure that the full potential of world expertise in the many fields of environment and conservation are brought to bear on these projects'*. Last but not least came *'the acquisition of financial support for the implementation of these projects'*.[1] The implication was that after 1981 IUCN would begin a comprehensive field programme.[9]

Lee Talbot's report to the General Assembly in Christchurch[1] was calmly confident. He had a lot of solid achievement to report – and said so, paying due tribute to David Munro as the architect of much of it. There seemed no need to make too much fuss of the financial crisis. Action had been taken. Thanks to IUCN economies and WWF's pledges a budget surplus for each of the three years ahead was on the cards. The need was for recommitment (and more money) from the membership, not recriminations. The members responded. They adopted a programme and an unprecedented number of resolutions which together amounted to *'an almost overwhelming agenda for action by the global conservation community'*.[51]

Hal Coolidge, by now Honorary President, was responsible for another report to the Assembly. He had been worried *'that IUCN's "track record" might be lost with the demise/departure of those involved in various stages of its history'*.[52] He argued that a history of the first 30 years of IUCN should be compiled. Sir Hugh Elliott, who finally retired as Senior Editor in June 1980, prepared a paper on *'the first quarter century of IUCN: looking back and looking ahead'*. Tony Mence was then commissioned by Hal Coolidge *'on a personal basis with a contribution from his Getty Prize money'* to write a history based partly on Elliott's text, and this was produced in September 1981 and circulated at the Christchurch General Assembly.[52,53]

The important new feature of the programme presented in Christchurch was that (thanks especially to the machinery created by Adrian Phillips) it was integrated, linking the work of the Commissions and Secretariat, and had a central rationale – the achievement of the long-range goals of the World Conservation Strategy. Moreover, the programme planning process included '*continuous consultations with IUCN's membership and the Commissions...Over 60% of the projects managed by IUCN in 1981 originated from proposals by members, and a similar percentage involves active participation by members in project implementation...*'[1] The CDC was seen as a mechanism for getting new action going on the ground. This programme integration, field operation, and close consultation with both the funding agencies and the IUCN membership marks the beginning of the 'modern phase' in IUCN.

One of the major thrusts of decision in Christchurch was that conservation programmes should also be integrated regionally. The various regional seas – the Caribbean, the Red Sea and Arabian Gulf, the Mediterranean, the Wadden Sea (part of the European North Sea), the South Pacific, and the Antarctic and Southern Ocean – were all highlighted. On land, Antarctica, the Sahel (increasingly drought stricken and desperate), South-east Asia, and areas of Africa with tropical forests were targeted.[51] There was also discussion at Christchurch about how the members of the Union – and especially the NGOs – could participate more effectively. One meeting produced the radical idea that IUCN should split into two allied unions – one governmental and the other non-governmental.[54]

Antarctica was the issue that made the New Zealand Government start to take IUCN seriously.[55] It had been agreed that Christchurch would be an appropriate place to establish an IUCN action plan for Antarctica and the Southern Ocean. But a paper commissioned by the American attorney and leading light in ASOC, Jim Barnes, was torn up by the Council who argued it was too long, failed to support the Antarctic Treaty as the best basis for conservation in the region, and sought a role for IUCN which went beyond the Union's capacity for action.[15] A certain cooling between IUCN and ASOC followed. A new paper by Peter Sand and Françoise Burhenne-Guilmin of the Environmental Law Centre was debated in Christchurch in a special open meeting chaired by Bob Boote and Derrick Ovington.

Bob Boote also chaired a group which prepared a resolution which defined the Union's Antarctic policy for many years to come.[56] In urging the Antarctic Treaty consultative parties to '*further enhance the status of the Antarctica environment*', it called expressly for a designation of the whole region '*which connotes worldwide its unique character and values and the special measures accorded to its planning, management and conservation*'. It urged that no mineral development should take place until the environmental risks had been evaluated and consideration given to complete prohibition of such activities. It called for better communication and the fostering of public awareness; for long-term ecological research and the establishment of a network of sites meriting special protection; for monitoring of the impact of tourism; and for a range of actions to ensure the effectiveness of CCAMLR (for which IUCN expertise was volunteered).[56] This recommendation, followed by others in successive General Assemblies, paved the way for the *Antarctic Conservation Strategy* agreed in 1990.[57]

The Christchurch General Assembly, of course, also got entangled in internal management matters – inevitably, given the upheavals that had preceded it. Some members wanted the Council to set up a special committee to examine how to improve management efficiency.[58] The Council did look at structure and functions, at how it could spend less time on finance and administration and more on discussing conservation issues and the planning of the programme, and – yet again – at '*whether IUCN's six Commissions, created over 25 years ago, were still suited to the present work of the Union and whether there was a need for new Commissions on such subjects as Population*'.[59–62] Meanwhile, after Christchurch, as after Kinshasa, the finances recovered slowly. The 1981 deficit proved less than feared, and the Bureau congratulated Lee Talbot on his strict financial control.[60] In January 1982 it was able to approve a new budget with accelerated repayment of the accumulated deficit.[60] This was made possible by WWF: Charles de Haes offered to reschedule and increase its payments so as to eliminate the deficit entirely by the end of 1982.[59]

The Bureau itself needed new leadership once Maurice Strong departed. The simplest course was to give the Chair to the President, to serve with the Vice-Presidents, Treasurer and five other Councillors. The result was to transform the Bureau from the rather distinctive and self-willed body Maurice Strong had created into a sub-committee of the Council (which is what it has remained). Moreover, in later years many of the things it had done were taken over by a new Finance and Administration Committee and Programme Advisory Committee, which met immediately before Council sessions and did much preparatory leg-work.[63]

This left the Bureau with a much-reduced work load, and it was proposed that it focus on the long-term perspective for IUCN as an institution.[64,65] It also had sensitive tasks – like finding a new Treasurer in 1982 to replace Don McMichael.[60] In due course Dr Dietrich von Hegel was persuaded to take the job, but he emphasized – as McMichael had done before him – that it would be better for the Treasurer to be based near to headquarters and readily available for urgent face-to-face consultation.[66] This change was made after the Madrid General Assembly in 1984, when Leonard Hentsch, a Swiss banker (and member of one of the oldest family banking firms in Geneva) was elected.[67]

A High at Bali...

The Commission on National Parks and Protected Areas was one of the most outstanding components of IUCN in the early 1980s. After Hal Eidsvik's departure, Jeffrey McNeely returned from South-east Asia to support Kenton Miller as Executive Officer, and they organized a systematic review of the world's existing protected areas. At six-monthly intervals, they produced new lists of possible additions, including world heritage sites and biosphere reserves. Jeremy Harrison of the Protected Areas Data Unit (PADU), backed up this work with maps and data management, and WWF, UNEP and UNESCO all provided funding.[68]

The Third World Conference on National Parks was held at Bali, Indonesia, in 1982.[68,69] Kenton Miller served as Secretary-General and Jeffrey McNeely as the Coordinator. The Congress undertook the first world-wide systematic review of the status of, and trends in, protected areas. It was regionally based, using Udvardy's classification (by this time CNPPA had enlisted a full tally of Regional Vice-Chairs), with PADU providing the maps and data. The success of the many years of effort by the conservation movement since the 1940s could be judged by the growth in the number and extent of protected areas – from some 750, totalling about 800 million hectares in 1940, to over 3000, with nearly 4000 million hectares in 1983. While IUCN could not claim the credit for all this, its steady promotion of the importance of such areas, and the support it gave to the world's 'parks people' undoubtedly had a major influence.[68,69]

Bali was a watershed for the Commission, for previously it had been led largely by protected areas experts from Europe and North America, but now the thrust turned south (no doubt impelled by Kenton Miller's own involvement in South America, and his University of Michigan seminars which welcomed a steady stream of people from the South). The Commission held an increasing number of regional working sessions: the total (since 1960) is now 51, 25 of them held in developing countries.[70]

The southward shift was stimulated in Bali by voices calling for new approaches. Walter Lusigi asked whether realistic conservation was possible in Africa, given political pressures and corruption. He urged that local communities must be involved – and that their limited consumption of wildlife in national parks should be accepted. (This led to his branding as a 'poacher's champion' by Perez Olindo, in their native Kenya, where all shooting of wild species was illegal.) His words fell on receptive ears, for following the World Conservation Strategy, IUCN was devoting increasing attention to sustainable resource management and sustainable wildlife use and was beginning to incorporate the concepts underlying biosphere reserves in its policies.[71,72] WWF was equally committed to the WCS, but was unable to abandon overnight all the 'old style' protected area projects, in which it had invested much money and effort, and which remained very attractive to public subscribers.

During the Congress, Cyrille de Klemm, a French environmental lawyer, suggested that a global convention covering all the world's habitats should be prepared – and this was the beginning of a process which led to the Convention on Biological Diversity ten years later.[68] Kenton Miller challenged the world conservation community to triple the world's coverage of protected areas and to safeguard ten per cent of each *biogeographic province* by the next World Congress in 1992 (this was a much sounder goal, ecologically, than the more usual proposal to protect 10 per cent of each *national territory*).[68] The Bali Congress was probably the most important meeting on protected areas ever held, and its action plan set the international agenda on protected areas for the whole of the following decade. It showed *'IUCN at its best – a convener, a leader, a promoter of great ideas, a facilitator of debate and team building...'*.[68]

The WWF Partnership

Official links between IUCN and WWF remained close in the period between 1980 and 1984. The Fund was the principal supporter of the Union's programme. It paid for the bulk of the field projects. It was the provider of managerial and financial services. Lee Talbot, as Director-General, and a number of other staff, including Jeffrey Sayer who ran the forest programme, had come across to IUCN from WWF.

The positive side of the relationship was illustrated by the arrangement (proposed by Prince Philip in 1981) that the Presidents should each be an *ex officio* Vice-President of the other organization.[48,60,75] At a Bureau meeting, held in London immediately after the WWF Executive Committee in June 1982, the two Presidents agreed to replace the old 'Grey Areas Committee' by an IUCN/WWF Coordination

Committee which would look at any problems such as '*overlap in functions and funding*'.[47] It was to consist of the Presidents, the Treasurers, one Vice-President from each organization, and the two Director-Generals, and the Chair would alternate between the Presidents.[47] The Committee started to meet that same year, but according to Prince Philip, the idea of alternating Chairs did not work very easily, largely because of Kassas' modesty. '*I would say to Kassas "Come on, it's your turn to take the Chair" but he always said "No, you take it, please"*'.[76] The two Presidents spoke of allocating target audiences for fund-raising, so that the organizations did not trip over one another's feet. Prince Philip even suggested that there might be a joint Executive Committee for the two organizations.

Prince Philip's capacity to produce challenging ideas was obvious at his first Bureau meeting. He suggested that the close relationship of the two partner organizations should be reflected in their names. IUCN, he said, should be renamed the World Conservation Union, and WWF the World Conservation Fund, while the shared headquarters should be the World Conservation Centre. He also suggested that the names of the specialized units might be made to conform – with a World Conservation Law Centre in Bonn and a World Conservation Data Centre in Cambridge.[47] The IUCN Council had been toying with a change of name to 'World Conservation Organization' before Christchurch, but in the face of members' criticism, dropped back to the dull formula 'IUCN, the World Conservation Organization'.[48] It did adopt the 'World Conservation Union' as a 'working title' in 1989 (and formally registered its right to the name in the USA and UK), while WWF renamed itself 'the World Wide Fund for Nature' in 1986 – a tongue-twisting elaboration which many of its supporters, including the Canadian and United States National Member Organizations, refused to accept.[77] Prince Philip's proposal might well have been better, but the only part that was implemented at the time was the name for the joint headquarters in Gland.

But there was a downside to the relationship. While the Joint Coordination Committee had its attractions, there was a danger that it would become a body making IUCN policy, thereby eroding the role of the elected Council and its Bureau.[14] Lee Talbot was concerned that with Mohamed Kassas deferring to Prince Philip, Dietrich von Hegel in close alliance with the WWF Treasurer, Louis Franck (and with the Finance Officer, Conrad von Ulm-Erbach, who had succeeded Stephan Suwald), and the IUCN Vice-President, Russell Train, also serving as President of WWF-US, the WWF side of the Committee was over-dominant.[14] At about this time Maurice Strong expressed a different worry – that WWF International had '*no real system of accountability to a constituency...*' in contrast to IUCN which had a well developed and democratic system. (He suggested that the remedy was to make WWF International more accountable by giving the national organizations more weight in the election of its trustees.)[78]

There were continuing niggles over finance. Both Hal Coolidge and Maurice Strong criticized WWF for not sharing the endowment raised by the 'Thousand and One Club'.[78,79] There was also friction between the Director-Generals and Secretariats. IUCN's financial dependence on WWF gave Charles de Haes a special reason for watching carefully over what the Union and its staff were doing. IUCN activities were a regular agenda item in his management group.[10] He has emphasized how important it was for him to be able to work effectively with IUCN, as a close partner and major recipient of WWF funding.[10] But he did not hesitate to question actions which he disliked. For their part, '*the staff of IUCN was greatly resentful of WWF meddling and put Lee Talbot under strong pressure to stand up to Charles de Haes. Sometimes this led to unnecessary confrontation...*'.[80] However, Talbot was succeeding in reducing IUCN's dependence on WWF: when he became Director-General the Fund was meeting 80 per cent of the Union's core costs but by the Northern autumn of 1982 the share had fallen to 20 per cent – much to Charles de Haes' surprise and delight.[14,41]

The officers of IUCN clearly wanted to maintain good relations with WWF, and disapproved of the friction between staff members. A questionnaire issued by Raisa Scriabine of IUCN drew a magisterial rebuke from the Treasurer, Dietrich von Hegel, who wrote to Lee Talbot that:

> *'IUCN people who criticize WWF do not take into account that the main difficulties of our relationship to WWF stemmed from the fact that IUCN failed to make sound management decisions in the past...And it was not IUCN, but WWF which prevented IUCN from bankruptcy and explosion and now gently helps IUCN to cover the accumulated deficit. Therefore all fears of too much "dependence" of IUCN upon WWF and other similar ideas are not helpful, even dangerous.'*[81]

Von Hegel welcomed the tighter linkage achieved through the roles of the two Presidents in the two organizations and urged that Council members should reject *'any suspicious statements by IUCN members against WWF'*.[81]

Another Change at the Top

One of the most sensitive tasks of any Council is the choice of a Chief Executive. At the time of the Christchurch General Assembly in 1981, nobody had any reason to expect that this duty would need attention for many years. Lee Talbot was in the saddle, he was young, energetic, strongly supported and had just resolved a financial crisis. But in November 1982 came a bombshell. The President reported that in a closed session held on the 23 November Dr Talbot had for personal reasons submitted his resignation as Director-General.[59] Why?

The first thing to emphasize is that there was no criticism of Lee Talbot's competence as an ecologist and professional conservationist, and the 'personal reasons' had nothing to do with his family life. Second, the Council strongly backed his management of the Union, including his tough actions in cutting the financial deficit.[59] On the face of it, the problem arose from the way in which he had drawn money from a fund established in connection with his salary, so as to meet cash flow needs for house-building without transferring reserves from the USA.[84] He repaid the money when called for. But the IUCN–WWF Joint Finance Group (which consisted of the two Treasurers, Dietrich von Hegel and Louis Franck, with Conrad Von Ulm-Erbach as Director of Finance), meeting in Paris on 3 November, expressed concern.[82] On the eve of the next IUCN Council meeting on 23 November von Hegel and von Ulm took the matter to Mohamed Kassas, who convened a meeting involving them, Wolfgang Burhenne, Luc Hoffmann and Lee Talbot himself. Mohamed Kassas confirms that he and the other IUCN officers were inclined to accept Lee Talbot's explanation.[83]

WWF took another view. There is a strong conviction in IUCN that they welcomed the opportunity to make a change. The issue exploded at a routine meeting of the Joint Coordination Committee – or, more strictly, the two Presidents, two Vice-

Presidents and the two Treasurers – on the day before the IUCN Council went into session.[83] Louis Franck, the Treasurer of WWF, said that unless the Director-General resigned, he could not support further payment of WWF money to IUCN.[83] Mohamed Kassas saw Lee Talbot and put the position to him. He, in turn, consulted Russell Train, who had been his boss at the Council on Environmental Quality and whom he counted as a friend, and was told that whatever the rights and wrongs of it, he was at the end of the road so far as acceptability to WWF was concerned, and should go with dignity.[85] Lee Talbot felt betrayed by his President and Treasurer, and resigned.[84] It was a sad end to 30 years of service to IUCN as Staff Ecologist, Commission Member, Board Member, Vice-President and Director-General. Everything happened in a tremendous hurry. It was all sewn up before the Council met, and they did not discuss the background or question the issues.[36]

So, in November 1982, IUCN once again had a void at the top. Kenton Miller was taken aside by Mohamed Kassas and Russell Train. '*Lee Talbot has just resigned*', they said. '*We are in an awkward position. We would like to name you as Director General at the Council meeting tomorrow.*'[86] Miller felt honoured, but insisted that there should be a proper electoral process.[87] Council duly met in closed session and heard of the resignation. Bob Boote recalls[88] that he asked whether it might be more efficient to make one person Director-General of both organizations, but this idea found little favour. Peter Sand was appointed Acting Director-General. Council members were asked to propose candidates by the first week in January 1983. The Bureau was to do the screening, and select more than one and fewer than four candidates for election by Council in a postal ballot (responsibility for appointment now rested with the Council, not the General Assembly).

The short list was again a strong one – with three very different candidates. Kenton Miller was Professor in the School of Natural Resources in the University of Michigan, Chair of the Commission on National Parks and Protected Areas, and had the outstanding achievements of Bali just behind him. Peter Thacher, one of the architects of the Stockholm Conference, had built a high international reputation as Assistant Executive Director of UNEP, as a skilled Chairman, a good speaker, and an experienced international politician. Brian Walker had been Director of OXFAM and was currently Director of the International Institute for Environment and Development. There were interviews in February 1983. Once again the Council chose the candidate it knew best – Kenton Miller – and the appointment was a popular one.[5] But he could not take up his post until the end of his teaching semester, although he commuted across the Atlantic every two or three weeks to discuss forward planning with groups of staff.[86] Because Peter Sand was leaving at the end of April 1983, Pierre Goeldlin, Swiss member of Council and Professor at Lausanne, was appointed Acting Director-General until the new DG could take up the post on 1 July.[89]

Lee Talbot took Kenton Miller aside. '*When you are Director General*', he said '*get some independent, outside advice on the financial services. There is something wrong. I have looked into it, but cannot find it...*'.[86] On the face of it, the advice may have seemed pessimistic, for Miller inherited a healthy financial situation. The deficit had been paid off, there was a reserve fund worth roughly SFr500,000 and the year's budget was 25 per cent higher than ever before, and fully covered.[14] And in recognition of Dr Miller's appointment, WWF–US voted a special grant of US$50,000 to help in the development of the World Conservation Plan which was to follow the WCS.[90]

9 Conservation for Development

A Time of Expansion

The period between 1982 and 1988 was one of continuing growth in international environmental activity. New international agreements were negotiated and signed – including major conventions on the law of the sea, the protection of the ozone layer, and the control of hazardous substances.[1] Conferences, action plans, regional agreements and national laws all multiplied. The Intergovernmental Panel on Climate Change was established. The theme of 'sustainable development' expounded in the World Conservation Strategy was seized upon, elaborated and publicized by the World Commission on Environment and Development.[2]

National conservation bodies were growing fast. By 1985 the National Wildlife Federation in the United States had 4.5 million members, the National Audubon Society 425,000 and the Sierra Club 363,000. In the UK, the National Trust (concerned with historic monuments as well as rural 'greenspace') had 1.3 million members and the Royal Society for the Protection of Birds 475,000. American membership of Greenpeace totalled 450,000: while in the UK it had only 50,000 members, WWF had 91,000 and Friends of the Earth 30,000. Most of these bodies doubled their membership in the following five years.[1]

The IUCN membership also grew considerably, thanks especially to the work of the Conservation for Development Centre, which increased the Union's visibility and relevance in developing countries. By the time of the General Assembly held in Madrid in 1984 the programme had become integrated, about a central theme – *'partnership in conservation: towards a World Conservation Plan'*.[3] The Technical Meetings covered IUCN's conservation achievements, limitations and opportunities, current conservation issues, and the steps that needed to be taken in preparing the world plan. There were also symposia on conservation and development (*'to clarify the relationship'*), Antarctica and the Southern Ocean and the categorization of threats to species. The programme for 1984–87 bore the general title 'Implementing the World Conservation Strategy'.[4]

The Madrid General Assembly saw something new – a contested election for the Presidency. Mohamed Kassas had come to the end of his second term of office. He had been warmly liked and highly regarded, and the Council voted to give him a special plaque in commemoration of his service.[5] Inspired by a feeling that the membership should have a democratic choice, it was resolved that two names would be put forward for the Presidency and for the Chair of each Commission.[6] The 'internal' Presidential nominee was a serving Vice-President, Dr Abdulbar al Gain, head of the Monitoring and Environment Protection Agency of Saudi Arabia, and well known in world climatological circles. But they wanted another candidate, and Mohamed Kassas was asked to find out whether Dr Monkombu Swaminathan, the world-famous Indian plant geneticist, Fellow of the Royal Society of London, honorary member of academies and holder of honours in many countries, and later recipient of the World Food Prize, would agree to stand.

He did. The candidates were both men of high calibre and rank in their countries. One represented the world of biological science: the other had experience in governmental administration and had been active in the UNEP Governing Council. One knew IUCN well, having been a Vice-President: the other had no links with the Union. The vote was narrow, but Dr Swaminathan (who was not at the Assembly) was elected, holding office until 1990. The election provoked long subsequent debate over whether it was seemly to expose very eminent people to the hurly-burly of the hustings – a debate that was to cause some anguish in 1990 and 1994.

Soon after his election, President Swaminathan issued a 'personal manifesto'. He emphasized that '*IUCN must change from a Euro-centric to an Earth-centric organization*'. He also stressed that '*to save the panda and the penguin, it is equally important to pay attention to the poor and the hungry...*'.[7] These themes recurred in speeches throughout his Presidency – in Ottawa in 1986,[41] San Jose in 1988 and at his final General Assembly in Perth in 1990.

Developing the World Conservation Strategy

The Conservation for Development Centre had been acclaimed in Lee Talbot's report to Christchurch as '*a major innovation*'.[8] It established itself steadily, if rather slowly. Mike Cockerell was strongly supported by Lee Talbot, Charles de Haes and Anders Forsse of SIDA: without this backing the venture might well have failed and IUCN '*might never have developed its field programmes, its regional and national offices or for that matter its theme programmes*'.[9]

There was considerable agonizing over how to fit the CDC into the fabric of IUCN – not surprisingly, for on the face of it, the fit was difficult. The Bureau had opined that the expertise the Centre needed would be drawn from IUCN's networks – which meant the Commissions.[10] The Chair of the Commission on Environmental Planning elected in Ashkhabad, Professor Peter Jacobs, argued that IUCN had little professional competence in development matters, and that his Commission should provide intellectual back-up and guidance.[10,11] Several Commissions wanted to assign members as participants in CDC projects,[12] and the six Commission Chairs made a bid to constitute the CDC Steering Committee.[13]

Maurice Strong and Mike Cockerell had a different vision. Strong was clear that CDC must develop both an operating and a project management capability, and he saw that this would raise questions of relationship with other parts of IUCN and with WWF, and especially with the Joint Project Management Group (which might well eventually be incorporated within the Centre). While recognizing why it had been decided to 'incubate' CDC as a subsidiary operation of IUCN, he remained of the view that it might eventually function as '*the operating and implementing arm of both organizations*', with its own Board made up of nominees of them both.[14] But these were longer-term considerations, and Mike Cockerell's urgent need was to get the action started. As he wrote in March 1983, '*the race against time, to make CDC fully operational and self-supporting before the start-up grant was depleted, has had a major influence on the programme and operational style of CDC...*'.[10]

He had problems convincing development assistance agencies, funds and foundations that IUCN, thought of as 'the nature organization', had something to offer them. Some insisted *'that their assistance structure does not allow for support to be given to GONGOs in Switzerland, even if this is simply a conduit to the developing world'*.[10] Another problem was scale: *'CDC had to go for projects of SFr 200,000 plus or it would not be able to operate'*.[9] In a note to Commission Executive Officers seeking proposals he asked that *'only projects of major significance reflecting priorities of the WCS should be considered, and these will normally be projects costing SFr300,000 or above'*.[15] Wolfgang Burhenne commented that the approach *'eliminates law, as the Law Programme works in SFr20,000 units'*.[13] Cockerell found that *'the response I got from the Commissions was almost totally unusable, largely because the individual priorities of the different Commissions were not packageable into fundable projects. The problem was that they were either too narrow, too academic or too small'*.[9] He went it alone, and this created friction between him and the Commission Chairs, who were not made members of his Steering Committee.[12]

CDC's work fell into three main categories. First, *'projects in the developing world advising development assistance agencies on how to ensure that conservation is built into their development projects'*. Second, *'projects in developing countries designed to help countries to achieve conservation'*.[10] Third, *'promoting international conventions and assisting developing country governments to take these on board within their own systems'*.[16]

The second category accounted for most of the initial programme, which was worth over US$2.75 million in April 1983, with another $7 million worth of projects in the pipeline. WWF supported a two-year follow-up to the WCS, and an information sheet *The World Conservation Strategy in Action* was issued with the IUCN *Bulletin*. The first 'basket' of projects included national conservation strategies in Nepal, Sri Lanka and Zambia.[10] The idea was that:

> *'CDC would persuade developing countries to prepare NCSs and would provide the technical assistance. CDC's programme would thus evolve...as a result of careful in-country planning, all components of each national programme having been approved for implementation by the governments and by the participating aid agencies. This seems obvious now, but at the time it certainly was not in people's minds that this was to be the main focus of CDC.'*[9]

Charles de Haes was extremely supportive, whereas Mostafa Tolba of UNEP wanted to take a more cautious line and focus on just two or three countries, until experience had been gained.[16]

The National Conservation Strategy programme took off. In the period between 1980 and 1986, strategies were prepared by some 30 states,[17] and the momentum continued right up to 1992 when the most ambitious of all the strategies, that for Pakistan, appeared.[18] IUCN did not have an institutional role in all of these: for example it played no part in the six-volume *Conservation and Development Plan for the UK* (although its British members did),[19] while the USA had completed its own analysis, the *Global 2000 Report to the President* before the WCS appeared (it was, indeed, very useful to the compilers of the WCS).[20] But by 1987, CDC had played a major part in strategies for Bangladesh, Botswana, Costa Rica, Jordan, Kenya, Mauritania, Nepal, Pakistan, St Lucia, Togo, Zambia and Zimbabwe. New projects were then expected in Belize, Colombia, El Salvador, Oman, Vanuatu and several of the Sahelian countries.[21]

On their own, national conservation strategies had limited value. Their main benefit was in alerting people to the importance of sustainable development, and in providing a framework, an agenda for action. For success, they had to involve a wide cross-section of government departments and agencies, including those concerned with economic development. In Nepal, an early break-through came when the Prime Minister and the Chairman of the National Planning Commission gave their support: in Pakistan the process was led by the Deputy Chairman of the Planning Commission.[22] It was also essential to reach down to local community level, and here the Botswana strategy broke new ground, being discussed in every village in the country.[13]

The World Bank, advised by Lee Talbot and François Falloux,[23] saw a model to copy. In 1987 they initiated National Environmental Action Plans (NEAPs). The first of these were deliberately done in countries without NCSs, and they copied the best features of an NCS, being done at all levels. That in Lesotho involved meetings and consultations with every principal village in the country. They were done to the countries' own timetables, taking from one to three years to complete. The aim was to ensure that each country had 'ownership' of its plan, and the Bank provided funding for follow-up and implementation. But the pattern changed. '*Unfortunately...the Bank decided to make NEAPs a requirement for a country to receive World Bank/IDA support. This made them donor-driven rather than country-driven and changed the character of some – but not all – of the subsequent NEAPs.*'[23] Some became little more than six-month 'quick fixes', done largely by visiting teams, and resented as a form of 'conditionality' – you did it or you did not get Bank assistance.[24] In some instances they were imposed on countries which had – or were preparing – NCSs, and this duplication led to friction between the Bank and IUCN teams.

CDC also supported resource surveys, environmental monitoring, training and management projects at sub-national and local community level.[10] As had been expected, the Strategies became the frameworks within which other actions to integrate conservation and development went forward. The Centre expanded. At the time of the Madrid General Assembly in 1984 it was no more than '*a small unit, entirely funded from its own project budget, a maverick among IUCN's established programmes and structures*'.[25] By the time of the Costa Rica Assembly in 1988 it had grown into '*an integral part of the Secretariat, working in increasingly close collaboration with the Commissions and theme programmes, with a growing network of field offices and with financial backing that is a significant factor in IUCN's financial viability...*'.[21] Mark Halle, previously a member of UNEP's Regional Office for Europe in Geneva and then a staff member of WWF and Personal Assistant to Charles de Haes, came across to IUCN as Mike Cockerell's deputy. A Consultant Register with 'electronically processed access' to some 1000 experts in relevant fields was prepared.

Another seed for future growth was sown in the first furrows of CDC development. Mike Cockerell wrote:

> '*Regionalization was very much on my mind when I was writing the basic CDC strategy document immediately before coming to IUCN for I could not see how aid agencies could be persuaded to fund a Swiss-based operation without developing country offices. We had to have permanent secretariat staff located in good Regional Offices, and*

> *discussions on these started at the New Zealand GA...Soon after this a*
> *formal proposal was presented to the Government of Zimbabwe for a*
> *regional office in Harare. I also discussed alternative possible*
> *locations for the Asian Regional Office in both Indonesia and Thailand*
> *on my way back from the GA but Asia was more difficult.'[9]*

The new offices proliferated. The first Regional Officer was appointed in Nairobi, under the agreement with Kenya on privileges and immunities.[26] In 1984 the CDC office in Zimbabwe opened.[25,27] The French Government provided funds for a Francophone Regional Officer for West Africa, based at Dakar in Senegal.[3,26,28] The use of non-convertible currencies to finance a Regional Officer for Eastern Europe was considered.[26] By 1987 the Nairobi office, led by Dr Rob Malpas, was financially self-sustaining and expanding fast. It was base for a Sahel unit as well as a team managing projects in East Africa. There were offices in Harare (for southern Africa), Dakar (for West Africa), San Jose, Costa Rica (for Central America) and Karachi (for Pakistan).[21] A joint programme in the Caribbean had been launched in partnership with the Caribbean Conservation Association, with an office in Barbados, and a similar initiative was being considered for the South Pacific.[21] A legal identity and presence had also been established in the USA so as to make IUCN eligible for grants and contracts from government, and allow tax exemptions for donors.

This expansion happened because IUCN gained the confidence of the official development assistance community. With the widening acceptance of the World Conservation Strategy, conservation had been recognized as an important component of development. Support for IUCN programmes followed, and this in turn shifted the centre of gravity of IUCN as a whole towards the part of the spectrum of activities in which CDC was located. In turn, CDC moved from project design (which could be done at headquarters) to on-the-ground implementation, which demanded professional staff located in the regions.[21]

But these new Regional and Country Offices were very much under the direction of the headquarters, linked to a series of regional desks established there. There was little devolution of power – and several office directors were expatriates from the North. A 23-year-old Englishman, Steve Bass, was the Union's first 'man in Nepal' (later transferring to Southern Africa): Rob Malpas, head of the Nairobi office, was also English; a Frenchman, Gerard Sournia, was in charge in West Africa; and a Swede, Johan Ashuvud, started the work in Central America (to be succeeded by a Latin American following his tragic death in an accident in 1988). It was not for some time that nationals of the developing world were appointed to lead the effort in their regions – commencing with Adolfo Mascarenhas (of Tanzania) followed by India Musokotwane (a Chieftain from Zambia) in southern Africa, and Aban Marker Kabraji in her native Pakistan. Because the offices had virtually no funds to build regional networks or convene regional meetings, their contact with IUCN members in their regions was severely constrained.

The creation of the Conservation for Development Centre had four inter-linked consequences for IUCN and for conservation. First, the Union began to attract serious money from official development assistance agencies for thematic programmes on such topics as tropical forests and wetlands as well as for conservation strategies. Second, the IUCN Secretariat became a real force in the execution of action. Third, as the overall programme got bigger, its balance changed and the Commissions ceased to be the dominant players – at least in expenditure terms. Fourth, and most important, IUCN began to evolve as the global conservation body with the widest-spreading roots and presence in the developing world. These were the ingredients of cultural transformation.

The Nordic countries, Norway, Sweden, Denmark and Finland, were among the few nations in the world that had heeded the United Nations call for all developed countries to allocate 0.7 per cent of their Gross Domestic Product to development assistance. They were keen to apply the lessons of the World Conservation Strategy. But they were not well equipped with delivery mechanisms that reached out to the grass roots of society in the poorer countries. Because IUCN worked with NGOs, it offered a real prospect of linkage with local bodies and communities.[29] The voluntary networks represented by the IUCN Commissions were also attractive as a pool of knowledge they could tap. So – influenced especially by key individuals such as the Swede, Mats Segnestam, who had led IUCN's marine programme before joining the Swedish International Development Agency, SIDA – they began to channel substantial funds through the Union. The Swiss and Netherlands agencies followed suit, together (to a degree) with those of Germany and France. Other nations with well-established systems of their own did not need to use this machinery. But they, and UN bodies like UNDP, did work in close collaboration with IUCN and many of them provided financial support to the NCS process.[16]

The second consequence followed. The Director-General was responsible for implementing the Agency contracts, and this could only be done through the specialist staff recruited for the purpose in CDC, with its regional desks at headquarters and its Regional or Country Offices, or in the headquarters units running thematic programmes like tropical forests, wetlands or (later) the Sahel. Although the General Assembly and Council approved the overall programme within which these activities slotted, what was done had to be endorsed by the donors and the Director-General was accountable for the proper implementation of their contracts. By 1988 the Secretariat was directing a substantial proportion of the overall programme.

The Commissions did benefit, as the resources available to IUCN as a whole grew. Some of them also began to raise their own funds, flowing directly into the offices of the Chair (and sometimes those of the Chairs of specialist groups) and allowing additional supporting staff there. But before about 1975 they had been the principal agents of programme implementation, and the main task of the Secretariat had been to support them. Strongly-minded Commission Chairs like Peter Scott or Hal Coolidge worked on the assumption that Commission Executive Officers worked for them rather than the Director-General.[30] Even after expansion began in the Budowski–Nicholls era, the Commission Chairs remained the principal group of conservation experts on the Council and had a major influence on the whole programme. Throughout Mohamed Kassas' time as President:

> '*as think fountains, the Commissions were the IUCN organs for identifying conservation issues and for gauging their extent and importance, outlining what needed to be done and should be done..., identifying the specific roles of IUCN and its programmes of action and activities...*'[31]

But as CDC evolved, it set up its own machinery for steering field projects, and separate advisory committees were appointed to guide the new theme programmes. While some Commissions remained world leaders, especially in species and habitat conservation, national parks and protected areas and environmental law, they were now only part of a much larger and more complex IUCN.

A lot of people did not like this transformation. Hal Eidsvik believes that '*as IUCN passed from a policy and technical assistance organization into a pseudo-Aid Agency it lost...much of its strength*'.[32] Marc Dourojeanni thinks that:

> '*from the 1960s to the '90s IUCN passed from the extreme protection-ism of nature to equally extreme human sustainable development, not stopping the pendulum in the right point of equilibrium which is more or less the conservation philosophy of the 1980s. The IUCN responsi-bility in human development is to care for the natural resources and the environment for the sake of the people. It is not...to promote devel-opment ('sustainable' if you want)...*'[33]

Michel Batisse is another who regretted the change in IUCN from an essentially scientific advisory body to an operational agency.

The steps towards regionalization brought the most profound change of all. The major worldwide environmental bodies – IUCN, WWF, Greenpeace and Friends of the Earth – all (inevitably) have their financial roots in the developed North but the first two, in particular, have always cast their fruit into the developing South. So have bodies like the US-based Nature Conservancy and Conservation International. The latter – with about 130 staff at its Washington DC headquarters – has national offices and activities in some 24 countries, and around 400 field staff, and has broadened from its traditional concentration of effort in Latin America to take in programmes in Africa and Asia. But none of these bodies can be described as 'Southern-based'. The progressive expansion of IUCN Regional and Country Offices gave the Secretariat an opportunity to link with the members in the developing world, listen to their needs and facilitate their actions.[22] It also stimulated the members to demand better links with, and services from, 'their' Regional and Country Offices and greater control over the IUCN programme in their regions. CDC was thus a springboard for the process of regionalization and decentralization that has been the dominant feature of the latest period of IUCN's history (see Chapter 11).

Towards a Second
World Conservation Strategy

In 1982 UNEP published a major review of trends in the world environment in the decade following the Stockholm Conference[34] and its Governing Council held a Session of Special Character to examine the world environmental situation. Two major initiatives were launched soon afterwards. One – proposed originally by Japan, and opposed by the Soviet Union and its communist allies – was the establishment of a World Commission on Environment and Development under the leadership of the Prime Minister of Norway, Mrs Gro Harlem Brundtland. Its seminal report, *Our Common Future*, published in 1987, gained wider circulation and publicity than any comparable document in recent years, and established the term 'sustainable develop-ment' in the global dictionary.[2] The second initiative – seen as a sop to the Soviets, who disliked the World Commission because it was not to be controlled by govern-ments – was an intergovernmental effort to prepare an environmental perspective to the year 2000 and beyond. It produced a rather dull document that was quickly buried in the UNEP archives.[35] But the World Commission report led directly to the UN

Conference on Environment and Development – UNCED or 'Earth Summit' – held
in Rio de Janeiro in 1992, 20 years after Stockholm.

IUCN also took stock of progress since the publication of the World Conservation
Strategy. A workshop on living resource management for sustainable development,
organized by the Commission on Environmental Planning, was held in Montreal in
April 1984.[25,36] The Commission Chairman, Peter Jacobs, and the former Director-
General, David Munro (who had been a consultant to CDC on national conservation
strategies and had been elected to the IUCN Council at the Madrid General Assembly
in 1984), were the driving force behind the International Conference on the World
Conservation Strategy, held in Ottawa in June 1986.[37] The conference was sponsored
by the Canadian Wildlife Federation, Environment Canada, UNEP and WWF and
took as its central theme 'conservation with equity' (also the title of the conference
volume, edited by Jacobs and Munro).[17]

Over 500 people, from 100 countries, attended.[17,38] President Kaunda of Zambia,
Mrs Victoria Chitepo, Minister of Natural Resources and Tourism in Zimbabwe, and
ministers from Canada and the UK were among the authors of papers – about half of
which came from the developing world. Maurice Strong was there as Special Adviser
to the Secretary-General of the UN. Mostafa Tolba delivered a World Environment
Day lecture. The conference reviewed the process of integrating conservation and
development, turned to the implementation of the WCS, considered alternative strategies for sustainable development, put national conservation strategies in context, and
concluded with an assessment of how to spread the message.

As follow-up, it was suggested that priority should go to the preparation by IUCN
of a revision of the WCS – not to replace it, but to add new thinking and to give
sustainable development a more 'human face'.[17,39,41] The transformation in thinking
meant, inevitably, that it would also have a 'Southern face', and that IUCN would
have to listen more closely to its Southern members and reflect their views in the
next major statement of world conservation policy. UNEP and WWF, the traditional
partners, were urged to back the new venture (which was costed at US$547,500). A
draft should be ready for the next Session of the General Assembly, or for launching
at the 'modest' celebrations that would mark the 40th anniversary of IUCN, probably
at Fontainebleau, in 1988.[39] The timetable, not surprisingly, proved wholly unrealistic, and 'WCS II' did not actually emerge until 1991.[40] Its story and content are
described in Chapter 10.

Conserving Species, Habitats and Protected Areas

The new emphasis on sustainable development was looked at askance by many IUCN
members. There was concern that the CDC was taking the Union out of its real
environmental niche.[33] But in the 1980s there was still a great deal of work in IUCN's
traditional fields of action. The Commission programme on ecology – or rather,
ecosystems – had three major aims: to identify sound management principles; to
stimulate awareness of the risks of bad management; and to derive practical bench-
marks and guidelines for good management. Key ecosystems including those of
tropical forests, freshwaters and coastal zones were highlighted. Sourcebooks on
terrestrial, freshwater, coastal and marine ecosystems (as detailed back-up to the
World Conservation Strategy) were in preparation. The output of publications was

diverse, and included a special series of 'occasional papers' (for example on *Natural Disasters and Ecological Processes* published in 1982 and on *Precipitation and Water Recycling in Tropical Rain Forests* produced in 1983). Another major publication had dealt with the global status of mangroves.[36] Perhaps the weightiest product of the triennium between the Christchurch and Madrid Assemblies was a *Directory of African Wetlands* (in collaboration with UNESCO).

The protected areas programme was vigorous, and on any basis of analysis, the Third World Congress on National Parks, held at Bali in 1982, had been an event of outstanding importance.[12,42] CNPPA, of all the Commissions, was the most regionalized in structure: it had to be, since it was concerned with action on the ground in all the world's biogeographical realms. It had Vice-Chairs for each region. One member was selected for each country – usually the head of the National Parks Service or the leader of a well-established NGO. Regional meetings were held between Sessions of the General Assembly. Southern membership started to grow. During Kenton Miller's tenure of the Chair the total reached about 300: under his successor, Hal Eidsvik, it advanced towards 700.[37] Soon there were more members in the developing world than in the North. When marine protected areas gained popularity, thanks especially to the energy of the Australian head of the Great Barrier Reef Marine Park, Graeme Kelleher, there was a further growth in membership from the tropical regions.[43]

Species conservation was also a massive venture. By 1983 the SSC network, now led by Grenville Lucas of the Royal Botanic Gardens at Kew in England, involved over 1200 individual specialists, 37 cooperating organizations, 48 honorary consultants, 100 IUCN member organizations and two major zoo associations.[25] There were 77 specialist groups (of which 13 were operated by the International Council for Bird Preservation and the International Waterfowl Research Bureau). The database at the Conservation Monitoring Centre was fully operational and was also IUCN's contribution to UNEP's Global Environmental Monitoring System (GEMS). The African Elephant and Rhino Specialist Group had assessed the significance of trade in ivory and horns. Large and small whales, Sumatran rhinos, giant sable antelope, kouprey, polar bear, kangaroos and harp and hooded seals were all high on the action list (perhaps depressingly, some had been there almost since IUCN began), and some of this work contributed to the UNEP/FAO Global Plan of Action on Marine Mammals.

It is a paradox of IUCN's history that despite the total dependence of all animal life on green plants, plant conservation had been largely neglected by the Union and the SSC. In Kenton Miller's time as Director-General, a new WWF/IUCN plants programme was established.[12] Dr Peter Raven of the Missouri Botanical Gardens – one of the first botanists to highlight the alarming losses of plant species likely to result from the accelerating clearance of tropical rain forests – agreed to chair a steering committee. Professor Vernon Heywood of Reading University in the UK was recruited to lead the programme. A Botanic Gardens Conservation Secretariat (BGCS) was established at Kew, England, and it prepared a strategy for *ex situ* plant conservation:[12] the BGCS later 'spun off' from IUCN to become a separate entity and focal point for the world's botanic gardens community.

Promoting Environmental Law, Education and Information

The Commission on Environmental Policy, Law and Administration worked, as ever, in close partnership with the Environmental Law Centre and the International Council for Environmental Law. Wolfgang Burhenne was once more Commission Chair, while his wife, Françoise Burhenne-Guilmin directed the ELC. By 1984 there were some 45,000 entries in the Centre's environmental law database; the World Charter for Nature had been promoted; the negotiation of a possible convention on Antarctic minerals (which most conservationists bitterly opposed) had been monitored; a lot of effort had gone into supporting CITES, Ramsar, Migratory Species and World Heritage Conventions, the three first of which had gained a number of parties; and IUCN had assisted in the drafting of a new regional instrument, the ASEAN Agreement.[25] The *Islamic Principles for the Conservation of the Natural Environment* had been published.[36]

The Union had also intervened in the hope of influencing the International Tropical Timber Agreement which was eventually adopted in Geneva in 1983, and set up its Secretariat in Yokohama, Japan.[44] Not only did IUCN wish to retain responsibility for the Secretariats of CITES and Ramsar, but it made a bid for that of the Migratory Species Convention as well, seeing '*these Convention Secretariats as components of a World Conservation Federation, with Headquarters in Gland*'.[36] With hindsight, much duplication and waste would have been avoided had governments accepted this common-sense idea: as it turned out, however, the three-cornered relationship between the parties, UNEP and IUCN brought increasing strains over CITES and despite detailed negotiations in 1984,[6] UNEP terminated the agency arrangement under which IUCN had managed the Secretariat, incorporating them in its own staff and subjecting them to its own increasingly interventionist management style.

Environmental education continued to be a subject of continuing policy debate. On the positive side, an illustrated booklet *Introduction to the World Conservation Strategy*, with a Foreword by the Indian Prime Minister, Indira Gandhi, was produced and national environmental education strategies were promoted in many countries. An illustrated *Glossary of Environmental Education Terms* was prepared. Curricula, exhibitions, meetings, seminars for teachers and discussions at conferences all spread the message, and out-of-school educational efforts involved the International Youth Federation and wildlife clubs, especially in Africa. IUCN/WWF education projects worth US$500,000 a year were implemented through such clubs in Cameroon, Kenya, Nigeria, Sierra Leone, Sri Lanka, Tanzania, Uganda and Zambia. And there was much influence below the surface: as a note on the history of the Commission on Education and Communication puts it, '*many of the Commission's most significant successes may be those which remain largely unseen and sometimes unacknowledged*'.[45]

But EduC (as the Commission called itself around 1980–84) had a rough road to Madrid. In the first half of 1983 there were serious differences with WWF, which wanted to start a new joint information division, guided by an Awareness Advisory Committee under David Attenborough. The IUCN Bureau sided with WWF, and the President, Mohamed Kassas, wrote to Al Baez in June 1983 asking him to make way for new leadership.[46] Naseeb Dajani, the Jordanian Executive Officer, was dismissed in September. A furore broke out, with numerous letters of protest to the President. Al Baez refused to go quietly, demanding to serve out his term until the General Assembly – and this drew a magisterial rebuke from Hal Coolidge.[47] For his part, Dr

Baez complained of '*a long series of WWF actions taken against the Commission on Education and its officers*'.[48] He also emphasized that the three Director-Generals with whom he had worked as Chairman had not addressed the role of education in IUCN with enough seriousness and stressed that an Executive Officer must be retained.[49] There was outrage at the summary dismissal of the only Commission Executive Officer from the South, and the International Youth Federation, which had just appointed Mohan Mathews from India as its first officer from the developing world, said that it would have to re-think its cooperation with IUCN.[50] By the Madrid General Assembly in 1984 lack of an Executive Officer for the Commission on Education and doubts over funding were said to have hamstrung work in that programme area.

Position statements were also issued for the information of members and as foundations for action. In 1983–84 there were eight, dealing with population and natural resources, conservation of Antarctica, mangrove ecosystems, ocean trenches, oil pollution and associated problems, salt marshes, the conservation and management of tidal flats and the use of pesticides.[36] Such statements were well balanced and more or less authoritative, but questions still arose over whether:

> '*IUCN has thought through how it goes about trying to get governments to pay attention to its message. Does it draw upon a coherent body of theory and practice in attempting to influence government policy? Is it funded, staffed and organized to undertake this work? Has it drawn upon the most experienced advisers in organizing its work? Has it decided how far it wishes to go beyond making policy declarations and providing scientific findings and perspectives?*'[51]

A working group chaired by Dr Gerald Lieberman of the Education Commission was established to prepare a proposal for action.[38] But there is no record of what it led to, and Mike McCloskey, who was instrumental in having the group set up, believes that it '*went off in a different direction and never dealt with this set of questions*'.[52] The Union also failed to take up a suggestion, made by Mohamed Kassas during his Presidency, that it should produce periodic overviews of the state of world conservation: instead this became one of the themes covered by the World Resources Institute's outstanding series of *World Resources Reports*.[53]

Promoting Special Conservation Issues

In the period between 1981 and 1987 the General Assembly and Council debated, and the programme embraced, several special issues that had become of wide concern among IUCN members. Antarctica, the Sahel, tropical forests, wetlands and human populations became the subject of special initiatives – the first and last of them driven by two energetic members of Council, Dr Geoffrey Mosley of Australia and Dr Russell Peterson of the USA. The former took the Chair of an Antarctica Coordinating Committee and the latter of an IUCN Population Task Force.[5] It is remarkable that all these special programmes were developed independently from the Commissions, and that where specialist advisory groups were set up for them, they were not part of the Commission structure. The non-involvement of the Commission on Ecology in the forests, wetlands, Antarctic and Sahel initiatives was surely another sign of its diminishing influence.

IUCN's interest in Antarctic affairs had begun with the CCAMLR negotiations and the special meeting at the Christchurch General Assembly. In 1984 a general statement on *Conservation and Development of Antarctic Ecosystems* was issued. The next step was to be the preparation of a conservation strategy in collaboration with the Antarctic Treaty partners.[54] But – much to Geoffrey Mosley's annoyance – the action dragged and proposals were not ready until 1986.[38] Recommendations on Antarctica were, however, adopted at successive Sessions of the General Assembly and there were workshops on the subject both in Costa Rica and at the following Assembly in Perth, Western Australia, in 1990. These recommendations are known to have influenced the decision to ban Antarctic minerals development and also the content of the all-important Environment Protocol to the Treaty.[55] But the Antarctic Conservation Strategy promised for 1987–88 did not actually appear until 1991, by which time these policies had largely been decided.[56]

In his farewell speech to the General Assembly in Madrid, Mohamed Kassas pleaded for the inclusion of deserts in the IUCN programme. The drought crisis in the Sahel region of Africa in the 1980s was the trigger for action by the development aid agencies. Mike Cockerell put together a plan for a major CDC effort, costed at SFr10 million per annum.[16] President Swaminathan set up a task force to review the need and the proposed response, and deliberately chose an African member of Council, Walter Lusigi of Kenya, to head it. The task force had a specific remit to examine the well-being of the human population.[7,54] But the report of the task force did not please Russell Peterson, who considered that the views expressed on population '*were directly at variance with those recommended by the Task Force on Population and Sustainable Development. In his capacity as Chairman of the Task Force he wished to publicly dissociate himself from this part of the Sahel report...*' Walter Lusigi was unmoved, retorting that the Sahel task force '*had considered population questions as it felt appropriate for the Sahel region*'.[39] Events were to prove him right: population pressures were not the driving force behind the Sahel crisis that had been assumed by many commentators.[57]

The Sahel Report led to one of the largest special IUCN programmes, designed to create a research, planning and training network for sustainable development, and envisaged as operating for 15 years, from 1986 to 2001.[38] It was important not only because it addressed a major environmental problem, but because it operated in countries with very limited capacity – and almost without NGOs. Per Ryden of the Swedish International Development Agency was recruited to lead it. The programme was IUCN's first large multiple-donor project, and coordination was achieved through a joint annual meeting. It paved the way for later framework agreements with the agencies.[16,29]

Concern over the destruction of tropical forests, the habitats for a high proportion of the world's species, led inexorably to demands that IUCN play a part in developing strategies for their conservation. The Tropical Forest Programme emerged from a debate in Madrid and was refined in further dialogue with FAO, the World Bank and the World Resources Institute. SIDA was satisfied that there was a niche for IUCN and put the money in. '*IUCN's credibility came from the fact that it was able to identify with on-the-ground conservation and through its centres, Commissions and members was in a very strong position for providing sound advice on many aspects of tropical forest conservation.*'[38] Jeffrey Sayer, who transferred from WWF to IUCN to run the Programme, set up a strong Advisory Group drawn from forest botanists, foresters and forest conservationists: again this was not part of the Commission on Ecology. Rather similarly the Wetlands Programme was prompted by evidence that drainage was accelerating their loss in many regions. It was funded by WWF, and Patrick Dugan who led it also set up another specialist Advisory Committee outside the Commission on Ecology.

A resolution at Ashkhabad had demanded that IUCN should do something about human population issues, and Bob Boote and Max Nicholson had established links with the IPPF which were later put on a more formal footing by Lee Talbot and also led to the journal *People and Planet*, in which IUCN became closely involved.[58,59] In December 1980, before the Christchurch General Assembly, Max Nicholson wrote to Bob Boote about '*saving the World Conservation Strategy from becoming bogged down and losing credibility*'.[60] He proposed a series of specific actions at Christchurch, one on population – and Bob Boote brought the matter up at a special General Assembly planning group on 14 January 1981, proposing that '*Resolutions on Hunger amended in manuscript to 'poverty' and Population problems be drafted by the June meeting of the Council*'.[61]

However, the niche for IUCN in population matters needed careful definition, and this was the job of the task force set up after Christchurch under Russell Peterson's chairmanship. IUCN needed to concentrate on activities within its field of principal expertise,[62] and clearly it could not do anything directly about human populations, a vast subject to which many expert bodies were contributing. What it could do (as Ashok Khosla, Council member from India, put it) was demonstrate how conservation could contribute to reducing the impact of human populations on resources. But for Dr Peterson, because population was *the* world issue, IUCN had to be in there with a broad programme. And he did go out and get a lot of the money, especially from the Andrew W Mellon Foundation: by June 1986 the last US$100,000 was in sight.[62] Perdita Huston was in due course appointed Coordinator of the Population and Sustainable Development Programme early in 1987.[63]

Another broad issue was raised in 1983 by Hal Coolidge. He wrote to Mohamed Kassas arguing that IUCN must address the fact that it had '*so far failed to have a significant impact on religious groups and religious thought although we share a common interest in nature and the environment with Buddhism and a number of other sects*'. He urged that a committee prepare a paper on the subject for the next General Assembly. He also urged that IUCN do more '*to unite biological development with the arts and humanities*', recognizing the value of exhibitions of nature paintings and sculptures in getting people interested in conserving their subjects.[64] Coolidge was by then an old and sick man, and his letter was possibly his last input to the work of a Union he had served, encouraged, prodded and rescued repeatedly for 35 years.

Supporting and Extending the Membership

In November 1982 Mohamed Kassas convened a meeting of the Commission Chairs and the Director-General to discuss the role of the Commissions as principal links with the world's scientific and technical communities, as 'think-fountains' and as implementers of parts of the approved programme. He wanted to make them work together better and also sought more balanced membership, from a disciplinary, geographical and gender standpoint. In July 1983 the President also followed up concerns expressed in Christchurch by the non-governmental members of IUCN. He again raised the notion that IUCN might split into separate governmental and non-governmental bodies – and provoked a series of vigorous thumbs-down gestures from Councillors. He had more success when he turned to IUCN's role in support of its NGO members.

Kassas pointed out that vigorous non-governmental bodies were mostly located in the Western developed countries and fell into two groups: scientific and activist. While both had counterparts in developing countries (such as India, where the Chipko movement was clearly both activist and effective) many such NGOs could not afford even the most modest IUCN subscription.[65] He was also worried that IUCN was not providing NGOs in developing countries with the support and encouragement they needed. He pressed for the creation of a membership unit, suggesting that it would help IUCN to mobilize the world conservation community just as ICSU did in the world of science.[65] This might also help implement a proposal by Charles de Haes *'that the 1984 programme should give more emphasis to the action that could be carried out by IUCN members'*.[44]

The membership unit was duly created – under Delmar Blasco, who came to IUCN in 1985 from Nairobi where he had led the Environmental Liaison Centre International – an analogous focal point for environmental organizations that wanted to build links with UNEP. And other opportunities for linkage emerged as the CDC programme became decentralized, with more and more staff working on the ground in developing countries. As Kenton Miller reported in 1988, *'whenever possible, CDC projects are implemented in connection with IUCN members in the country or region. This association, directly or indirectly, leads to the strengthening of the partner institution and to increasing its influence.'*[21] He went on to illustrate the point by explaining that the CDC programmes in Central America were all carried out jointly with the Tropical Agricultural Research and Training Center (CATIE).

The need to make the Union a true network, supporting the membership, was widely acknowledged. But the development of Regional and Country Offices was hampered by lack of resources. CDC funds were very tight. Its embryonic offices in developing countries were largely staffed by consultants because there was no guarantee of long-term financial viability.[16] In 1984, when the Union had a total staff of 83, only two were based in the developing world (both in Nairobi). By 1987 the total Secretariat numbered 110, and 12 were spread between five developing world offices, but most of them, too, were consultants.[21] By 1990, however, two-thirds of the staff were based outside Switzerland, and if those on secondment to the reconstituted World Conservation Monitoring Centre are discounted, half of them were located in the developing world.[66] It was the beginning of a process which has gained momentum ever since.

Despite the work of the membership unit, the membership in the developing world still felt little affinity with a distant headquarters in one of the richest countries in the world. They wanted their Regional Offices to become foci for their meetings and communications, and IUCN as a whole to be a facilitating and networking organization. Very slowly – and always constrained by lack of unrestricted money – the Secretariat responded. Members' meetings and newsletters were initiated. In parallel, several Commissions – whose total numbers almost doubled between the Christchurch and Madrid General Assemblies, to reach over 3000 people by 1984 – set up their own regional networks. National Committees – at the start confined to Australia, Canada, the Netherlands, South Africa New Zealand, the UK and the USA – were encouraged. And the *Bulletin* was recognized as a key instrument for network-building, with a circulation in both English and French to about 4000 recipients (many of whom passed it on to others). There was a target list of 1000 journalists for press material.

But this was just a start. In his report to the Madrid General Assembly, Kenton Miller spoke of a huge unrealized potential in the membership network.

> *'Many activities in the programme could and indeed should have been implemented by member organizations with their own funding. A strengthened sense of unity and solidarity might have forged a greater capacity to deal with the complex issues facing people and their environment. And it must be said that competition among members, excessive expectations...and the late payment of dues have limited the ability of staff and volunteers to execute the Union's wishes completely and promptly.'*[25]

He probably had in mind a point he had made to Council – that many IUCN members in the developed world had budgets much larger than that of the IUCN Secretariat, and could do more through the Union if they wanted to.[36]

But how far did these processes alter the 'culture' of IUCN and make it less 'Northern' in its central ethos? Even at the time the World Conservation Strategy was gaining acclaim, to many Southern environmentalists IUCN appeared too rigid, too North-dominated and too 'establishment'. In the mid-1980s, when the CDC was extending its influence, the rhetoric of old-style conservation was still heard on many lips. There were very few headquarters Secretariat members from the developing world. The few that came – like Delmar Blasco, who was one of the first with Spanish as his mother tongue – felt strongly that real links with the membership had still to be built and that much had to be done to make the Secretariat multicultural.[67]

Another issue was how far the Union could speak for its members, and how far it needed to have a cohesion of identity, ensuring that the members were truly like-minded. The first issue came to the fore in 1985, when Greenpeace, by then a full member of IUCN, applied for consultative status at the International Maritime Organization. IMO had a rule excluding bodies that were members of organizations that themselves had consultative status – as IUCN did. Could IUCN represent the interests of Greenpeace? Wolfgang Burhenne told IMO *'that since IUCN represented the views of its membership as a whole, it could not represent those of individual members'*.[38] Very well – but this inevitably led to parallel presences and diminished the notion of a *Union* that could speak for all its constituents. And the ruling was at a variance with what had happened in the CCAMLR negotiations, when the IUCN delegation had been a channel through which the views of the Antarctica and Southern Ocean Coalition had been put to the meeting.

Greenpeace was admitted to IUCN at the Madrid General Assembly – after a battle among the electorate. Several State members, among whom Canada was outspoken, opposed – chiefly because of the illegality of some of Greenpeace's operations. Several non-governmental members were passionate supporters. The debate became raucous. Mohamed Kassas brought down his gavel. *'This is what we're going to do'*, he said. He read out the names of the most vociferous pros and antis. *'You will meet with me in ten minutes' time'*, he announced, naming a room. Kenton Miller took over the Chair, and the President walked out. He came back in due course and announced that *'we have applied eastern democracy, and in so doing we have accepted the application of Greenpeace to be a member of IUCN!'* Down came the gavel with the crack of a pyramid-overseer's whiplash. That was it.[43]

The argument was, of course, over the appropriateness of admitting a campaigning body that could be a thorn in the side of governments. But Greenpeace had gained respect around the Pacific Rim, including Latin America, for its opposition to French nuclear tests in the Pacific atolls. Alone among NGOs it had established a base in Antarctica, meeting the tests that would, were it a state, have qualified it for consultative status under the Antarctic Treaty. While very much a guerilla force in the conservation army, there is no doubt that its direct action won wide public respect in a way that even the best argued and most eloquent scientific presentation could not do.[43] Greenpeace International remained an IUCN member until 1996, when it withdrew (ostensibly for financial reasons): Greenpeace (Australia) remains within the fold.

There were tests for admission, to make sure that members all belonged in the same church, even if it was a very broad one. Applicants had to endorse the aims of the Union, and the principles of the World Conservation Strategy. In 1986 Council decided that they should also endorse the World Charter for Nature (which, in theory, would have excluded the United States from membership since it had voted against the Charter).[39] There was also continuing debate over changing the name to 'The World Conservation Union' – though this gave rise to translation problems in both French and Spanish. Less contentious, it was agreed that the bilingual letter-block logo which had come into general use should become the Union's formal emblem. The 'flaming artichoke' (Figure 3.1) was extinguished.[39]

The General Assembly has always been a crucially important means of sustaining the cohesion of IUCN and supporting the membership. It is unique in providing not only for the formal business of elections, resolutions and approval of programme and budget, but in offering an opportunity for conservationists from all over the world to meet, join in workshops, and forge informal and personal links. The Union had adopted the UN rule that where a conference was held away from headquarters, the host country should meet the extra costs involved (which meant those of providing the meeting place, facilities (including those for interpretation between the two official languages, French and English) and travel and subsistence of the Secretariat).[68] But as the Assembly got bigger, attracting many hundreds of people, it also became more expensive and was beyond the means of many developing countries. The problem came to a head between 1981 and 1987, when first Costa Rica and then Brazil withdrew their initial offers to host the 1984 Session, leaving Spain as the eventual (and generous) venue. The Bureau wondered whether this global wandering was efficient, and whether it might be better to stay near to the headquarters in Geneva or Lausanne.[26] In the event, although Costa Rica itself had very limited funds to offer, a fund-raising basket did allow an Assembly in San Jose in February 1988.[69]

Finance and Partnership – Again!

When Kenton Miller reported to Madrid, a rosy glow seemed to suffuse IUCN's financial sky. Income had exceeded expenditure in 1981, 1982 and 1983. Money had been credited to a general reserve and a contingency account.[25,68] While UNEP and WWF support remained crucial, *'governments and government agencies became an increasingly important source of income for IUCN, almost doubling their contribution during the report period. This increase largely reflects the successful operation of the Conservation for Development Centre.'*[25] But the donors insisted that the membership should pay their share of the expanding programme, and in Madrid, the

Council secured an increase of 15 per cent per annum for each of the three years in the 1984–87 triennium. The pill was sugared by Pierre Goeldlin's announcement that after four years of negotiation, the Swiss federal authorities had approved a tax-exempt status for IUCN which would permit saving in costs of about SFr300,000 to 400,000.[39,70] In 1984 there was an unprecedented bonus – a surplus of nearly SFr2 million of what the Council was told was unrestricted money. Unused to such largesse, they decided to go out and spend some of it, though over half did go into reserve.[54]

Support for the Commissions was strengthened. By November 1985 all except Ecology had Executive Officers[38] and that niche was filled in 1986 when Dr Frédéric Briand was appointed.[62] Money was secured from the Rockefeller Brothers fund to support Commission on Environmental Planning initiatives in Eastern Europe, which were to become a major programme and an important influence on the trend to new democracy, because many environmental NGOs were focal points for people opposed to communism.[62] The operational side of the partnership with WWF also ran smoothly. By 1984 IUCN was managing some 496 projects supported by the Fund, with a total cost of US$8.5 million.[25] Latin America and the Caribbean had the most – about 170 – with Africa next with 110, and Asia and the Pacific with about 95. The least activity was in North America and Greenland, with four projects – not because these areas were unimportant but because the national conservation organizations there had the capacity to tackle their problems without outside help. There were nearly 80 global and inter-regional projects.

But in May 1985 came a portentous announcement.

> '*The Director General informed the Council that WWF had decided to take over complete responsibility for the management of its field projects and would now be establishing its own Project Management Department. IUCN would nonetheless continue to provide technical advice on request for the WWF projects. In the meantime IUCN would continue to manage its own projects...*'.[54]

The operative date was to be 1 July 1985 – only two months ahead.

The decision did not come out of the blue. Mike Cockerell (now styled Director of Operations) was reorganizing his division, and had been discussing with WWF how their projects should be managed. He thought the change made sense. Because the WWF portfolio included so many tiny projects, it needed a different kind of management from the larger units operated by CDC.[13] Moreover,

> '*it was not simply a matter of IUCN managing their projects for them. It was the whole process of reviewing the hundreds of unsolicited requests for grants and assistance and recommending to WWF which things should be funded. The 350 or so projects really were an assortment of unrelated items taken from the incoming mail rather than a pro-actively designed programme.*'[71]

It is commonly said that the change was caused by restiveness on the part of the WWF national member organizations. They were the front-line fund-raisers, and they had been expanding fast. They wanted to control the expenditure of the money they raised, and questioned why they should give large sums to their international headquarters only for it to be passed on to IUCN or other recipients.[72] The answer appeared to be for WWF International itself to become a fully-fledged conservation service organization, managing its own programme.[73] This would help provide the *'greater clarity to the outside world about relations between IUCN and WWF'* which Charles de Haes believed to be necessary.[54] As part of the reconstruction, WWF also decided to 'phase down' core support for IUCN from SFr1.5 million to SFr0.5 million between 1988 and 1991, again because *'WWF was under an obligation to report to its donors and needed to be able to identify specific areas on which funds were spent'*.[62] However, the Council was assured that this cut in core funding need not reduce the total amount of support for collaborative ventures, because these had tangible purposes that could be reported to donors. Broadly speaking, this assurance was honoured.[74]

Under both Stephan Suwald and Conrad von Ulm-Erbach, the joint financial services operated with a minimal staff of only three accountants. None the less, the auditors reports were unqualified, and during von Ulm's tenure (which ended in 1986) IUCN's financial affairs appeared healthy.[85] But Leonard Hentsch – the first professional banker to serve as IUCN Treasurer – concluded that the joint services were not working to IUCN's advantage.[12] One problem was that the two organizations were very different. WWF was cash-rich, with a steady stream of income from which it was accumulating large reserves. IUCN had negligible reserves and depended on membership dues and projects to generate much of its funds. Project management demanded tight controls, and Mike Cockerell set up his own separate accounting system for CDC, including records of staff time used on each project.

Matters came to a head in 1986, when Hentsch, Miller and Cockerell concluded that IUCN simply had to detach its business from WWF. There were *'some nasty small group discussions with the Presidents and Treasurers'*.[12] but separation was eventually agreed.[13,75,76] Kenton Miller wrote to Lee Talbot that *'after all this digging and exposure a great deal of sympathy has surfaced among Councillors for past DGs. No-one ever understood! Now they know.'*[77] The next step was to rebuild a more constructive relationship. WWF *'invited IUCN to work together with WWF to determine what were the areas of overlap between their programmes, and to decide which organization was best suited to carry out which function'*.[69] In May 1987 Luc Hoffmann emphasized to the Council that *'IUCN could continue to count on WWF's support, though it would increasingly be given on the basis of paying for specific services'*.[63] The result was that IUCN and WWF could stand back from one another, and that mutual recriminations would no longer erupt every time there was a financial problem.

The separation did not prevent another IUCN financial crisis in 1986 and 1987. The audited accounts for 1985 showed that expenditure had exceeded income by over three quarters of a million Swiss francs. The 'surplus' carried forward from 1984 had been nowhere near as large as at first thought.[62,85] In November 1986 the Treasurer reported that over SFr1.7 million in membership dues was still outstanding.[39] The Council set up a budget committee chaired by the President, to *'take a detailed look at the budget and fund allocations'*.[39] The Director-General was told to come forward in May 1987 with a revised budget which would generate a surplus of SFr500,000, but several state members (including Canada and the UK) said bluntly that they would not accept the significantly higher dues that some Councillors advocated.[39] Wolfgang Burhenne, as Chair of CEPLA, *'expressed deep concern that IUCN ran the risk of losing one-third of its members with this proposed increase'*.[39]

The atmosphere had become increasingly nasty as 1986 gave way to 1987. The pressures on the leadership were intense. Staff were demoralized. And as the new financial system began to work, and as information improved Kenton Miller received disquieting reports. Knowledge did not bring tranquillity, and the Commission Chairs and some staff were resentful of Mike Cockerell's tough financial management (some, perhaps, recalling old grudges from the time of CDC's birth, or even hearing an echo of Frank Nicholls from far away). Chris Shorrock, the Assistant Director-General who had been responsible for management, prepared to depart. Kenton Miller had a long talk with President Swaminathan and in April 1987 announced that he would also be leaving. The President urged him to stay on until after the General Assembly, to be held in Costa Rica early in 1988.[43]

If IUCN was indeed to take full responsibility for its own financial affairs, it needed its own manager. Mike Cockerell, who had more business experience than anyone else in the Secretariat, was made Deputy Director-General (Management) with effect from 1 June 1987. Jeffrey McNeely, Director of Programmes, was made Deputy Director-General (Conservation), and given responsibility for the content and quality of scientific elements of the work of all units. Mark Halle took over as head of CDC. Mike Cockerell set up his own financial management spreadsheets and began the process of tracking what was happening. He and François Droz began the separation from the WWF services.[13] But he was uneasy. '*I do not believe that management has the tools necessary for adequate decision-making*', he wrote to Kenton Miller on the day after taking over his new responsibilities. He set out the minimum information he needed, expressing doubts about how far funding for the various units – especially theme programmes and Commission Executive Officers – could be relied on.[78] He was concerned about the Accounts Unit, saying that it '*appeared to be in a state of chaos and anarchy, with three out of the four staff members threatening to resign*'.[79] The financial status of the units in the UK had never been evaluated.

What was clear was that IUCN was heavily in the red, and although the Bureau demanded a reduction in the deficit of almost half a million Swiss francs in 1987 and the creation of an operating reserve of some SFr2.5 million, they offered no practical ideas about how to do it. Mike Cockerell had to pick up the whole finance system and shake it. Only a little over six months before the General Assembly gathered, the Council found itself responsible for an organization that once more faced insolvency; had been through a crisis of confidence with one of its principal partners, WWF; and now had to find a new Director-General.

Another Change of Leadership

President Swaminathan was given the job of searching for a new DG. He canvassed views – including staff opinion. A number of names came forward including those of Dr Francesco di Castri, then in a prominent position in UNESCO, and Dr Martin Holdgate.[7] In May 1987 Wolfgang Burhenne and Mohamed Kassas approached Holdgate, who was leading the UK delegation to the UNEP Governing Council in Nairobi. '*Kenton Miller is leaving IUCN*', they said; '*would you be interested in becoming the next Director General?*'[80]

Martin Holdgate was a biologist who had worked in Antarctica and had been on the IBP CT Committee. He and Bob Boote had served together as the two Deputy

Directors of the British Nature Conservancy under Max Nicholson and Duncan Poore. But for the past 18 years he had spent most of his time in the UK Department of the Environment, as Chief Scientist and head of the side of the department dealing with environmental protection. He had been deeply involved in UNEP, and had been President of its Governing Council. He combined a science background with a great deal of administrative experience. But he had been on the fringes of IUCN, whereas all his predecessors had been very much 'IUCN people'. There was an element of mutual gambling in such an appointment.

President Swaminathan considered all the names put forward.[7] He consulted the staff. He discussed the options with Wolfgang Burhenne, José Furtado and Leonard Hentsch who had been given the job of helping him finalize the terms of appointment of the new DG. He reported to Council. In September 1987, Holdgate received a formal telegram welcoming him to the job: he negotiated terms with José Furtado (who had been charged with the task as the Council member resident in Britain), visited Gland and met staff, and arranged to leave the British Civil Service at the end of January 1988 so that he could attend the General Assembly with only his future responsibilities on his mind.[80]

The circumstances of Kenton Miller's resignation clearly troubled the President. Three out of the four Director-Generals of IUCN had left prematurely after internal turmoil. Was IUCN (as some alleged) ungovernable? Dr Swaminathan asked Miller to convene a meeting of the former DGs to explore the reasons for their departure. Miller invited Cameron Sanders, IUCN's first (voluntary) representative in the United States, pioneer in establishing the Union's office in Washington DC and tireless promoter of US state membership, to arrange it. He in turn asked David Runnalls, then Director of IIED in North America, to provide facilities: Gerardo Budowski, Ray Dasmann, Duncan Poore, David Munro, Lee Talbot and Kenton Miller duly assembled.[7,43,81]

Everyone except Gerardo Budowski said that their chief difficulty had been the relationship with WWF. For Talbot and Miller, the heart of the problem had lain in the joint financial services.[43] By the time the meeting convened, that problem, at least, had been dealt with. But there were other reasons why IUCN appeared ungovernable. They were related to the separation of powers. For the Union was not like a normal company where the shareholders elect the Board, the Board appoints the Chief Executive, and the Chief Executive hires the staff and runs the business. In IUCN the ultimate authority rested with the General Assembly – a vast, amorphous 'shareholders meeting'. The ex-DGs criticized the process of selecting Councillors. People who were popular in their regions were chosen, rather than people who would make up a board with a balance of qualifications. Individual Councillors tended to ride their pet hobby-horses (like population or Antarctica), so that the Director-General was pressed to implement conflicting demands (and sometimes threatened if he declined). '*The Council did not behave as a Board of Trustees should. Instead the members all pulled for their own corners. Instead of being like a Prime Minister, as Wolfgang Burhenne alleged, the Director-General was more like an insect caught in a spider's web, drawn and dangled by those forces*'.[43]

Management was made more difficult because the programme was run partly by the Director-General and partly by the Chairs of the Commissions. The latter were elected by, given mandates by, and reported to, the General Assembly: they were thus constitutionally independent of the Council although they served on it. They had a strong voice in the selection of a Director-General (and if all six lined up, could block the appointment of anyone who might be a challenge). In law the Commission

Executive Officers reported to the DG, but the Chairs none the less treated them as 'their' staff. The structure appeared designed to cause conflict. Don McMichael had proposed to alter this in 1977 by having the new Statutes provide for appointment of Commission Chairs by the Council, not the General Assembly: small wonder that he had not been appointed Director-General! Kenton Miller gave Martin Holdgate a marked-up copy of Machiavelli's *The Prince* (which had been presented to him by WWF Australia) as an aid to survival.[43] Holdgate decided to form his own opinions, believing that IUCN politics could not be more devious than those of Sir Humphrey Appleby's Whitehall, where he had worked for over 15 years.

A Question of Place

The financial crisis in 1986–87 had been over 'unrestricted money', and the volume of project work had mounted none the less. Both IUCN and WWF had grown so that their elbows jostled in the World Conservation Centre, which they shared equally. A floor of a rather ugly modern industrial building just across the road – the Norwood building – had been taken. It had red-painted corrugated cladding and became known as 'the Kremlin'. Kenton Miller moved his office there. Charles de Haes stayed behind in the centre, nick-named 'the White House'. The physical separation did nothing to help harmony, and the problems led Kenton Miller to raise with the Bureau the issue of whether the Secretariat was housed in the most efficient and economical way.[69]

He was told to find out just what the formal rights in the joint headquarters building were, what help the Swiss might give with new accommodation, and whether there was any prospect of other countries offering to host the Union.[69] He held long discussions with the Syndic (Chief Executive) of Gland,[12] and also contacted the Dutch. On 5 May 1987, Drs Jaap Pieters, head of the Netherlands Directorate of Nature Conservation, Environment Protection and Fauna Management in the Ministry of Agriculture and Fisheries, came with his colleague Nico Visser to offer the Bureau a new, free, headquarters, almost certainly at The Hague.[63,82]

They made another presentation to the Council in September.[83] Drs Pieters emphasized that the Netherlands did not wish to compete with the Swiss Government, but were acutely aware of the financial pressures on IUCN. They estimated a move should allow a saving of 20 per cent in IUCN salaries without any reduction in the staff standard of living. The Dutch Government would either finance the purchase of a building in the centre of The Hague, in direct rail contact with Schipol airport, or guarantee the rent of one for 30 years. They would also offer assistance in putting IUCN's financial affairs in order.[82] '*A larger percentage of the funds provided by IUCN members would be available for conservation by locating IUCN's Headquarters in the Netherlands*'.[82]

The Council also heard from the Swiss, represented by Pierre Goeldlin and Dr Wilhelm Schmidt, head of the Section on International Environmental Affairs from the Foreign Ministry in Berne. Dr Goeldlin reminded them that Switzerland had been chosen in 1960 for its neutrality, the strength of the international community located there, and the fact that IUCN's original working language, French, was spoken there. In 1987, Switzerland was supporting four IUCN programmes and spending SFr2.2 million on projects managed by IUCN. It had granted tax-exempt status. The federal authorities and those of the Canton of Vaud were aware of the need for more space and two sites were being looked at – one in Gland, near the lake (where the land would need to be purchased from a private owner) and the other at Yverdon les Bains some 45 minutes away from Geneva by rail and autoroute, where a site was available and where a building would be constructed and provided free of charge.[83]

The Council decided to remit the further analysis of these offers to a sub-group, chaired by President Swaminathan, who invited Martin Holdgate to serve as a member once he had become Director-General Elect.[7] The group visited possible office sites in The Hague. It found the arguments finely balanced. The Dutch were offering buildings that would unquestionably be suitable, and at least one of which would be available almost at once. In either Swiss case, there would be a delay while the building was constructed. But the possible economies gained by a move to the Netherlands had to be balanced against the upheaval and the certain loss of some staff with family ties in Switzerland. The move would take IUCN away from WWF and from the international organizations in Geneva, including a UN headquarters. It would also take IUCN away from a non-colonial country that prided itself on its neutrality.

The sub-committee recommended that the Swiss offer be accepted and their advice was confirmed by Council in mail ballot, and subsequently when the Council met in Costa Rica on the eve of the General Assembly. Two powerful dissenters, Russell Peterson and Richard Steele, felt that the desperate financial situation made the Dutch offer overwhelmingly advantageous.[84] They were outvoted, and the General Assembly confirmed the Council's decision to remain in Switzerland.

10 The Web Extends

Renewal in Costa Rica

The Seventeenth IUCN General Assembly in Costa Rica was a cheerful affair. This was partly because the difficult issues seemed to have been resolved; partly because Costa Rica is a warm, welcoming and relaxed country as well as a stunningly beautiful one; and partly because – although over 800 people turned up, stretching the facilities to the limit – the atmosphere remained that of a family gathering with time for informality and for outings. Relaxation was evident after the opening ceremony in the downtown theatre, when the President of Costa Rica, Oscar Arias, Dr Swaminathan and Prince Philip walked through the streets to the host country reception along roads guarded by nothing more military than boy scouts with staves.[1]

An IUCN General Assembly is almost always a time of renewal. That in San Jose allowed the difficulties of 1987 to be reviewed and put in perspective.[1] In Kenton Miller's report, achievements were far more evident than problems.[2] Most of the 'core' activities agreed in the Madrid programme had been carried out. The Sahel programme – called for by Mohamed Kassas in his valedictory address in Madrid – was operational. Work in the developing world was expanding, with the creation of five Regional or Country Offices. Many governments had been helped with National Conservation Strategies and laws. There had been a vigorous contribution to CITES and Ramsar, and to a number of international meetings. There had been input to the World Commission on Environment and Development. An agreement had been established with the ICSU Scientific Committee on Antarctic Research. A Botanic Gardens Conservation Strategy had been prepared. Working arrangements had been established with the European Economic Community and efforts in Central and Eastern Europe had increased. The Norwegian Agency for International Development (NORAD) had asked IUCN to advise on conservation and development priorities, and similar links were being forged with other development assistance agencies. The Ottawa conference had led to the decision to proceed with a revision of the World Conservation Strategy, covering aspects neglected in the original. Some 85 publications had been issued.

The Assembly heard calls for new action. President Arias spoke of the dangers posed by the decrease of biodiversity. *'Loss of habitat and diversity of species will also have tragic economic consequences'*, he said. *'Improvement in the quality of commercially profitable cultivated plants, especially edible ones, increasingly depends on germplasm from plants in the wild. Wild species form the basis of more than half the medical products in the world, revenues which amount to tens of million dollars a year.'*[3] President Swaminathan proposed a global network of 'Brundtland

Centres' to promote integrated technologies for development, following the principles set out by the World Commission on Environment and Development.[4] Prince Philip called for a new relationship with WWF – '*less dependence, more interdependence*' – and urged IUCN to improve the flow of knowledge between conservation organizations, so that each would know what the others were doing.[5] The World Bank and UN Fund for Population Activities promised closer cooperation.

There were 14 workshops – most of them dynamic and important in clarifying avenues to the future. One called for 15 regional task forces to examine obstacles to marine conservation. Others addressed Antarctica, the Sahel, islands, tropical forests (and the timber trade), wetlands, plants, biodiversity, protected areas, restoration of habitats, population and sustainable development, economics, building of human capacities, and the role of traditional knowledge. Conservation databases, national data centres, and the reconstruction of the Conservation Monitoring Centre, received a lot of attention.[6] Over a hundred resolutions were adopted.

The General Assembly did two other vital things: it balanced the budget and approved a new programme for the coming triennium. As the Assembly gathered, the Council was still in the thick of agonizing financial debate because the final accounts for 1987 showed that the performance over the year had been one million Swiss francs worse than Council had demanded. Mike Cockerell's round of reviews had ended just before the Assembly and one of the last of them revealed a substantial accumulated loss at the Conservation Monitoring Centre.[7,8] Dr Russell Peterson (who had chaired the Budget Advisory Committee) rubbed in the salt by emphasizing that this meant a cumulative deficit of 1.8 million Swiss francs in unrestricted funds. It was true (as Leonard Hentsch said) that as of 1 January 1988, the membership owed SFr4.5 million in dues, but if these were to be applied to clearing the deficit the programme for the year would be squeezed flat. Mike Cockerell explained that things were now improving because of tighter controls, but that did not obviate the immediate need to substitute a new document for the one all the delegates had been given for approval.

The revised version cut SFr890,000 overall. It greatly reduced the income projections. It cut support for the Commissions, leaving the Commission on Education just SFr29,000 for the whole of 1988. The discussion was uncomfortable. Leonard Hentsch, the Treasurer, was treated by some as the scapegoat for the muddle and was at one stage excluded from the Council discussions.[9,10] Martin Holdgate, guessing that there might be horrors yet to creep out from under the stones, asked for, and got '*flexibility to reallocate funds within the budget as necessary*'.[11] He also demanded (borrowing a pet phrase from Mostafa Tolba) that whenever a proposed General Assembly resolution called upon the Director-General to undertake new activities, the words '*within available resources*' should be inserted, giving him an escape hatch if the money simply was not there.

The General Assembly workshops looked hard at the need for data and information. It was obvious that the Conservation Monitoring Centre could have an important role, both in supporting IUCN Commissions and international conventions and in helping members, especially in the developing world, to create their own data centres. But it was in financial difficulties, and badly housed in an old soil research station and temporary huts at Cambridge and rented accommodation at Kew (which the Botanic Gardens would want back one day). Dr Robin Pellew, its new Director, spoke of an out-of-date database and computers.[12] IUCN did not have the resources to rebuild it, but WWF had indicated that it was willing to help. A meeting held in London under the Chairmanship of T A P Walker, Chairman of WWF–UK, and

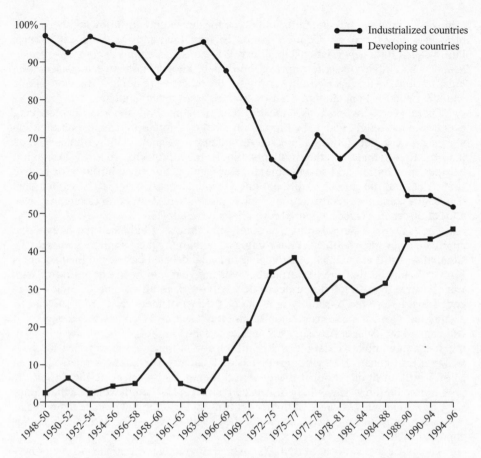

Figure 10.1 *The increasing representation of developing countries at meetings of the IUCN Executive Board and Council, 1948–96.*

attended by Martin Holdgate as IUCN Director-General Designate, emphasized that the real issue was long-term funding, especially to modernize equipment and data handling systems.[13] Prince Philip proposed that CMC should be reconstituted as a joint venture between IUCN, UNEP and WWF, and the General Assembly workshop endorsed this approach.

There were two pieces of good news. Julia Ward, who had lived in Switzerland and been deeply concerned for the welfare of Swiss birds, left 40 per cent of her residuary estate to IUCN, 40 per cent to WWF and 20 per cent to ICBP. It was estimated that it might bring in SFr2 million – a sum slightly larger than the accumulated deficit in unrestricted funds, and a guarantee of solvency. And thanks to some good footwork in the corridors by 'Buff' Bohlen and David Runnalls, a group of North American members (notably the Canadian International Development Agency, WWF–US and the Ford Foundation) offered to give money to a governance fund which would enable Councillors from developing countries to attend Council meetings.[11,14,15]

The result was a much stronger and more balanced Council, in which the voice of the South was heard clearly in the debate.[16,17] From 1988 to 1994 some 44 per cent of those attending Council were from the developing world, and 56 per cent from the North (between 1994 and 1996 the balance adjusted further to 48:52) against a theoretical ratio of 50:50 if Commission Chairs are taken into the equation. The change in turn permitted regular reports from Regional Councillors on what was happening in their regions, and sparked debate about regional priorities.[18] Regional conservation strategies were seen as an excellent way to address major environmental systems such as the Amazon, the Andes and the Himalayas.[16,18] All this increased IUCN's attractiveness to potential Southern members, most of whom had scanty resources but needed an international organization through which to build bridges with the rest of the world.[16]

A New Start in Latin America

The Costa Rica General Assembly was important as the stimulus to a major increase in Latin American involvement in IUCN. Despite the holding of the Third General Assembly in Venezuela, the part played by Enrique Beltran of Mexico and Bill Phelps of Venezuela as early Council members, the early initiative to support the Charles Darwin Foundation in the Galapagos Islands and a major regional conference at San Carlos de Bariloche in Argentina in 1968,[19] that involvement had been uneven. Africa and southern Asia had been seen as the continents with the highest conservation priorities and most of the world's 'charismatic megafauna' – and were the continents of greatest interest to European ex-colonialists, whose influence on the infant IUCN had been so great.[20] The situation changed as concern over Amazonian deforestation mounted between 1975 and 1985. Equally, IUCN became more attractive to prospective Latin American members when the WCS, and the Ottawa Conference of 1986, placed emphasis on conservation for people. Even then, expansion was hampered because the funding agencies did not give much priority to supporting environmental action in the relatively rich countries of South America.[16]

It helped that Kenton Miller knew Latin America well and spoke fluent Spanish (he delivered his Director-General's report to the Assembly in that language). For in the past, IUCN had not appeared welcoming to Latin Americans. Marc Dourojeanni of Peru, who served on the Council and as a Vice-President in the late 1970s,

> '*cannot forget the feeling of being just a southern ornament in the meetings in Morges and Gland...Most other Latin American Commission and Council members felt very often alike. Our English was too poor to follow discussions and speak, and we were unable to get a reaction to what we were saying. We were, for years, simply ignored. From that point of view, Miller and his new staff meant a crucial change.*'[21]

Yolanda Kakabadse confirms that when Latin American organizations like Fundacion Natura in Ecuador became members of IUCN '*all we got was publications!*'.[16] A Session at the Costa Rica Assembly, organized by Mark Halle, displayed Central American conservation issues and actions.[1] The special knowledge of indigenous peoples was highlighted in a presentation of how the Kuna people of Panama were developing new partnerships with developed country botanists to catalogue and use traditional herbal medicines. Following the Assembly, Yolanda Kakabadse and the

Brazilian Regional Councillor, Jose Pedro de Oliveira Costa, championed the cause of an IUCN presence in South America[18] and built awareness not only of what IUCN could offer Latin America, but what its conservationists could offer the rest of the world, given the continent's outstanding natural and human resources.[22]

The action did not stop when the delegates went away. The tiny Project Office in Costa Rica was converted to a full Regional Office and expanded rapidly. Soon, there were projects on conservation and sustainable development in Guatemala, Honduras, Panama, Nicaragua and Costa Rica itself.[23,24] But the members demanded more than project work. In 1990 the first meeting of IUCN members in Latin America, held at Chorlavi in Ecuador, agreed to link the various National Committees into a continental network and sowed the seeds for effective regional participation. Many Latin American members attended the 1990 General Assembly in Perth, Western Australia, and that proved the start of a major movement to strengthen National Committees, press for the establishment of a Regional Office in Quito, and alter the whole pattern of dialogue with the international headquarters in Gland.[25] In 1991 – to carry the story forward – the members met again in Santa Marta, Colombia, and designed a regional programme, and then, at Parati in Brazil, they chose their regional candidates for Council.[26]

Under New Management

Back from Costa Rica, Martin Holdgate got the new programme moving. He was surprised and rather depressed by what he found in IUCN. On 24 October 1988 he wrote a note to all staff punningly entitled '*six months of Glandular fever*'. He admitted that at times he had doubted his wisdom in coming to IUCN. He identified four primary causes of the malaise in the Union: a lack of team spirit and corporate identity in the Secretariat; uneven professional output and opportunity; lack of a coherent organizational structure; and both a lack of resources and inefficiencies in how the resources to hand were used. He described the staff as '*a commensalism of energetic individualists...each doing his or her allotted (or more exactly, self-selected) tasks with minimal linkage to the work of others (and at times considerable ingenuity in keeping potential interference at a safe distance)*'. He was worried at the lack of ecological talent. He thought that the programme was developed too opportunistically and was too broad for the team's strengths, doubting the wisdom of including politically fashionable topics like population and the role of women. There was no fund-raising prospectus explaining what IUCN wanted to do and why it was the body to do it. There was no strategy for achieving the mission – which itself was ill-defined. The roles of both the President and Council needed review.[27]

But at least the tight financial controls worked. In 1988 non-project income exceeded core expenditure by SFr550,000. In the same year the World Conservation Trust received SFr1.35 million from Julia Ward's bequest. The result was that the assets now covered the deficit, so that IUCN was technically solvent. Because of this, the deficit could be treated as an internal loan, to be repaid (with interest) over ten years. The line was held in 1989, when core income and expenditure balanced, with a modest transfer of SFr113,000 towards the operational reserve.[23,28] But holding the line took a good deal of managerial time. And while the management system Mike Cockerell had devised succeeded, he was recurrently unpopular with heads of cost centres when, like a recording angel with trumpet blaring, he flew by with accusations of financial sin![29]

The tight money situation squeezed the Commissions badly, and the Chairs grumbled. Hal Eidsvik, as Chair of CNPPA, was particularly concerned with the effect on the next World Congress on National Parks, to be held in 1992. He pointed out that such gatherings, only held once a decade, were a major responsibility as well as a major opportunity. The 1992 Congress would *'emphasize the role of protected areas in the conservation of biological diversity, the economic value of protected areas to society, and the basis for more effective management'* – all highly topical and important in shifting the emphasis from narrow aspects of park management to the wider theme of 'parks for people'.[28] But proper preparations would cost SFr1.5 million – and this meant either securing a special grant or cutting something else. There was another complication: Kenton Miller had signed a formal agreement to hold the Congress in Panama, but political developments now made that look impracticable. Yet the Panamanians expected the agreement to be honoured. In the end, a deal was done under which, with Panamanian protests and IUCN promises to maintain a programme initiative in Panama, the Congress was switched to Caracas in Venezuela.[30]

The Commission Chairs had reason to complain. Those that had well-defined programmes and really efficient networks were highly cost-effective because the volunteer experts gave their time freely. Several Commissions were making a special effort to recruit more members in developing countries and to establish regional networks. Some – notably SSC – had funds of their own, secured by Chairs or the leaders of specialist groups, to augment the pittance doled out by IUCN. Investment of 'unrestricted' IUCN money in a small staff supporting SSC, CNPPA or CEPLA clearly paid large dividends because of this large 'gearing' – estimated at not less than 10:1. But while Chairs and Commission members devoted much personal time and effort, they could not be expected to maintain their commitment if it did not seem valued. If tasks were given to Commissions, resources must be provided or the volunteers who form Commission networks would be disappointed and the programme targets would not be met.[30]

There were two particular problems. First, while government members all said how important the Commissions were, few donors were willing to fund them. Second, 'unrestricted' money was the most precious resource at the disposal of the Director-General, and it had to be used not only for Commissions but for any work the Regional Offices did to provide support to the members in their areas. The programmes the Commissions on Sustainable Development, Ecology and Education wanted to carry out proved unattractive to donors. The Executive Officers of the first two were transferred to other work, funded by contracts, while M A Partha Sarathy, the dynamic Indian Chair of the Commission on Education and Communication, set up his own Commission Office in Bangalore, paid for partly from the allocation to him as Chairman and partly from his personal resources.

Forty Years On

The Union was forty years old in 1988. The original idea had been for a 'modest' celebration, but soon after Martin Holdgate arrived it became clear that the Councillor from France, Jean-Claude Lefeuvre, and the Francophone staff members, led by

Frédéric Briand, the Executive Officer for the Commission on Ecology, wanted more. Holdgate and Briand visited Paris and met the new French Environment Minister, Brice Lalonde, the new Director-General of UNESCO, Federico Mayor, Michel Batisse, the 'father' of the Man and Biosphere Programme of UNESCO, Bernd von Droste, now UNESCO's main link with IUCN, Mireille Jardin, who was at the heart of UNESCO's preparations to support the 'celebration', and Serge Antoine of the Environment Ministry.

The result was a positive and profile-raising event.[31] It began in Switzerland with a reception at the University of Lausanne, addressed by René Felber, head of the Department of Foreign Affairs of the Swiss Federation, Marcel Blanc, President of the Council of the Canton of Vaud, Luc Hoffmann on behalf of WWF and Monkombu Swaminathan. It moved on to the Salle des Colonnes at Fontainebleau where IUPN had been founded. An international seminar on '*Man and Nature – the next 40 years*', led by Jacques Lesourne, produced a general declaration and a series of ten-year and forty-year '*goals and objectives for world conservation*'.[32,33] The participants were photographed on the 'Escalier des Adieux' just as the founding fathers had been. UNESCO (with the support of the Fondation Yves Saint-Laurent) generously laid on a gala for a thousand people, at which Jose Carreras and Barbara Hendricks sang.

The chief formal event was held in the French Government's conference centre in Avenue Kleber. There was a morning of 'tributes to the founders of IUCN'. Michel Rocard, the Prime Minister of France, spoke of his country's commitment to securing for all people their basic right to a healthy environment. Recognizing that '*our planet needs to be managed in the best interests of the human beings who inhabit it*', and that '*protection of the environment calls for global solutions that transcend selfish, short-sighted behaviour*', he went on to advocate a new international organization '*devoted exclusively to the environment, an organization which would federate, amplify and rationalize all efforts and be empowered to enforce its recommendations*'.[34] Her Majesty Queen Noor of Jordan (who has been a dedicated patron of IUCN over recent years), H H Sayyid Shabib bin Taimur, Minister of Environment of Oman, and Federico Mayor of UNESCO, added their tributes. Mostafa Tolba of UNEP sent a congratulatory message. And Jean-Paul Harroy, 'Grand Old Man' of IUCN, recalled some of the great names he had known in the past – Julian Huxley, Charles Bernard, Roger Heim, Harold Coolidge, Jean Baer, Marguerite Caram, Victor van Straelen and Pieter van Tienhoven. President Swaminathan and Martin Holdgate responded and French Environment Minister Brice Lalonde concluded the session.[34]

Like the Roman god Janus, the meeting looked forward as well as back. In the afternoon six speeches – from six different regions – addressed the challenges of the coming 40 years. Syed Babar Ali of Pakistan, Victoria Chitepo of Zimbabwe, Ted Means (of the USA but representing the indigenous peoples of the western hemisphere), Emil Salim of Indonesia, Alvaro Umaña of Costa Rica and Klaus Töpfer of Germany set out their perspectives. Jacques Lesourne of France reported on the workshop at Fontainebleau. The somewhat breathless participants were then rushed by bus to a reception at the Muséum Nationale d'Histoire Naturelle, where the Declaration of Fontainebleau was handed to President Mitterrand.[18,34]

The Second Step: the Perth General Assembly and Afterwards

By the time Martin Holdgate came to report to the Eighteenth General Assembly, held in the resplendent facilities of the Burswood Conference Centre in Perth, Western Australia, from 28 November to 5 December 1990, IUCN was in a phase of rapid growth.[14] There were now 62 State members, 108 government agency members and over 400 non-governmental members. The total annual budget had increased from SFr19 million in 1987 to SFr32 million in 1990 and was still growing fast.[14,35] The World Conservation Trust had benefited by a second bequest, from Juliette Nicollier, to add to Julia Ward's earlier generosity and stood at SFr2 million. Agreement had been reached with the Swiss Confederation, Canton of Vaud and Commune of Gland on the site and funding of a new headquarters. About SFr4.5 million a year was flowing directly into the Commissions (notably SSC), and was managed by the Chairmen outside IUCN's accounts. Some cost centres had overspent and had to be temporarily bailed out from the operational reserve, but the management system now made tight control possible and the overspends were clawed back.[14]

The Secretariat had also grown, from 110 in 1987 to 190 in 1990.[14] The good news was that most of the growth had been away from the Swiss headquarters, where personnel had only increased from 59 to 66. The biggest growth had been in Nairobi, Karachi and San Jose, where staff now totalled 22, 18 and 11 respectively, with another 24 spread around locations such as Katmandu, Harare, Dakar, Dhaka, Bamako, Colombo and Managua. Thirty-six nationalities were represented, although developed countries (especially the British, Swiss and North Americans) predominated. Regionalization still had a long way to go, but the broadening of the Union was emphasized in Perth by the adoption of Spanish as the third official language[36] and by a decision to adopt '*The World Conservation Union*' as a '*short descriptive title*'.[37] The CDC, led by Mark Halle, had been renamed Field Operations Division, and he himself was styled Director of Development. He had initiated annual gatherings for regional and country representatives, and the third of them was held at Yanchep, just outside Perth, on the eve of the General Assembly.[38]

Despite the remoteness of its location – Perth prided itself on being 'the most isolated capital city in the world' – about 1500 delegates, observers and journalists turned up.[38] It was the biggest IUCN gathering ever. The Australian hosts did IUCN proud (and at a cost to themselves of between two and three million Australian dollars). The Prime Minister, Bob Hawke, opened the session: the Duke of Edinburgh made a warmly supportive speech, and the Australian Commonwealth Minister for Arts, Sport, Environment, Tourism and Territories, Ros Kelly, was so positive in her commitment that she moved her private office to Perth for the duration. The Government of West Australia was energetically involved – though a fair part of their time was spent in wrangling with their own conservationists about proposals for mining in national parks.

The theme was 'Conservation in a Changing World'. There were 12 workshops, covering a very wide range of topics. Five dealt with environmental situations – arid lands, tropical forests, wetlands, marine environments and Antarctica (where the long-promised Antarctic Conservation Strategy was discussed in detail, prior to publication early in the following year). Six others dealt with cross-cutting themes: the impact of population growth and life styles, conserving biological diversity, critical issues in protected area management, wildlife utilization, global change and its implications, and harmonizing industrial development and environmental protection. The final workshop was on the World Conservation Strategy for the 1990s (with a special session on the role of women).[38]

There was something positive to record under almost all the 98 sub-headings in the programme Kenton Miller had put forward in Costa Rica. But '*IUCN could have done a lot more had resources been to hand and circumstances easier*'. That was particularly so for the Commissions where SSC's 80 specialist groups, CNPPA's 400 active members, organized by regions, and CEPLA's 200 or so distinguished international lawyers had achieved much – but where lack of support had hampered the output of the Commissions on Ecology, Sustainable Development and Education.

The programme was summarized under five headings: conservation and development, conservation science, biological diversity, habitat and protected areas management and programme support and services. Twenty-five reports of various kinds had been published under the first heading, 22 were out or about to appear in the second, 69 in the third, including a mass of output from SSC, 18 in the fourth and five in the final section. The diversity of publications is an index to the breadth of the work. Among the volumes produced, *From Strategy to Action* recorded IUCN's evaluation of the Brundtland report; the first volume of IUCN *Sahel Studies* had appeared; Jeff McNeely's *Economics and Biological Diversity* broke new ground; eight titles in the Tropical Forest Programme's special series had been issued; a massive three-volume inventory of *Coral Reefs of the World* flanked an equally massive three volumes on *Significant Trade in Wildlife* and a major Red Data Book on Dolphins, Porpoises and Whales. One of the first ever 'glossy' volumes from IUCN, *The Last Rain Forests*, had been produced by a commercial publisher; there had been a revision of the *UN List of National Parks and Protected Areas*, and a massive *Directory of Asian Wetlands* was paralleled by numerous other directories, including one of IUCN members.[38]

The Sahel project became operational in 1988, and reached a peak of effort in the early 1990s. It was the biggest single element in the programme, and potentially the most controversial. 'Everybody' knew that the disasters in the region were the result of unprecedented drought and soaring human populations. But Per Ryden and his team found that what may have been unusual was not the drought, but the high rainfall period between 1920 and 1970. Despite the drought, production in the region had actually increased (or at worst held level) between 1961 and 1987. The real problem was the limitation in the resource base – which was deteriorating under pressure. Even though its productivity could be increased, it could not both support the people and provide the cash crops the governments had been depending on to fund development. The land could be restored, but the key lay in finding development pathways that did not depend on the natural resource base.[39,40] Sustainable development – as so often – had to be part of a total political process.

One of the notable features of the new programme was its emphasis on 'the social sciences', including economics.[18] If conservation policies were to work in the real world, it was clearly essential to understand the human dimension of development.[38] The Director-General was worried about a lack of social science expertise in the Secretariat, and wondered whether the Commission on Sustainable Development (as the Commission on Environmental Planning had been renamed) might provide linking philosophy.[30] The need to build environmental values into the economic equations had been emphasized in Ottawa, and Jeffrey McNeely settled to the matter almost single-handed. In 1988 he published a book, *Economics and Biological*

Diversity: Developing and Using Economic Incentives to Conserve Biological Resources, which argued cogently that the benefits from the sustainable use of wild species could outweigh those from more traditional land uses including timber extraction and agriculture.[41] In this he repeated a conclusion that went right back to near the start of IUCN, to the African mission of Julian Huxley and the field work of the Talbots and Ray Dasmann.

Sustainable use was a highly topical issue in Perth. A special number of the *Bulletin* issued just before the Assembly pointed out how greatly societies all round the world depended on wild plants and animals for foods, medicines and many other essentials.[42] But five questions were highlighted: Is wildlife use ethically justifiable? Is wildlife use really compatible with conservation? Can wildlife use projects be justified if they compete with traditional activities like farming? What makes a sustainable use project successful? And, what standards should IUCN apply when setting up a project?

These are not all easily answerable. One problem is that scientific concepts have been borrowed too uncritically from fisheries, importing the idea of '*maximum sustainable yield*' – which itself begs a host of questions.[43] The debate in Perth brought out the range of views – from 'hands off' (typical in NGOs in rich countries that did not have a tradition of wildlife use, or a need to develop it) to the view in many African countries that wildlife use was essential and a positive contribution to conservation because it made the species valuable. A recommendation opined that the '*ethical, wise and sustainable use of some wildlife...can be consistent with and encourage conservation...*'[44] and called on the Director-General, in consultation with the SSC, to develop guidelines (which needed to take account of the genuine difference in conditions on land and in aquatic habitats and between different regions and countries). This was the genesis of the special programme led by Dr Steve Edwards (who had previously headed the SSC team) from a base in Washington DC. It was undoubtedly another development that increased IUCN's relevance to the needs of many developing countries.

Communications were another issue. Many people attending the 40th anniversary celebrations in October 1988 had '*questioned IUCN's lack of influence with decision-makers and with the media*'.[30] Jeffrey McNeely was concerned that while IUCN was producing a vast quantity of printed materials, distribution was poor.[28] The Director-General wanted to build on the anniversary and strengthen communications, and Mike Cockerell wanted to put the financing of publications on a stronger footing by creating a special fund. Both agreed on the need for a head of communications, but financial stringency prevented recruitment until 1990, when John Burke was appointed.[28,45]

Policy statements brought other questions. It was agreed that the Union should prepare and publish these on important conservation topics. But sometimes there was controversy. Two Regional Councillors from southern Africa, for example, took exception to a joint statement with WWF supporting the ban on the ivory trade, arguing that Zimbabwe, in particular, was a special case with elephant herds increasing at 5 per cent per annum, tight control of poaching, and a need to help finance conservation by selling the ivory that was inevitably collected from culled animals and victims of natural mortality (this topic was to run and run through the CITES meetings in Lausanne and Kyoto until a limited concession to southern Africa was made in Harare in 1997). Another statement on marine protected areas, although based on General Assembly resolutions, was remitted for further work in CNPPA before it could be adopted.[35,45]

Perth showed IUCN in transition. It attained an unprecedented political prominence. The attendance had risen to a level at which the informal, family, atmosphere
gave way to one closer to that of an intergovernmental conference (perhaps the
magnificent, but daunting, auditorium of the Burswood Centre had something to do
with that). The theme of sustainable development was to the fore, as outgoing
President Swaminathan emphasized in his opening address. '*Unless the penguin and
the poor evoke from us an equal concern, conservation will be a lost cause. There
can be no common future for humankind without a better common present.
Development which is not equitable is not sustainable in the long term.*'[46] In his final
President's message he emphasized that:

> '*the future of humanity depends on our ability to incorporate in devel-
> opmental programmes the principles of sustainability and equity and
> considerations of efficiency and profitability...The time is therefore
> ripe for adopting a global compact on the equitable and sustainable
> use of environmental resources in the form of an integrated Law of the
> Biosphere at the UN Conference on Environment and Development
> scheduled to be held in Brazil in June 1992.*'[47]

But the Assembly demanded a balance between sustainable development and more
traditional conservation. Prince Philip, speaking as President of WWF and patron of
IUCN, called on IUCN to '*stand up and champion nature*', adding that:

> '*I do not believe that we can achieve any significant success if we try
> to cope with every one of the very many issues that need to be tackled.
> The issue of preventing the steady decline of biological diversity is
> quite big and complicated enough without getting involved in matters
> beyond the professional knowledge and expertise of the conservation
> movement...*'[48]

Many members, especially from Australia and other developed countries, echoed
his words. '*The current mission statement tends to overemphasize the use of nature
and natural resources rather than their conservation*', said Phillip Toyne of the
Australian Conservation Foundation.[49] The old dichotomy in IUCN was still
apparent.

The message of change was strengthened by the election of Sir Shridath
Ramphal, unopposed and by acclamation, as the new President. 'Sonny' Ramphal
was a Guyanan, descended from Indians who had been taken to South America as
indentured labourers in the days of British colonial rule. A brilliant lawyer, he had
played a leading role in the writing of the constitution for his newly-independent
country, and he served as its first Attorney-General, before becoming Secretary-
General of the Commonwealth. In putting him forward as its sole nominee for the
Presidency, the Council was marking a transition in the leadership of IUCN from a
long sequence of distinguished scientists to a world statesman renowned for his
eloquence, and one fully committed to sustainable development.

There was, as the membership soon discovered, no finer orator in the business.
And in his first speech he made it clear that he saw things very much as the outgoing
President did. '*You could hardly expect me to accept the Presidency of IUCN and not
ensure that development plays a major part in its considerations*', he stressed.

'Sustainable development, so far as developing countries are concerned, has to begin with development. There is nothing to sustain if there isn't development. And where there is no development it has to become the priority, moving people away from the terrors of poverty. A preoccupation with poverty and a concern about the poor have therefore to be part of our concern, whether we belong to IUCN or to any other organization.'[50]

Branching Out

The most remarkable feature of the period between 1988 and 1994 (though it continued after the latter date, as Chapter 11 shows) was the beginning of a shift in emphasis from the headquarters of IUCN to its regions, and the emergence of members' groupings as new foci of power. Whereas much of IUCN's history had been headquarters-centred, it now became truly world-centred.

The regional presence began in East Africa in 1985. By 1988 there were 14 staff, led by Rob Malpas and based in a rented modern building that rose somewhat incongruously from a landscape of rutted lanes, fields and partly-built new structures on the edge of the Nairobi National Park (Martin Holdgate once saw three black rhinoceros from Rob Malpas' office window). Their stated role was *'catalyzing effective conservation action, developing new and innovative projects, promoting conservation awareness and...supporting the efforts of others'*.[51] The principal supporters of the diverse programme of field projects were WWF, the Frankfurt Zoological Society, the Nordic development assistance agencies (especially NORAD) and the European Economic Community.

In Kenya, a national conservation strategy was being prepared. In Tanzania, there was work on a regional conservation strategy for the Serengeti National Park, a conservation and development project for the Ngorongoro caldera and conservation area, sustainable forest management in the Usambara Mountains of Tanzania and coastal resource management nearby at Tanga. In Uganda, the emphasis was on a national wetlands survey and the restoration and sustainable management of the country's severely depleted forests, not least on the great volcano of Mount Elgon. Across the regional boundary in Zaire, WWF and the Frankfurt Zoological Society supported a rehabilitation project in Garamba (home to the world's last population of the northern sub-species of white rhinoceros), and there was a gorilla conservation project in Kivu. The office was also home for a Sahel unit, working closely with Per Ryden's headquarters team.[52]

Expansion in East Africa was paralleled by developments in both western and southern Africa. By 1992, when a special report in the *Bulletin* reviewed the branching-out process,[53] there were staff in Botswana, Burkina Faso, Chad, Ethiopia, Guinea Bissau, Kenya, Mali, Niger, Senegal, Tanzania, Uganda, Zambia and Zimbabwe. There were activities in Angola, Malawi, Mozambique and Namibia. The offices were themselves 'branching out' to provide services to IUCN's membership as well as to run projects. In southern Africa, India Musokotwane had established a Regional Advisory Council involving government and NGO representatives. In West Africa the Niger office was base for seven people working to promote sustainable resource management (with WWF backing in the important Aïr Teneré Reserve), was the centre of a network of IUCN presences in Mali, Burkina

Faso, Chad, Senegal and Mauritania, and was conducting training and issuing educational bulletins.

IUCN's work in Pakistan also started in 1985 – in a temporary office provided by Syed Babar Ali, later IUCN Councillor and Vice-President, and later still Prince Philip's successor as President of WWF International. From 1987 onwards, growth was rapid so that by 1992 Aban Marker Kabraji headed a team of 30 staff, most of them at the national headquarters in Karachi but with others in Islamabad. The central role was '*to serve IUCN members, Pakistan Government agencies and NGOs, helping them to draw up, launch and carry out environment and development projects*'.[54,55] They were involved in 15 projects. The largest project of all, the National Conservation Strategy, ran from 1988 to 1991 before submission to the Federal Cabinet, to be followed by implementation through a range of sustainable resource management projects at village community level. These spanned the whole country, from the mangroves of the Indus delta to the villages around Gilgit and Hunza, under the soaring peaks of the Karakoram Himalaya, where IUCN worked with the Aga Khan Rural Support Programme. A Journalists Resource Centre and an educational awareness programme were part of the action.

The Latin American programme also 'took off'. It started in meso-America (the six countries of Central America and Mexico). Wetlands, mangrove woodlands, wildlife management, marine and coastal resources and the development of a database for resource inventory were all highlighted. Again, training, capacity building, environmental law and education were in demand alongside sustainable resource use and conservation projects on the ground. But there were problems. During a visit to Mexico for a conference on national biodiversity conservation in 1992, Martin Holdgate was told bluntly by Arturo Gomez Pompa, Vice-Chair of SSC, and Rodrigo Gamez of Costa Rica, that IUCN was undermining its own members by competing for project finance. The members made it clear that they saw IUCN's mission as '*not to conduct field projects but to strengthen the capacity of our members to do so*'.[56] The meso-American office (ORMA) had to be reconstructed and in 1992 it was complemented by IUCN–SUR, the South American office in Quito, Ecuador which provided a focus for regional meetings, support to a regional committee, and encouragement of national programmes formulated by members in Argentina, Bolivia and later Ecuador, Peru and Venezuela.[57]

And so on. In Oman, Saudi Arabia, Jordan, North Africa, Nepal, Sri Lanka, Bangladesh, Indo-China and the Pacific Islands the IUCN presence was growing – the number of contacts and activities was becoming bewildering.[52,58,59] No single history could do justice to all this work in a book of publishable dimensions. Nor was the effort restricted to developing countries. Australia and New Zealand have long had active IUCN National Committees promoting cooperation between members. An East European Regional Committee of the Commission on Education has been functioning since 1966, and laid the foundations for cooperation among environmentalists in the area – immensely difficult under the communist regimes, especially as they strove to conceal the seriousness of the environmental situation.[60]

A wider Eastern European programme began in 1988, following an appeal from four specialists from the region who attended the Costa Rica General Assembly.[61] With Rockefeller Brothers Fund 'start up' finance it became operational in 1988 and played an important part in strengthening emergent NGOs that also had a role in the overthrow of communism. Between 1988 and 1993 the programme had four main themes: ecosystem conservation, management and restoration; promotion of sustainable sectoral policies, for example for agriculture and tourism; institutional strengthening; and the provision and dissemination of information. IUCN offices were set up in Bratislava, Budapest, Moscow, Prague and Warsaw. Since 1992 the programme has broadened into a pan-European effort.[62]

A New World Conservation Strategy

In the period between 1990 and 1992, IUCN made what history is likely to record as three substantial contributions to worldwide thinking about the environment.

The first was the publication and launch of the 'World Conservation Strategy for the 1990s' in 1991 under the title *Caring for the Earth*.[63] This had been planned as an update of the WCS, in the light of the conclusions of the Ottawa Conference, and it had a difficult beginning. Soon after the Costa Rica General Assembly, a compiler was engaged to write the text, only to withdraw after six weeks because she had doubts about the concept.[30] David Munro came to the rescue, resigning from the Council to take the job on, with Robert Prescott-Allen, author of the original strategy, in support.[23]

They planned a far more open and participatory process than that adopted for the original strategy.[28] By February 1990 there had been regional consultations in Southeast Asia and Latin America, with further sessions planned in India, Africa and the USA, and special workshops on topics of major concern. When Council debated the text in May 1990, there were, however, numerous criticisms, some of which echoed old times. It was argued that the new strategy '*would be useful for Northern populations but was not a document for the South. Many issues had not been addressed such as pollution, wastage, consumerism, the effects of military strife and the relations between countries*'.[35] The text should consider '*the basic causes of deterioration and look closely at the social and economic strategies which caused instability*'. It should '*set out the steps to be taken in such a way that local people could participate in the conservation movement*', and '*address the imbalance between North and South: the terms of trade and inequity in the distribution of resources. Conservation could not be achieved within systems which did not take account of these elements.*'[35] If Council could argue so vigorously, it was not surprising that the workshop and plenary debate at the General Assembly in Perth were lively!

The Director-General was authorized to revise the text and get it out to the members.[45] The aim was a launch on World Environment Day, 5 June 1991, a year before the opening of the UN Conference on Environment and Development, to be held in Rio in June 1992, 20 years after Stockholm. The final text was the result of partnership between David Munro, Robert Prescott-Allen and Martin Holdgate. It was ready in mid-1991 – four months behind schedule. The Preface was signed by Mostafa Tolba as Executive Director of UNEP, Charles de Haes as Director-General of WWF, and Martin Holdgate as Director-General of IUCN.[63,64]

Caring for the Earth: a Strategy for Sustainable Living is a very different document from the original World Conservation Strategy, although it echoes its main themes. It is, unashamedly, a social and political document. As its introductory user's guide states, its aim is '*to help improve the condition of the world's people*' through two processes.

> '*One is to secure a widespread and deeply-held commitment to a new ethic, the ethic for sustainable living, and to translate its principles*

into practice. The other is to integrate conservation and development: conservation to keep our actions within the Earth's capacity, and development to enable people everywhere to enjoy long, healthy and fulfilling lives.'

Caring for the Earth states nine principles for a sustainable society:

1   *Respect and care for the community of life.*
2   *Improve the quality of human life.*
3   *Conserve the Earth's vitality and diversity.*
4   *Minimize the depletion of non-renewable resources.*
5   *Keep within the Earth's carrying capacity.*
6   *Change personal attitudes and practices.*
7   *Enable communities to care for their own environments.*
8   *Provide a national framework for integrating development and conservation.*
9   *Create a global alliance.*[64]

The first principle is ethical: it *'reflects the duty of care for other people and other forms of life, now and in the future. It means that development should not be at the expense of other groups and later generations.'* The second follows: *'the real aim of development is to improve the quality of human life. It is a process that enables human beings to realize their potential, build self-confidence and lead lives of dignity and fulfilment.'* There follows a confident (and controversial) assertion: *'economic growth is an important component of development, but it cannot be a goal in itself, nor can it go on indefinitely'*.[64]

The next three principles turn to the ecological foundations of sustainable development: *'conservation-based development needs to include deliberate action to protect the structure, functions and diversity of the world's natural systems on which our species utterly depends'*… the life of non-renewable resources such as minerals, oil, coal and gas needs to be extended *'for example, by recycling, by using less of a resource to make a particular product, or by switching to renewable substitutes where possible'* and *'policies that bring human numbers and life-styles into balance with nature's capacity must be developed alongside technologies that enhance that capacity by careful management'*.[64]

Finally, the strategy turns to the human actions necessary, at individual, community, national and international level:

> *'people must re-examine their values and alter their behaviour. Societies must promote values that support the new ethic and discourage those that are incompatible with a sustainable way of life'* …
>
> *'properly mandated, empowered and informed communities…play an indispensable part in creating a securely-based sustainable society'*
>
> *'a national programme for achieving sustainability should involve all interests, and seek to identify and prevent problems before they arise. It must be adaptive, continually re-directing its course in response to new needs'* …
>
> *'if we are to achieve global sustainability a firm alliance must be established among all countries. Lower income countries must be helped to develop sustainably and protect their environments. Global*

*and shared resources, especially the atmosphere, oceans and shared
ecosystems can be managed only on the basis of common purpose and
resolve.'*[64]

Thus isolated, the central rhetoric of *Caring for the Earth* does, indeed, sound like
many another green manifesto. But what distinguished the strategy was that, for the
first time, it worked the principles into practical suggestions for action – first under
each of the nine guiding themes and then sectorally for energy; business, industry
and commerce; human settlements; farm and range lands; forest lands; fresh waters;
and oceans and coastal areas. It concluded with implementation, listing 132 actions
and 113 specific targets by set dates.[64] The latter are none the less valuable for the
challenge they pose – though it is clear that a large number of those set for the years
up to and including 2000 either have not been or will not be met.[65]

One unfulfilled dream came from President Swaminathan – the creation of an
environmental amnesty organization:

> '*characterized by political neutrality, professional integrity and credi-
> bility, to monitor natural heritage abuses. While human rights
> violations affect individuals, human heritage violations impair life
> support systems such that genetic damage may result in future genera-
> tions. Natural heritage violations undermine the livelihood security of
> present and future populations, particularly of the poor. Environment
> Amnesty would bring to public notice prominent cases of damage
> resulting from the desire of some to make personal profit out of public
> property.'*[66]

Caring for the Earth was launched in 65 countries worldwide on 21 October 1991.[67]
The print run was (for IUCN) vast – 27,000 copies in English, 8000 in French and
12,000 in Spanish. A special version in English was also produced for commercial
sales.[16] The Australian Committee for IUCN and WWF Australia supplemented it
with a special brochure, issued on the day of the launch and aimed at the individual
citizen, under the title *What on Earth can I do? – a Personal Action Guide to
Sustainable Living.*[68]

Caring for the Earth did not have the impact of the original World Conservation
Strategy. There were probably three reasons for this. First, the launch took place only
a little over six months before the Rio 'Earth Summit'. Second, this was a period
when the world was supersaturated with green rhetoric. Third, it was, in essence, an
elaboration of a widely accepted theme (although some reviewers found it impossibly Utopian)[69] whereas the WCS had broken really new ground. But over the years,
it has gained recognition as one of IUCN's weightier products. Its message is the
same as that of the Earth Summit, and of the hundreds of pages of *Agenda 21*,[70] and
is now almost universally accepted, but its conversion to action is halting and bedev-
illed by quibbles over interpretation, some apparently designed to allow inaction to
be presented in a politically more advantageous light.[65]

New Thinking about National Parks and Protected Areas

The Fourth World Congress on National Parks and Protected Areas was held in Caracas, Venezuela, from 10 to 21 February 1992. The preparations had exercised Hal Eidsvik, Chair of CNPPA from 1988 to 1990 and his successor, 'Bing' Lucas of New Zealand, for the following two years. It was clear that a new approach was needed: in June 1989 Eidsvik commented that '*the concept of National Parks was becoming increasingly difficult to sell. For this reason CNPPA was emphasizing the value of various other categories of protected area*'.[28] The Congress was designed to consider not only how to strengthen protection for protected areas, but also the improved management of lands outside such areas.

The political omens for the Congress were unpropitious. Only two weeks before the opening ceremony, there had been an abortive *coup d'état* against the President of Venezuela, Carlos Andres Perez. Some nervous governments were cautioning their nationals against travel. The President of IUCN, Sonny Ramphal, who knew Perez well, disagreed and the meeting went ahead – with ringing '*words of solidarity...in my capacities as President of IUCN, as a son of neighbouring Guyana, as a friend of Venezuela and its President*' in his speech to the opening ceremony.[71] All went well – just. For 'C A P' was toppled in a second coup a few weeks after the Congress concluded.

The Congress itself was a great event – on a scale comparable with that of a General Assembly.[72] Indeed, it broke all records, attracting 1840 participants from 133 countries, and receiving over 1000 papers including important regional reviews. Thanks especially to the work of Kenton Miller as Chair of the Congress Steering Committee, Jeffrey McNeely as leader within the Secretariat, and the Venezuelan Organizing Committee, all went smoothly. And the message was indeed new and distinctive. It was that parks and protected areas should not be seen as '*islands set aside from human use*' but as positive assets to the communities living in and around them, and to the nations in which they were situated. '*The Congress concluded that properly managed protected areas make important contributions to human welfare, warranting far greater attention than they are now receiving.*'[73]

As Walter Lusigi put it, '*the most fundamental and basic justification for support of protected areas...is that they support life renewal processes which are responsible for the survival of humanity and without which we die...*'[74] Sonny Ramphal stressed the need to find ways of ensuring that protected areas provided more benefits to local people, for '*if local people do not support protected areas, then protected areas cannot last*'.[75] Claude Martin, then Deputy Director-General of WWF, but soon to succeed Charles de Haes, was equally clear.

> '*Approaches to reconcile the needs of local people with protected areas have often been top-down and unsympathetic to the constraints of local people. The strategy was too often "to build support" among them, "to educate them" and "to integrate them" rather than a genuine participatory process.*'[76]

The Congress produced a Declaration urging all governments to integrate protected areas within their national strategies; to ensure that their national networks safeguarded a full range of ecosystems; to involve all sectors of society, but especially local and indigenous peoples, in the planning, establishment and management of protected areas; and to strengthen international cooperation that would help developing countries establish such areas and safeguard their biodiversity. The action plan called for 15 specific initiatives to those ends, and there were 20 major recommendations.[73]

The Declaration and action plan were handed by President Carlos Andres Perez to Maurice Strong, Secretary-General of the UN Conference on Environment and Development, for onward transmission to Rio four months later. Maurice Strong welcomed the message, saying that '*until nations and people that depend on biological diversity for their economic well-being can see that their economic interests are served by sustainable development of ecosystems, the accelerated loss of species will continue.*'[77] The 23 recommendations, volumes of workshop conclusions and invaluable informal interchanges between participants have had a lasting influence on how protected areas are treated within the wider context of land and water management.

A Major Campaign for Biodiversity

The period between 1988 and 1994 saw an increasingly powerful and effective campaign for the conservation of the world's biological diversity. It had several strands – of which the two most important were the development of a global biodiversity strategy and the drafting of a new international convention.

The idea of a convention was first ventilated at Bali in 1982, and carried forward in both the Species Survival Commission and the Commission on Environmental Policy, Law and Administration (of which Cyrille de Klemm, proponent of the notion at Bali, was a member). Following a resolution of the General Assembly in Madrid demanding '*a preliminary draft for a global agreement on the conservation of the world's wild genetic resources...*',[78] the Environmental Law Centre and the Commission on Environmental Law prepared successive draft texts over the period between 1984 and 1989.[79] These texts:

> '*concentrated on the global action needed to conserve biodiversity at the genetic, species and ecosystem levels, and focussed on in situ conservation within and outside protected areas; it also included the provision of a funding mechanism to alleviate the inequality of the conservation burden between the North and the South*'.[79]

The UNEP Governing Council had begun to take an interest in this subject in 1987. Several national delegations, including the United States, expressed concern at the untidiness of the international legal machinery – with the Ramsar Convention dealing with wetlands, the Bonn Convention tackling migratory species, CITES dealing with trade in threatened species, the World Heritage Convention safeguarding outstanding natural sites, but no measure concerned with biodiversity in its entirety. The Governing Council called on the Executive Director to set up a working group to explore '*the desirability and possible form of an umbrella convention to rationalize*' all these activities.[79] But the working group, which first met late in 1988, soon concluded that an umbrella convention would not work and what was needed was a new global treaty on biodiversity conservation which would build on the existing measures.

The IUCN and UNEP initiatives converged. The process was, however, an untidy one, with some in-fighting between UNEP and FAO, which drafted its own text.[80] The content of the proposed measure broadened, for it was clear that many developing countries were suspicious of a 'Northern' initiative to impose a conservation convention that might impede their use of their own natural resources. They were fearful that their natural wealth might be collected, developed and exploited, for example in pharmaceuticals, with negligible returns to their own economies. They therefore sought the inclusion in the Convention of measures to regulate access to genetic resources and their use in industry, including biotechnology. Taking all the inputs, UNEP prepared a new draft which was eventually laid before an intergovernmental negotiating committee in February 1991. It focussed especially on the living resources which were so large a part of the wealth of developing countries, and the benefits they could secure through their conservation and sustainable use.[18,79] The negotiations were complicated by the need to allay suspicions and ease tensions, and were often highly charged politically, so that IUCN and other expert groups contributed largely in technical discussions 'in the corridors' and as supporters of the UNEP Secretariat, but in the end the text was adopted in Nairobi on 22 May 1992 in time for signature at the UN Conference on Environment and Development in Rio de Janeiro in June of that year.[79]

Laws only work if there is understanding of the matters to which they apply. The underlying needs and principles of biodiversity conservation were discussed in many meetings during the 1980s. Kenton Miller, José Furtado, Cyrille de Klemm, Jeffrey McNeely, Norman Myers, Michael Soulé and Mark Trexler contributed a joint paper to the Global Possible Conference, convened by the newly-formed World Resources Institute (WRI) at Wye in Maryland in May 1984, setting out the needs and the actions that should be taken.[81] When he left IUCN Kenton Miller went to the WRI to take this initiative forward. A wide-ranging partnership involving WRI, IUCN, the World Bank, UNEP, WWF and Conservation International convened meetings, issued reports and stimulated debate. In 1989, Kenton Miller and Walt Reid of WRI produced a book on the scientific basis for conserving biodiversity entitled *Keeping Options Alive.*[82] A multi-author report, *Conserving the World's Biological Diversity* followed in 1990,[83] and in 1992 the *Global Biodiversity Strategy* was published by WRI, IUCN and UNEP in consultation with FAO and UNESCO.[84]

The *Global Biodiversity Strategy* set out 85 necessary actions – but highlighted five that would be catalytic and cheap. The first was the completion and adoption of the Convention. Second, a decade of concerted effort was demanded – and it was suggested that the UN designate 1994–2003 as the international biodiversity decade. Third, an international panel on biodiversity conservation was proposed, bringing intergovernmental, governmental and non-governmental interests together to maintain the dialogue. The fourth need was for global monitoring and an early warning system to detect threats and mobilize action. Finally, and critically, action integrating biodiversity conservation into national planning was essential.[84]

What happened about these five key actions? For completeness, the story of what must rank as one of the world's major conservation efforts is carried forward here to 1996 even though it breaks the strict time-sequence of the book. The Convention made outstanding progress. The text attracted an unprecedented number of signatures in Rio on 5 June 1992, and entered into force only 18 months later, on 29 December 1993.[79] The UN did not designate a special decade – but it scarcely mattered, for the momentum has been kept up regardless. Agenda 21, the vast compendium of actions for a sustainable future adopted in Rio, called on all states to adopt the Convention and to prepare and implement national strategies for biodiversity conservation.[70] Many complied. IUCN itself convened the panel the strategy had called for. The stream of publications from IUCN and its partners flowed on, almost as a minor torrent. The Environmental Law Centre produced a guide to the Convention:[79] in 1992 the World Conservation Monitoring Centre published a compendium of information on the status of the Earth's living resources[85] and in 1994 it marked the first Conference of Parties with a data sourcebook (published in partnership with IUCN, UNEP and WWF).[86] And in 1995 UNEP delivered the mightiest tome of all – a thousand-page *Global Biodiversity Assessment* edited by the former IUCN Chief Plant Scientist, Vernon Heywood, with Jeffrey McNeely and Kenton Miller among the contributors.[87] The World Conservation Monitoring Centre became a focus for BCIS – the Biodiversity Conservation Information System. Biodiversity conservation is now a major component of IUCN's endeavour, spearheaded by the Chief Scientist, Jeffrey McNeely. Its renewed emphasis marks something of a return by IUCN to its original intellectual heartland.

The 'Earth Summit': All Streams Lead to Rio

Caracas, the biodiversity initiative and *Caring for the Earth* (together with myriad other streams of action) all flowed into the international environmental ocean at the United Nations Conference on Environment and Development (UNCED) held in Rio de Janeiro in June 1992, 20 years after Stockholm.

Like Stockholm, UNCED had a Preparatory Committee, chaired in a dynamic, forceful, and often entertaining way by Ambassador Tommy Koh of Singapore. Maurice Strong, as Secretary-General, was scarcely less energetic than he had been 20 years earlier on the road to Stockholm – and the two dominant energies sometimes sparked off one another, for Tommy Koh was very much in charge of the formal sessions. The Committee was much bigger than that for Stockholm, and being 'open ended' allowed the attendance of virtually all governments. The non-governmental community was allowed into the room to listen, but had only limited opportunity to participate.

IUCN approached Rio in much the same way as Gerardo Budowski had handled Stockholm. It got into dialogue with Maurice Strong's Secretariat, and helped to prepare documents for the Preparatory Committee (notably on biodiversity, forests and marine environments) which in turn helped to shape Agenda 21.[70] In parallel, Sonny Ramphal was commissioned by Strong to write the 'background book' for the Conference, and produced an eloquent plea for global citizenship, *Our Country the Planet*.[88] IUCN also produced a position paper, circulated to all its members, addressing the themes of the conference.[89] At Rio itself, Martin Holdgate was one of 16 people from the non-governmental world allowed to address the intergovernmental plenary session – through the invitation of Maurice Strong and of Yolanda Kakabadse who was responsible in the Secretariat for relations with the non-governmental movement. He argued that certain GONGOs and NGOs, as representative of major groups in their field and with much expertise to contribute, should have entry to the intergovernmental debates – so long as they got a mandate from their groups.[90]

In 1992 governments were still unsure of how to cope with the vast, and at times unruly non-governmental movement. It would clearly have been quite impossible for all the 10,000 or so people from the non-governmental world who crowded into Rio to have access to the formal sessions, and still less to speak in a tight agenda which was, moreover, primarily one of intergovernmental negotiation. Hence the parallel environmental forum – a kind of super-fringe – at which ideas (some of them quite radical) could be exchanged. It was a much bigger and more sophisticated affair than the forum in Stockholm, and its campus by the sea in the heart of Rio had something of the atmosphere of a trade fair, with exhibits of the work of many participants. As Sonny Ramphal commented afterwards, it was truly a global forum because only Earth flags were in view: governments met behind national flags, which is why their meeting was an intergovernmental conference.[20]

UNCED was popularly termed 'Earth Summit' because it attracted an unprecedented assembly of heads of state and government. It gave global environmental issues their highest profile ever. The Convention on Biological Diversity and the Framework Convention on Climate Change were opened for signature, and an unprecedented number of states signed up.[70,79,91] It also took decisions which affected the status of UNEP. For it recommended the UN General Assembly to set up a new body – a Commission on Sustainable Development (CSD) – as an intergovernmental (and especially ministerial) forum for debate on the interlinked issues of environmental, economic and social policy. CSD had higher status and a broader mandate than the UNEP Governing Council, and UNEP itself entered into a difficult period in which its influence and its financial base both waned. Indeed the steady growth of IUCN meant that it came to disburse a comparable amount of funds to UNEP, while WWF, with an annual income of about US$300 million, vastly surpassed both. Most other conservation and environment bodies also continued to expand: the National Wildlife Federation in the United States passed the five-million member mark in 1990 while Greenpeace (USA) had two million adherents.[91] The power and influence of the non-governmental sector was growing.

At the time, many participants were unsure as to whether Rio was a success or failure. David Runnalls, IUCN Regional Councillor for North America and the Caribbean, thought it was both – because it did focus world attention on the environment for a full week and put some real agreements in place, but failed to measure up to the imperative of funding sustainable development in the South.[92] Angela Cropper of Trinidad and Tobago, head of governance in IUCN headquarters, castigated it for failing '*to recognize that poverty is the single most debilitating constraint on the majority of humanity in responding to the imperatives of sustainable development*'.[93] But with hindsight it is clear that Rio did make a difference – even if deeds still lag far behind fine words, and some major challenges have still not met with response. For IUCN and its members, perhaps the most encouraging thing is that the area of biological diversity has emerged as one of the most active of the post-Rio initiatives. If conservation can be highlighted as a foundation of sustainable development, then IUCN's pendulum will again rest in its proper position.

A New Headquarters at Last!

In 1988, the Costa Rica General Assembly had endorsed the Council's recommendation that the IUCN headquarters should stay in Switzerland. But it was not until February 1989 that the Syndic of the Commune of Gland offered a suitable site only five minutes' walk from the building shared with WWF. It would be rent free for 50 years. The Bureau liked it, and the President and Director-General wrote to the Swiss authorities asking for action. Although negotiations were difficult because the Canton of Vaud were displeased by the Union's refusal to move to Yverdon,[28] thanks to the efforts of Pierre Goeldlin, Raymond Junod, Robert Briod, Wernher Stern (the Chancellor of the Canton), and Walter Gyger in the Ministry in Berne, Vaud were persuaded to contribute SFr5 million and the Federal Government contributed SFr12.5 million. The Director-General was made responsible for arranging an architect's competition, and a design by Hans Schaffner of Lausanne was chosen. The 1990 General Assembly was assured that an excellent IUCN headquarters was now genuinely in sight.[94]

One reason for staying in Gland was to maintain links with WWF, which were progressively reforged as a new, mutually supportive, partnership.[95] Martin Holdgate and Charles de Haes got on well together, consulting informally on many problems. WWF continued to make a core contribution of SFr500,000 per annum for the 1988–90 triennium as well as supporting SSC's Species Conservation Officer and a number of joint activities including the World Conservation Strategy for the 1990s, the Fourth World Protected Areas Congress and the World Conservation Monitoring Centre (WCMC).[35]

WCMC was the latest, and perhaps most tangible, expression of the partnership between IUCN, WWF and UNEP. It became a new legal entity, governed by a Board with two Directors from each of the partners and a neutral Chairman (a well-known businessman, Rudolph Agnew, appointed in 1989). The partners each contributed £200,000 a year as core funds, and this allowed a start to be made on modernization of computers and data management systems. By November 1989, half the income of the Centre was coming from these core funds and half from contracts. The staff were IUCN staff, on secondment, but it was clear that they would at some future date transfer to direct employment under the Board. In May 1990 the partners funded a new building to replace the old Soil Research Station and ramshackle huts.[35] WCMC pulled the formerly separate data units into a coordinated team, created a geographical information system as part of the integrating frame, and set out to establish itself as a unique resource in support of world conservation.

There was also harmony over what to do when IUCN moved out of the shared headquarters. Legally, the building belonged to WWF, but IUCN had a right to occupy half of it, and had it been sold the proceeds would have been split equally: WWF therefore agreed to make a payment to IUCN for its residual interest in the building and this was put aside as a 'Headquarters Facility Fund' whose interest would be used for maintenance. IUCN offered WWF use of its new, larger, conference facilities and its canteen, and it was agreed that it would maintain one library for use by both bodies. The relationship became one of partnership for the good of conservation, as it always should have been.

Many members of the Union gave money to help equip the building, or articles to be displayed in it. A foundation stone was laid on 9 April 1991, and speaking on that occasion, the President, Sonny Ramphal, trotted out a suggestion which has yet to be realized. '*We are all familiar with the clock...indicating that humanity is only a few minutes away from nuclear disaster*', he said. '*Perhaps on this building we should have another clock showing how close we have come to environmental disaster. But it is not IUCN's job tamely to observe the seconds ticking away. It is our job to turn that clock back...*'.[96]

By October 1991 the shell was complete, and on 3 November 1992 the finished building – a long, low, well-lit and airy structure faced in pale grey limestone, with a grassy meadow on its roof and a 'wild garden' at its side – was duly opened by the

President of the Swiss Confederation, René Felber.[97] It bore the Union's third official logo – a stern block of letters – adopted in May 1992 (Figure 3.1). As if to rebut Martin Holdgate's quotation from the late Professor C Northcote Parkinson that *'when an organization moves into a gleaming new headquarters, it is a sure sign that the end is nigh'*, the occasion was celebrated by a symposium on the future of IUCN.[98]

The symposium asked four questions. First, what kind of organization should IUCN be? Second, what should be its style of work? Third, how far should it work alone and how far in partnership? Fourth, how could the members be involved in the choice of priorities for action? The conclusion was that the Union must base its work on its mission and be driven by its membership. It must continue to decentralize, and link Regional Councillors, Regional and Country Secretariat Offices and Commission members at country and regional level. It must strengthen the role of regional and national institutions in its governance. It should build stronger partnerships with its NGO membership, but must also reinvigorate its working links with the UN agencies, with multilateral development banks, bilateral official development agencies, the business community and the scientific community. It must greatly improve its communications and must be an effective advocate for the views of its members.

Charles de Haes had been invited to speak on 'What does the world expect of IUCN?' and he had gathered material by circularizing the membership. Some vigorous views emerged. *'First, IUCN must offer leadership, building on the work already started in* Caring for the Earth *by promoting sustainability.'* Second, IUCN's chief role remained the provision of a global forum for the conservation world. It must continue to build bridges between governmental and non-governmental sectors, and facilitate the exchange of views on global environmental issues. Third, it should decentralize its staff and regionalize its programmes. It must concentrate on networking, improve communication and information flow among the members, and give members more say in its decisions. Fourth, it must sustain its scientific expertise and its identity as a powerful and highly respected technical NGO devoted to nature conservation. It should not be distracted by too much involvement in sustainable development.[99]

Aban Marker Kabraji of Pakistan asked *'What can IUCN deliver?'* She pointed out that it is *'a diverse grouping of Governments and NGOs…a series of impressive networks of volunteers…and a Secretariat which has outreach, with staff and programmes in the regions…'*.[100] Its complex structure gave it particular opportunities. It could provide its members with advice, drawing on the expertise that is its heartland. Through its networks, it could supply the latest knowledge. It offered a neutral forum for traditionally opposed groups. It could build partnerships of influence with the UN family, multilateral and bilateral agencies and national bodies. Through a participatory process like that used to develop conservation strategies it could reinforce the strengths of participatory democratic planning. Through training, education and public awareness programmes it could facilitate changes in attitudes and behaviour.[100] Decentralization was important, but should not be thought of as only a 'Southward' process: some of the most difficult problems lay in the North where new approaches to conservation, and new cooperation, needed to be established.

Mark Halle, Director of Development, looked forward. He saw *Caring for the Earth* as providing the essential new conceptual base for the Union's mission. But IUCN had to understand who its constituency was – and while the membership had a central place, others also needed support. He called for a change in governance, with encouragement of members' organizations at regional and country levels. The headquarters role in a decentralized Union should increasingly be one of coordination, support and synthesis. In the field, IUCN should retreat from direct implementation of projects, instead supporting its members and partners in their operations. Finally, he urged '*abandoning, once and for all, the safe haven of nature protection for the infinitely more difficult but rewarding world of sustainable development*'.[101]

Changing Course in Buenos Aires

The decision to hold the Nineteenth Session of the IUCN General Assembly in Argentina was actually taken in Rio. There were two bidders for the event – Argentina and Mexico – and the former got in first. Sonny Ramphal and Martin Holdgate were bidden for a meeting with President Carlos Saúl Menem, who confirmed an invitation. But meanwhile, Holdgate had also been invited to an audience with President Carlos Salinas de Gortari of Mexico, and sensed that a second invitation was on its way. To avoid embarrassment, President Salinas was warned in advance that IUCN was minded to accept the Argentine offer for 1993, but would be very interested in a Mexican invitation for another year. The meeting passed off civilly, on that understanding. But the fact that IUCN was now seen as important enough to warrant two invitations delivered by heads of state in person was not lost on anyone.

The Buenos Aires General Assembly in January 1994 again broke records for size – despite the remoteness of the venue and the high costs of travel and living. President Menem, President Sanchez de Lozada of Bolivia and Sir Shridath Ramphal took the platform in an opening ceremony in the beautiful Teatro Colón, and over 1100 participants, from 109 countries, together with 144 IUCN staff joined in the formal sessions in the welcome cool of the Sheraton Conference Centre. Over 700 representatives of the Press were accredited.[102,103] There were ten workshops, the themes including environmental ethics, the sustainable use of wildlife, the conservation of biological diversity, the nature of carrying capacity, empowering and involving communities in care for their environment and the global role of IUCN. 98 resolutions and recommendations were adopted'.[102] Several publications resulted – including a book written by Martin Holdgate drawing on the workshops and evaluating progress in converting *Caring for the Earth* into action.[65]

The General Assembly heard a story of continued growth. Between 1990 and 1994 the total IUCN membership had risen from 592 to 788.[14,104] The USA became a state member in 1990[80] and the Soviet Union in 1991.[11] The Union's standing in Japan rose in 1993, following the award of the Blue Planet Prize by the Asahi Glass Foundation[105] and a series of very visible accompanying ceremonies in Tokyo. Thanks to the energetic efforts of Akiko Domoto, Member of the Diet (Japanese Parliament) and IUCN Regional Councillor, Japan eventually became a state member despite IUCN General Assembly resolutions critical of 'scientific whaling'. There was a dramatic growth in membership in the developing world, so that although Western Europe remained the region with the most members, they accounted for only 31 per cent of the total and Europe and North America together for only 42 per cent. Central and South America had the second largest regional total, with Africa third.

However, there was a problem. As members came pouring in at one end, a number dropped out at the other because they could not or would not pay their dues. The Statutes said that any who were 12 months in arrears lost their rights as voting members, and after two years their remaining rights could be rescinded. But the application of this rule in Perth led to a drop in the number of state members from 65 to 53, with government agencies falling from 116 to 90 and NGOs from 506 to 436. Martin Holdgate expressed his worries to Council.[11] One concern was that the lapsed state members included some in which the Union was working actively (especially in Africa). Another was the inherent contradiction between on the one hand seeking to be a Union open to all states, agencies and organizations committed to conservation, and on the other dependence on members' dues to maintain the flow of the most precious of all resources – unrestricted funds. Over the following years several solutions were proposed: there might be a category of 'dormant' member, still kept in touch through the *Bulletin* and circulars;[11] states might pay by providing facilities and services in kind and allowing IUCN to redeploy the money saved; developed countries might sponsor developing countries by meeting their dues; or payments in non-convertible currencies might be accepted if they met local IUCN expenses and saved Swiss francs. But the conundrum was never quite resolved, and still has not been.

The scale of the Union's activities had also increased. The budget had risen from SFr19 million in 1987 to 52 million in 1994, thanks to the support of development assistance agencies.[14,106,107] The Secretariat both increased and dispersed: in 1987 there were 110 staff, 12 of whom were based in the developing world,[14] but by the start of 1994 they totalled 464, of whom 339 were based away from headquarters, most of them in developing countries.[63] In 1988 well over 80 per cent of the expenditure of IUCN was managed from headquarters: in 1994 some 40 per cent was managed from the Regional and Country Offices. These trends continued (indeed accelerated) in the following years.[108]

Success had not been unmixed. Martin Holdgate reviewed 71 programme elements and commented on failures as well as successes. He rated the completion and publication of *Caring for the Earth* and the *Strategy for Antarctic Conservation* as highlights, together with the provision of advice to governments on national conservation strategies. Work on promoting the role of women in natural resource management, the integration of population issues in IUCN's work, and on evaluating and planning for global change were marked as less successful. Efforts at relating the knowledge and culture of the world's indigenous people to the programme of IUCN was another area of uneven success, despite the cooption of a Council member, Cindy Kenny Gilday of the Dene nation in Canada, to spearhead this process and lead a task force.

The area of conservation of biological diversity, led by Jeffrey McNeely, was rated highly, and especially the publication of the *Global Biodiversity Strategy*. The broad areas of species conservation and of conservation in major biomes had gone well, but lack of funds had impeded the establishment of a new arid lands programme. Regionalization had pressed forward in Central and Eastern Europe, South America, eastern and southern Africa and parts of Asia and the Pacific, and work in North America had been strengthened, but the Caribbean, Western Europe and the Mediterranean basin, West and Central Africa and the Sahel were areas where less had been done than hoped, and there had been problems in Central America making a reconstruction of the regional office necessary.[63]

This kind of unevenness is no more than the normal stock in trade of any international programme, but once again the support to the Commissions was uneven: strong teams backed SSC, CNPPA and the Commission on Environmental Law (as CEPLA had become under its new Chair, Parvez Hassan of Pakistan), but the other three had not had either the support or the output hoped for. Indeed, the role of the Commissions had been an issue of recurring vexation throughout Martin Holdgate's six years as Director-General. In Perth, concern had led to adoption of a resolution calling for a review, and Council appointed David Munro and Gabor Bruszt (a

Swedish consultant) to '*review critically the purpose, objectives, terms of reference, work plans, activities and output of the Commissions, expert groups and other voluntary networks*'.[17]

The pair duly reported at Buenos Aires. Their main points were that the programmes of the Commissions should be an integral part of the overall work of the Union; that the Secretariat should provide adequate support (in the shape of one full-time officer, increased to two by the Assembly); that each Commission should be subject to regular review; that each Commission should have defined performance indicators; and that more should be done to increase the regional diversity and regional involvement of Commission members.[109] The mandate of the Commission on Education and Communication '*should be confined to the provision of policy advice on the formulation, funding and modalities of the Education Programme*', while the Commission on Environmental Strategy and Policy (the successor of the Commission on Sustainable Development) '*should continue to elaborate a more clear and focussed role and a more manageable mandate*' and the Commission on Ecology should be abolished, giving way to a Scientific and Programme Advisory Board.[109] The last proposal was too much for the General Assembly. A small but vociferous pressure group argued that ecology was so fundamental to the Union that a Commission *must* be retained. It was. What became the Commission on Ecosystem Management took slow shape during the following triennium, to be launched at the Montreal World Conservation Congress in 1996.

Two debates from the Perth General Assembly were renewed in Buenos Aires. One was the longest-running saga in the whole history of the Union – the balance to be struck between nature protection and sustainable development. It had rumbled through the 1990s despite the supposed commitment of all IUCN members to the World Conservation Strategy, and the general acceptance of *Caring for the Earth*. It had surfaced at the special symposium to mark the opening of the new headquarters in November 1992.[98] The polarization affected the Council, some of whose members were cool about admitting organizations whose focus was strongly on sustainable development and vigorously opposed the admission of members that favoured the hunting of animals, even if this was controlled so as to be strictly sustainable and was backed by research and habitat conservation.[17]

As before, the most vociferous champions of strict nature protection came from the United States and Australia, while the outspoken champions of sustainable development and the sustainable use of wildlife came from Africa, Asia and Latin America. Tariq Banuri, head of the Sustainable Development Policy Institute of Pakistan, was disturbed to find many IUCN members espousing what he called '*Noah's Ark conservation*', and even more by sensing that *Caring for the Earth* was not truly a consensus document in IUCN because those who demanded that any use of natural resources must be '*ecologically sustainable*' tended to equate the latter condition with a demand for '*zero ecological change*'.[110] The Sustainable Use Programme, led by Stephen Edwards (and with a linked SSC specialist group) put forward guidelines, but there was no consensus on them and many people argued they would have to be related to particular environmental, social and local circumstances.

The second debate also cut deep into the ethics of the conservation movement. *Caring for the Earth* recognized that much of the development process was driven by the private sector of business, industry and commerce, and emphasized the need to make their activities sustainable. Mike Cockerell, and the Treasurer elected in Perth, Don Person (an American citizen who was senior partner in the Geneva branch of a major accountancy firm), saw the establishment of a corporate sector of associate membership as a means both of linking IUCN with the chief movers of worldwide development and as a source of valuable finance. But the membership – spearheaded by Australian non-governmental members who were fighting domestic battles especially with their minerals industry – wanted none of it. The workshop in Perth on harmonizing industrial development and environmental protection had been confrontational, and the Chairman, Michael Royston, author of a pioneering book that argued that *Pollution Prevention Pays*,[111] received a verbal 'roughing-up' from his audience. The notion of corporate associate membership had been thrown out. Despite this, Martin Holdgate built links with the Business Council for Sustainable Development, chaired by a charismatic Swiss, Stephan Schmidheiny. BCSD championed 'ecoefficiency' as a principle for modern business, and produced a report, entitled *Changing Course,* for the Rio Conference.[112] After Rio the dialogue continued, despite further negative splutters from the greener wing of the membership in Buenos Aires.

WWF shared none of these inhibitions. Charles de Haes put their position clearly to the IUCN Council in 1991, when he drew attention to *'the importance of collaborating with industry'* and commented that *'many of the Board members of WWF were leaders of industry and were able to promote a dialogue on industry and the environment'.*[11] It was not really until after 1996, when business leaders including Stephan Schmidheiny figured prominently in an open forum and discussion at the World Conservation Congress in Montreal, that David McDowell was able to promote ties with industry openly, convening (for example) a major workshop on the environmental impact of large dams that involved construction and engineering companies, environmental scientists and the World Bank.[113]

The biggest debate at Buenos Aires was over the strategy of the Union – an issue that had really been in gestation throughout the six years of Martin Holdgate's service, but was demanded specifically by a resolution adopted in Perth and had been brought to completion through an intensive process of discussion in the Secretariat (led by Angela Cropper, as head of strategy) and interaction with a Council strategic planning group led by Jay Hair of the USA. The strategy asked five key questions: What distinctive contribution could IUCN make to the solution of the complex problems of environment and development? What specifically should it seek to do? How should it approach its objectives? How should it mobilize and allocate its resources? And with whom, through whom and for whom should it work?[114]

The mission of IUCN was restated – after a lot of argument – as *'to influence, encourage and assist societies throughout the world to conserve the integrity and diversity of nature and to ensure that any use of natural resources is equitable and ecologically sustainable'.* The first point of emphasis is important: IUCN should work with and through those it influences, encourages and assists. Second, by stating the conservation of nature as the primary aim, the traditional goals of the Union are upheld. Third, while demanding that any use of natural resources be sustainable, the statement makes clear that there is no obligation to use all such resources, and that such use must meet the criteria of equity (presumably between social groups today and between generations), and ecological sustainability. Some have seen this statement as a partial victory for 'nature protectionists' over 'sustainable developers'. The problem is that a number of these concepts are ill-defined or scientifically undefinable. The statement is likely to be the cause of further debate and argument.

The strategy (and the revised Statutes later adopted in Montreal) make it clear that IUCN will perform its mission primarily by *'harnessing the strengths of its members, Commissions and other constituents'*. It will *'strengthen the institutional capacity of its members'*, promote enhanced cooperation between governmental and non-governmental members, encourage research, and *'provide a forum for discussion of conservation issues'*. It will develop expert networks and information systems and undertake a wide range of promotional and supportive activities. It will mobilize the Union's distinctive strengths to influence international environmental policies and the development of international law.[114] The programme of the Union, which *'must integrate the work of the Commissions and the Secretariat'*, has to provide the scientific understanding on which sound conservation depends.

So far, so familiar. But the strategy broke new ground in emphasizing the essential need to continue regionalization and decentralization, and to recognize the central role of the membership in determining the policies of the Union. The importance of National Committees was upheld. New definitions of the roles and responsibilities of the President, Vice-Presidents, Regional Councillors, Director-General and Secretariat were agreed.

Problems with the Presidency

There was an unhappy argument over the Presidency on the road to Buenos Aires. Shridath Ramphal completed his term of three years in 1993, and the Council had to consider whether to nominate him for a second term, as had become normal in IUCN in recent years.

There was genuine debate over the kind of President the Union needed. Many saw the value of having a recognized world figure at the head of the Union, and valued Sonny Ramphal's magnificent oratory. Others felt that a President who would make promoting the Union his or her principal concern, and would spend more time organizing the work of the Council, was needed at that juncture. Some hankered after a scientist with a professional track-record in nature conservation. There was an equally strong view that so long as the Director-General came from the developed world, the President should come from a developing country, and although Martin Holdgate was due to retire in 1994, having completed six years in office, by the time the Council came to consider its nomination of President it seemed most likely that his successor would also come from the North. Matters were forced to a head in the Council meeting in May 1993, when members had to decide who to nominate to the General Assembly. Vice-President Al Gore wrote on behalf of the US state member nominating Dr Jay Hair for the job.

Hair was a wildlife biologist who had been associate professor of zoology and forestry at North Carolina State University, Special Assistant in the US Department of the Interior, and Executive Vice-President and later President and Chief Executive Officer of the National Wildlife Federation – America's biggest conservation organization, with about six million members.[115,116] He had served for three years on the IUCN Council, had chaired the Business Committee, and was known to have ideas about making the Union and the Council more effective. Council had to balance his claims against those of Ramphal – orator, world statesman, Guyanan (albeit long resident in England) and also a skilled Chairman. What to do?

Ramphal made it clear that he did not seek re-election, but would accept it if it was the unanimous wish of the Council, and if there was no contest. His words were forceful:

> *'At this time in 1990 when the Council of IUCN was considering the future of the Presidency of the Union I did not seek it. Nor did I at any time later. Had there been a contest at Perth or in the approaches to it, I would not have been in it. I accepted the Presidency as an act of service to the cause of environment and development on the strength of the opinion of others whose judgement I respected that by doing so I might help a little. I hope I have done so...I do not seek a renewal of the Presidency now. I am not a candidate in a contest for it. I thought I should make that clear. I hope you consider it helpful that I do so.'*[109]

Council was thrown into a spin. Many members wanted a developing country candidate. Many favoured giving the membership a choice – but Ramphal had refused to argue his candidacy on the hustings. Jay Hair was willing to take part in an election process, and was not willing to withdraw. Council could not duck the issue. In the end, Jay Hair's name went forward as the sole candidate, but there were some awkward moments in Buenos Aires when developing country delegates, among whom Tariq Banuri was fierily eloquent, argued that a developing country candidate should have been chosen and that the General Assembly should have had a choice. Such was the arcane constitution of IUCN that the Assembly was not able to consider other names at that stage: should they have decided not to elect Jay Hair the new Council would have had the task of selecting a President from among its members after the Assembly.

Jay Hair made an emotional speech, emphasising his dedication to the Union and to the task he saw before him. He was elected, having undertaken to serve one term only and to ensure that when he left there would be a choice of candidates of whom at least one would come from a developing country and one of whom would be a woman. Sir Shridath Ramphal bowed out with dignity, and there was consensus that nothing like it should be allowed to happen again.

11 Power to the Members

A Changing World

The nature and context of environmental affairs changed in the late 1990s. The environmental problems worrying the world were bigger and more pervasive than those that had been top of the priority list at Stockholm in 1972. The Intergovernmental Panel on Climate Change, which brought together most of the world's top climatologists, concluded that the human augmentation of 'greenhouse gas' concentrations in the atmosphere was indeed altering world climate. Under the Framework Convention on Climate Change, which entered into force soon after Rio, governments began to take action to cut back emissions from the developed world. Action to eliminate the use of chlorofluorocarbons, the principal destroyers of stratospheric ozone, was taken under the Montreal Protocol to the Convention on the Protection of the Ozone Layer (and its London Amendment). The entry into force of the Convention on Biological Diversity brought further demands for action by governments.

But there were major changes in the organization of world affairs. The United Nations had been founded on the premise that the nation state was the essential building block of global society. Fifty years later, society was more complicated. Supranational groupings like the European Union, or MERCASUR, the Common Market of the Southern Cone of South America, emerged and became powerful trading and negotiating units. The boards of the biggest global multinational corporations presided over economies larger than those of many states. International environmental conventions and agreements had their own impact on trade, and there was debate over their compatibility with global trading agreements administered by the World Trade Organization.[1]

Then again, there was a tide of decentralization within states. More and more decisions on environmental matters were devolved to local level. Local Agenda 21s became a feature of many national strategies for sustainable development. Biodiversity conservation action plans had a strongly local component. All this posed challenges to the conservation community – although it was in many ways pre-adapted, because the involvement of local communities, whether inside or outside protected areas, had been recognized as essential for many years, and almost all of the projects undertaken by IUCN, WWF and other organizations were done in partnership with the people on the ground.[1,2]

The conservation world may have been dismissive of the results of Rio, but in fact the conference led to a mass of international and national action. The Commission on Sustainable Development set out to review the implementation of

Agenda 21, debating the major sectors – including environmental components like atmosphere, oceans, freshwaters and forests – in a regular sequence. It opened its debates – and especially the less formal inter-sessional meetings where much of the work of preparation was done – to representatives of non-governmental 'major groups'. Consortia of organizations, among which IUCN and WWF were prominent, got together to coordinate their arguments and prepare presentations to government representatives. In 1996 an Intergovernmental Panel on Forests was established, not only to review the implementation of this part of Agenda 21 but to address the thorny perennial – should there be a new forests convention as some had called for? IUCN and its partners were active in organizing presentations to the panel, as well as participating in its debates. They also faced up to the need to build their links with the new supranational groups of states, and with the world of business, industry and commerce.

Empowering the Members

The need for change in IUCN's approach coincided with a change at the top. Martin Holdgate retired in April 1994, after a little over six years in the job. After a world-wide search by a Council sub-committee chaired by 'Bing' Lucas, in October 1993 the Council selected a historian and diplomat, David McDowell. He was at the time New Zealand Ambassador to Japan, had served previously as his country's Permanent Representative to the United Nations in New York and High Commissioner to a range of developing countries (India, Bangladesh, Nepal, Fiji and Kiribati),[3] had been a senior member of the Commonwealth Secretariat, had run the New Zealand development assistance agency in a period of fast expansion in the 1970s, had been a well-known member of the UNDP Governing Council in the late 1980s, and had headed two government agencies in Wellington – the Department of Prime Minister and Cabinet and the Department of Conservation. He was able to attend the Assembly in Buenos Aires, and see at first hand what he had let himself in for. And the staff and membership were able to see him – an unforgettably towering figure, almost two metres tall, looming above the crowd as the shape of things to come.

The message to the new Director-General from the membership in Buenos Aires was, as David McDowell has put it:

> '*blunt and clear. The membership requires that the Union be Mission-led and constituency driven. This means, inter alia, that the members are to be in the driving seat, not the Secretariat nor any other element inside or outside the Union. It also means that strengthening the capacity of the members, individually and collectively, to influence societies to conserve nature is to be a primary objective, as is their greater involvement in the formulation and execution of the Union's programme...*'[4]

The consequence had to be a great strengthening of networking in general (and in particular among the membership), better support for volunteer networks (notably the Commissions), stronger alliances with global partner organizations and a more integrated and catalytic method of working. There was to be a more proactive approach to the advocacy of policies. There was to be more emphasis on gender and

North–South equity in appointments, especially at senior levels in the Secretariat. The Union's resource base needed to be widened (partly because official governmental development aid agencies could not be expected to pay for all the activities the membership wanted), and the Secretariat, Commissions and programme had to be further regionalized and decentralized. '*All this adds up to a revolution. What the General Assembly sought was not simply fundamental change in procedures, ways of operating and global distribution of human and financial resources, but a whole change of mindset across the Union*'.[4]

That message came home even more clearly when David McDowell began to travel around the world and meet the membership in their home territories – and almost as soon as they assumed office both he and the new President did a great deal of travelling.[3,5]

> '*In informal conversations in Africa, the Andes and Asia – most often at night, usually over food – the accumulated resentments of the years came out. Many members did not feel it was their organization. It was owned and dominated by Europeans and North Americans. It was a "white old boys club". It was more interested in birds and mammals than people. It paid lip service to regionalization, but the real money and power lay in Gland. An impact on conserving natural resources would not be made on the shores of Lac Leman but out there where the real biodiversity lay – in the developing world...*'[3]

The strategy the members adopted in Buenos Aires endorsed the process of decentralization, but did not elaborate the guiding rationale. This was debated after the Assembly by a joint Council and Secretariat Task Force on Regionalization and Decentralization. Significantly – for the fast-growing Latin American membership was often in the forefront of the drive for a more membership-driven programme – the task force was chaired by the Regional Councillor from Bolivia, Alexandra Sanchez de Lozada.[6] It redefined 'regionalization' as '*the process of structuring the work of the Union within a regional framework that takes account of regional heterogeneity and targets members' needs on the ground*'. 'Decentralization' was defined as '*a process of devolving greater responsibility for the preparation and implementation of the Programme of the Union to Regional and Country Offices of the Secretariat and, where possible, to the regional and national structures of the membership and Commissions*'.[6]

The task force called for three actions – the decentralization of the Secretariat by establishing offices around the world; the delegation by the Director-General of authority for coordinating the development and implementation of regional and national components of the programme; and the devolution of responsibility for identification and pursuit of priorities at regional and national level from the Secretariat to members and Commissions (working through a consultative process).[6] The result would be a Union programme developed through a 'bottom up' consultative process.

The Commissions were swept up into this process. Prior to Buenos Aires, only CNPPA, CEL and CEC had a regional structure but it was now clearly necessary for all Commissions to engage in dialogue with the members at regional and national level. Many of them, moreover, had in the past been overwhelmingly 'Northern' in their composition, and this also needed to change. The task force called for field projects and regionally-focussed technical activities to be managed from Regional and Country Offices. '*By late 1996 only global projects of major strategic importance should be managed from Headquarters.*'[6] Moreover:

> '*in implementing the programme every possible effort should be made to devolve responsibility to the members. Wherever a member or Commission network has the technical and managerial capacity to implement a project directly, the Secretariat should encourage it to do so, reducing its own role to one of providing technical support and advice.*'[6]

This was a mandate for a radically different kind of decentralization from that followed, cautiously, in the period between 1984 and 1994. Although this had led to great expansion in Regional and Country Offices, increasing employment of people from the South, and much more networking, liaison and support for members, that process had been carefully controlled by the central Secretariat.[7] Capacity to support the membership had been constrained by the fact that most of the funds were earmarked for operational projects. In some regions there had even been tension because IUCN appeared to be bidding for such project funds against its own members.[8,9,10] The message David McDowell got was that the regional members in the South now wanted to decide their own programme priorities. They saw National and Regional Committees as policy-making bodies, closely linked to Regional Offices and members of Commissions in the regions.

Action followed. By the end of 1996 the Secretariat numbered 820, spread around the Swiss headquarters, seven Regional Offices, 21 Country Offices and 14 Project Offices. Most of this strength was in the developing world (there were only five bases, including headquarters, in the North).[11] Most of these offices were headed by nationals of the countries concerned – or at least of the regions in which they lay. A beautiful new Eastern African Regional Office, the Wasaa Centre, standing in one of the finest gardens in the region and with an adjacent small area of natural woodland, was opened in March 1995 by the President of Kenya, Daniel arap Moi.[12] Members from the whole region met there to draw up a new regional programme. In the same period, a new office for Central Africa opened at Brazzaville (Congo) and new machinery for coordination in West Africa was announced.[13]

The headquarters was slimmed from 135 to 109 staff, partly to help pay for this expanding network, but the truly global professional units like those dealing with biodiversity and coastal and marine conservation were strengthened. In 1988, nearly 90 per cent of the Union's expenditure had been managed from headquarters: it was still above 60 per cent in 1994, but had dropped to 42 per cent by 1996. All the larger non-global programmes were now managed by Regional or Country Offices.[3,14] This in turn altered the pattern of work among headquarters staff, making them coordinators and supporters of decentralized efforts rather than hands-on managers of work on the ground. But decentralization had to be accomplished without fragmentation.[4,15] Membership structures had to be developed, if they were to make a coherent input into programming. Regional and Country Offices also had to show their ability to take decisions and handle money before responsibilities could be devolved to them. Coordination was provided by the regional support group which represented the regions at headquarters.[4]

The membership made it clear that they wanted the Councillors they elected to have a decisive role in determining the policies of their Union. Jay Hair, in bidding for the Presidency, had emphasized his commitment to reforming the governance of

IUCN.[16] Council members wanted the Council to be the place where policy was developed in a consultative way.[3] That in turn meant a review of the role of the business, membership, policy and programme committees. The Commissions once again emerged as important 'think fountains' (to use Mohamed Kassas' term, with its suggestions of dynamism and sparkle) and they received a 40 per cent increase in funding in 1995.[5] A Commission 'summit', led by the President at the mountain retreat, Sonloup, above Montreux in 1995, not only defined their role but set out eight principles '*for promoting partnership between the 3 pillars of IUCN – the Commissions, Members and the Secretariat*'.[17] But although there was consensus on the need to strengthen the Council, nobody doubted that the Director-General must remain in command of the Union's operations, and must play a proper part in building new policies.[3] The importance of partnerships was also recognized, and it was agreed in 1994 that IUCN should forge strong links with the Convention on Biological Diversity, the Global Environment Facility, the World Bank, UNDP and UNEP.[5] Agreements were in due course signed and closer relationships were established with the Secretariat of the CBD.[18,19]

Jay Hair, as President, found himself devoting a quarter of his time to IUCN in his first year of office.[5] He went to East Africa, with Vice-President Perez Olindo, to discuss IUCN activities with the leaders of the countries concerned. He represented IUCN at the Central American Ecological Summit in October, when heads of state signed a Central American Alliance for Sustainable Development. He joined the IUCN delegation to the Conference of Parties to CITES in the following month.[5] In 1995 he was in East Africa again, for the opening of the new Wasaa Centre. He met IUCN members, saw the Prime Minister of Ethiopia and senior figures in Addis Ababa, went on another mission to the Russian Federation, the Czech Republic, Slovakia and Hungary[17] and attended the pan-European ministerial conference on 'Environment for Europe' in Sofia, Bulgaria.[20] In the following year he paid a visit to Cambodia, where he met King Norodom Sihanouk and the Ministers of Environment and Foreign Affairs, and Vietnam where he had talks with the Deputy Prime Minister, the Minister of Science, Technology and Environment and various key officials.[21]

A New Programme

Regionalization meant that more and more effort went into working with communities on the ground. The IUCN Secretariat, member organizations and experts drawn from the Commission networks cooperated with a great diversity of local groups.[14] Devolution to the regions put the work of the Union under the members' as well as the donors' microscopes. Relevance and value for money were scrutinized. It was clear that at regional level the emphasis had to be on ecosystems and natural resources and their sustainable use, and that at global level the Union had to make a distinctive input to world policy.

Most of the world's states had signed the Convention on Biological Diversity in Rio. They now had to implement it. The Convention demanded the conservation of genetic, species and ecosystem diversity and the sustainable and equitable use of biological resources – very much the heart of IUCN's and WWF's mission. Many countries, following Rio, adopted national strategies for both sustainable development and biodiversity conservation. IUCN's expertise was in high demand –

especially because the Union had shown that it knew how to integrate conservation with development that met human needs.[14,19] The biodiversity component of the Union's programme focussed on ecosystem management, protected areas, species, and sustainable use.[22] Jeffrey McNeely's Biodiversity Policy Division drew together outputs from regional and global programmes, and linked IUCN to other bodies, especially so as to support the implementation of the Convention.

WWF's approach was very different, but complementary. In October 1996 it launched its Living Planet campaign which defined, and sought to protect, some 200 areas, termed '*the Global 200 Ecoregions*'. It called on governments, institutions, businesses and individuals to make '*gifts to the Earth*' in the shape of new protected areas, better policies and practices, more sustainable styles of living, and finance.[23] It promoted sustainable use schemes, especially in the forests and oceans. The Marine Stewardship Council (a joint initiative between WWF and the multinational corporation Unilever) was set up to certify products of sustainable fisheries. The Forest Stewardship Council similarly certified that timber and other products came from sustainably-managed forests. A new joint forest programme was set up with IUCN. WWF supported WCMC to produce the first digital map of the world's remaining forest cover.[24]

As the founding fathers of IUCN had understood, making ecology relevant and applicable is a central task in conservation. The Buenos Aires General Assembly had refused to abolish the Commission on Ecology. Instead, it decreed that a Commission on Ecosystem Management be created, but this made slow progress in the following two years, and it was not until 1996 that a symposium on the principles of ecosystem management was convened by the Deputy Chairman of the Commission, Professor Ed Maltby, at his Institute of Environmental Research at Royal Holloway College, London. The symposium was partly funded by a small trust endowed by the late Miss Mary Sibthorp, and the paper resulting from it – including a set of ten guiding '*Principles for Ecosystem Management*' – was discussed at the World Conservation Congress in Montreal.[25,26] The Commission also looked at the criteria for defining threats to ecosystems and planned a Red List of endangered ecosystems.[14]

The massive species conservation programme was the natural heart of the Union's programme on biodiversity. By 1996 SSC had 7000 volunteers in 110 specialist groups.[11] In 1996 a new *Red List of Threatened Animals* was published,[27] in partnership with BirdLife International (formerly ICBP), The Nature Conservancy, Conservation International and the World Conservation Monitoring Centre. A new list of over 30,000 threatened plants was nearing completion, also by WCMC. More than 40 action plans for particular species or groups were available.[14] The new threat of 'recombinant biogeography' – the increasing mingling of species formerly separated by ocean and climate barriers as a result of universal human transport of seeds, fruits, living plants, supposedly useful animals and the pathogens and invertebrates that are inadvertently carried along with them – became a focus for additional action by the SSC.[28]

Habitat conservation is clearly the key to maintaining biodiversity: that is why it has been highlighted so strongly in the WWF Living Planet campaign. The CNPPA (or World Commission on Protected Areas, WCPA, as it became in 1996 in Montreal) – now with over 800 members – followed up the Caracas Congress with action plans, including a major scheme for protected areas in Europe, launched in 1994.[29] It began – belatedly – to give the biosphere reserve programme more emphasis, setting up a Vice-Chairman for Biosphere Reserves. In 1995 the Commission also published a major report on the priority sites for marine protected areas and the procedures for their management.[30] Forests and wetlands continued as the two biggest global programmes managed by the Secretariat, and the emphasis in the former was very much on sustainable management and use – recognizing the immense worth of non-timber resources, especially to local communities, and the need to value these properly and take due account of the rights of forest communities when decisions are taken about national policies.[31] Efforts were also made to strengthen work on marine conservation.

Much greater attention was also given to human-centred conservation. The 'message from the South' had been heeded, with considerable growth in the programme on the Sustainable Use of Species, led by Dr Steve Edwards in Washington DC. The Law Commission helped newly-independent Eritrea draw up new environmental laws. The IUCN office in meso-America helped the governments of the region to prepare a new plan for conservation and sustainable development under the Central American Alliance for Sustainable Development, adopted in 1995.[14] Globally, IUCN played a major role (in partnership with other sponsors) in the creation of ICTSD, the International Centre for Trade and Sustainable Development. A new programme on environmental economics began in 1995. The Commission on Education and Communication became more active.

Data and information are at the heart of any biodiversity strategy, and in 1996 BCIS, the Biodiversity Conservation Information System, was established '*to support environmentally-sound decision-making affecting the status of biodiversity and landscapes at international, regional and national levels through the cooperative provision of data, information and expertise*'. By the end of the year it linked 1400 sources of biodiversity data and over 10,000 specialists in 173 countries. It involved the IUCN Secretariat and three Commissions – SSC, WCPA and CEM. The other partners were BirdLife International, Botanic Gardens Conservation International, Conservation International, The Nature Conservancy, TRAFFIC International and WCMC.[14] Its Secretariat was based at the World Conservation Monitoring Centre, but had its own steering committee separate from the WCMC Board.

And How to Pay for It

A recurrent problem in IUCN is that the funds available from donors do not match the pattern of membership needs and priorities. As Michael Cockerell pointed out in April 1994, '*only 8 per cent of the total income came from membership dues while the remaining 92 per cent came largely from development assistance agencies*'.[32] Early in the triennium there were complaints that only 1.5 per cent of the budget was allocated to work in Latin America despite the unprecedented growth of membership there and the region's extraordinary biodiversity. North Africa, West Asia and Western Europe all protested at their low allocation of resources. More needed to be done in East Asia because of the environmental impact of the region's rapid economic growth (the need has become greater recently, after the economic upheavals in the region, which struck just as climatic upsets brought massive fires to parts of Indonesia). Regional task forces to deal with issues especially relevant to indigenous people's concerns were suggested. The Programme Committee decided to look at '*geographical gaps in the programme*',[32] but the choice was to go slow on regionalization, and disappoint the members, or to risk over-committing scarce unrestricted funds. The whole issue of raising funds for adequate regional support became a recurrent debating topic.

The triennium started in robust financial health, but there was an alarm in 1995 when an operating deficit was projected. In November, Council agreed to withdraw SFr1.1 million from the substantial reserves, while demanding that it be repaid as quickly as possible.[17] In practice, tight control of expenditure averted the deficit, and both unrestricted and restricted income exceeded expenditure throughout the triennium, which ended with the unrestricted, undesignated fund balance (amounting to genuinely 'free' money) at an all-time high of SFr3.9 million.[33] However, much was said about the need to find new sources of finance, even though corporate membership was still ruled 'off limits'.[17]

Long memories must have stirred a little in 1995 when the Business Committee reported that it *'had considered a proposal for the development and marketing, in collaboration with the US mint, of a series of IUCN Ocean Conservation Coins'*![17] There is no record that anyone told them about that long-dead golden goose, the Conservation Coin Collection, and Council allocated SFr100,000 to launch the venture! In April 1996, the President produced a new idea: the establishment of a fund-raising subsidiary, the World Conservation Trust, to be incorporated as a legal entity in the United States and governed by an independent Board (including the President and Director-General).[21] This notion evolved separately from that of an

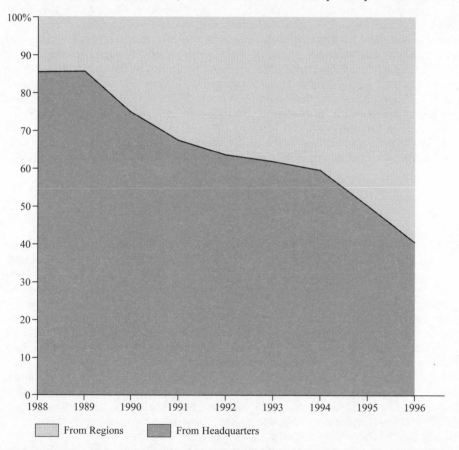

Figure 11.1 *Decentralization: the rising proportion of expenditure managed from Regional and Country Offices.*

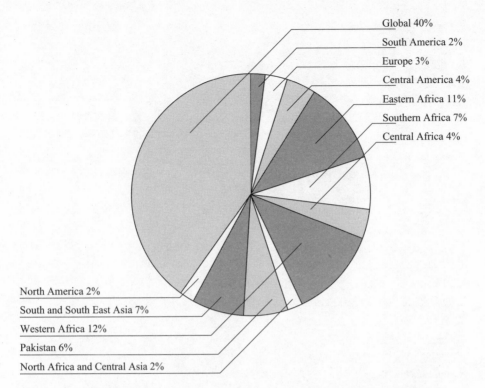

Figure 11.2 *The distribution of IUCN expenditure by region, 1994–96.*

overall fund-raising strategy elaborated at a special summit of Council members and senior staff: clearly the issues were being taken very seriously, but with some uncertainty over approach and outcome.[21]

The review of the Statutes – required by the Buenos Aires General Assembly – was approached with understandable trepidation. When in 1977 it had last been attempted in any wholesale way, it had taken a Special Session of the General Assembly and protracted wrangling, about which Wolfgang Burhenne still spoke with all the drama of a battle-scarred veteran. Now it was to be dealt with in no more than two days, as a kind of extension to the General Assembly in Canada in 1996. And it was to be much more radical than in 1977, dealing with the Statutes, the rules of procedure of the General Assembly and the regulations as three interlinked entities. The only way was to consult the membership fully, interchange drafts with them well in advance, and try to defuse all potential bombs long before the debate in Montreal.

The job was given to Parvez Hassan, the Chair of the Commission on Environmental Law, supported by a team that included a Councillor from each region. The detailed textual work was remitted to a legal drafting group led by Professor Nick Robinson, Vice-Chair of CEL, and involving Wolfgang Burhenne, Jacques Morier Genoud, the Swiss lawyer who represented the host country on the Council, José Martinez Aragon, a Spanish lawyer who worked for the European Commission, and Martin Holdgate as a Special Adviser. The presence of Francophone and Hispanophone lawyers meant that English, French and Spanish texts were prepared in parallel, and Nick Robinson refused to let an article go by until the versions in all

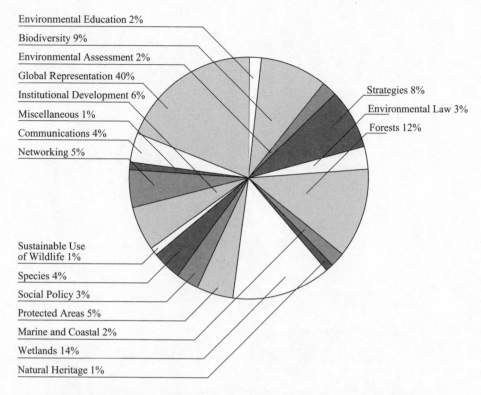

Environmental Education 2%
Biodiversity 9%
Environmental Assessment 2%
Global Representation 40%
Institutional Development 6%
Miscellaneous 1%
Communications 4%
Networking 5%

Strategies 8%
Environmental Law 3%
Forests 12%

Sustainable Use
of Wildlife 1%
Species 4%
Social Policy 3%
Protected Areas 5%
Marine and Coastal 2%
Wetlands 14%
Natural Heritage 1%

Figure 11.3 *The distribution of IUCN expenditure by subject, 1994–96.*

three languages had been collated. It was slow, but it worked well enough.[34] However, one of the primary aims of the exercise was supposed to be the definition of new and more logical IUCN regions. The Committee and the Council argued the options one way and another and various innovative new groupings, with representation on Council designed to reflect the strength of the membership in each region, were examined but in the end inertia ruled. It was decided to advise retention of the existing units, but the labels were altered, 'East Europe' becoming 'East Europe, North and Central Asia' and Latin America becoming 'Meso and South America'.[35]

The First World Conservation Congress

In Buenos Aires, Tom Lee, Deputy Minister from Canada, and David McDowell had discussed the possibility that Montreal might be the venue for the following session of the General Assembly, to be entitled the First World Conservation Congress. The Canadian offer was duly made to the plenary, but a final decision was deferred to allow other possible bids to be presented and considered. The Canadian offer was formally accepted by the new President of IUCN in May 1994.[32]

Montreal was quite different from all previous IUCN General Assemblies.[36] It was vastly bigger, to start with – over 3000 people were involved in one part or another of the ten-day programme. It was really three conferences linked into one.

CONFERENCE ONE

Conference One dealt with the normal domestic business of IUCN, rendered abnormal by the devotion of two days to the approval of the new Statutes, rules of procedure for the General Assembly, and regulations. Thanks to skilled chairmanship by Jay Hair, to the thorough work of Parvez Hassan's Statutes Review Committee and Nick Robinson's drafting group, and to the effective communication with the membership throughout the process, the texts sailed through remarkably smoothly within the allotted time. This Conference also adopted 111 resolutions and recommendations – again, without the same trauma as in Buenos Aires, thanks to the skilled use of 'contact groups' to resolve differences, and firm Chairmanship in the plenary sessions. Conference One also elected a new President in succession to Jay Hair, who had stood firmly by his promise not to seek a second term, to give the Congress at least two candidates to choose between, and to ensure that at least one was from a developing country and one was a woman. In fact the election was contested between two developing country candidates – Yolanda Kakabadse of Ecuador and Parvez Hassan of Pakistan – and the former won, giving IUCN its first female President.

Reporting to Conference One, David McDowell described impressive progress on decentralization.[4] The relevance of the Union was confirmed by the continuing growth in membership, reaching 855 in 134 countries by the end of 1996, and an upwards climb in its budget.[14] But there were stresses. Speaking to Council in April 1996 about the conclusions of his independent review of the programme and Commissions, Leif Christoffersen (a Norwegian who was also a consultant to the World Bank) commented that '*on the one hand, the membership had been considerably strengthened by the growing number of Regional and National Committees while on the other, members, especially States, had expected too much from IUCN and subsequent disillusionment led to arrears of dues*'.[21]

The programme still showed apparent imbalances, partly because of the preoccupations of donors.[4] Some 40 per cent of expenditure was on global topics, with Africa (eastern, southern, central and western) taking 34 per cent of the remaining budget, as against only 2 per cent for South America, 4 per cent for Central America and under 15 per cent for the whole of Asia. There was also apparent imbalance between themes: there was no obvious logic in the assignment of 26 per cent of the budget to forests and wetlands, when marine and coastal took only 2 per cent, species 4 per cent, sustainable use of wildlife 1 per cent and environmental law 3 per cent. And although allocations to the Commissions had quadrupled, there were still gaps between what the membership (and the Council and Director-General) wanted, and what could be done.

The publications list is one index of the Union's productiveness.[4] In the period 1994–96 an astonishing 131 titles were added to the list – and some of these were weighty volumes, such as the three-volume *Guide and Strategy for the Conservation of Centres of Plant Diversity*, the 1993 revision of the *UN List of National Parks and Protected Areas*, and the four-volume *Global Marine Representative System of Protected Areas*. Others were useful handbooks like the *Guide to the Convention on Biological Diversity*, the *Handbook for the Planning and Implementation of Strategies for National Sustainable Development*, a new 1994 *Red List of Threatened Animals*, the *Action Plan for the Conservation of Dolphins, Porpoises and Whales* and several other action plans. Three volumes on Antarctic conservation appeared, dealing with protected areas, sub-Antarctic islands and the impacts of tourism, all published jointly with SCAR, the Scientific Committee on Antarctic Research. There

Year	Number	Year	Number
1948	1	1973	19
1949	1	1974	14
1950	2	1975	16
1951	2	1976	25
1952	2	1977	11
1953	2	1978	13
1954	4	1979	13
1955	4	1980	23
1956	4	1981	25
1957	3	1982	23
1958	2	1983	29
1959	2	1984	56
1960	7	1985	51
1961	3	1986	49
1962	5	1987	58
1963	4	1988	57
1964	6	1989	66
1965	6	1990	68
1966	3	1991	90
1967	11	1992	119
1968	14	1993	155
1969	11	1994	92
1970	9	1995	119
1971	13	1996	122
1972	14	1997	145

Figure 11.4 *IUCN publications: 50 years of continuous publishing.*

were numerous analyses of issues like the impact of climate change, and papers on the management of particular areas. The Commission on Environmental Strategy and Planning (CESP) produced a 272-page book, *A Sustainable World: Defining and Measuring Sustainable Development*, based on its workshop in Buenos Aires.[37] And a group of distinguished international lawyers convened by the Commission on Environmental Law completed the draft of a proposed new, global legal instrument – a *Covenant on Environment and Development* – which was launched in 1995, the UN's 50th anniversary year, at a UN Congress on Public International Law.[5,38]

CONFERENCE TWO

Conference Two, however, was what many members came for. It held 49 workshops, grouped in ten 'streams' – enhancing sustainability; conserving vitality and diversity; adapting protected areas management to new challenges; sharing nature's bounty; implementing strategies for sustainability; involving people in conservation; using economics as a tool for conservation; acting on global issues; learning from Canadian experience; and engaging members and partners. One workshop, which caught everyone's attention, was literally dramatic – a 'total theatre' presentation involving drama, dance and mime entitled 'Guardians of Eden' which presented the dilemmas of

African conservation in a moving and memorable way.[39] It showed '*how theatre could bridge the communications gap between people from different parts of the world, with diverse views*'[39] and suggested that '*a Festival of Conservation Arts and Drama might move more hearts and minds than a million discourses on sustainable use or saving biodiversity*'.[40]

The workshops were all pulled together by Jeff McNeely, who stressed the real value of such events – the exchange of experience between people from all over the world. He drew some general conclusions: '*We need to build a stronger constituency through providing benefits to more people*', he emphasized.

> '*We need to show the linkages between biodiversity loss, ecological degradation and human health, and between trade and environment. We need to link up with the private sector. We need to use economic tools. We need to consider water as the ultimate constraint on development. We need to focus more on alien species and on restoration ecology. We need to give more attention to climate change.*'[41]

He thought that IUCN might contribute especially by raising new issues and defining what the public priorities might be. He stressed the need for scientifically credible information and positive examples of best practice. IUCN could provide a forum for discussion of issues not yet on the public agenda. It could promote new partnerships between different sectors. It should monitor and evaluate success and failure, and it should continue to promote the exchange of views. McNeely's conclusions were debated in a 'panel of panels' chaired by the Union's former President, Shridath Ramphal and involving Keith Bezanson, Director of the International Development Research Centre in Canada, Ashok Khosla, head of Development Alternatives in India, Julia Carabias, Minister of Environment in Mexico, Marie-Angelique Savané, head of the African Section of the UN Fund for Population Activities and Anders Wijkman, Director of the UNDP Policy and Programme Support Bureau.[42] They concluded that a sustainable life style was imperative, and demanded changes in social, administrative, political and economic systems. The positive links between economic growth and environmental protection had to be emphasized. Population issues had to be addressed positively, within the envelope of development for a new, environmentally-friendly life style.

The workshops and panels thus returned, time and again, as *Caring for the Earth* had done, to the human heart of conservation and development. The old face of IUCN appeared, however, in some of the resolutions and recommendations – and in the argument when they were debated.

Resolutions provide an important opportunity for a member, or group of members, to bring an issue before the world conservation community and seek global support for their views. The adoption of a resolution (a motion addressed to IUCN by a Congress or General Assembly, as the sovereign parliament of the members), moreover, defines the policy of the Union and while it may not fetter the discretion of the Council and Director-General it clearly imposes an obligation on them to act in conformity with it. Recommendations, addressed to governments or other recipients outside IUCN, are clearly not binding, but they too have considerable moral force. It is not surprising, therefore, that many members, especially from the non-governmental sector, come to an Assembly or Congress with the adoption of a resolution or recommendation high on their priority lists. Some see it as the most important action of all. And that importance has little to do with the capacity of the Secretariat to implement what is agreed – the value for NGO members lies in a document they can use at home.[43] Over the years the number of proposals brought before an Assembly has mounted steadily, from under 20 a session at the start to well over 100. The subjects covered have ranged very widely, although the principal themes – general issues of conservation, ecology, species, protected areas, development, education, law and the administration of the Union – have been constant elements.[44]

Such motions can readily be partisan (that can sometimes be their value in getting some specific action taken by a reluctant authority). Sometimes, they can clash. In Montreal, there were (for example) three draft recommendations on the use of wildlife.[45] Two pointed the same way – endorsing the work of the Union (and especially SSC) on the development of principles, guidelines and practices that '*would enhance the sustainability of use of wild fauna and flora*'. The other would, effectively, have banned the consumptive use of wild mammals, birds, reptiles and amphibia – regardless of the fact that these were staple sources of protein for local people in many parts of the world, notably in Africa. Even after amendment in an informal 'contact group' it sought to impose conditions that would have gravely hampered any commercial consumption of wildlife (including fisheries). It was voted down. So was a motion on environmental degradation in the Niger delta which, while addressing the need for good practice and attention to human rights on the part of the oil industry (which everyone accepted), had political overtones that government delegations in particular thought inappropriate for IUCN.

That was another problem. To succeed, a motion has to have a simple majority in favour of it in both the governmental and non-governmental 'chambers' of membership. This is wise, for it maintains the balance between the two components, whose presence is one of IUCN's distinctive features. But where a motion strongly favoured by NGOs is blocked by governments, there can be rancour. Where, on the other hand, governments do not block a motion but make subsequent statements that distance themselves from it, and hence undermine its standing, other kinds of criticism result. The wise course is for members at all times to be sensitive to one another – but that is easier said than achieved in the heat and pressure of a session that has perhaps three days to debate over a hundred proposals. The sheer volume of the motions for consideration, even with much corridor work in 'contact groups', makes it virtually impossible for all of them to receive the balanced discussion they merit.

Other motions put forward in Montreal were less contentious, but addressed local conservation issues on which delegations from distant lands could scarcely form a view. Some opined on policy issues which were peripheral to IUCN's mandate and mission – such as nuclear energy or the management of household wastes. Yet others sought to strengthen sections of the IUCN programme, or boost other activities in support of the membership in particular regions or in particular Commissions (often bidding to distort the balance of effort proposed in the triennial programme as a separate agenda item before the Congress). Costs were rarely considered by sponsors: David McDowell estimated that the motions '*proposed in Montreal would cost the Union several million francs to be implemented. This put him in an impossible position...*'.[46] While it was customary to insert the phrase '*within available resources*' to make it clear that some actions simply could not be taken, this was (rightly) seen as unsatisfactory. Sponsors of motions themselves incurred a responsibility for helping to implement their proposals. The Secretariat prepared an analysis for Council of who could implement what, at what cost.[46] Many delegates left feeling that something more had to be done to ensure that the Congress in future adopted motions that were clearly the business of IUCN, that would clearly advance conservation and sustainable resource use, and that did not duplicate or contradict the conclusions the Congress reached in its debate on the overall programme.[46]

CONFERENCE THREE

Conference Three was an open session of panel discussions on the big issues of the time. The first considered communications.[47] The environmental writer, Lloyd Timberlake, presided over a panel that included David Bellamy, the well-known British botanist and broadcaster, Kalpana Sharma, Indian journalist, and Claude Martin, Director-General of WWF International. Timberlake emphasized that '*environmentalists are too narrow-minded. We enjoy talking to our own kind too much, we have a hard time reaching out to business, to the legal profession, to groups we don't normally associate with – and we will have to get better at this.*' David Bellamy argued that '*the green movement must begin to use its political clout and voice its opinions*' and that IUCN, with 7000 scientists in its networks and 800 organizations in membership '*should be the people the world actually believes when it makes a decision*'. Kalpana Sharma urged the need to develop environmental understanding among journalists, and Claude Martin commented that mass communication is a professional activity that conservationists were often not very good at.

The second panel examined the relationship between environmentalists and business: it was chaired by Stephan Schmidheiny, and involved William Ruckelshaus (once head of the US Environment Protection Agency), Edgar Asibey of Andes Pharmaceutical, Jean Monty of Northern Telecom in Canada, and Elizabeth Dowdeswell, Mostafa Tolba's successor as Executive Director of UNEP.[48] They emphasized that '*environmental protection is good business*', that '*business people should realize that their enlightened self-interest is consistent with the principle of sustainable development*' and that '*we are now seeing new approaches to dialogue and partnership, built on the linked concerns of business and consumers*'. David McDowell was encouraged to go away from Montreal to build a new relationship between IUCN and the business community.

The third panel looked at how sustainable development could be financed.[49] Maurice Strong took the Chair, and was supported by Jean-François Richard, Vice-President of the World Bank, Gus Speth, the Administrator of UNDP and founder and former head of the World Resources Institute, Tessa Tennant, Director of the Global Care Fund for a major group of investment managers, and Enrique Garcia, head of the Andean Development Corporation. As Maurice Strong stressed, '*sustainable development will not happen without financing, and financing will not take place if sustainable development is not financeable*'. Gus Speth was equally definite: '*there'll be no sustainable development without development. We need more development assistance, not less.*' And Jean-François Richard spoke of the strong, emerging, correlation between environmental and economic success. The message that people should focus on '*capitalism for conservation*' and incorporate social factors in environmental protection reinforced that from the business panel, and strengthened the call for IUCN to build its links with the commercial world, which is the engine of development. A few head-shaking nature protectionists clearly wondered what the Union was coming to.

The fourth panel, chaired by Martin Holdgate, was on more familiar ground (indeed it had been demanded by some of the greener Council members as an antidote to all this commercial stuff).[50] It addressed nature in the 21st century. The panel brought together Ed Ayensu of Ghana, former head of the Scientific and Technical Advisory Panel to the Global Environment Facility, Sylvia Earle, well-known American marine biologist and conservationist, and José Sarukhan of Mexico, who had convened his country's national conference on biodiversity conservation. They concluded that some of the human impacts on the natural world were unstoppable: conservation had to be made compatible with growth. But – linking back to the commercial debates – they stressed that:

> *'environmental protection...is a requirement for long-term growth and sustainable development. It is financially and environmentally sound, and indeed good practice, to include pollution control at the design stage in any development venture. Everybody wins if we protect the wild oceans, the common heritage. Everybody loses if we don't, and we will not succeed unless we work at community level.'*

Jeffrey McNeely tied many strands together in a discussion paper on *Conservation and the Future: Trends and Options towards the Year 2025*.[51] Tidied up after the Congress, and published in 1997, this reviewed ten inter-related areas where significant changes were bound to affect conservation:

1   the growth in human populations, and continued inefficiency in resource use;
2   the threat to cultural diversity from the growth of the global market and universal information technology;
3   increasing recognition that national security has major environmental dimensions (especially relating to water supplies);
4   the likelihood that climate change will pose a profound challenge to the adaptive capacities of societies;
5   the continuing threat of pollution;
6   the recognition that economics is central to all conservation issues, and that economic tools must be adopted by conservationists;
7   the institutional changes in the world, as central governments weaken, multi-national corporations grow in size and strength, and non-governmental organizations proliferate;
8   the widening gap between rich and poor, which is aggravated by differences in the availability of technology;
9   the growing power of information and communications;
10   the losses of biodiversity, which conservationists can and must address and mitigate, even if they cannot halt them.

McNeely saw the answer in adaptive management, and emphasized the need for IUCN and other conservation organizations to monitor trends, to develop practical solutions in the shape of management policies, plans and techniques, and to promote them through environmental assessment, advisory and mediation services. It must prepare for a diversity of possible futures, because there is no certainty.

While uplifted by the spirit and stimulation of one of the biggest meetings of environmentalists ever held, David McDowell was not enthusiastic about the programmatic products of the Congress. He felt that it did not provide enough ideological direction or programmatic priority. He came away convinced that the Union must focus its work more sharply and make a greater impact on the big conservation and development issues. Like Martin Holdgate before him, he was also worried that the Secretariat was still not working as a sufficiently integrated, cross-sectoral team (he set out these concerns a year after Montreal in a memorandum entitled *Lifting the Union's Game*, which has echoes of Holdgate's *Six Months of Glandular Fever*).[52]

The Congress was closed by two speeches – from Jay Hair as outgoing President and Yolanda Kakabadse as his successor. Jay Hair was typically up-beat. '*I think without question this has been the most energized, exciting and useful meeting ever held by IUCN* ' he proclaimed. He felt that the time was right for new endeavours.

> '*I've never seen the world's attention more focussed on the need to achieve an ecologically sustainable future…Harmonizing the needs of humankind with the need to protect the environment and conserve natural resources will be the issue of the 21st century. Society is gradually understanding this. That is why I feel so encouraged that IUCN is coming into its own, in the excellence of its secretariat staff, the interaction and involvement of our members, and the way we are reorganizing ourselves through a decentralized process. I think the Union is positioned beautifully to provide inspired leadership to bring the world together.*'[53]

Yolanda Kakabadse was also positive and forward-looking. '*Sustainable development is not just about the environment*', she said, '*it is also a philosophy*'. The Congress had brought a vast diversity of people together, and had emphasized the need to communicate the message more clearly. It had given a strong mandate '*to involve more people from the private sector, from banks, from industries, from trade organizations at a national and international level, in order to discuss what sustainable development is about and how we work together in solving the problems of the world today…The challenge is to create an awareness of what we are really talking about. For we are not talking about protecting a few species or some national protected areas and reserves. We are talking about life and death.*'[54]

12 The Balance Sheet

The close of the World Conservation Congress is also a convenient point at which to close the narrative record of 50 years of history. Fifty years from the first excursion in the Swiss Engadine to that immense gathering in Montreal. What has it really meant? What have been the strengths and weaknesses, successes and failures of global action for conservation? How successful has IUCN been?

This must be a section of interpretation. I must therefore start with a 'disclaimer'. The preceding chapters have described the history of IUCN and the parts of the conservation movement with which it has interlocked as objectively as possible, drawing on publications, the extensive records of General Assembly sessions and Council and Bureau meetings, and the memories of people who have played key parts on the green stage over the past half-century. But the interpretation can only be a matter of personal judgement. As one consequence, this chapter is written using the first person, whereas the chronicle of events when Martin Holdgate was Director-General has been more or less impassive!

Success or Failure?

On some evaluations, the world conservation movement has failed.[1] Greenhouse gas concentrations in the atmosphere continue to rise. The ozone-depleting substances continue to erode our protective screen even though further emissions are being curbed. There is still too much pollution in the world and it threatens to be a scourge of newly-industrializing countries unless they are helped to install the latest technology. Biodiversity is in decline, and further losses are inevitable as forests are cut or burned, coral reefs destroyed, intensive agriculture expands, and species are transported around the world, leaping ancient biogeographical barriers.[2]

But the real test is one we cannot apply. How much worse would all this have been had there been no global conservation movement?

We can only hazard a guess, but my guess is much, much worse.[3] Without the efforts at intergovernmental level led by UNEP, UNESCO, FAO and latterly the CSD, reinforced by the conventions and other agreements of the past 50 years,[4] and without the Global Environment Facility and the vast mass of projects supported by WWF, IUCN and many other conservation bodies, surely the world's habitats, soils, waters, forests and seas would be in an even worse state.

What about the specific contribution of IUCN? That is much more difficult. The world environmental movement is an interlocking whole, and it is hard to dissect out the contribution of any one component. It is especially difficult with IUCN because it is a green web – a Union of members – in which much of the action takes place through the parts. The principal test of the value of IUCN must be – have the members, partners and third parties who have used the concepts and information it has supplied been able to do more than they could have done without it? Had time allowed, I would have researched this aspect by asking them, and it remains a promising area of future study (preferably addressed by region and subject area).

As it is, so far as I know the only attempted evaluation is that conducted by Charles de Haes, who received 70 replies from a questionnaire sent to IUCN members and others in 1992.[5] Most of them saw '*IUCN as a very positive force, but a force to be channelled in certain definite directions*'. The aspects the respondents valued most were the Union's contributions to nature conservation, its scientific expertise and the expert support it can provide, its role as a forum and network linking a broad spectrum of governmental and non-governmental elements, and its leadership in major ventures such as the *World Conservation Strategy* and *Caring for the Earth.* The things the respondents did not like were the centralization of power and action at headquarters, elements of competition with members when it came to funding for projects, and any tendency for IUCN to become a development agency.

My own judgement is that IUCN has been outstanding in nine particular respects.

First, the Union has made a unique contribution by bringing together nearly half the world's states (including virtually all the most influential ones), many of the most powerful government agencies concerned with conservation, and virtually every significant international and national non-governmental conservation body.

Second, its General Assemblies and Technical Meetings have for 50 years been the unchallenged forum for worldwide discussion of conservation. Although the Governing Council of UNEP and the Commission on Sustainable Development are now the principal places for intergovernmental consideration of environmental issues, the World Conservation Congress is unique in the breadth of its agenda, the flexibility of its discussions, and the contacts it facilitates.

Third, well over a thousand resolutions and recommendations adopted in General Assembly have fed into and influenced a mass of decisions at international, regional, national and sub-national levels and greatly strengthened the hands of non-governmental conservation organizations.

Fourth, the Union has made an immense contribution to a half-century of evolving conservation philosophy. It has drawn on new thinking in ecology, and applied it to the conservation of species and habitats and the management of natural resources. It has published a mass of major works. The *World Conservation Strategy* of 1980 was one of the seminal environmental documents of the half-century. *Caring for the Earth* and the *Global Biodiversity Strategy* – also partnership products – are documents of the first importance.

Fifth, IUCN's voluntary networks – especially in the fields of species conservation, protected areas and environmental law – are the world's largest, most productive and most authoritative bodies in their fields.

Sixth, IUCN's classification of categories of threatened species, and its Red Data Books, Red Lists and Action Plans, have won universal acceptance, and have been used by all significant conservation bodies in their own campaigns.

Seventh, its classification of categories of protected areas, the *UN List of National Parks and Protected Areas* which it compiles, and the conclusions of the four World Congresses on Parks and Protected Areas which it has convened stand as global authorities.

Eighth, no other body – even in the United Nations system – can rival IUCN's record as a promoter and drafter of new national and international conservation law. As Nicholas Robinson, current Chair of CEL has put it, '*IUCN's contribution is unique. It defined the opportunities and established the legitimacy of environmental law. Others have emulated, but copying is the best compliment.*'[6]

Ninth, the worldwide programme of the Union – again in partnership with others – is making an outstanding contribution to the conservation of biological diversity and biological resources, and to meeting the needs of human communities for development that is sustainable because it uses those resources in an equitable and ecologically sound way.

The Basis for Success

IUCN's success depends on what it is not as well as what it is.[7] It was not set up as world director of conservation but as a *facilitator*. It was not designed to lead, but (as the most recent mission statement says) *to influence, encourage and assist*. Its greatest strength lies in its ability to work as an equal partner with diverse peoples, institutions and governments.[7] It was modelled on the kind of cooperation well established in science – for example in the International Council of Scientific Unions. In the beginning, it had no bureaucracy, and relied on networks of professional people for its creative thinking. The 'value added' of the original Union lay in its ability to convene the world's best ecologists to provide new insights, clear definitions of concepts, problems and priorities, logical explanations of what needed to be done, compendia of information and methods that could be used by practitioners. As David Bellamy put it at Montreal, it was meant to bring together *the people the world actually believes when it makes a decision*.[8]

I consider that the key to the Union's success has lain in its capacity to provide knowledge, techniques and support. A few words on each in turn.

Knowledge

One of IUCN's first activities was to record the state of nature in many parts of the world through pooling the knowledge of member organizations and individual scientists. This led on to monitoring: to defining the status of ecosystems and species and the rates and causes of change. The Species Survival Commission, the World Commission on Protected Areas and their predecessors were at the front of this action, and the World Conservation Monitoring Centre is the repository of the databases they, the Secretariat of the Union and the Centre's own staff have built up over the years. Without survey and monitoring everybody is 'flying blind' and IUCN's first great contribution was surely to gather and interpret the information without which world conservation would have been purely intuitive and reactive. This work continues, and the Biodiversity Conservation Information System, as the world's network for biodiversity information, is the latest opportunity for a major contribution.[9]

Linked to survey and monitoring, there must be explanation. This is where ecology comes in. Julian Huxley, right at the beginning, saw the need to harness ecology as a service to development, and the roots of what we now call 'sustainable development' can be found in his writings and those of other pioneers like Frank

Fraser Darling, Ray Dasmann and Thane Riney. The Commission on Ecology compiled up-to-date reviews of what was known about many key ecosystems. More recently, the need to understand social systems – whether of people who follow traditional ways of life or of modern technological societies – has become evident. Ecology has had to be joined by economics, and the social sciences – and with the recognition of the paramount need for a new ethic has come linkage with philosophers, humanists and theologians. There are challenges to the Union today to maintain its essential expertise in these fields – and the Commission on Ecosystem Management has a major task ahead in '*linking science with society*'[10] and restoring itself as the voluntary network to which applied ecologists wish to belong. As the Programme Committee said in Montreal, IUCN has to excel as a knowledge-based institution.[11]

TECHNIQUES

Conservation and sustainable development are social activities, not theories and IUCN can take pride in the undoubted fact that it has been the world pioneer and leader in the development both of concepts and methodologies. The conceptual roots of today's 'new' emphasis on the importance of biodiversity extend right back to the start of the Union's history. It was Peter Scott, as Chairman of SSC, who established the Red Data Books and associated Action Plans. Today over 5000 threatened animals and 30,000 threatened plants appear in the Red Lists, and there are 40 Action Plans for plant and animal groups.[12] The classification of categories of threatened species which SSC has developed is used universally. IUCN, through the specialist groups of SSC and the central Secretariat, backed up by the databases of WCMC and in partnership with the information gathering networks of TRAFFIC and WWF, provides the principal authoritative advice to the Convention on International Trade in Endangered Species.[13] They can and should do the same for the Convention on Biological Diversity.

Then again, it was IUCN (thanks initially to the vision and energy of Hal Coolidge) that secured the mandate from the United Nations to prepare and regularly revise the *UN List of National Parks and Protected Areas*, and this has been done using the unique network of 'parks people' provided by WCPA. This list, too, is linked to a taxonomy for protected areas, and IUCN's classification is accepted as authoritative worldwide. The Union's support to the World Heritage Convention – which now has over 500 cultural and natural sites on its list – is another model. The practical knowledge of protected area management that the Union has fostered is an indispensable weapon in the armoury of biodiversity conservation.

Law is a sphere of knowledge, but legal instruments are, in their essence, techniques – ways of ensuring that societies behave in certain ways. It was the Centre for Environmental Law, led, cajoled (and at times financed), by Wolfgang and Françoise Burhenne, that brought together the first (and still the most comprehensive) environmental law database in the world. It was the Commission on Environmental Law and CEPLA, its predecessor, that linked the voluntary services of hundreds of the world's top environmental lawyers to prepare texts of new legal instruments. The Convention on International Trade in Endangered Species, the Convention on Biological Diversity, the Convention on Migratory Species and the World Charter for Nature all began on the drawing boards of IUCN. So did a host of regional agreements, including those for Africa, the ASEAN region and the South Pacific, and some specific measures such as that for the protection of polar bears. Now the Covenant on Environment and Development is following.

And it was IUCN that produced the World Conservation Strategy, though it was its African members and UNEP that gave the impetus to its evolution from a nature conservation document into one that struck a new balance between conservation and development. The WCS was the spring from which 'sustainable development' as a concept has flowed. It established more cogently than ever before the cardinal principle that conservation can only succeed if pursued within the context of development that caters for people, and safeguards the resources on which future societies will depend. It led on to the notion of conservation with equity between people and generations, and to the imperative of environmental ethics, both elaborated in *Caring for the Earth*. It led to practical techniques for national conservation strategies, most of them guided and encouraged by IUCN Secretariat services.[14] The thinking and approach of Agenda 21, of national strategies for sustainable development, of the World Bank's National Environmental Action plans and many others stemmed from the WCS, and from the efforts of David Munro, Robert Prescott-Allen, Duncan Poore, Ray Dasmann and their colleagues – criticized and at times startled by Reuben Olembo and his colleagues in Nairobi.

SUPPORT

For the membership, support has perhaps been the greatest advantage and it works in several ways. First, small societies around the world feel strengthened simply by being a member of IUCN and able to link with its networks, draw on its expertise, meet one another in its Assemblies and workshops, and propose resolutions and recommendations that advance their causes back home. As Anis Mouasher of Jordan has put it, '*as a result of our membership...we consider ourselves part of a global movement*'.[15] The label 'Member of IUCN' is not only an acknowledgement of admission to the top global professional organization, but a veiled warning that any government or agency that pushes such a body around is liable to end up at the receiving end of condemnation by a significant world community. And increasingly, as regional forums and gatherings, National Committees and regional programmes and Regional Offices have proliferated, IUCN is gaining capacity to provide practical support on the ground where conservation is done.

Resolutions and recommendations are part of the support mechanism. Their importance can easily be underestimated by people working in governments, or by members of the IUCN Secretariat (who are conscious of the ephemeral nature of many of them and the immense burden of work they impose on those servicing a General Assembly). But for many non-governmental members, especially in the developing countries, they can be a lifeline. There can be no better testimonial than the following, from the distinguished Brazilian ecologist and conservationist, Paulo Nogueira-Neto:

> '*To me, the most important meeting I took part in in IUCN was that of Banff, in 1972...I presented a Resolution proposal declaring the island "Ilha de Cardoso" and also three spectacular neighbouring groves (practically the last significant ones) of our biggest tree in SE Brazil, as areas of world importance for conservation. This was very important for us in Brazil because these areas had only a small protection. The people who were directing the meeting were against my proposals, saying that they needed more details. They had a good argument but I*

*strongly stated that we needed an immediate decision in order to protect that island and the groves of jequetiba trees (*Cairinia strellensis*)*

The Assembly, to my surprise and joy, approved my request in a general vote. It was my first big achievement in an international meeting. I felt deeply gratified. It was for me a moment of very strong emotion, as I seldom felt in my life. It also showed that a modest member from a developing country could receive the approval of a majority made of people from several developed countries...This resolution of IUCN had a broad effect in Brazil. The areas mentioned became State Parks, in large part because of this support.'[16]

The example could be replicated many times over. I believe that getting the process right, so that IUCN resolutions and recommendations carry as much authority as possible, is an important task for the future.

The Commissions are also important support mechanisms. Specialist and working groups of many kinds assemble committed experts from all round the world to pool knowledge and develop techniques. The support works two ways – to the individuals, who gain effectiveness by being linked into respected networks of this kind, and to the world community that gets the best available analyses and proposals. IUCN can offer a mechanism for convening, a platform for the exposition of collective thinking, a central Secretariat that provides administrative linkage and operational continuity, and a publications outlet for the final conclusions. There is no other conservation organization in the world that operates voluntary networks of this kind, on anything like this scale. Many people would agree that '*IUCN works best when it engages its volunteer networks substantively.*'[17] And by drawing such expertise together it can contribute authoritative statements to third parties like CITES.[13]

In the past 50 years, the weaknesses of some Commissions and the management of all of them have been the subject of agonized reviews. The Commissions on Ecology (now CEM), Sustainable Development (now CEESP) and Education (now CEC) have ben criticised and reconstituted. While all have successes to record (CEC, for example, has had an important supportive role in Central and Eastern Europe) they have not 'taken off' in the same way as the other three.

My own view is that one problem has been that people attending General Assemblies have assumed that because a subject is important, IUCN must have a Commission for it. That is nonsense. A Commission is a voluntary assembly of experts who maintain continuing programmes within the broad mandate of the Union. The test is activity and productivity. The networks that have succeeded are those central to the mission of IUCN and not duplicated elsewhere: they thus provide a natural focus for professionals in their spheres. That is why SSC, WCPA and CEL (and their diverse acronymic predecessors) have achieved their reputation. That is why the Commission on Ecology has slithered downhill in the past 20 years, when it ceased to be a natural focus for ecological scientists – and why CEM has a steep hill ahead of it. That is why CEP/CSD/CEESP has struggled: it has not made itself the natural focus for the world's top environmental planners, environmental economists or thinkers about sustainable development. That is why the Commission on Education has had so uneven a track record. I believe that it lost its way when it failed to position itself within UNESCO–UNEP–IEEP, working on well-defined tasks agreed as the right niche for IUCN – something it is now trying to do in relation to CSD and Agenda 21.[18]

This question of niches is in my view more important than the matter of governance. It is true that the constitution of IUCN makes the Commissions inflexible. It has proved almost impossible to close down those that are ineffective, because each has its own loyal 'supporter's club' at the General Assembly, and the direct election of Chairs and assignment of mandates by the Assembly gives them immense independence. The SSC, in particular, with the vast proportion of its funding coming from outside IUCN directly to its Chair or Specialist Groups, operates as a semi-independent entity.[17] But while I believe that it would have been wiser, as was proposed in 1977, to give the Council responsibility for appointing Commission Chairs and for approving their programmes, any defects of governance have not impeded the success of those Commissions whose niche is clear. Now regionalization is forcing the Commissions to build much closer links with the membership, and I believe that this will greatly strengthen their supportive value.

Dilemmas and Debates

IUCN's dilemmas seem to me to have largely been over balance: between being a facilitator or an implementer; between being a cautious, government-dominated body and a lively NGO; between being a nature conservation body or one promoting sustainable development; between North and South (and between being centralized or dispersed); between independence and partnership; between being the champion of conservation in the public's eye, or a wise shadow behind the publicists. These five dilemmas are explored in the following sections.

Facilitator or Implementer?

IUPN/IUCN, in the years before 1972, worked as a facilitator. It relied on Commissions and their subordinate specialist groups to develop ideas, methods and action plans. The knowledge 'on tap' in the Commissions, plus the database in the central library inherited from the International Office for the Protection of Nature, were drawn on by the small, central Secretariat to provide advice and help to members. The same system gave the infant WWF the support it needed in vetting applications for its funds. The main task of the Secretariat was to stitch the whole together by organizing General Assemblies and other meetings, answering queries and keeping information flowing through the network by means of the newsletter or *Bulletin*. A specialist advisory organization of this kind posed no threat to the UN agencies like UNESCO, with whom there was easy partnership.

In the mid-1970s, and even more after the World Conservation Strategy appeared in 1980, IUCN changed character. It retained its networks (indeed SSC, CNPPA and CEPLA grew in strength, energized by dynamos like Peter Scott, Hal Coolidge and Wolfgang Burhenne). But the expansion of the Secretariat under Gerardo Budowski, and still more the creation of the Conservation for Development Centre, impelled by Maurice Strong and Michael Cockerell, transformed its character. IUCN became an operational agency managing an immense number of projects, and more and more of them were related to sustainable development. New Secretariat-led thematic programmes multiplied. Field offices proliferated. Project work dominated the programme. Even though most of the money was spent in the developing world, and the donors of funds were enthusiastic about institution-building, in practical terms shortage of unrestricted money inhibited the building of links to and for the members.

Some people believe that this change was damaging, and '*confused the Union's intellectual identity. The founding fathers wanted it to work in support of the membership. The field operations are distorting its mission.*'[19] '*As IUCN passed from a policy and technical assistance organization to a pseudo-aid agency it lost in my view much of its strength.*'[20] Today, with regionalization and decentralization an accomplished fact (and supported by donors) these problems should be nearing solution. But this will only be so if the Union '*realizes it must be guided from the regions, understanding their politics and societies. It must be good on the ground and react quickly to situations. It should involve wildlife clubs and build new ethics. There needs to be a new dynamism*'.[21] As David McDowell has recognized, '*decentralization is not just a political approach. It is at the country level that biodiversity will be conserved. And IUCN can do more to convene groups among countries with shared problems – as in the Zambezi basin – than the more inhibited UN can*'.[22]

My own view is that IUCN must be both facilitator and implementer. It must help its members to work more effectively. But it must do some things itself, in both the Secretariat and the voluntary networks. It must have enough professional 'critical mass' to support its status as an expert body, developing authoritative statements and perfecting techniques, policies, laws and strategies. The SSC and WCPA must stay at the forefront of world efforts to conserve biodiversity. This is where the Union stands quite distinct from WWF: '*IUCN has a unique role in policy development, as a GONGO. WWF will never be a policy developer.*'[23] '*IUCN must continue in its pioneering global role as a force shaping international policies, standards and practices for nature conservation.*'[15]

> '*Already the Global Environment Facility is being approached by governments from around the world seeking support to implement "bioregional management" projects, working at "ecosystem scales", establishing new "institutional arrangements" with stakeholders across whole landscapes, managing wildlife for local benefit and use. This is what IUCN is pushing now, and SSC and WCPA are leading the charge.*'[24]

And it must continue to provide expert Secretariat help to its members on the ground, supporting the thorn- and grass-roots of conservation.

GOVERNMENT-DOMINATED OR NGO?

It is often said that 'IUCN is a membership organization' – but the meaning of the phrase is less clear. But it is true that IUCN – unlike WWF, or Greenpeace or Friends of the Earth – has a constitutional structure that makes the Secretariat accountable to the Council and the Council and Commissions to the General Assembly of all the members. The latter thus determine the broad policies – and adopt the resolutions and recommendations that express aspects of that policy.

The Union needed a broad and large membership to carry credibility. The tests for admission have always been gentle – adoption of the mission statement and Statutes, and most recently acceptance of the World Conservation Strategy and *Caring for the Earth* as documents expressing the ethos of the Union. This has permitted a great diversity of organizations to join. Hunting organizations came in as founder members, welcomed so long as they showed a clear concern for the conservation of their quarry and its habitats. Bodies concerned primarily to advance sustainable development were also welcomed provided they showed a clear commitment to conservation and did work to safeguard natural resources as well as encourage good land use, good farming or well-planned settlements. Forestry bodies joined, provided that they met the rules of good forest management.

In my view, this breadth is important and the members and Councillors should be wary of allowing their prejudices to exclude bodies that could contribute – and be influenced – better inside than outside. I believe that IUCN should admit not-for-profit bodies in the world of business, industry and commerce, provided that they are truly committed to sustainable development. For the corporate sector is today the principal agent of investment, development and environmental resource use, disposing of wealth and power greater than that of many governments. IUCN was not founded as a club, but as an agent for achievement, and its goals will not be achieved unless it builds links with the corporate sector and strengthens its environmental sensitivity.

The founding fathers saw clearly that if the Union was to succeed it must attract a sufficient 'critical mass' of bodies carrying out conservation around the world. They needed natural history and nature protection societies, the new governmental agencies for conservation and the State members who, in the end, determined the policies that would make conservation possible. There was a second reason for wanting State members – money. But state membership grew very slowly because governments did not want to commit themselves to providing that money. Although the Group of Seven leading industrial powers, together with China and Russia, are all now State members, the United States, Japan, China and Russia have all joined since 1988. In 1996, less than half the total membership of the United Nations adhered as State members of IUCN and many of the world's poorest countries have been lost because of either inability to pay dues, or an insufficient priority to so doing. And although they may be State members, and have many national NGOs in membership, the biggest and richest Northern countries have given less to IUCN than many smaller countries with a stronger conservation ethic – among whom the Nordic countries stand pre-eminent. The quest for State members as golden egg-layers proved misplaced, and IUCN needs to make clear that it wants them for what they can do for conservation, not simply for their money.

Equally, it has to retain harmony between government and NGO members. Given the constitutional requirement that a vote can only succeed in a General Assembly if carried in both governmental and non-governmental 'chambers', there is little risk of one sector dominating the other, and this should give a sense of security. But something does need to be done about resolutions and recommendations. In recent years there have been too many occasions when governments have sat out a debate while non-governmental advocates press their causes, simply declaring when the motion is adopted without a vote that 'had there been a vote my delegation would have opposed'. And when governments do feel stirred to vote down a motion that non-governmental groups desire, the latter rarely accept the decision with understanding or good grace. It is a dangerous and widening crack that must not be permitted to threaten the security of the edifice.

PROTECTION OR SUSTAINABLE USE?

The conversion of IUPN into IUCN in Edinburgh in 1956 seemed to legitimize the presence in the Union of organizations who believed that conservation was about managing and using nature and natural resources as well as protecting what we would now call biodiversity. The World Conservation Strategy seemed to secure the position beyond doubt. Ottawa and *Caring for the Earth* placed conservation in its social context. The expanding programme in the developing world, with its emphasis on national conservation strategies and practical approaches to sustainable resource use seemed to mean that sustainable development was accepted as mainstream business of IUCN. Speaking to the symposium at the opening of IUCN's new headquarters in 1992 Mark Halle urged the Union to abandon '*once and for all, the safe haven of nature protection for the infinitely more difficult but much more rewarding world of sustainable development*'.[25]

Others differed strongly. But those who stressed the need to keep IUCN firmly rooted in nature protection were not seeking to deny the social context or the need for sustainable development. Their belief was in a balance that also emphasized the continuing importance of protecting areas and species, and of putting the interests of nature first, at least in some places.[26] In the debate over the mission of IUCN, first in Perth and then in Buenos Aires, the ultimate compromise reflected the two viewpoints by stating that the goal was '*to conserve the integrity and diversity of nature and to ensure that any use of natural resources is equitable and ecologically sustainable*'.[27] The word 'any' is important, because it implies that there is no obligation to use all the resources of nature for human benefit.

The debate has had its bitter moments, and there has been a degree of polarization, with some members, largely from developed countries, opposing the use of wildlife while others, especially in the developing world, stress the imperative of sustainable development and the '*inescapable reality that wild species and ecosystems are used*' and that such use is vital to human welfare.[28] Some protectionist members have felt that the Secretariat was too much in the sustainable use camp and that they were being '*betrayed by staff who were wilful and only heard their own ideas*'.[26]

It is not that lively debates on such issues are wrong – the reverse. The issue is what motivates the debate. In my view, IUCN should focus on what makes for sound conservation practice and conforms with an underlying conservation ethic. In some countries, the will of the community may mean that wildlife is not exploited for human gain. In others, forests, fisheries and wild animals and birds may be resources of great value, and the social ethic may be wholly at ease with their humane and sustainable harvesting. Both approaches – and many intermediaries between them – are compatible with sound conservation. IUCN's role is to stress the need to care for the Earth and its rich diversity of life, and to advise and guide on good practice rather than seek to impose one community's set of value judgements on another.

A NORTHERN CLUB?

It has been argued that IUCN has always been 'North-dominated' and remains so.[29] The Union certainly evolved very much within the envelope of European and North American thinking, and most of the first members and the active individuals came from those continents. But they looked South, appreciating the importance of science-

Figure 12.1 *Attitudes to nature. Gerald Watterson's sketch in 1962 still has topical relevance.*

based conservation for the newly independent colonies and other states of the developing world. The early field missions and the special projects in Africa and Asia demonstrated that commitment. And many in the South may well have shared the perspective of Anis Mouasher of Jordan, namely that:

> '*whilst IUCN was undoubtedly a northern initiative, we in the 'south' could see that the people involved had a clear picture and understanding of conservation and, most importantly, were prepared to help conserve nature in different parts of the world, not just their own. In other words, we did not find them patronising.*'[15]

Eskandar Firouz of Iran[30] and Paulo Nogueira-Neto of Brazil[16] are among those who also felt that North-South issues were not a matter of contention in IUCN in the 1960s and early 1970s.

Perhaps one reason why it was not an issue is that '*after the Second World War a small technical elite arose in developing countries such as India, Pakistan, Brazil and Iraq, who had been educated as scientists in the industrialized world*'.[31] These scientists pushed for accelerated programmes of advanced industrial development that mirrored those in the North – including nuclear science and nuclear energy. Something rather similar happened in conservation. The leading conservationists in many developing countries were educated in the North and transferred Northern concepts, including the notion that 'real' national parks should be built on the Yellowstone model, and be people-free. Eskandar Firouz considers that '*we were rather more paternalistic in the mode and manner of implementing or imposing our conservation programmes than our northern colleagues*' but that otherwise there was not much of a difference.[30] India provides some evidence of this conceptual transfer: at independence in 1947 it had fewer than half a dozen wildlife reserves, but by 1997 there were more than 400, covering 4.3 per cent of the country.[32] According to Zafar

Futehally, '*without the thrust of IUCN/WWF the environmental movement which is now fairly strong in India...would not have taken shape*'.[33] But some argue that IUCN and WWF transferred some of the wrong concepts. Traditional human use of species and resources in protected areas was excluded, causing local hardship and antagonism. According to Ramachandra Guha, this change was the result of pressures from city dwellers, foreign tourists, biologists wanting to save wilderness and species for the sake of 'science', officials in wildlife departments and international conservation agencies (including IUCN).[32]

The fact is that debates raged in both North and South. In Peru there was a particularly bitter antagonism between protectionists, championed by Felipe Benavides, and 'sustainable users', including Marc Dourojeanni, then IUCN Council Member and Vice-President, over the management of vicuña.[34] Many emerging Southern non-governmental conservation bodies were concerned with the human dimension, and warmly espoused the message of the World Conservation Strategy.[21] More and more bodies concerned with sustainable resource use rather than with nature conservation in the narrow sense have joined the IUCN membership. The largest number of members is now in the South.[35]

Which does not mean that the end of the debate is near. At the Buenos Aires General Assembly Tariq Banuri of Pakistan attacked Northern over-emphasis on the 'Noah's Ark' approach to conservation, stressing that '*species survival and protected areas were but a means to an end – the end being that human beings behaved in a sustainable manner*'.[36] Pressures on land in many developing countries are becoming more intense as larger and more educated populations demand higher standards of living, and there is an imperative to grow more food. Kenya, for example, has lost half its wildlife territory to human occupation in the past two decades.[21] IUCN needs to champion a North–South dialogue that will promote integrated land use (as called for in Agenda 21) and place the conservation of biodiversity and biological resources in the wider context of action to combat poverty and support development and economic growth. My own view is that with only 12 per cent of IUCN's Secretariat now at headquarters, with field representatives in the majority on the Management Board,[37] with a strong regional voice in the Council and Commissions, with strong regional and national infrastructure, and with a conservationist from Latin America in the Presidency, the North–South issue can be laid to rest.

INDEPENDENCE OR PARTNERSHIP?

IUCN and the UN are children of the same period: a time when hope rested in new international partnerships. It was conceived of as a partnership organization, drawing many state and non-governmental entities together in an association that would strengthen them all, and speak for conservation in a fast-changing world. And throughout its history it has been a partnership body. Virtually all its publications acknowledge that fact.

UNESCO was the partner of greatest importance in the early years, and has remained a staunch supporter, especially of work on biosphere reserves and the World Heritage Convention. UNEP was a major supporter from around 1973, had an immense influence on the World Conservation Strategy, was a partner in many other major reports and has helped time and again to get developing country people to General Assemblies and other meetings. FAO, UNDP, the World Bank, multilateral regional banks, governments, their bilateral development assistance agencies, major NGOs...the list is an enormous one. Outside the governmental world, ICBP (now BirdLife International) has been the expert ornithological partner from the beginning, and Fauna and Flora International, Conservation International, the World Resources Institute, the Frankfurt Zoological Society, The Nature Conservancy and many others have been close collaborators. Many IUCN members have joined with the Secretariat and Commissions in joint ventures, and are therefore partners. Today almost all the action on the ground is undertaken with or through members.

The partnership with WWF has been special, and at times turbulent. It was, of course, IUCN's chronic inability to attract income from its membership, and the limitations of finance from the UN agencies, that made people like Peter Scott and Max Nicholson conceive the idea of the WWF as a means of tapping personal and corporate donations for conservation. Although some SFr43 million has flowed into IUCN over the years[38] (and although WWF certainly saved the Union from bankruptcy twice), my personal judgement is that for one reason or another, the original plan failed. WWF itself has, of course, been an immense success story and has undoubtedly done a vast amount for world conservation.[39] On any conservative estimate it has raised at least US$3 billion for the cause. But it did not rescue IUCN from recurrent financial crisis. Since 1982 (or thereabouts) the Fund has supported less than 15 per cent of the work of IUCN: in 1993 it contributed under 4 per cent of the Union's 'operating income' and from that year onwards, although it has contributed as much as SFr1 million to supporting IUCN activities in some years, it has ceased to be identified as a funding source in the Union's audited accounts.[40] Three-quarters of IUCN's money has come from governments and their agencies and from international organizations such as the UN system, development banks and the European Union.[12,40]

I believe that the most serious mistake was to think that these two disparate bodies could be run in tight double harness. The merging of administration and finance in the new shared headquarters in Gland was logical in concept, but proved disastrous in practice. The two organizations were too different in their governance, culture, incomes and management needs. And when things went wrong, there were those in IUCN who – no doubt recalling the antagonisms at the times of the rescue operations in 1976 and 1981 – scented conspiracy. My personal experience dates from the later period, when the management of the two bodies had been separated and IUCN was not significantly dependent on WWF, and I found only cooperation and goodwill. But I can see that in the period between 1975 and 1987 friction was almost inevitable, because of the way the system was structured. Partnerships only work when there is mutual benefit, between freely-associating equals. The IUCN–WWF partnership only worked smoothly when the original concept of WWF's founders had been relegated to history. Yet I agree with Charles de Haes that '*neither IUCN nor WWF could have achieved anywhere near the success it has without the other*'.[41]

My own view is that the stated antithesis between 'independence' and 'partnership' is a false one. IUCN must indeed be independent – as it is constitutionally and legally – but it must continue to work in partnership, and be willing to strike up new partnerships where these will advance its mission. That is current policy – it has brought new links with the World Bank, the Global Environment Facility and with the business world, and it is right.

CHAMPION OR SHADOW?

Perhaps IUCN's greatest weakness has been in communications. If the Union is really the most authoritative body in the world when it comes to the conservation of nature and natural resources, why do the world's media hardly ever quote it, or even approach it? The Press is full of statements by WWF, by Friends of the Earth and by single-issue pressure groups. They are enlivened by photographs of Greenpeace activists festooning oil rigs with their chained persons. They carry stories of every inevitable objector to every environmental modification – giving the zaniest such opponent weight equal to that of the most rational developer. Only once every three years, at the time of Congress or Assembly, does a mass of media people gather and report interesting stories from IUCN, but these are like the stories purveyed at the time of the annual meetings of the American Association for the Advancement of Science and its British counterpart – they are for 'the heavies' and they lack passion. They appear somewhere on the inside pages, low down towards the corners.

There are, I think, several reasons for this situation. First, IUCN is obviously quite different from all other environmental bodies. It is the *only* 'organization of organizations' spanning governmental and non-governmental spheres. It has by far the broadest programme of activities. The result is that there has been no distinctive image: a body concerned with everything is often celebrated for nothing. Look at any of the lists of activities reported to General Assemblies, or highlighted in the resolutions they generate. Every topical environmental issue is there (together with a vast number of obscure ones). Yet does their discussion by IUCN make world headlines? No – because they do not have the impact of a well-documented single-issue report that is promoted with passion. IUCN tends to weigh scientific evidence and state its conclusions in measured tones: none of the language of disaster and imminent death.

And the communication process is very different. IUCN has always been cautious about its statements. They have been weighed and debated by Council. They are rarely issued as immediate responses to an alleged 'environmental emergency'. Even where they are topical, they are commonly rather dull. Moreover, IUCN is generally at pains not to condemn anyone – especially a State or government agency member. It has always worked by undercover persuasion rather than public campaigns. Even its most critical resolutions and recommendations are conveyed by the Director-General to their targets in discreet letters rather than blazoned across angry headlines. And this is not simply because it would be painful if golden geese stopped laying. It is because the Union relies on its members to act responsibly, and seeks always to work by influencing their conduct in the right direction. IUCN brings its findings and resolutions to the attention of governments whose shelves may be centimetres deep in them: other bodies scream energetically at the world's press (often with a distorted message whose impact is all the greater for the exaggeration). Blazing attacks that the media will treat as 'news' are counter-cultural for IUCN.

None the less, it could do a lot better. It could become the trusted source of authoritative briefings for serious journalists who want to know whether the tropical forests will *really* all be gone in 30 years, or the Antarctic ecology destroyed by ozone depletion, or the soils of Europe sterilized because flatworms imported from New Zealand are eating all the earthworms. Such briefings could have another benefit: they could make the more popularist IUCN members (and even more, the wilder non-members) a little more cautious about the press releases they distribute. If they knew that every such story was likely to be checked back with IUCN, they might have slightly greater regard for the truth. And we can hope that in a more educated century ahead, even if truth does not sell newspapers, lies will increasingly rebound to their discomfort. IUCN must speak clearly but precisely, for its knowledge is of immense importance to the future of the world.

The Way Ahead

One of the main values of a history is that it reflects the past, as an object lesson for the future. What, then, can and should the world learn from the past of IUCN – The World Conservation Union?

First, that if it did not exist it would have to be invented. There is a manifest need for a body that can convene the world's environmental organizations – state and non-state – and help them debate, pool knowledge and cooperate.

Second, that there is a lot of room for improvement. Too many conservation bodies are happier talking to one another than facing outwards. There is no point in conservationists talking while nature is destroyed. And that means talking with those who are not yet conservationists – who do not see the need for sustainable development. It means recognizing that the private sector of business, industry and commerce is the dominant agent of transformation in today's world, and needs the knowledge that IUCN can provide in order to avoid destruction that will harm everyone's long-term interests. The World Conservation Strategy succeeded because it captured the diversity within IUCN, blended its insights and those of the Union's partners, and launched new thinking about the interdependence of conservation and development at a critical time.[42] It follows that IUCN must face outwards and assert its place in the creation of some of the policies that will be most important for the future of humanity within the world of nature.

Third, IUCN should lead the environmental movement away from in-fighting and rivalry. Individual conservation bodies should stop pretending that they are the only significant force for good in the world. Partnerships should not only happen but be publicized as a strength for all involved. Members and partners of IUCN should see that publicizing their involvement in the Union is an asset, not a blurring of the image. This is already beginning to happen in the *ad hoc* alliances that coordinate inputs to bodies like the UNCSD.

Fourth, the regionalization process is (rightly) unstoppable, but the implications must be recognized. Regional forums will gain importance as places where policy and programme are debated, and the world congresses will become unique meeting-grounds for discussion of global issues. They will find that different regions (and different areas and communities) have genuine differences in need and perspective. It follows that IUCN will very likely pursue different policies in different places, and divergences in values and priorities must be respected. It is imperative that it avoids cultural arrogance between North and South.

Fifth, given commitment and individual energy and ability, much can be done against great odds. IUCN's history has been dominated by individuals who have carried their visions to fruition, often without much money and despite constitutional and bureaucratic barriers. The most important need for the future is to attract and empower more people of vision.

IUCN is not an easy body to lead. There are problems of governance, authority and accountability. But while recurrent crisis has been a feature of its history, and has to be reported in any objective account, it should not be made too much of. Large and complex institutions are prone to recurrent crises.[22] The important thing is that IUCN – like many other war-torn bodies – has gone on working despite the buffetings and undoubted traumas it has suffered. In one sense its complexity is its strength: as in many an ecosystem a blight may devastate one element, but the others can continue to flower and fill in the gaps.

The First World Conservation Congress showed IUCN at a turning point. Its power of convening people from many ways of life is well established. It could form an outstanding expert group to consider almost any topic. Its President and Director-General have access to heads of state and senior ministers. Although never wealthy enough to do half what it wanted, in 1998 the budget for the total activities of the Union was over SFr90 million, it had a worldwide Secretariat, and had made major strides in balancing North–South interests.[43] The policies the membership wanted were in place. The direction of evolution was clear. The founding fathers, staggering from deficit to deficit, with a handful of people at their disposal, would (one hopes) have been well satisfied. But they might have been astounded, too.

A1 Presidents, Secretary-Generals and Director-Generals of IUPN and IUCN

Presidents

1948–54	Charles Bernard (Switzerland)
1954–58	Roger Heim (France)
1958–63	Jean Baer (Switzerland)
1963–66	François Bourlière (France)
1966–72	Harold Coolidge (USA)
1972–78	Donald Kuenen (Netherlands)
1978–84	Mohamed Kassas (Egypt)
1984–90	Monkombu Swaminathan (India)
1990–94	Shridath Ramphal (Guyana)
1994–96	Jay Hair (USA)
1996–	Yolanda Kakabadse (Ecuador)

Secretary-Generals

1948–55	Jean-Paul Harroy (Belgium)
1955–58	Tracy Philipps (UK)
1959–60	M C Bloemers (Netherlands)
1961–62	Gerald Watterson (UK)
1962–66	Hugh Elliott (UK)
1966–70	Joe Berwick (UK)

Director-Generals

1970–76	Gerardo Budowski (Venezuela)
1976–77	Duncan Poore (UK) (Acting)
1977–80	David Munro (Canada)
1980–82	Lee Talbot (USA)
1982–	Pierre Goeldlin (Switzerland) (Acting)
1982–88	Kenton Miller (USA)
1988–94	Martin Holdgate (UK)
1994–	David McDowell (New Zealand)

Notes

Preface: The Conservation World's Best-kept Sectret

1 Nicholas Robinson (Chairman, IUCN Commission on Environmental Law). Discussion with MWH in December 1997.
2 Zafar Futehally (former Honorary Secretary of the Bombay Natural History Society, IUCN Council member and Vice-President). Letter to MWH dated 9 June 1998.
3 Eskandar Firouz (former Deputy Prime Minister and Minister with responsibility for the Environment, Iran and former IUCN Vice-President and Councillor). Letter to MWH dated 12 April 1998.
4 Marc Dourojeanni (former IUCN Regional Councillor for Latin America and Vice-President of IUCN). Letter to MWH dated 8 April 1998.
5 IUCN (1997) *A Pocket Guide to IUCN, The World Conservation Union*. Gland, Switzerland and Cambridge, UK: IUCN. Figures for 1998 provided by J A McNeely on 15 June 1998.
6 Aban Kabraji (1993) What can IUCN deliver? In Holdgate, M W and Synge, H (Eds) *The Future of IUCN, The World Conservation Union*. Gland, Switzerland and Cambridge, UK: IUCN. In this article Kabraji argues that the major conservation challenges of the future lie in the North, and that IUCN has a major role in their solution.
7 Nicholson, E M (1990) A perspective of IUCN. Unpublished note.
8 Van Schuylenberg, P (1997) *La Mémoire des Belges en Afrique Centrale. Inventaire des Archives Historiques Privées du Musée Royal de l'Afrique Centrale, de 1858 á nos jours*. Tervuren: Musée Royal de l'Afrique Centrale.
9 Liamine, Nathalie (1989) *L'Union Internationale pour la Conservation de la Nature et de ses Ressources, 1948–1988. Mémoire de Maîtrise présenté sous la direction de Monsieur le Professeur Frank*. Université de Paris – Nanterre. U E R d'Histoire. Session d'Octobre 1989.

Chapter 1: The Springs of Conservation.

1 Cindy Kenny-Gilday (1994) Comment in *IUCN Bulletin*, (2) p. 20.
2 Martin, P S (1971) Pleistocene overkill. In Detwyler, T R (1971) *Man's Impact on Environment*. New York: McGraw-Hill.
3 Leakey, R B (1981) *The Making of Mankind*, London: Michael Joseph.
4 Fraser, J G (1987) *The Golden Bough. A Study in Magic and Religion*. Abridged edition. London: Papermac.
5 Kemf, Elizabeth (1993) *The Law of the Mother*. San Francisco: Sierra Club.
6 Jeffrey McNeely (1998) Letter to MWH, 16 March.
7 Groombridge, B (Ed) (1992) *Global Biodiversity. Status of Earth's Living Resources*. London Chapman and Hall.

8   Tacitus, *Annals* XIV, xxx. Quoted in Dillon, M and Chadwick, N K (1967) *The Celtic Realms.* London: Weidenfeld and Nicholson.
9   David McDowell (1998) Comments to MWH on 15 June.
10   Garmonsway, G N (Ed) (1953) *The Anglo Saxon Chronicle.* London: Dent and New York: Dutton. Everyman series. Extract from the Laud (Peterborough) manuscript for 1087, recalling the life and deeds of King William I.
11   E M Nicholson (1998) Letter to David McDowell, 14 June.
12   Portas, P (Ed) (1988) The stirring of awareness. In: Forty years in conservation. *IUCN Bulletin*, Special Issue, vol 19, 7–12, p 5.
13   Allen, T B (1987) *Guardian of the Wild. The Story of the National Wildlife Federation.* Bloomington & Indianapolis: Indiana University Press.
14   McCormick, J (1989) *The Global Environmental Movement. Reclaiming Paradise.* London: Belhaven Press.
15   Thomas, K (1983) *Man and the Natural World. Changing Attitudes in England, 1500–1800.* Harmondsworth: Penguin.
16   McNeely, J A and Wachtel, P S (1988) *The Soul of the Tiger. Searching for Nature's Answers in Exotic South-East Asia.* New York: Doubleday.
17   Plato. Critias, III. Quoted in Thirgood, J V (1981) *Man and the Mediterranean Forest.* London: Academic Press.
18   Pliny the Elder. Quoted in Hughes, J D (1975) *Ecology in Ancient Civilizations.* Albuquerque: University of New Mexico.
19   Ashby, E and Anderson, M (1981) *The Politics of Clean Air.* Oxford: Clarendon Press.
20   Büttikofer, J (1947) Statement on the international protection of nature and report on the work preparatory to the establishment of an international organization for the protection of nature. Paper delivered to the Brunnen Conference in 1947. Published in Büttikofer, J (1947) *International Conference for the Protection of Nature.* Basel: Swiss League for the Protection of Nature as acting agency for the Provisional International Union for the Protection of Nature.
21   Michel Batisse (1998) Comments sent to MWH on 13 March.
22   Fitter, Richard S R (1978) Letter to H F I Elliott enclosing sections of his draft book, *The Penitent Butchers* written for the seventy-fifth anniversary of the Fauna Preservation Society. In Elliott archives at IUCN. The book itself was published by Collins in 1979.
23   White, Gilbert (1788) *The Natural History of Selborne.* Reprinted with notes by Richard Kearton, 1924. Bristol: Arrowsmith.
24   Rousseau, Jean Jacques (1909) *Discourse on Inequality.* Harvard Classics, vol 24. New York: P F Collier and Son. Cited in Shabecoff (Note 28).
25   Emerson, Ralph Waldo (1909) *The American Scholar.* Harvard Classics, vol 5. New York: P F Collier and Son. Cited in Shabecoff (Note 28).
26   Wordsworth, William (1798) Lines...composed a few miles above Tintern Abbey, on revisiting the banks of the Wye during a tour, July 13, 1798. Published in numerous anthologies and this passage in Harrison, G B (Ed) (1949) *A Book of English Poetry.* The Penguin Poets.
27   Wordsworth, William (1810) *A Guide through the District of the Lakes in the North of England.* Fifth Edition. Kendal: Hudson and Nicholson.
28   Shabecoff, P (1993) *A Fierce Green Fire: the American Environmental Movement.* New York: Hill and Wang.
29   Crosby, A W (1986) *Ecological Imperialism. The Biological Expansion of Europe, 900–1900.* Cambridge: Cambridge University Press.
30   Darwin, Charles (1845) *The Voyage of the Beagle.* Everyman edition. London: Dent, 1955.
31   Skottsberg, C (1960) Remarks on the plant geography of the southern cold temperate zone. *Proc Roy Soc Lond B*, 152, 447–457.
32   Darwin, C (1859) *On the Origin of Species by Means of Natural Selection or the Preservation of Favoured Races in the Struggle for Existence.* Numerous editions and reprints.
33   Marsh, George Perkins (1864) *Man and Nature; or, Physical Geography Transformed by Human Action.* New edition edited by D Lowenthal (1965): Cambridge, Mass: Harvard University Press.

34 Bramwell, A (1989) *Ecology in the 20th Century. A History.* New Haven and London: Yale University Press.

35 Haeckel, E (1894) *Monism as Connecting Religion and Science. The Confessions of Faith of a Man of Science.* London & Edinburgh.

36 Holdgate, M W (1994) Ecology, development and global policy. *Journal of Applied Ecology*, 31, 201–212.

37 Huxley, T H (quoted by Bramwell (Note 34) from J Durant, 1977, *The Meaning of Evolution. Post Darwinian Debates on the Significance for Man of the Theory of Evolution, 1858–1908*. Cambridge PhD thesis).

38 see, for example, Tansley, A G (1950) *The British Islands and their Vegetation.* Cambridge: Cambridge University Press.

39 Fitter, Richard (1998) Discussion with MWH on 8 February.

40 Gille, Alain (1998) Comments sent to MWH on 8 March.

41 Sheail, J (1976) *Nature in Trust*. London: Blackie.

42 Lt Gustavus Doane. Report to Congress on the potential for a National Park at Yellowstone. Quoted by E M Nicholson; lecture on 'The challenge for a new Renaissance', September 1997.

43 Portas, P (Ed) (1988) Historic landmarks, 1885–1987, in forty years of conservation. *IUCN Bulletin* vol 19, 7–12, p 13.

44 IUCN (1994) *1993 United Nations List of National Parks and Protected Areas.* Cambridge, UK and Gland, Switzerland: IUCN.

45 Nicholson, E M (1997) Personal recollection; quoted in lecture on 'The challenge for a new Renaissance', September.

46 Pinchot, G (1910) *The Fight for Conservation*. New York: Doubleday.

47 Morris, E (1979) *The Rise of Theodore Roosevelt.* New York: Coward, McCann and Geoghegan.

48 Fox, S (1981) *John Muir and his Legacy. The American Conservation Movement.* Boston: Little, Brown & Co.

49 McCloskey, M (1998) (Chairman, Sierra Club). Discussion with MWH on 18 March.

50 Republicans for Environmental Protection (REP) (undated) Teddy Roosevelt on conservation; compilation of statements by President Theodore Roosevelt, 1858–1919. Note provided to MWH by J A McNeely, December 1997.

51 Waterson, M (1994) *The National Trust. The First Hundred Years.* London: BBC Books and the National Trust.

52 Sheail, J (1981) *Rural Conservation in Inter-war Britain.* Oxford: Clarendon Press.

53 Sheail, J (1987) *Seventy Five Years in Ecology. The British Ecological Society.* Oxford: Blackwell Scientific Publications.

54 Rothschild, M and Marren, P (1997) *Rothschild's Reserves. Time and Fragile Nature.* Balaban, Essex: Harley Books.

55 Thomas, J A (1997) *The Rothschild Nature Reserves. An Assessment of the Value and Feasibility of Proposed Habitat Restoration.* Furzebrook, Wareham, Dorset: Natural Environment Research Council Centre for Ecology and Hydrology.

56 Liamine, Nathalie (1989) *L'Union Internationale pour la Conservation de la Nature et de ses Ressources, 1948–1988. Mémoire de Maîtrise présenté sous la direction de Monsieur le Professeur Frank.* Universite de Paris – Nanterre; U E R d'Histoire; session d'Octobre.

57 Curry-Lindahl, Kai (1978) Background and development of international conservation organizations and their role in the future. *Environmental Conservation*, vol 5, no 3, 163–169.

58 Halle, Mark (1997) Discussion with MWH on 29 May.

59 Sarasin, Paul (1913) Exposé introductif. In *Procès verbal de la Conférence International pour la Protection de la Nature. Berne, 17–19 Novembre 1913.* Sarasin refers, *inter alia*, to a letter he had received from J Waterschoot van der Gracht in 1912 about the destruction of the Ona people of Tierra del Fuego by sheep farmers and the bounty hunters they hired.

60 Goeldlin, Pierre (1994) *La Ligue Suisse pour la Protection de la Nature (LSPN), 'mère spirituelle' de l'Union mondiale pour la nature (UICN). Quelques pages d'histoire. Lausanne, le 18 Novembre.* Note in IUCN archives.

61   Acte de Fondation d'une Commission consultative pour la Protection internationale de la
      Nature. Signed at Berne 19 November 1913. Reproduced in Portas, P (Ed) (1988) *Forty
      years in conservation. IUCN Bulletin*, vol 19, 7–12, p 6.
62   Wyss, K J (1914) *Recueil des Procès-Verbaux de la Conférence Internationale pour la
      Protection de la Nature*, Berne.
63   Pelzers, E (1994) Historical background on the Netherlands Commission for
      International Nature Protection, the Foundation for International Nature Protection and
      the Office International pour la Protection de la Nature. Translation by J A Boddens
      Hosang from article in *Mededelingen* no 29, 1994, of the Netherlands Commission for
      International Nature Protection. Copy in IUCN archives, Gland.
64   Franklin Delano Roosevelt. The Wildlife Week Proclamation. Reproduced in T B Allen,
      op cit, Note 13 (Appendix 3).
65   Talbot, Lee M (1988) Discussion with MWH on 18 March and detailed notes provided
      on that occasion.
66   Leopold, Aldo S (1933) *Game Management*. New York: Scribner.
67   Leopold, Aldo S (1948) *A Sand County Almanac*. New York: Oxford University Press.
68   Talbot, Lee M (1983) IUCN in retrospect and prospect. *Environmental Conservation*, vol
      10, no 1, 5–11.
69   Biographical note on Harold Jefferson Coolidge, in *Proceedings, First World Conference
      on National Parks*, Seattle, Washington, June 30–7 July 1962. Washington DC: US
      National Park Service and Department of the Interior.
70   Harold J Coolidge: a chronology. Note circulated in July 1998 with material by Interlock
      Media Inc, in connection with their compilation of a documentary film, *The Harold J.
      Coolidge Chronicles*, based on the film shot by Coolidge in Africa and Asia.
71   Brewer, G (1947) Intervention in the third plenary meeting at the Brunnen Conference of
      1947. In J Büttikofer, op cit, Note 20.
72   Shabecoff, Philip (1996) *A New Name for Peace. International Environmentalism,
      Sustainable Development and Democracy*. Hanover and London: University Press of
      New England.
73   Rothschild, The Hon Miriam (1997) Conversation with MWH on 2 July.
74   Harroy, J-P (1983) *IUCN Bulletin*, vol 14, nos 4–6, p 35.

Chapter 2: The Path to Union

1   Gille, Alain (1998) Letter and commentary, 8 March.
2   McCormick, J (1989) *The Global Environmental Movement: Reclaiming Paradise*.
      London: Belhaven Press.
3   Sheail, J (1995) War and the development of nature conservation in Britain. *J. Environ.
      Management*, 44, 267–283.
4   Sheail, J (1987) *Seventy Five years in Ecology. The British Ecological Society*. Oxford:
      Blackwell Scientific Publications.
5   Sheail, J (1996) From aspiration to implementation. The establishment of the first
      National Nature Reserves in Britain. *Landscape Research*, 21, no 1, 37–54.
6   Osborn, Fairfield (1948) *Our Plundered Plant*. New York: Random House.
7   Pelzers, E (1994) Historical background on the Netherlands Commission for
      International Nature Protection, the Foundation for International Nature Protection and
      the Office International pour la Protection de la Nature. Written for *Mededelingen* no 29
      of the Netherlands Commission of International Nature Protection, and translated for
      IUCN by J A Boddens Hosang.
8   Bernard, C (1947) Opening statement to the Brunnen Conference. In Büttikofer (1947)
      op cit Note 23.
9   Bernard, C (1946) Opening address to the Basel meeting. In Büttikofer (1946) op cit
      Note 20.
10   Nicholson, E M (1988) Letter to David McDowell, 14 June.
11   Anon (1936) Un grand Colonial: Charles Bernard. *L'Illustré*, no 29, pp 923–924.
12   Burhenne, Wolfgang (1998) Discussion with MWH, 16 February.

13 National Parks Committee (England and Wales) and Wild Life Conservation Special Committee (1946) Report on a visit to inspect the Swiss National Park, 30 June to 7 July 1946. Document NPC/89 and WLC/48. Paper supplied to MWH by Dr John Sheail.

14 The foreign participants in the 1946 tour were: UK – John Berry (Scottish Wildlife Conservation Committee), Lord Chorley (National Parks Committee for England and Wales), Richard Fitter (Wild Life Conservation Special Committee for England and Wales), Max Nicholson (ditto), Robert Grieve (Scottish National Parks Committee) and William Arnold-Forster (Council for Protection of Rural England and Society for the Promotion of Nature Reserves). Belgium – Antoine Freyens, Louis Gavage and Louis Thiry. Czechoslovakia – Rudolf Maximovic (Conservator-General for Nature Protection). France – Robert Etchecopar (Secretary-General of the French Ornithological Society). Norway – Erling Christophersen (Norwegian Societies for the Protection of Nature). Netherlands – W G van der Kloot (Ministry of Education), Pieter van Tienhoven (President of the Society for Nature and President of the International Office for the Protection of Nature).

15 Fitter, Richard (1998) Discussion with MWH, 8 February.

16 Nicholson, E M quoted by J McCormick, op cit Note 2.

17 Nicholson, E M (1997) Conversation with MWH, 21 July.

18 Bernard, Charles. Short article on the beginning of IUPN, in *IUCN Yearbook*, 1973. Morges, Switzerland: IUCN.

19 Bernard, C J and Büttikofer, J (1946) Memorandum on behalf of the Swiss League for the Protection of Nature to the President and Members of the Swiss Federal Council, 20 August 1946. Copy in IUCN archives.

20 Büttikofer, J (1946) *Report on the Conference for the International Protection of Nature (Basel, June 30-July 7, 1946)*. Basel: The Swiss League for the Protection of Nature.

21 Letter referenced as Inv no 18 by Pelzers, op cit Note 7.

22 Berry, John. Formerly scientist to the Scottish Hydroelectricity Board, later Director of Nature Conservation in Scotland and then Director of the Nature Conservancy in Scotland. Telephone conversation with MWH, 7 June 1997 and letters to David McDowell, 24 June 1998 and to MWH, 29 June 1998.

23 Büttikofer, J (1947) *International Conference for the Protection of Nature. Proceedings, Resolutions and Reports. Brunnen, June 28th – July 3rd 1947*. Basel: Provisional International Union for the Protection of Nature. Acting Agency: Swiss League for the Protection of Nature.

24 Letter from G F Herbert Smith to E M Nicholson,11 February 1947. File CAB 124 1062, Proposed International Organization for the Protection of Nature. 1597/15/1. In UK Public Record Office. Transcripts supplied to MWH by Dr John Sheail.

25 Gille, Alain (1993) Interview with Sylvie Wabbes of IUCN; transcript and original tape in IUCN archives.

26 Huxley, Julian (1946) *UNESCO. Its Purpose and its Philosophy*. Paris, UNESCO, 6 December. Essay published 'as a separate signed document as a statement of his personal attitude' and 'in no way an official expression of the views of the Preparatory Commission'; copy supplied to MWH by Dr Michel Batisse.

27 Huxley, Julian (1973) *Memories*. New York: Harper and Roe.

28 Letter from Dr Joseph Needham (UNESCO) to Dr J H Westermann (IOPN); 9 January; 1947 copy in IUCN archives.

29 Letter from Julian Huxley, Director-General of UNESCO, to J Büttikofer, Swiss League for Protection of Nature, 28 March 1947. UNESCO reference 4.4025; copy in IUCN archives.

30 Letter from E M Nicholson to Julian Huxley, 25 April 1947. File CAB 124 1062, Proposed International Organization for the Protection of Nature; 1597/15/1. In UK Public Record Office; transcripts supplied to MWH by Dr John Sheail.

31 Letter from Julian Huxley to G F Herbert Smith, 24 April 1947. File CAB 124 1062, Proposed International Organization for the Protection of Nature; 1597/15/1. In UK Public Record Office; transcripts supplied to MWH by Dr John Sheail.

32 Letter from E M Nicholson to G F Herbert Smith, 20 June 1947. File CAB 124 1062, Proposed International Organization for the Protection of Nature; 1597/15/1. In UK Public Record Office; transcripts supplied to MWH by Dr John Sheail.

33   Letter from Pieter van Tienhoven to Charles Bernard, 30 April 1947. Copy in IUCN archives.

34   Letter from Victor van Straelen to Charles Bernard, 12 June 1947. Copy in IUCN archives.

35   Gille, Alain (1964) Message de l' UNESCO. Victor van Straelen, 1889–1964. *Flambeau. Revue Belge des Questions Politiques et Litteraires*, no 2, pp 65–69.

36   Harold Coolidge (1964). Note of appreciation of Victor van Straelen. *Flambeau. Revue Belge des Questions Politiques et Litteraires*, no 2, p 69.

37   Letter from Charles Bernard to Victor van Straelen, 16 June 1947. Copy in IUCN archives.

38   Eleen Sam (1947) Memorandum to Dr Joseph Needham, UNESCO. Report on the Brunnen Conference for the International Protection of Nature – 28 June to 3 July 1947. Internal memorandum,15 July. This memorandum is initialled on each page by Dr Charles Bernard and J Büttikofer, presumably to authenticate it as a record. Carbon copy in IUCN archives.

39   Pierre Goeldlin (1998) Discussion with MWH, 15 June.

40   Statements by van der Haagen and J H Westermann in the second plenary meeting, 30 June 1947. In Büttikofer (1947), op cit Note 23.

41   Rothschild, The Hon Miriam (1997) Conversation with MWH, 2 July.

42   Statement by Charles Bernard in the fourth plenary meeting of the Brunnen Conference. In Büttikofer (1947), op cit Note 23.

43   Statement by Professor Bressou to second plenary meeting of the Brunnen Conference. In Büttikofer (1947), op cit Note 23.

44   Statement by Dr John Ramsbottom to second plenary meeting of the Brunnen Conference. In Büttikofer (1947), op cit Note 23.

45   Statement by Professor Vinding Kruse to second plenary meeting of the Brunnen Conference. In Büttikofer (1947), op cit Note 23.

46   Statement by Mr Brewer (USA) in the third plenary meeting of the Brunnen Conference, on 1 July 1947. In Büttikofer (1947), op cit Note 23.

47   Memorandum from E M Nicholson to Ministry of Education, 18 July 1947. File CAB 124 1062, Proposed International Organization for the Protection of Nature. 1597/15/1. In UK Public Record Office; transcripts supplied to MWH by Dr John Sheail.

48   Letter signed by Dr C J Bernard and J Büttikofer on behalf of the Swiss League to the President of the Swiss Confederation and Members of the Federal Council, 25 July 1947. Copy in the IUCN archives.

49   UN (1950) *Proceedings of the United Nations Scientific Conference on the Conservation and Utilization of Resources, 17 August–6 September 1949*. Lake Success, New York: United Nations Department of Economic Affairs.

50   Bernard, Charles. Letter to George E Brewer, 9 March 1948. In UNESCO archives. Copy supplied to MWH by Dr Pierre Lasserre.

51   Conference pour l'etablissement de l'Union Internationale pour la Protection de la Nature. Renseignements Généraux. Document preparé par le Secretariat de l'UNESCO pour le Gouvernement française. Fontainebleau, France, 30 september–7 octobre 1948. Photocopy in IUCN archives.

52   *International Union for the Protection of Nature. Established at Fontainebleau, 5 October 1948.* Record of the Conference and Constitution. Brussels: IUPN, 1948.

53   Charles Bernard (1948) Letter to Professor Urbain, 25 March. In UNESCO archives. Copy supplied to MWH by Dr Pierre Lasserre.

54   Michel Batisse (1998) Letter and commentary to MWH, 13 March.

55   Repartition des responsabilités et ordre du jour des Préparatifs pour la Conférence de Fontainebleau, 30 Septembre–7 Octobre 1948. Typescript in IUCN archives.

56   Draft, 7 July 1948, inviting international organizations to be represented at the Constitutive Conference of the International Union for the Protection of Nature, to take place at Fontainebleau from 30 September to 7 October 1948. In IUCN archives.

57   Letter from G F Herbert Smith to E M Nicholson, 18 June 1948. File CAB 124 1063, Proposed International Organization for the Protection of Nature. 1597/15/2. In UK Public Record Office; transcripts supplied to MWH by Dr John Sheail.

58 Memorandum by E M Nicholson, 30 June 1948. File CAB 124 1063, Proposed International Organization for the Protection of Nature. 1597/15/2. In UK Public Record Office; transcripts supplied to MWH by Dr John Sheail.

59 Letter from E M Nicholson to Sir John Maud, Permanent Secretary, Ministry of Education, 7 August 1948. File CAB 124 1063, Proposed International Organization for the Protection of Nature. 1597/15/2. In UK Public Record Office; transcripts supplied to MWH by Dr John Sheail.

60 Julian Huxley (1948) Notes for opening speech to the Conference for the establishment of the International Union for the Protection of Nature, Fontainebleau, 30 September. Original in J S Huxley papers, Rice University, Texas, USA: photocopy in UNESCO archives; copy supplied to MWH by Dr Pierre Lasserre.

61 Julian Huxley (1948) Scientific management of wild life. Notes for speech at Conference for the establishment of the International Union for the Protection of Nature, Fontainebleau, 2 October. Original in J S Huxley papers, Rice University, Texas, USA: photocopy in UNESCO archives; copy supplied to MWH by Dr Pierre Lasserre.

62 Mence, Tony (1981) *IUCN: How it Began, How it is Growing Up*. Morges, Switzerland: IUCN.

63 IUCN (1974) The first quarter century of IUCN: looking back and looking ahead. In *IUCN Yearbook, 1973*. Morges, Switzerland: IUCN.

64 E M Nicholson (1998) Letter to MWH, 14 January.

65 Liamine, Nathalie (1989) *L'Union Internationale pour la Conservation de la Nature et de ses Ressources, 1948–1988. Mémoire de Maîtrise présenté sous la direction de Monsieur le Professeur Frank*. Universite de Paris – Nanterre. U E R d'Histoire. Session d'Octobre.

66 Talbot, Lee M (1983) IUCN in retrospect and prospect. *Environmental Conservation*, vol 10, no 1. pp 5–11.

67 Julian Huxley (1948) Letter to E M Nicholson, 12 August. In UNESCO archives; copy supplied to MWH by Dr Pierre Lasserre.

68 Harroy, Jean-Paul. Autobiographical note. Extract provided to MWH by Mme Mady Harroy, courtesy of Françoise Burhenne-Guilmin.

69 Harroy, Jean-Paul (1988) The early years. Article in: Forty years in conservation. Special Issue of the *IUCN Bulletin*, vol 19, 7–12, pp 15–17.

70 Memorandum by E M Nicholson, 30 June 1948. File CAB 124 1063, Proposed International Organization for the Protection of Nature. 1597/15/2. In UK Public Record Office; transcripts supplied to MWH by Dr John Sheail.

71 Letter from P G van Tienhoven to Victor van Straelen, 12 October 1948, cited in Pelzers, op cit Note 7.

72 Aldous Huxley (1948) Letter to Julian Huxley dated 25 July. In UNESCO archives; copy supplied to MWH by Dr Pierre Lasserre.

Chapter 3: The Union Established

1 Liamine, Nathalie (1989) *L'Union Internationale pour la Conservation de la Nature et de ses Ressources, 1948–1988. Mémoire de Maîtrise présenté sous la direction de Monsieur le Professeur Frank*. Universite de Paris – Nanterre. U E R d'Histoire. Session d'Octobre.

2 Jean-Paul Harroy. Autobiographical note. Extract provided by Mme Mady Harroy, courtesy of Françoise Burhenne-Guilmin.

3 Harroy, J-P (1988) The early years. Article contributed to Forty years of conservation. Special Number, *IUCN Bulletin*, vol 19, 7–12, pp 15–17.

4 Shabecoff, Philip (1993) *A Fierce Green Fire. The American Environmental Movement*. New York: Hill and Wang.

5 E M Nicholson (1959) Money for nature. Typescript contrasting the size and diversity of the natural history movement in Britain with the paucity of money available to support those bodies.

6   List of founding members of IUPN (5 October 1949). In Forty years in conservation. *IUCN Bulletin,* Special Issue, vol 19 (7–12), 1988, centre section, pp 4–5. The United States members of IUPN included most of the major national conservation bodies: the American Committee for Wildlife Protection, American Geographical Society, American Nature Association, American Ornithologists Union, Boone and Crockett Club, Conservation Foundation, Izaak Walton League, National Audubon Society, National Parks Association, National Research Council, National Wildlife Federation, New York Zoological Society, Wilderness Society, Wildlife Management Institute. The admission of the Sierra Club is recorded in the minutes of the sixteenth session, first sitting, fiftieth meeting of the Executive Board held in Edinburgh,19 June 1956.

7   Anonymous (probably Jean-Paul Harroy) (1956) Report on the activities of the Union for 1954–56. In: *Proceedings of the Fifth General Assembly, Edinburgh, 20–28 June 1956.* Brussels: IUCN.

8   McCormick, J (1989) *The Global Environmental Movement. Reclaiming Paradise.* London: Belhaven Press.

9   United Nations (1950) *Proceedings of the United Nations Scientific Conference on the Conservation and Utilization of Resources, 17 August–6 September 1949.* Lake Success, New York: United Nations Department of Economic Affairs.

10   Huxley, Julian (1949) Chapter VI: protection of nature. In: *Report of the Director General.* Paris: UNESCO.

11   The Hon Miriam Rothschild FRS (1997) Conversation with MWH on 2 July.

12   E M Nicholson. Memorandum to UK Foreign Office, 10 August 1949, with a brief for the British participants in the Technical Conference on the Protection of Nature. File CAB 124 1065, Proposed International Organization for the Protection of Nature. 1597/15/4. In UK Public Record Office; transcripts supplied to MWH by Dr John Sheail.

13   Harroy, J-P (1949) *Activity of the International Union for Protection of Nature, from its Establishment until 1 July 1949.* Brussels: IUPN.

14   Minutes, IUPN Executive Board (1949) Second session, second sitting, fourth meeting, Brussels, 18 March. In IUCN archives. Note that the early sessions of the IUPN Executive Board adopt a complicated and confusing numbering system. Each session (*session*) was divided into several sittings (*réunions*), minuted separately, but an overall numerical sequence of meetings (*séances*) was also recorded.

15   Alain Gille (1997) Letter to MWH dated 31 July. In IUCN archives.

16   Alain Gille (1993) Tape recorded interview with Sylvie Wabbes of IUCN; transcript in IUCN archives.

17   E M Nicholson (1997) Conversation with MWH on 21 July.

18   UNESCO (1950) *International Technical Conference on the Protection of Nature, Lake Success, 22–29 August 1949. Proceedings and Papers. Edited by the Secretariat of the International Union for the Protection of Nature.* Paris and Brussels: UNESCO.

19   Harroy, J-P (1950) *Activity of the International Union for the Protection of Nature from its Establishment until 1 January 1950.* Brussels: IUPN.

20   Section on science and conservation. In: *1973 IUCN Yearbook.* Morges: IUCN.

21   IUPN (1948) *International Union for the Protection of Nature. Established at Fontainebleau, 5 October 1948.* Brussels: IUPN.

22   Michael J Cockerell (1995) The future of IUCN membership. Internal paper 5 October. In IUCN archives.

23   Letter from G F Herbert Smith to E M Nicholson, 18 June 1948. File CAB 124 1063 1597/15/2. In UK Public Record Office; transcripts supplied to MWH by Dr John Sheail.

24   Correspondence between E M Nicholson and others between April 1956 and April 1957 relating to the proposal that the UK become a state member of IUPN. File CAB 124 1599, International Union for the Conservation of Nature and Natural Resources, 1955–65. 15/1/01. In UK Public Record Office; transcripts supplied to MWH by Dr John Sheail.

25   Letter from H G Maurice to E M Nicholson, 10 October 1948. File CAB 124 1064, Proposed International Organization for the Protection of Nature. 1597/15/4. In UK Public Record Office; transcripts supplied to MWH by Dr John Sheail.

26 Huxley, Julian (1970) Remarks at an award ceremony during the Eleventh Congress of the World Wildlife Fund in London in November. Quoted in: Forty years of conservation. Special Number, *IUCN Bulletin*, vol 19, 7–12, 1988, p 10.

27 E M Nicholson (1998) Letter to David McDowell, 14 June with comments on the near-final text of this book.

28 Julian Huxley (1948) Letter to E M Nicholson, 12 August. In UNESCO archives, document 13.40253; photocopy provided to MWH by Dr Pierre Lasserre.

29 E M Nicholson (1998) Letter to MWH, 17 January.

30 Alain Gille. Echos-actualité. J-P Harroy est décédé en juillet dernier. *Le Courrier de la Nature*, no 155, Janvier-Fevrier 1996.

31 In *IUPN Bulletin*, vol I, no 4.

32 Minutes, Bureau of the IUPN Executive Board, Paris, 21 and 22 March 1950. Copy in IUCN archives.

33 Michel Batisse (1998) Letter to MWH, 24 June, with detailed commentary on near-final text of this book.

34 IUPN (1950) *Proceedings and Reports of the Second Session of the General Assembly Held in Brussels, 18–23 October 1950*. Brussels: IUPN.

35 Lee M Talbot (1998) Commentary provided to MWH, 18 March.

36 Harroy, J-P (1952) Report of the Secretary-General. In: *Proceedings and Reports of the Third General Assembly, Caracas (Venezuela), 3 to 9 September 1952*. Brussels: IUPN.

37 Minutes, IUPN Executive Board, eighth session, fourth sitting, twenty-second meeting, Caracas, 9 September 1952. In IUCN archives.

38 Minutes, IUPN Executive Board, second session, third sitting, fifth meeting, Brussels, 19 March 1949. In IUCN archives.

39 UIPN/IUPN (1951) *État de la Protection de la Nature dans le Monde en 1950*. Publié avec le concours financier de l'UNESCO.

40 Harroy, J-P (1954) Report of activities for the years 1952–1954. *Proceedings and Papers of the Fourth General Assembly, Copenhagen (Denmark), 25 August to 3 September 1954*. Brussels: IUPN.

41 The publications referred to were reports of the Technical Meetings held in Caracas and Salzburg, the Caracas General Assembly, and a volume on hydroelectricity and nature protection which was an additional product of the Technical Meeting held in Caracas. In addition, there was *A Guide to Conservation*, written by Laurence E Palmer (and published in Spanish as well as English, thanks to a grant from UNESCO), an addendum to the volume on *The Position of Nature Protection Throughout the World* and a first volume in a new IUPN Pro Natura Series entitled *Les Fossiles de Demain*, published by a commercial publisher at its own expense. An *Atlas of Nature Reserves in the World* was being prepared together with a book on *Preservation of Fauna in Semi-arid Areas.*

42 Gille, Alain (1998) Letter and commentary on draft text of this book, 8 March.

43 Under the expanded schools programme, educational leaflets on nature protection were distributed in Argentina, Cameroon, Ecuador, French West Africa, Greece, Italy and Mexico. The Belgian Congo, France, Madagascar, Peru and Turkey were to follow. Austria, Belgium, Canada, three regions in Italy and Indonesia had run programmes without financial help. The Gold Coast, Libya and Thailand were considering action. Progress continued in 1952–54. The film strip and lecture notes were completed, the French version of the text and the preparation of the film being done by Mme Caram. Material was produced for a travelling exhibition in Indonesia and for other exhibitions. School material was produced for Ecuador, France, Madagascar, Greece, Laos and Italy, although UNESCO had ceased to finance this work.

44 Report of the Secretary-General, Tracy Philipps, to the General Assembly, Athens, 1958. In: *Proceedings of the Sixth General Assembly of IUCN, Athens, 1958*. Brussels: IUCN, 1960.

45 Wolfgang Burhenne (1998) Discussion with MWH on 16 February.

46 Michel Batisse (1988) Letter to MWH and commentary on draft text of this book, 13 March.

47 IUCN (1994) *The 1993 United Nations List of National Parks and Protected Areas*. Gland, Switzerland and Cambridge, UK: IUCN.

48   Minutes, IUPN Executive Board, sixth session, first sitting, fourteenth meeting, Paris, 30 April 1951. In IUCN archives.
49   Minutes, Bureau of the Executive Board of IUPN, Paris, 27 March 1952. In IUCN archives.
50   Minutes, IUPN Executive Board, fourth session, first sitting, tenth meeting, Brussels, 17 October 1950. In IUCN archives.
51   Minutes, IUPN Executive Board, eleventh session, first sitting, thirty-first meeting, Brussels, 14 January 1954. In IUCN archives.
52   Minutes, IUPN Executive Board, twelfth session, seventh sitting, fortieth meeting, Esbjerg, Denmark, 2 September 1954. In IUCN archives.
53   Minutes, IUPN Executive Board, second session, fourth sitting, sixth meeting, Brussels, 19 March 1949. In IUCN archives.
54   In 1952 the administrative budget was only US$9500, the operative budget $14,000 and the total $23,500. In 1953 and 1954 the administrative budget stayed constant at $10,500 while the operative budgets were $24,500 and $22,500, giving totals of $35,000 and $33,000. The 1952 figures appear in minutes, IUCN Executive Board, seventh session, first sitting, seventeenth meeting, The Hague, 20 September 1951. The projected 1953 and 1954 figures are in the minutes, IUPN Executive Board, eighth session, fourth sitting, twenty-second meeting, Caracas, 9 September 1952. In IUCN archives.
55   Minutes, IUPN Executive Board, seventh session, second sitting, eighteenth meeting, The Hague, 21 September 1951. In IUCN archives.
56   Michel Batisse (1988) Note on UNESCO finance to IUCN, 1948–1966. Information supplied to MWH by Dr Batisse, March.
57   M C Bloemers. Report of the Secretary-General to the Seventh General Assembly, Warsaw, June 1960. In IUCN archives.
58   Minutes, IUPN Executive Board, eleventh session, third sitting, thirty-third meeting, Brussels, 15 January 1954. In IUCN archives.
59   Minutes, IUPN Executive Board, thirteenth session, first sitting, forty-first meeting, Bussels, 7 January 1955. In IUCN archives.
60   Minutes, IUPN Executive Board, twelfth session, fourth sitting, thirty-seventh meeting, Copenhagen, 24 August 1954. In IUCN archives.
61   Minutes, IUPN Executive Board, sixth session, second sitting, fifteenth meeting, Paris, 30 April 1951. In IUCN archives.
62   The other jury members were Darthea Speyer, Assistant Cultural Officer of the US Embassy in Paris, M C Bloemers of the Netherlands Ministry for Education, Arts and Sciences, Alfredo de Canas, artist and publicist of Montevideo, G H Rivière, Curator of the Musée des Arts et Traditions Populaires in Paris and M Dorival, Assistant Director of the Museum of Modern Art in Paris.
63   *IUPN Information Bulletin*, vol III, no 1, February 1954.
64   IUCN/World Bank (1997) *Report of the Symposium on Large Dams.* Gland, Switzerland and Cambridge, UK: IUCN.
65   *IUPN Bulletin*, vol I, nos 5–6, 1952.
66   Minutes, UNESCO Executive Board, 1953. Quoted by J-P Harroy in his report to the Copenhagen General Assembly, op cit Note 40.
67   Walter Lusigi (1998) Discussion with MWH on 17 March.
68   Grzimek, Bernhard (1960) *Serengeti Shall not Die.* London: Hamish Hamilton.
69   In the period between 1948 and 1958, over 90 per cent of those attending IUPN/IUCN Executive Board meetings came from the developed countries. The picture did not begin to change until around 1966, when developing country attendance rose to about 40 per cent of those present. Data provided by Fiona Hanson (see Figure 10.1).
70   Minutes, IUPN Executive Board, ninth session, second sitting, twenty-fourth meeting, Brussels, 6 January 1953. In IUCN archives.

Chapter 4: A Time for Science

1   E M Nicholson (1997) Conversation with MWH on 21 July.
2   The Hon Miriam Rothschild FRS (1997) Interview with MWH on 2 July.

3   Anon (1956) Report on the activities of the Union for 1954–56. In: *Proceedings of the Fifth General Assembly, Edinburgh, 20–28 June 1956*. Brussels: IUCN.

4   *IUPN Bulletin*, vol III, 1954.

5   Minutes, IUPN Executive Board, thirteenth session, third sitting, forty-third meeting, Brussels, 8 January 1955. In IUCN archives.

6   List of officers, Executive Board members and Secretary-Generals, 1948–73. In *1973 IUCN Yearbook*. Morges, Switzerland: IUCN.

7   Minutes, IUPN Executive Board, fifteeth session, first sitting, forty-seventh meeting, Brussels, 13 January 1956. In IUCN archives.

8   Jean-Paul Harroy. Autobiographical note. Extract provided by Mme Mady Harroy, courtesy of Françoise Burhenne-Guilmin.

9   Coolidge, Harold J (1960) Foreword to Talbot, Lee M (1960) *A Look at Threatened Species* – see Note 13.

10   Minutes, IUPN Executive Board, ninth session, fourth sitting, twenty-sixth meeting, Brussels, 7 January 1953. In IUCN archives.

11   Minutes, IUPN Executive Board, thirteenth session, first sitting, forty-first meeting, Brussels, 7 January 1955. In IUCN archives.

12   *IUPN Bulletin*, vol IV, nos 5–6, December 1955.

13   Talbot, Lee M (1988) Discussion and written commentary provided to MWH on 18 March.

14   Talbot, Lee M (1960) *A Look at Threatened Species. A Report on Some Animals of the Middle East and Southern Asia which are Threatened with Extermination. Survival Service Field Mission of 1955 and Subsequent Inquiries.* London: The Fauna Preservation Society for the International Union for Conservation of Nature and Natural Resources.

15   John Berry. Telephone conversation with MWH, 30 May 1997, amplified by letters to David McDowell, 24 June 1998 and to MWH 29 June 1998.

16   Correspondence between E M Nicholson and others between April 1956 and April 1957 relating to the proposal that the UK become a State member of IUPN. File CAB 124 1599, International Union for the Conservation of Nature and Natural Resources, 1955–65. 15/1/01. In UK Public Record Office; transcripts supplied to MWH by Dr John Sheail.

17   Office note dated 1 April 1957. NC/M/57/26. In file CAB 124 1599. International Union for the Conservation of Nature and Natural Resources 1956–66. UK Public Record Office, 15/1/01; transcript supplied to MWH by Dr John Sheail.

18   Robert E Boote. Telephone conversation with MWH on 12 January 1998. Bob Boote had just joined the Nature Conservancy at the time of the 1956 General Assembly, where he acted as 'Max Nicholson's bag-carrier'.

19   Talbot, Lee M (1983) IUCN in retrospect and prospect. *Environmental Conservation*, vol 10, no 1, pp 5–11.

20   Talbot, Lee M. *Notes of the Name of the IUPN*. Paper circulated at the Edinburgh General Assembly in 1956. Copy provided to MWH by Lee Talbot on 18 March 1998.

21   Alain Gille. Tape-recorded interview with Sylvie Wabbes of IUCN in 1993; transcript in IUCN archives.

22   Wolfgang Burhenne and Françoise Burhenne-Guilmin. Discussion with MWH on 16 February 1998.

23   Minutes, IUCN Executive Board, sixteenth session, third sitting, fifty-second meeting, Edinburgh, 20 June 1956. In IUCN archives.

24   Harroy, J-P (1988) The early years. Article contributed to Forty years of conservation. Special Number, *IUCN Bulletin*, vol 19, 7–12, pp 15–17.

25   Minutes of the forty-eighth meeting of the IUCN Executive Board, Brussels, 13 January 1956. In IUCN archives.

26   Report of the Secretary-General, Tracy Philipps, to the General Assembly, Athens, 1958. In: *Proceedings of the Sixth General Assembly of IUCN, Athens, 1958*. Brussels: IUCN, 1960.

27   Minutes, IUCN Executive Board, eighth session, first sitting, fifty-seventh meeting, Brussels, 8 November 1957. In IUCN archives. It was at this meeting that Alain Gille

was able to report a proposed increase in support from US$1500 to $5000 annually for the 1959–60 biennium.

28   Michel Batisse (1998) Letter to MWH, 13 March, with detailed summary of UNESCO financial support for IUCN, 1948–66, supplemented by a letter, 24 June 1998, with detailed comments on the near-final text of this book.

29   Minutes, IUCN Executive Board, sixteenth session, first sitting, fiftieth meeting, Edinburgh, 19 June 1956.

30   Roger Heim. President's report to General Assembly, Athens, 1958. In: *Proceedings of the Sixth General Assembly of IUCN, Athens, 1958*. Brussels: IUCN, 1960.

31   Minutes, IUCN Executive Board, seventeenth session, first sitting, fifty-fifth meeting, Brussels, 15 February 1957. In IUCN archives.

32   Report by the Secretary-General, M C Bloemers. In: *Proceedings of the Seventh General Assembly, Warsaw, June 1960*. Brussels: IUCN.

33   The lists of topics and of personalities taken from the minutes of a number of meetings of the IUCN Executive Board. Minutes held in the IUCN archives.

34   Walter Lusigi (1998) Discussion with MWH on 18 March.

35   Pelzers, E (1994) Historical background on the Netherlands Commission for International Nature Protection, the Foundation for International Nature Protection and the Office International pour la Protection de la Nature. Written for *Mededelingen* no 29 of the Netherlands Commission of International Nature Protection, and translated for IUCN by J A Boddens Hosang.

36   Minutes, IUCN Executive Board, seventeenth session, second sitting, fifty-sixth meeting, Brussels, 16 February 1957. In IUCN archives.

37   IUCN (1974) *IUCN Yearbook, 1973*. Morges: IUCN.

38   Minutes, IUPN Executive Board, fourteenth session, second sitting, forty-fifth meeting, London, 11 July 1955. In IUCN archives.

39   Rapport d'activité de la Commission d'Ecologie, 1955–1958. In IUCN archives.

40   Minutes, IUCN Executive Board, eighth session, second sitting, fifty-eighth meeting, 9 November 1957. In IUCN archives.

41   Minutes, IUCN Executive Board, twentieth session, third sitting, sixty-third meeting, Athens, 11 September 1958. In IUCN archives.

42   Minutes, IUCN Executive Board, nineteenth session, second sitting, sixtieth meeting, Brussels, 2 May 1958. In IUCN archives.

43   Report of the Commission on Ecology, 1958–1960. In IUCN archives.

44   Bourlière, François (Ed) (1961) *Ecology and Management of Wild Grazing Animals in Temperate Zones. Proceedings of the 8th Technical Meeting of IUCN, Warsaw, 15–24 July 1960*. Morges, Switzerland: IUCN.

45   Curry-Lindahl, Kai (1978) Background and development of international conservation organizations and their role in the future. *Environmental Conservation*, vol 5, no 3, pp 163–169.

46   Jeffrey A McNeely (1977) Letter to MWH, 18 September.

47   Minutes, IUCN Executive Board, twentieth session, second sitting, sixty-second meeting, Athens, 10 September 1958. In IUCN archives.

48   Minutes, IUCN Executive Board, twentieth session, fourth sitting, sixty-fourth meeting, Athens, 16 September 1958. In IUCN archives.

49   *World Lists of National Parks and Equivalent Reserves*. Morges and Gland, Switzerland and Cambridge, UK: IUCN.

50   Alain Gille (1964) Victor van Straelen, 1889–1964. Message de l'UNESCO. *Flambeau: Revue Belge des Questions Politiques et Littéraires*. 47 Année, no 2, mars-avril 1964, 65–69.

51   Malcolm Gracie (1986) *The International Union for the Conservation of Nature and Natural Resources: What it is and What it has Done to Promote the Growth and Development of Certain Rules and Principles of Contemporary International Law*. Thesis: Macquarie University School of Law, June 1968. Copy kindly supplied to MWH by Françoise Burhenne-Guilmin.

52   Françoise Burhenne-Guilmin (1998) Memo to David McDowell, 31 March.

53 Pearsall, W H (1962) Paper in Le Cren, E D and Holdgate, M W (Eds) *The Exploitation of Natural Animal Populations*. British Ecological Society Symposium No 2. Oxford: Blackwell.

54 Julian Huxley (1960) *The conservation of wild life and natural habitats in Central and East Africa. Report on a mission accomplished for UNESCO, July–September 1960.* Paris: UNESCO.

55 Julian Huxley (1960) Summary of main lines of proposed report to UNESCO on conservation of wild life and natural habitats in Central and East Africa. Typescript in IUCN archives bearing the initials EBW, in the handwriting of E Barton Worthington.

56 Huxley suggested that there were seven positive factors:
   i)   the discovery that large areas of wild land produce more meat, and can produce a greater profit, if managed for game cropping rather than given over to domestic stock;
   ii) recognition that large areas of forest are necessary to protect watersheds from erosion;
   iii) appreciation of the economic value of wildlife in National Parks and Reserves through tourism;
   iv) increasing interest in African wildlife in Europe and North America;
   v)   recognition of the importance of studying the ecology of African wild lands and large wildlife before it is too late;
   vi) increasing realization in African countries of the prestige value of national parks, and
   vii) realization that African people themselves derive enjoyment and interest from seeing and studying wildlife.

57 The members were: François Bourlière of France (Vice-Chairman), Frank Fraser Darling, Bernhard Grzimek, Jean Baer, Theodore Monod, Leonard Beadle, Sayid Kamil Shawki of Sudan, David Wasawo of Kenya and William Banage of Uganda.

58 Tony Mence (1998) Written comments on draft texts and discussion with MWH, 3 February.

59 Grzimek, Bernhard (1961) Winning the fight for Africa's game. *Daily Telegraph*, 21 August.

60 No less than four people have assured MWH that they drafted Dr Nyerere's speech! The overwhelmingly important thing is that Dr Nyerere, an African statesman of world stature, made these forceful words his. They have continued to influence African conservation down the years. The text of the Arusha Manifesto will be found in several publications including Omar, J A (1996) Opening remarks on *Community-based Conservation in Tanzania*, Kayera, J A (Eds) IUCN Species Survival Commission Occasional Paper No 15, Gland, Switzerland and Cambridge, UK: IUCN.

61 College of African Wildlife Management, Mweka, Tanganyika. Brochure issued soon after its establishment. Copy supplied to MWH by E M Nicholson.

62 Alain Gille (1988) Letter to MWH, 8 March, with detailed commentary on draft texts of this book.

63 Guha, Ramachandra (1997) The authoritarian biologist and the arrogance of anti-human-ism. Wildlife conservation in the Third World. *The Ecologist*, vol 27, no 1, 14–20.

64 Talbot, Lee M (1957) Wilderness overseas. *Sierra Club Bulletin*, 42, no 6.

65 Report on the Ngorongoro Workshop in 1989. *IUCN Bulletin*, vol. 21, no 1, March 1990, p 11.

66 United Nations General Assembly Resolution A RES/1831/XVII/Economic, 8 January 1963.

67 *Ecological and Chemical Pesticides*. New York: The Conservation Foundation, 1960.

68 IUCN (1958) *Union Internationale pour la Conservation de la Nature et de ses Ressources. Dixième Anniversaire, 1948–1958. De Fontainebleau à Athènes et Delphes.* Brussels: IUCN.

69 Mady Harroy (1997) Letter to Alain Gille, 4 September, in which she speaks of the destruction of the IUPN archives by Jean Baer.

70 Minutes, IUCN Executive Board, twenty-fourth session, third sitting, eighty-third meeting, Warsaw, 15 June 1960. In IUCN archives.

71   Minutes, IUCN Executive Board, twenty-fourth session, fourth sitting, eighty-fourth meeting, Warsaw, 18 June 1960. In IUCN archives.
72   Minutes, IUCN Executive Board, twenty-fourth session, sixth sitting, eighty-sixth meeting, Cracow, 24 June 1960. In IUCN archives.
73   E B Worthington: also section on 'A new name and a new home' in *IUCN Year Book 1973*. IUCN, Morges, Switzerland.
74   Minutes of Special Executive Meeting held at the Buffet de la Gare, Lausanne, Switzerland on 10 January 1961. In IUCN archives.
75   Minutes of the IUCN Executive Board, Morges, 27–29 April 1961. In IUCN archives. This was the first meeting of the 'new series', but was not numbered.
76   Minutes, IUCN Executive Board, thirty-sixth session, first and second meetings, London, 2 and 3 October 1965.
77   H F I Elliott. Secretary-General's Report for 1960–1963. *Proceedings of the Eighth Session of the General Assembly, Nairobi, September 1963.* Morges: IUCN.
78   Minutes of the IUCN Executive Board, Morges, 18–19 November 1961. Second meeting of the 'new series'. In IUCN archives.

Chapter 5: The New Ark Puts to Sea

1   Scott, Peter (Ed) (1965) *The Launching of the New Ark. First Report of the World Wildlife Fund.* London: Collins.
2   Harroy, Jean-Paul (1988) The Early Years. *IUCN Bulletin, Special Issue: Forty Years in Conservation*, vol 19, 7–12, pp 15–17.
3   McCormick, J (1989) *The Global Environmental Movement. Reclaiming Paradise.* London: Belhaven Press.
4   Talbot, Lee M (1998) He told MWH on 18 March that Peter Scott had told him that he and Max Nicholson had decided to take action to provide support for IUCN while travelling home from an IUCN Executive Board meeting in 1960.
5   Scott, Peter (1966) *The Eye of the Wind. An Autobiography* revised edition. London: Hodder and Stoughton.
6   Max Nicholson's meeting was attended by Victor Stolan, Julian Huxley, Peter Scott, Guy Mountfort, Phyllis Barclay-Smith (of the ICBP), Lt Col Boyle of the Fauna Preservation Society (and Commission for the Survival Service), Aubrey Buxton (head of Anglia Television and himself a wildlife photographer and film-maker), Lord Hurcomb (another keen ornithologist, Nicholson's former boss in the Civil Service and Chairman of the Nature Conservancy), Sir Landsborough Thomson (then President of the Zoological Society of London), the Marquis of Willingdon (President of the Fauna Preservation Society) and Barton Worthington (Nicholson's deputy at the Conservancy).
7   E M Nicholson (1998) Letter to MWH, 25 June, with comments on near-final text of this book.
8   Ian MacPhail (1998) Discussion with MWH on 3 March. MacPhail provided MWH with a typescript account of events entitled *The Launching of the New Ark*.
9   Tony Mence (1998) Written comments on draft texts and discussion with MWH on 3 February.
10   Tony Mence (1981) *IUCN: How it Began, How it is Growing Up*. Gland: IUCN.
11   *IUCN Yearbook, 1973*. Morges, Switzerland: IUCN, 1974.
12   Headings for a contract between World Wildlife Fund and IUCN. Paper dated 16 August 1961. In WWF archives.
13   *Save the World's Wildlife.* First WWF promotional brochure. Layout by Ian MacPhail, Foreword by HRH Prince Bernhard of the Netherlands, drawings by Peter Scott. Contains the text of 'The World Wildlife Charter' (which is a completely different document to the World Charter for Nature, adopted by the United Nations General Assembly 20 years later).
14   The Hon Russell Train (1988) Discussion with MWH on 18 March.
15   Wolfgang Burhenne and Françoise Burhenne-Guilmin (1998) Discussion with MWH on 16 February.

16　Ian MacPhail (1997) Note to MWH in August.
17　Talbot, Lee M (1988) Discussion and written commentary provided to MWH on 18 March and 24 June.
18　HRH The Prince Philip, Duke of Edinburgh (1997) Conversation with MWH, 24 July.
19　De Mattos-Shipley, H, Lyons, J, Belsham, C, Harding, D and Johnston, M (Eds) (1996) *WWF. Changing Worlds. 35 Years of Conservation Achievement.* London: Banson.
20　Charles de Haes (1998) Discussion with MWH on 10 March.
21　Simon, Noel M. IUCN: its policy, goal, strategy and tactics. Paper submitted to the IUCN Executive Board, twenty-eighth meeting, 24–26 November 1962. In Elliott papers, IUCN archives.
22　The policy of IUCN. Paper drafted by Ed Graham and edited by Peter Scott, 19 April 1963. In Elliott papers, IUCN archives.
23　E M Nicholson. Letter to H F I Elliott,11 March 1963. In Elliott papers, IUCN archives.
24　E M Nicholson (1997) Conversation with MWH on 21 July.
25　Minutes, IUCN Executive Board, Morges, 27–29 April 1961. In IUCN archives. Unnumbered first meeting of the 'new series'.
26　Minutes, IUCN Executive Board, Morges, 18–19 November 1961. Unnumbered second meeting of the 'new series'. In IUCN archives.
27　Minutes, IUCN Executive Board, third meeting, Morges, 15–17 May 1962. In IUCN archives. This is the first meeting of the new series to bear a number.
28　H F I Elliott. Secretary-General's Report for 1960–1963. Proceedings of the Eighth Session of the General Assembly, Nairobi, September 1963.
29　Rapport de la Commission d'Ecologie, 1960–1963. In IUCN archives.
30　G V T Matthews (1993) *The Ramsar Convention on Wetlands. Its History and Development.* Gland: Ramsar Convention Bureau. Photocopy supplied to MWH by Dr Luc Hoffmann, who added comments in letters dated 14 and 27 August 1998.
31　Talbot, Lee M and Talbot, M H (eds) (1966) *Conservation in Tropical South East Asia.* IUCN Publications, New Series, no 10, pp 1–550. Morges: IUCN.
32　The first text of what became the Agreed Measures was prepared by Martin Holdgate and Brian Roberts of the UK Scott Polar Research Institute in 1960 and brokered by Roberts at the Antarctic Treaty Consultative Meeting. The First Symposium on Antarctic Biology in Paris in June 1962 was convened by the Working Group on Biology of the Scientific Committee on Antarctic Research, and its proceedings were published as Carrick, R, Holdgate, M W and Prevost, J (1964) *Antarctic Biology – Biologie Antarctique.* Paris: Editions Hermann.
33　Proceedings, Conference on the Conservation and Management of Temperate Wetlands: Les Saintes Maries de la Mer, 12–17 November 1962.
34　Proceedings, Symposium on Ecological Research in National Parks, Zurich, May 1961.
35　National Parks Service, US Department of the Interior (1964) *First World Conference on National Parks.* Washington DC: US Government Printing Office.
36　M McCloskey (1998) Discussion with MWH on 18 March.
37　Marc Dourojeann (1988) Letter to MWH, 8 April.
38　Letter from Peter Scott to Noel M Simon, 22 August 1962. In Elliott papers, IUCN archives.
39　Liamine, Nathalie (1989) *L'Union Internationale pour la Conservation de la Nature et de ses Ressources, 1948–1988. Mémoire de Maîtrise présenté sous la direction de Monsieur le Professeur Frank.* Université de Paris – Nanterre. U E R d'Histoire. Session d'octobre.
40　John A Burton (1998) Memorandum to Kevin Grose, Head, Information Management Group, IUCN, 4 June, entitled '*Towards a bibliography and catalogue of the IUCN loose-leaf Red Data Books*'.
41　E M Nicholson (1998) Letter to MWH, 30 June, with comments on near-final text of this book.
42　Claude Martin (1998) Letter to David McDowell, 24 June, with table of statistics setting out WWF's core and other non-project contributions to IUCN.
43　Manuscript memorandum by Jack F Lipscomb, 10 August 1963. In Elliott papers, shelf 21.0, headquarters policy 1962–65; IUCN archives.

44   Manuscript letter from Jack F Lipscomb to H F I Elliott, 12 July 1963. In Elliott papers, shelf 21.0, Headquarters policy 1962–65; IUCN archives.

45   Letter from H F I Elliott to Jack F Lipscomb,16 July 1963. In Elliott papers, shelf 21.0, Headquarters policy 1962–65; IUCN archives.

46   Letter from Peter Scott to Luc Hoffmann, 25 August 1963. In WWF archives. Copy supplied to MWH by Dr C Martin.

47   Blondel, Jacques. *François Bourlière, 21 December 1913 – 10 November 1993.*

48   Letter from Fred M Packard, Secretary of the International Commission on National Parks to Noel Simon of IUCN, 25 February 1964. In IUCN archives.

49   Peters, Rudolph (1975) Statement. In: Worthington, E B (1975) *The Evolution of IBP. International Biological Programme 1.* Cambridge: Cambridge University Press.

50   Waddington, C H (1975) The origin. In: Worthington, E B (1975) op cit Note 54.

51   Letter from G Watterson to H Ellenberg,17 May 1961. In IUCN archives.

52   Letter from J D Ovington to H Ellenberg,18 May 1962. In IUCN archives.

53   Letter from H Ellenberg to J D Ovington, 1 June 1962. In IUCN archives.

54   Worthington, E B (Ed) (1975) *The Evolution of IBP. International Biological Programme 1.* Cambridge: Cambridge University Press.

55   Nicholson, E M. Conservation. In: Worthington, E B (1975) op cit Note 54.

56   Martin Holdgate. Personal recollection (as a member of SCIBP, 1966–68).

57   Conservation Terrestrial (CT). Substance of the programme. In: Worthington, E B (1975) op cit Note 54.

58   Peterken, G F (Ed) (1968) *Guide to the Check-Sheet for IBP Areas*, Oxford: Blackwell Scientific Publications for SCIBP.

59   Duncan Poore (1998) 'Notes on IUCN' and discussion with MWH on 20 February.

60   Paper submitted to the thirty-third session of the IUCN Executive Board, Morges, 26–28 June 1964. In IUCN archives.

61   Letter from F Bourlière to H F I Elliott, 28 July 1964. In Elliott papers, shelf 21.0, Headquarters policy 1962–65; IUCN archives.

62   Letter from David C Martin to J G Baer, 11 June 1965. In IUCN archives.

63   Statement after a meeting to discuss IBP/IUCN relationships, held on 25 September 1965. In IUCN archives.

64   Report of the Commission on Ecology, 1958–1960. In IUCN archives.

65   Rapport d'activité de la Commission d'Ecologie, 1956–1958. In IUCN archives.

66   Report of the Commission on Ecology, 1966–1969. In IUCN archives.

67   IBP CT Newsletter, November 1971.

68   Report of the Commission on Ecology, 1970–1972. In IUCN archives.

69   Jeremy Harrison, World Conservation Monitoring Centre. Conversation with MWH on 6 January 1998.

70   IUCN (1975) *World Databook of National Parks and Protected Areas.* Prepared under the supervision of R F Dasmann. Morges: IUCN.

71   Report of the Commission on Ecology, 1973–1975. In IUCN archives.

72   Minutes, IUCN Executive Board, thirty-sixth session, first and second meetings, London, 2–3 October 1965. In IUCN archives.

73   Anis Mouasher, President, Royal Society for the Conservation of Nature, Jordan. Letter to MWH,15 April 1998.

74   Peter Scott (1965) Letter to the Hon Stewart L Udall, 27 January. In IUCN archives.

75   Michel Batisse (1998) Letter to MWH, with commentary, 13 March. Includes note on the establishment of UNDP.

76   Michel Batisse (1998). Detailed commentary on the near-final text of this book, with letter to MWH, 24 June.

77   Raymond F Dasmann (1998) Letter and notes sent to MWH, 17 January.

78   UNESCO (1970) *Use and Conservation of the Biosphere.* Report of the Intergovernmental Conference of Experts on the Scientific Basis for the Rational Use and Conservation of the Resources of the Biosphere. Natural Resources Research Series, vol X, Paris: UNESCO.

79   Bourlière, F and Batisse, M (1978) Ten years after the Biosphere Conference: from concept to action. *Nature and Resources*, XIV, 3, 14–17.

80 UNESCO (1993) *The Biosphere Conference 25 Years Later.* Paris: UNESCO.
81 Michel Batisse (1997) Biosphere reserves. A challenge for biodiversity conservation and regional development. *Environment*, 39 (5), October, 7–33.
82 Maldague, M (1984) The Biosphere Reserve concept: its implementation and its potential as a tool for integrated development. In: di Castri, F and Hadley, M (Eds) *Ecology in Practice. Part I: Ecosystem Management.* Dublin: Tycooly International and Paris: UNESCO, pp 376–402.
83 Duncan Poore (1998) Letter to MWH, 20 June 1998, with commentary on the near-final text of this book.
84 McNeely, J (1982) Why biosphere reserves? An introductory note. IUCN *Bulletin*, 13, p 59.
85 Michel Batisse (1998) Letter to MWH, 2 February.
86 Walter Lusigi. Discussion with MWH on 18 March 1998.
87 Kenton Miller (1998) Letter to MWH, 2 February, with detailed commentary on many issues covered in this chapter.
88 UNESCO/UNEP (1984) *Conservation, Science and Society.* Proceedings of the First Conference on Biosphere Reserves. Natural Resources Research Series, vol XXI. Paris: UNESCO.
89 George A Knox, first Secretary-General and later President of INTECOL. Conversation with MWH on 26 August 1997.
90 International Association of Ecology. A note on its activities. In Appendix B on the activities of ICSU Unions and associated groups, in Holdgate, M W and White, G F (Eds) (1977) *Environmental Issues.* SCOPE Report 10. London: John Wiley & Sons.

Chapter 6: The Environmental Explosion

1   Eric Ashby (1982) Report to the global shareholders. Review of Holdgate et al (1982) op cit Note 9. *New Scientist.*
2   McCormick, J (1989) *The Global Environmental Movement. Reclaiming Paradise.* London: Belhaven Press.
3   Robert Prescott-Allen. Discussion with MWH on 21 March 1998.
4   Patrick Moore (one of the founder-members of Greenpeace) (1998) Letter to MWH, 16 March.
5   Rachel Carson (1962) *Silent Spring.* London: Hamish Hamilton.
6   Lee M Talbot (1998) Commentary and discussion with MWH on 18 March. Talbot recalled, as interesting background to the publication of *Silent Spring*, a meeting in the fall of 1955 with Paul Brooks, the Editor in Chief of Houghton Mifflin Company. Brooks asked whether Talbot thought the environmental impact of pesticides was really an important issue, since he had an author who wanted to write a book about them. Talbot told him that he thought they were a major environmental problem, and said that IUPN had considered them at several meetings, initially at Lake Success, and had held a symposium about their impact. Brooks asked Talbot to get him a copy of the symposium proceedings and said that he was going to urge the author (Rachel Carson) to go ahead.
7   Paul Ehrlich (1968) *The Population Bomb.* New York: Ballantine.
8   Commoner, Barry (1971) *The Closing Circle.* New York: Alfred Knopf.
9   Holdgate, M W, Kassas, M and White, G F (1982) *The World Environment, 1972–1982.* Dublin: Tycooly, for UNEP.
10 Curry-Lindahl, K (1978) Background and development of international conservation organizations and their role in the future. *Environmental Conservation*, vol 5, no 3, pp 163–169.
11 Patrick Moore. Discussion with MWH, October 1996.
12 Michael McCloskey. Discussion with MWH, 18 March 1998.
13 Shabecoff, Philip (1993) *A Fierce Green Fire. The American Environmental Movement.* New York: Hill and Wang.
14 David Runnalls. Conversation with MWH, 3 December 1997.

15 Goldsmith, E, Allen, R, Allenby, M, Davoll, J and Lawrence, S (1972) *Blueprint for Survival*. Boston: Houghton Mifflin.
16 Meadows, D H, Meadows, D L, Randers, J and Behrens, W (1972) *The Limits to Growth*. London: Universe.
17 Michael J Cockerell (1995) The future of IUCN membership. Internal paper, 5 October; in IUCN archives.
18 Claude Martin (1998) Memo to David McDowell, 24 June, including detailed statistics of payments from WWF to IUCN.
19 E M Nicholson (1988) Letter to MWH, 30 June with comments on the near-final text of this book.
20 Richard Sandbrook. Conversation with MWH, December 1997.
21 Elliott, H F I. Secretary-General's Report for 1960–1963. Proceedings of the Eighth Session of the IUCN General Assembly, Nairobi, September 1963.
22 Minutes, IUCN Executive Board, thirty-ninth session, Lucerne, 2 July 1966. In IUCN archives.
23 H F I Elliott (1965) Letter to Mme Eleen Thierry-Mieg, 2 March. In IUCN archives.
24 H F I Elliott (1965) Letter to François Bourlière, 24 February. In IUCN archives.
25 Letter from Max Newman to H F I Elliott, 30 July 1965. In Elliott papers, IUCN archives.
26 HRH The Prince Philip, Duke of Edinburgh. Conversation with MWH on 24 July 1997.
27 Wolfgang and Françoise Burhenne. Discussion with MWH on 16 February 1998.
28 Charles de Haes (1998) Telephone conversations with MWH on 24 and 31 July 1998, and written comments on the near-final text of this book.
29 Elliott, H F I (1966) Secretary-General's Report. In: *Proceedings, Ninth General Assembly of IUCN, Lucerne, Switzerland, 25 June–2 July 1966*. Morges: IUCN. WWF figures supplied in 1998 give the 1963 subvention to IUCN as SFr186,297 and that for 1965 as SFr108,781 so the cut may have been less serious than Hugh Elliott alleged at the time.
30 E J H Berwick (1974) Brief statement of reminiscence in *1973 IUCN Yearbook*. Morges: IUCN .
31 Letter, Fritz Vollmar to H F I Elliott, 28 July 1965. In Elliott papers in IUCN archives.
32 Letter, Peter Scott to H F I Elliott, 19 July 1965. In Elliott papers in IUCN archives.
33 IUCN (1974) *1973 IUCN Yearbook*. Morges, Switzerland: IUCN.
34 Minutes, IUCN Executive Board, fortieth session, Morges, 5–6 November 1966. In IUCN archives.
35 Minutes, forty-first session of the IUCN Executive Board, Morges, 8–9 April 1967. In IUCN archives.
36 The Hon Russell Train. Discussion with MWH, 18 March 1998.
37 Walter Lusigi. Discussion with MWH, 18 March 1998.
38 Minutes, IUCN Executive Board, forty-second session, Morges, 1–2 November 1967. In IUCN archives.
39 Gerardo Budowski. Conversation with MWH, 29 November 1997.
40 Robert E Boote. Discussion with MWH, 19 February 1998.
41 Letter, Lenore Smith (International Commission for National Parks) to Noel Simon of IUCN, 19 January 1966. In IUCN Elliott papers.
42 Minutes, IUCN Executive Board, special meeting, UNESCO, Paris, 1 July 1969. In IUCN archives.
43 Gerardo Budowski and Frank Nicholls. Report on the work of the Union since the Tenth General Assembly. In *Proceedings of the Eleventh General Assembly of IUCN, Banff, Canada, 11–16 September 1972*. Morges, Switzerland: IUCN, 1972.
44 Mence, Tony (1981) *IUCN: How it Began, How it is Growing Up*. Booklet prepared for IUCN General Assembly in Christchurch, New Zealand.
45 Duncan Poore (1998) Notes on IUCN and discussion with MWH, 20 February.
46 World Commission on Environment and Development (1987) *Our Common Future*. Oxford and New York: Oxford University Press.
47 Papers supplied to MWH by Gerardo Budowski.
48 Kenton Miller (1998) Letter to MWH, 2 February 1998, with detailed commentary on many issues covered in this chapter.

49   Frank Nicholls (1998) Letter to MWH,10 July 1998, with comments on the near-final text of this book.
50   Raymond F Dasmann (1998) Draft chapter of an unpublished autobiography, kindly supplied to MWH under cover of letter, 17 January.
51   Dasmann, Raymond F (1994) *Environmental Conservation*, 5th edition. John Wiley and Sons. (Includes text of Cocoyoc Declaration.) The first edition of this important book appeared as early as 1959.
52   Gerardo Budowski (1998) Letter to David McDowell, 25 June, commenting on near-final text of this book.
53   IUCN (1971) *IUCN Yearbook, 1971.* Morges: IUCN.
54   Biographical note on Maurice Strong. *The Globe and Mail Report on business*, 25 October 1997.
55   Shabecoff, Philip (1996) *A New Name for Peace. International Environmentalism, Sustainable Development and Democracy.* Hanover and London: University Press of New England.
56   Ward, B and Dubos, R (1972) *Only One Earth. The Care and Maintenance of a Small Planet.* London: Andre Deutsch.
57   United Nations: Report of the Secretary-General to the Third Session of the Preparatory Committee (UN Doc A/CONF.48/PC.11). New York: United Nations, 1971, quoted by J McCormick (1989) op cit Note 2.
58   Raymond F Dasmann (1998) Letter and notes sent to MWH, 17 January.
59   Gerardo Budowski (1998) Letter to MWH, 27 May.
60   Maurice Strong (1973) Article in *IUCN Bulletin,* January.
61   IUCN (1972) *IUCN Yearbook, 1972.* Morges: IUCN.
62   Gerardo Budowski (1982) A certain pre-event anxiety. *Uniterra,* 1, pp 5–6. Quoted by J McCormick (1989) op cit Note 2.
63   Michel Batisse (1998) Letter and commentary sent to MWH,13 March.
64   Max Nicholson (1966) Paper on conservation for science of a series of Pacific Islands, 13 October; following Eleventh Pacific Science Congress, September 1966. In IUCN IBP papers.
65   G V T Matthews (1993) *The Ramsar Convention on Wetlands. Its History and Development.* Gland: Ramsar Convention Bureau. Photocopy supplied to MWH by Dr Luc Hoffmann, with added comments in letters, 14 and 27 August 1998.
66   Eskandar Firouz. Discussion with MWH,15 June 1998.
67   Gracie, Malcolm (1986) *The International Union for the Conservation of Nature and Natural Resources: What it is and What it Has Done to Promote the Growth and Development of Certain Rules and Principles of Contemporary International Law.* Thesis for the degree of Bachelor of Law, Macquarie University, Sydney, Australia. Copy supplied to MWH by the IUCN Environmental Law Centre.
68   Meyer, R L (1976) Travaux Préparatoires for the UNESCO World Heritage Convention. *Earth Law Journal,* 2, p 45.
69   Batisse, M (1992) The struggle to save our World Heritage. *Environment*, vol 34, no 10, pp 12–32.
70   Michel Batisse (1998) Letter to MWH, 24 June with detailed commentary on near-final text of this book.
71   Wolfgang Burhenne. Discussions with MWH on 28 January and 16 February 1998. Burhenne believes that the long time-interval between the development of the draft of what became CITES and the convening of the intergovernmental negotiating session was a consequence of the long-running debate over which of the two Chinese Governments should represent their country at the UN. Until the matter was resolved the USA could not convene the conference in Washington. IUCN was itself in difficulties, for it had admitted a government agency in Taiwan to membership. The seating of the People's Republic of China at the UN in 1971 brought pressure for organizations like IUCN to drop their Taiwanese members if they wanted continuing UN agency support. The Statutes were amended, restricting membership to bodies based in a '*State Member of the United Nations, its Specialized Agencies, the International Atomic Energy Agency or a Party to the Statutes of the International Court of Justice*'.

72   Robert Prescott-Allen (1998) Letter to David McDowell and Martin Holdgate,15 July
     1998 with comments on near-final text of this book. Robert Prescott-Allen points out
     that these two axes can be used to group both conservationists and the policies they
     espouse. 'Preservation and animal rights' fall in the corner of the matrix that gives prior-
     ity to nature and wildlife and rates nature above people. 'Deep ecology' is concerned
     with the whole ecosystem, and again is more concerned with it than people. Sustainable
     development is concerned with the whole ecosystem and gives at least equal importance
     to people. Sustainable wildlife use is narrower, but accepts that people's interests in
     wildlife are as important as the interests of the wildlife itself. In this book, the term
     'protectionist' is applied generally to those who put nature (whether wildlife or ecosys-
     tems) first and 'conservationist' to those at least equally concerned with people.
73   E U Curtis ('Buff') Bohlen. Discussion with MWH,19 March 1998.
74   Jan Cerovsky (1977) Brief notes from the History of the IUCN Commission on
     Education. Paper 3 April. In IUCN files.
75   Tony Mence (1998) Written comments on draft texts and discussions with MWH, 3
     February.
76   Peter Jackson (1998) Letter to MWH, 15 June. His article on Operation Tiger appears on
     p 30 of de Mattos-Shipley *et al* (1996), op cit Note 77.
77   De Mattos-Shipley, H, Lyons, J, Belsham, C, Harding, D and Johnston, M (Eds) (1996)
     WWF. Changing Worlds. 35 Years of Conservation Achievement. London: Banson.
78   Harold J Coolidge (1981) Letter to Mohamed Kassas, 2 December. Copy provided to
     MWH by Professor M Kassas.
79   Maurice Strong (1998) Letter to David McDowell, 26 July.
80   Dasmann, R F, Milton, J P and Freeman, P F (1973) *Ecological Principles for Economic
     Development.* London, New York, Sydney and Toronto: John Wiley for IUCN and the
     Conservation Foundation, Washington DC.
81   Kenton R Miller. Discussion with MWH,17 March 1998.
82   Marc Dourojeanni (1998) Letter to MWH, 8 April.
83   Françoise Burhenne-Guilmin (1998) Letter to MWH, 31 March.
84   Eskandar Firouz (1998) Letter to MWH,12 April.
85   Zafar Futehally (1998) Letter to MWH, 9 June.
86   Gerardo Budowski. Conversation with MWH, 29 November 1997. He confirmed a story
     often told in IUCN about an incident involving Maurice Strong. The latter was in
     Caracas and wanted a meeting with the President of Venezuela, Carlos Andes Perez. The
     official channels were unhelpful. He found himself bemoaning the fact to Budowski at a
     cocktail party. The latter used his contacts as a senior Venezuelan scientist and soon
     afterwards Strong was bidden to a special lunch with the President. He expressed his
     sense of obligation, and while this did not cause the partnership between IUCN and
     UNEP, it did help establish the contacts.
87   Peter Thacher (former Assistant Executive Director of UNEP). Discussion with MWH
     on 14 June 1998.
88   Ursula Hiltbrunner. Discussion with MWH, June 1997.
89   Charles de Haes. Discussion with MWH,10 March 1998.
90   Pierre Goeldlin. Discussion with MWH,15 June 1998.
91   Claude Martin. Discussion with MWH, 4 December 1997.
92   Gerardo Budowski and Frank Nicholls (1975) Report of the Work of the Union since the
     Eleventh General Assembly. In: *Proceedings, Twelfth General Assembly, Kinshasa,
     Zaire, 8–18 September 1975.* Morges: IUCN.
93   The history of the IUCN Environmental Law Service and the Environmental Law
     Information System, ELIS, is described in several IUCN documents including
     Environmental Law Service (1996) available from IUCN Environmental Law Centre,
     Adenauerallee 214, D–53113 Bonn, Germany and *Environmental Law Information
     System*, ELIS (1994) from the same address.
94   Minutes, IUCN Executive Committee, twenty-fourth meeting, Morges, 9–11 February
     1977. In IUCN archives.
95   Minutes, IUCN Executive Board, fifty-fifth session, Morges, 1–3 May 1975. In IUCN
     archives.

96 Delmar Blasco. Discussion with MWH, December 1997.
97 Duncan Poore (1998) Letter to MWH, 20 June with detailed commentary on the near-final text of this book.
98 Michel Batisse. Message of greetings from UNESCO to the General Assembly of IUCN in Banff, 1972. Copy supplied by Michel Batisse.
99 Hal Eidsvik. Discussion with MWH, 23 March.
100 Mike McCloskey (1998) Letter to MWH 2 July commenting on near-final text of this book.
101 Minutes, IUCN Executive Board, fifty-sixth session, first sitting, Kinshasa, 7 September 1975. In IUCN archives.
102 Luc Hoffmann (1998) Letter to MWH,14 August.
103 Duncan Poore. Typed transcript of a note dictated at the time of the Kinshasa General Assembly and made available to MWH, August 1997.
104 Hal Eidsvik (1998) Letter to MWH, 22 January.
105 Minutes, IUCN Executive Board, fifty-sixth session, third sitting, Kinshasa, 16 September 1975. In IUCN archives.
106 Minutes, IUCN Executive Committee, twenty-second meeting, Morges, January 31–1 February 1976. In IUCN archives.

Chapter 7: A Strategy for World Conservation

1   Tolba, M K, El Kholy, O, El Hinnawi, E, Holdgate, M W, McMichael, D F and Munn, R E (Eds) *The World Environment, 1972–1992*. London: Chapman and Hall.
2   Editorial comment. *IUCN Bulletin*, New Series, vol 7, no 1, January 1976.
3   E Max Nicholson. Quoted in Jon Tinker (1976) op cit Note 17.
4   Duncan Poore. Discussion with MWH, 20 February 1998, and notes on IUCN, 1976, sent as a basis for that discussion.
5   Donald J Kuenen. Memorandum to Executive Board,12 November 1975, setting out his analysis of the events in Kinshasa. Copy supplied to MWH by Professor M Kassas.
6   Minutes, IUCN Executive Board, fifty-eighth session, Morges, 13–15 May 1976. In IUCN archives.
7   Minutes, IUCN Executive Committee, twenty-second meeting, Morges, 31 January–1 February 1976. In IUCN archives.
8   Raymond F Dasmann (1998) Letter to MWH,17 January and draft chapter of unpublished autobiography kindly supplied with that letter.
9   Charles de Haes (1998) Telephone conversations with MWH on 24 and 31 July and detailed comments on the near-final text of this book.
10 Minutes, first meeting of the IUCN Management and Finance Committee, Morges, 17–18 January 1976. In IUCN archives.
11 Tony Mence. Written comments on draft texts and discussion with MWH on 3 February 1998. At the time of the imposed pay cuts in 1976, Tony Mence wrote a poem entitled 'The Brush-Off' which is of historical interest as it shows the inter-organizational bitterness of the period. These verses were read to the staff of IUCN at coffee break shortly after 'Black Friday' when they had been forced to agree to salary cuts or be sacked. Some of the words would not be used today, but the verses should be read in the context of their time. Tony Mence retains the copyright of these verses, which appear here with his permission.
    'Tell me', said the young man, bright and starry eyed
    'What is conservation, and how is it applied?'
    We told him that it's something that keeps the world alive,
    Maintaining its diversity and capacity to thrive
    We told him that it's something affecting everyone
    And that we develop strategies whereby it can be done
    He thanked us most politely and bade us all good day,
    Picking up his haversack and going on his way

He went, in fact, to WWF[1] and asked when let inside
'What is conservation, and how is it applied?'
They looked on him with pity, as on the blind or deaf,
'The aim of conservation is – promoting WWF!
And as to how we do it, that obviously depends
On the thickness of your wallet and the status of your friends!
Conservation's not for commoners and as you'll soon be shown
We've Ambassadors and Admirals for keeping up the tone.'
'D'you deal in oil or chemicals? or do you own a bank?
Have you got a title? – or other kind of rank?
If so, we'll have the pleasure – when your pedigree's explored -
Of appointing you to office as a member of our Board,
And you can have the privilege – every now and then
Of confounding dangerous heresies put out by IUCN[2]
To counteract suspicion that our influence derives
From raping the environment or wedding wealthy wives!'

'Are you a social climber? Perhaps you have a yen
To occupy a station above your fellow men?
To associate with Princes? and Rockefellers too?
And have the most respected names pass time of day with you?
We offer you the answer – ten thousand dollar sub –
Then come right in and join us, and welcome to the club!
And when you've got your membership, we'll tell you right away
Our views of conservation – whatever you may say!'

'Or if your means are modest, you assist us quite a lot
By buying model monsters designed by Peter Scott[3]
To help us purchase Landrovers – perhaps some Unimogs
With Panda stickers on them to distribute to the wogs;
Pretending that we're helping them, but if they only knew
We make them sign agreements that tell them what to do
Our lack of understanding doesn't worry us a bit,
We've struck a blow for WWF and scored another hit!'

'Thank you' said the young man, wise and narrow-eyed
'For explaining conservation, and how it is applied
Reposing in my haversack is everything I've got –
So just let me have a monster designed by Peter Scott
Until I've made my fortune and can reap my due reward
Of a handle to my surname and a seat upon your Board
And let me have some stickers, for these can be the means
Of maintaining full diversity among my pairs of jeans!

[1] 'WWF' must be pronounced in the French manner 'vay vay eff' in order to scan!
[2] 'IUCN' must similarly be pronounced 'wee see en'!
[3] Peter Scott had been convinced by underwater photographs taken by an American investigator, Dr Rines, that there was some large creature lurking in the depths of Loch Ness in Scotland. One frame of the film appeared to show a diamond-shaped (rhomboid) flipper. Scott and Rines gave the legendary monster a scientific name, *Nessiteras rhombopteryx*, or 'Ness Monster with rhomboid paddles'. There was immense scepticism in the scientific world, especially as no new and convincing photographs were forthcoming and the position was not eased when some wag discovered that the name was an anagram of 'monster hoax by Sir Peter S'. Though he acted in all sincerity, the episode undoubtedly undermined Peter Scott's credibility in the scientific world.

12 Luc Hoffmann (1998) Letter to MWH, 14 August.
13 Raymond F Dasmann (1976) Letter to Lee Talbot,12 February 1976; copy provided to MWH by Dr Lee Talbot.
14 Gerardo Budowski (1976) Note, January 1976, entitled 'My future position in Latin America'. In papers supplied to MWH by Professor M Kassas.
15 Donald J Kuenen (1976) Memorandum to the Executive Board, 2 February. Copy supplied to MWH by Professor M Kassas.
16 Duncan Poore (1975) Letter to Professor Donald Kuenen, 26 November. In: Poore's possession.
17 Jon Tinker (1976) IUCN: crisis and opportunity. *New Scientist*, 13 May, pp 349–350.
18 Ursula Hiltbrunner. Discussion with MWH, June 1997.
19 Françoise Burhenne-Guilmin (1977) Letter to Sir Hugh Elliott, 7 November, describing the history of the Convention on Migratory Species.
20 For 1976–77, WWF agreed to pay a regular subvention of SFr900,000, and promised an additional SFr200,000 and help in raising as much again, if IUCN would make economies of SFr300,000. In fact it paid more than had been promised: the 1976 support for core and IUCN programmes exceeded SFr2 million (information from Claude Martin: Note 45).
21 Between October 1976 and February 1977 there was a running debate over the adequacy of IUCN staff salaries, and the comparisons to be used to fix them. In February 1977 it was agreed that the scales based on the UN should be replaced by new ones tied to the Swiss Civil Service. The Swiss Federal Office of Personnel evaluated the posts in IUCN and the Extraordinary General Assembly approved the new scales, which were applied from 1 January 1977. WWF decided to apply the IUCN criteria to its own staff where practicable.
    WWF agreed to pay for: professional review of projects proposed to WWF; scientific monitoring of projects included in the WWF conservation programme; further development of the WWF marine programme, 1977–78; preparation of the WWF conservation programme, 1977–78 within the scope of IUCN's global conservation plans and programme; provision of scientific advice to WWF on critical conservation issues as they arose. There was also to be discussion of work on environmental education and to evaluate the effectiveness of selected projects that had already been completed (Note 23).
22 Minutes, IUCN Executive Committee, twenty-fourth meeting, Morges, 9–11 February 1997. In IUCN archives.
23 Memorandum from the Staff Liaison Committee to Professor Donald Kuenen, 2 July 1976. In IUCN archives.
24 Minutes, IUCN Executive Committee, twenty-third meeting, Morges, 7–8 October 1976. In IUCN archives.
25 Minutes, IUCN Executive Board, fifty-ninth, sixtieth and first sessions and IUCN Council, first session, WHO, Geneva, 18 and 22 April 1977. In IUCN archives.
26 Charles de Haes. Discussion with MWH,10 March 1998.
27 Jeffrey A McNeely (1997) Letter to MWH, 23 October.
28 Mohamed Kassas (1977) Letter to Professor Donald Kuenen,10 January. Copy supplied to MWH by Professor M Kassas.
29 Donald J Kuenen (1976) Confidential memorandum to Executive Committee and search committee for DG, 27 September. Copy supplied to MWH by Professor M Kassas.
30 Mohamed Kassas (1976) Letter to Professor Donald Kuenen, 23 November. Copy supplied to MWH by Professor M Kassas.
31 Lee M Talbot (1977) Letter to Professor Donald Kuenen, 8 February, declining consideration for the post of Director-General. Copy supplied to MWH by Professor M Kassas.
32 Don McMichael (1998) Letter to David McDowell, 29 June, with comments on the near-final text of this book.
33 Michael J Cockerell (1998) Letter to MWH,14 January.
34 Duncan Poore (1977) Presentation of progress report. In: *Proceedings of the Thirteenth (Extraordinary) General Assembly, Geneva, Switzerland, 19–21 April 1977*. Morges: IUCN.

35   Duncan Poore (1977) International Union for Conservation of Nature and Natural Resources: a dynamic strategy. *Environmental Conservation*, 1977, pp 119–120.

36   Donald Kuenen. Transcript of part of speech as President at the Extraordinary General Assembly of IUCN in April 1977. In the possession of Duncan Poore.

37   Maurice Strong (1998) Letter to David McDowell, 26 July 1998.

38   Maurice Strong (1977) Memorandum to Duncan Poore, 2 May. In the possession of Duncan Poore.

39   Minutes, IUCN Bureau; open first session, Morges, 31 May 1977. In IUCN archives.

40   Minutes IUCN Bureau, third meeting, Morges, 10–11 February 1978. In IUCN archives.

41   David Munro. Conversation with MWH, 20 March 1998.

42   Duncan Poore (1998) Letter to MWH, 20 June, with commentary on the near-final text of this book.

43   Jon Tinker (1978) Comment: IUCN and the Third World. *New Scientist*, 12 October 1978.

44   Reuben Olembo (1998). Letter to MWH, 9 April.

45   Claude Martin (1998) Letter to David McDowell, 24 June, with comments on near-final text of this book, and including details of WWF payments to IUCN.

46   David Munro. Report of the Director-General on the work of the Union since the Thirteenth Extraordinary General Assembly. Proceedings of the Fourteenth IUCN General Assembly, Ashkhabad, 1978.

47   Jeffrey A McNeely. Conversation with MWH, 30 May 1997.

48   Fiona Hanson. Note dated 27 February 1998 with table and figure of North–South balance in voting membership of the IUCN Executive Board/Council.

49   Eskandar Firouz (1998) Letter to MWH,12 April.

50   Michel Batisse (1998) Commentary on draft text, supplied under cover of a letter to MWH, 13 March.

51   Robert Prescott-Allen. Telephone conversation with MWH in July 1997 and lengthy discussion on 19 March 1998.

52   Minutes, IUCN Council, third meeting, Ashkhabad, USSR, 26 September, 28 September and 3 October 1978. In IUCN archives.

53   Lee M Talbot (1998) Detailed written commentary and discussion with MWH,18 March. Commentary in IUCN archives.

54   Hal Eidsvik. Discussions with MWH, 22–23 March 1988.

55   Kenton R Miller. Discussion with MWH,17 March 1998.

56   Kenton R Miller (1998) Letter to David McDowell, 24 June, with comments on near-final draft of this book.

57   Walter Lusigi. Discussion with MWH, 28 March 1998.

58   Marc Dourojeanni (1998) Letter to MWH, 8 April, and comments,18 June.

59   IUCN statement on the draft text of the proposed convention submitted to the 1977 session of the Third UN Conference on the Law of the Sea.

60   Meeting of Commission Chairmen and Deputy Chairmen, Morges, 31 January– 2 February 1978. Copy made available by Duncan Poore.

61   Jan Cerovsky (1977) Brief notes from the history of the IUCN Commission on Education. Note dated 5 April 1977. In IUCN files. The files also contain an anonymous paper, 'IUCN–CEC Historical Notes'.

62   Minutes, IUCN Bureau, sixth meeting, Morges, 12–13 March 1979.

63   Minutes, IUCN Council, fifth meeting, Morges, 25–27 June 1979. In IUCN archives.

64   Minutes, IUCN Council, sixth meeting, Gland, 5–7 November 1979. In IUCN archives.

65   Talbot, Lee M (1981) *Achievements, 1978–1981*. Report of the Director-General to the Fifteenth Session of the IUCN General Assembly, Christchurch, New Zealand, October 1981. Gland: IUCN.

66   Commission on Ecology. Report to the 1978 Session of the General Assembly. Paper GA78/18. In IUCN archives.

67   Hugh Synge (1987) *The History of TPC and TPU, 1970–1986*. IUCN Threatened Plants Unit. Copy supplied to MWH by the author.

68   Minutes, IUCN Council, seventh meeting, Gland, 27–28 July 1980. In IUCN archives.

69   Kenton Miller (1998) Letter to MWH, 2 February, with detailed historical commentary.

70 Minutes, IUCN Council, eighth meeting, Gland, 10–12 November 1980. In IUCN archives.
71 International Council on Environmental Law. Brochure published by the Office of the Council, Adenauerallee 214, D–53113, Bonn, Germany.
72 Minutes, IUCN Bureau, fifth meeting, Morges, 7–8 November 1978. In IUCN archives.
73 Minutes, IUCN Council, second meeting, Morges, May 4–6 1978. In IUCN archives.
74 IUCN/WWF (1979) Shared Headquarters. Note in *Environmental Conservation*, p 110.
75 Minutes, IUCN Bureau, tenth meeting, Gland, 15 March 1980. In IUCN archives.
76 Richard J Herring (1981) Memorandum to members of IUCN Council, 29 May. Copy made available to MWH by Dr David Munro.
77 Burhenne, Wolfgang E and Irwin, Will A (1986) *The World Charter for Nature. La Charte Mondiale de la Nature. Part I: Legislative History. Part II: Commentary.* 2nd revised edition, May 1986. Berlin: Erich Schmidt Verlag.
78 Scott, Peter (Ed) (1965) *The Launching of the New Ark. First Report of the World Wildlife Fund.* London: Collins.
79 Mike McCloskey (1998) Letter to MWH, 2 July, with comments on the near-final text of this book.
80 Fiona Hanson. Interview with MWH on 30 May 1997.
81 The Elizabeth Haub Foundation for Environmental Law and Policy is a charitable (not for profit) foundation established in Germany, the USA and Canada.
82 Mohamed Kassas (1997) Letter to MWH, 22 June.
83 Robert Prescott-Allen (1998) Letter to David McDowell and Martin Holdgate,15 July, with comments on the near-final text of this book.
84 Minutes, IUCN Council, fourth meeting, Ashkhabad, USSR, 5 October 1978. In IUCN archives.
85 IUCN (1980) *World Conservation Strategy. Living Resource Conservation for Sustainable Development.* Gland, Switzerland: IUCN.
86 David A Munro (1979) Guest editorial: towards a world strategy for conservation. *Environmental Conservation*, vol 6, no 3, pp 169–170.
87 Talbot, Lee M (1980) The world's conservation strategy. *Environmental Conservation*, vol. 7, no 4, pp 259–268.
88 O M El-Tayeb (1979) Internal memorandum to R Olembo, 30 March, entitled 'Comments by evaluation consultants on World Conservation Strategy', UNEP. Copy supplied to MWH by Robert Prescott-Allen.
89 M D Gwynne (1979) Internal memorandum to Mona Bjorklund, 23 April,entitled 'Decision-maker's pack – World Conservation Strategy', UNEP. Copy supplied to MWH by Robert Prescott-Allen.
90 World Commission on Environment and Development (1987) *Our Common Future.* Oxford: Oxford University Press.
91 Minutes, first meeting of the Technical Advisory Committee on World Conservation Strategy II, Washington DC, 29–30 October 1987. IUCN/UNEP/WWF.
92 Guha, Ramachandra (1997) The authoritarian biologist and the arrogance of anti-humanism. Wildlife conservation in the Third World. *The Ecologist*, vol 27, no 1, pp 14–20.
93 Waldheim, Kurt (1980) Statement on the occasion of the launching of the World Conservation Strategy on 5 March 1980. New York, Office of the Secretary General.
94 Minutes, IUCN Bureau, tenth meeting, Gland, 15 March 1980. In IUCN archives.
95 Independent Commission on Development Issues (the Brandt Commission) (1980) *North–South: a Programme for Survival.* Cambridge, Mass: MIT Press.

Chapter 8: After the Strategy

1 Talbot, Lee M (1981) *Achievements, 1978–1981.* Report of the Director-General to the Fifteenth Session of the IUCN General Assembly, Christchurch, New Zealand, October 1981. Gland: IUCN.

2   Munro, David A (1979) Guest editorial. *Environmental Conservation*, vol 6, no 3, pp 169–170.
3   Jeffrey McNeely (1988) Letter to MWH, 27 March.
4   Conservation for Development Centre. Perspective Paper, April 1983. Paper CDC-MJC/MH/eef/ek/8/4/820026v. Document supplied to MWH by M J Cockerell.
5   Michael J Cockerell. Discussion with MWH,18 February 1998.
6   Marshall Robinson (Vice-President of the Ford Foundation). Letter to Maurice Strong, 24 April 1978.
7   Conservation and Development. Council Paper UC78/53, November 1978. Referred to and quoted, op cit Note 4.
8   Mark Halle. Interview with MWH, 30 May 1997.
9   Michael J Cockerell (1998) Letter to MWH, 14 January.
10   Charles de Haes. Discussion with MWH,10 March 1998.
11   Minutes, IUCN Bureau, tenth meeting, Gland, 15 March 1980. In IUCN archives.
12   Minutes, IUCN Bureau, fifth meeting, Morges, 7–8 November 1978. In IUCN archives.
13   Minutes, IUCN Bureau, sixth meeting, Morges, 12–13 March 1979. Percy H C Lucas, a distinguished New Zealand conservationist, is known as 'Bing' because as a young man (and Bing Crosby enthusiast) he was compère of a local radio show entitled 'Swing with Bing'.
14   Lee M Talbot (1998) Detailed written commentary and discussion with MWH,18 March.
15   Minutes, IUCN Council, ninth meeting, Gland, 8–10 June 1981. In IUCN archives.
16   de Mattos Shipley, H, Lyons, J, Belsham, C, Harding, D and Johnston, M (Eds) (1996) *WWF. Changing Worlds. 35 Years of Conservation Achievement.* London: Banson for WWF.
17   Minutes, IUCN Council, sixth meeting, Gland, 5–7 November 1979. In IUCN archives.
18   Antarctic and Southern Ocean Coalition. Papers prepared as input to negotiations of Convention on the Conservation of Antarctic Marine Living Resources.
19   David Munro. Conversation with MWH, 20 March 1998.
20   Minutes, IUCN Council, seventh meeting, Gland, 27–28 July 1980. In IUCN archives. NGOs of the Western kind did not exist in China. The Society for Environmental Sciences, although headed by a government member, was an informal body and provided a 'non-governmental' way for China to have relationships with IUCN when it did not want State or government agency membership.
21   Tony Mence (1998) Written comments on draft texts and discussion with MWH, 3 February.
22   Minutes, IUCN Council, fifth meeting, Morges, 25–27 June 1979. In IUCN archives.
23   Michael McCloskey. Discussion with MWH,19 March 1998.
24   Minutes, IUCN Executive Committee, twenty-third meeting, Morges, 7–8 October 1976. In IUCN archives.
25   Minutes, IUCN Council, second meeting, Morges, May 4–6 1978. In IUCN archives.
26   Humphreys, D (1996) *Forest Politics. The Evolution of International Cooperation.* London: Earthscan.
27   United Nations Economic and Social Council (1997) Report of the Intergovernmental Panel on Forests on its Fourth Session, New York, 11–21 February 1997. Document E/CN17/1997/12, 20 March.
28   The Agreed Measures for the Conservation of Antarctic Fauna and Flora became effective in July 1966. Texts are printed in the *SCAR Manual,* second edition (1972) Cambridge (UK): Scott Polar Research Institute.
29   Robert E Boote. Note supplied to MWH together with his report on the Canberra Conference on Antarctic Marine Living Resources and copies of his statements at that conference on behalf of IUCN.
30   Robert E Boote. Telephone conversation with MWH on 12 January 1998.
31   Robert E Boote. Conference on Antarctic Marine Living Resources, Canberra, 7–20 May 1980. Information note to Council. Copy supplied to MWH by Robert Boote on 19 February 1998. (Note: In the paper and others of this period Boote's initials are cited as R A and one paper gives his full name as Robert Arvill Boote. This deliberate error was made because he had recently published a successful paperback on *Man and Environment* under the pen-name Robert Arvill.)

32 Minutes, IUCN Council, eighth meeting, Gland, 10–12 November 1980. In IUCN archives.
33 Minutes, IUCN Bureau, fourth meeting, Morges, 4 May 1978. In IUCN archives.
34 A dossier of papers loaned to MWH by Professor Mohamed Kassas includes strong letters of support for Lee Talbot from WWF–US, the New York Zoological Society, the Natural Resources Defense Council and the African Wildlife Leadership Foundation. He was also supported by Peter Scott.
35 Wolfgang Burhenne and Françoise Burhenne-Guilmin. Discussion with MWH on 16 February 1998.
36 Hal Eidsvik. Discussion with MWH on 23 March 1998. Hal Eidsvik was elected to IUCN Council at Christchurch in 1981, a year after stepping down as Executive Officer for CNPPA.
37 Adrian Phillips. Discussion with MWH on 5 February 1998.
38 Minutes, IUCN Bureau, eleventh meeting, Gland, 10 October 1980. In IUCN archives.
39 Adrian Phillips. Memorandum entitled 'The events of 14 and 17 November 1980' and written at the time. Copy given to MWH by Professor Phillips on 5 February 1998.
40 Richard J Herring (1981) Memorandum to members of IUCN Council, 29 May 1981. Copy made available to MWH by Dr David Munro.
41 Charles de Haes (1998) Detailed commentary on the near-final text of this book, sent to MWH over the period 31 July–3 August 1998.
42 Richard J Herring. Manuscript notes among papers supplied to MWH by Dr David Munro.
43 Lee M Talbot (1981) Letter to Adrian Phillips,10 July. Copy supplied by Professor Adrian Phillips. The letter also explains Lee Talbot's efforts to find a new appointment for the African member of staff, John Kundaeli.
44 Minutes, IUCN Bureau, twelfth meeting, Gland, 24 July 1981. In IUCN archives.
45 Estelle F Viguet. Conversation with MWH, 29 May 1997.
46 E O A Asibey (1981) Letter to Dr Lee Talbot, 27 July. Copy made available to MWH by Professor M Kassas.
47 Minutes, IUCN Bureau, fourteenth meeting, London, 11–12 June 1982. In IUCN archives.
48 Minutes, IUCN Council, tenth meeting, Christchurch, New Zealand, 12–22 October 1981. In IUCN archives.
49 Claude Martin (1998) Letter to David McDowell, 24 June, with details of WWF's financial contributions to IUCN.
50 Michael J Cockerell (1998) Letter to MWH, 22 June, with detailed comments on the near-final text of this book.
51 Miller, Kenton R (1984) Report of the Director-General to the Sixteenth Session of the IUCN General Assembly, Madrid, November 1984.
52 Mence, Tony (1981) *IUCN: How it Began, How it is Growing Up.* IUCN (presented to the General Assembly in Christchurch, New Zealand).
53 Letter from Tony Mence to MWH dated 4 July 1997 explaining the background to the history of IUCN produced in 1981, op cit Note 52.
54 Mohamed Kassas (1983) Conservation NGOs. Memorandum to IUCN Councillors,10 July. Copy kindly made available to MWH by Professor M Kassas.
55 Percy H C 'Bing' Lucas (1997) Note to MWH.
56 Resolution 15/20. Antarctica Environment and the Southern Ocean. Adopted at the Fifteenth Session of the IUCN General Assembly, Christchurch, New Zealand, 11–23 October 1981. This resolution speaks of the 'Antarctica Environment', which is a curious confusion of terms. 'Antarctica' normally means the continental land mass, while 'the Antarctic' is the wider region. Wolfgang Burhenne[35] states that the wording was chosen to make the resolution applicable to the whole region and not just the Antarctic Continent and the adjacent seas south of 60 degrees South (the Antarctic Treaty area). If interpreted literally, it has the contrary effect.
57 IUCN (1990) *A Strategy for Antarctic Conservation.* Gland, Switzerland and Cambridge UK: IUCN.
58 F van Rijkevorsel (1981) Statement to the 11th meeting of the IUCN Council, Christchurch, New Zealand, 23 October. In IUCN Archives.

59   Minutes, IUCN Council, twelfth meeting, Gland, 23–26 November 1982. In IUCN archives.

60   Minutes, IUCN Bureau, thirteenth meeting, Gland, 18–19 January 1982. In IUCN archives.

61   Boote, Robert E. Draft paper on Review of Structure and Funding of IUCN, for discussion at January 1982 Bureau meeting. In IUCN archives.

62   Minutes of the sixteenth meeting of the IUCN Bureau, Gland, 22–23 June 1983. In IUCN archives.

63   Minutes, IUCN Council, eighteenth meeting, Gland, 15–16 May 1985. In IUCN archives.

64   Minutes, IUCN Council, nineteenth meeting, Gland, 14–15 November 1985. In IUCN archives.

65   Summary record, IUCN Bureau, nineteenth meeting, Prangins, 13 November 1985. In IUCN archives.

66   Minutes, IUCN Bureau, fifteenth meeting, Gland, 20 January 1983. In IUCN archives.

67   Minutes, IUCN Bureau, eighteenth meeting, Gland, 2 October 1984. In IUCN archives.

68   Kenton Miller (1998) Letter to MWH, 2 February, with detailed historical commentary.

69   McNeely, J A and Miller, K R (Eds) (1984) *National Parks, Conservation and Development.* Washington DC: Smithsonian Institution Press. This volume reports on the Third World Conference on National Parks and Protected Areas, Bali, 1982.

70   David Sheppard (1998) Note to MWH, 25 March.

71   Michel Batisse (1998) Letter to MWH, 24 June, with detailed comments on the near-final text of this book.

72   Walter Lusigi. Discussion with MWH,18 March 1998.

73   Genetic Resources. Recommendation 15/10. *Resolutions and Recommendations of the 15th Session of the IUCN General Assembly, Christchurch, New Zealand, October 1981.* The Recommendation called for a study that might provide the basis of an international arrangement for the conservation of genetic resources. Cyrille de Klemm was doubtless aware of that text when he spoke in Bali.

74   Recommendation 19/38. Targets for Protected Areas Systems. *Resolutions and Recommendations of the 19th Session of the General Assembly of IUCN – The World Conservation Union, Buenos Aires, Argentina, 17–26 January 1994.* Gland: IUCN. The Fourth Congress, held in Caracas, Venezuela in 1982 had urged that protected areas should cover a minimum of 10 per cent of each biome by the year 2000. The Buenos Aires recommendation repeated that call and urged governments to protect substantial percentages of the major natural regions or biomes and their plant and animal communities within their territories.

75   Mohamed Kassas (1981) Letter to HRH Prince Philip, Duke of Edinburgh, December, inviting him to become a coopted member of IUCN Council and a Vice-President. Copy made available to MWH by Professor M Kassas.

76   HRH Prince Philip, Duke of Edinburgh. Conversation with MWH on 24 July 1997.

77   Minutes, IUCN Council, twentieth session, Ottawa, 7–8 June 1986. In IUCN archives.

78   Maurice Strong (1982) Letter and memorandum to Charles de Haes and Lee Talbot, 13 July. Copy made available to MWH by Professor M Kassas.

79   Harold Jefferson Coolidge (1981) Letter to Mohamed Kassas, 2 December. Copy made available to MWH by Professor M Kassas.

80   Mark Halle (1997) Letter to MWH, 6 October.

81   Dietrich von Hegel (1982) Letter to Lee Talbot, 4 February. Made available to MWH by Professor M Kassas.

82   Conrad von Ulm-Erbach. Confidential memorandum regarding his criticisms of Dr Lee Talbot and detailing the steps leading to the latter's resignation. In the possession of the IUCN Director-General.

83   Mohamed Kassas (1998) Letter to MWH,17 April, and telephone commentary on 24 April.

84   Lee M Talbot. Commentary to MWH, 24 June 1998.

85   The Hon Russell Train. Discussion with MWH,18 March 1998.

86   Kenton Miller. Discussion with MWH,17 March 1998.

87   Kenton Miller (1998) Letter to David McDowell, 24 June, with comments on the near-final draft of this book.
88   Robert E Boote (1998) Discussion with MWH,19 February, and letter to David McDowell,15 June.
89   Kenton Miller (1983) Letter to Mohamed Kassas,11 March, detailing arrangements for the interregnum between his appointment as Director-General and his arrival to take up the post. Copy made available to MWH by Professor M Kassas.
90   Minutes, IUCN Council, thirteenth meeting, Gland, 8–11 November 1983. In IUCN archives.

Chapter 9: Conservation for Development

1   Tolba, M K, Ek Kholy, O, El Hinnawi, E, Holdgate, M W, McMichael, D F and Munn, R E (Eds). *The World Environment, 1972–1992.* London: Chapman and Hall.
2   World Commission on Environment and Development (1987) *Our Common Future.* Oxford: Oxford University Press.
3   Minutes, IUCN Bureau, seventeenth meeting, Gland, 15 February 1984. In IUCN archives.
4   *Implementing the World Conservation Strategy.* IUCN's Conservation Programme, 1985–1987. IUCN Programme Series No 1/1985. Gland: IUCN.
5   Minutes, IUCN Council, seventeenth meeting, Madrid, 15 November 1984. In IUCN archives.
6   Minutes, IUCN Council, fourteenth meeting, closed session, Gland, 6–8 June 1984. In IUCN archives.
7   Monkombu Swaminathan (1998) Letter to David McDowell, 25 June, commenting on near-final text of this book.
8   Talbot, Lee M (1981) *Achievements, 1978–1981.* Report of the Director-General, IUCN Fifteenth General Assembly, Christchurch, New Zealand, October 1981. Gland: IUCN.
9   Michael J Cockerell (1998) Letter to MWH,14 January.
10   Conservation for Development Centre (1983) Perspective paper, April. Paper CDC-MJC/MH/eef/ek/8/4/820026v. Document supplied to MWH by M J Cockerell.
11   Minutes, IUCN Council, fifth meeting, Morges, 25–27 June 1979. In IUCN archives.
12   Kenton Miller. Letter to MWH dated 2 February 1998, with detailed commentary on draft of this book.
13   Michael J Cockerell. Discussion with MWH,18 February 1998.
14   Maurice Strong (1982) Letter and memorandum to Charles de Haes and Lee Talbot dated 13 July. Copy made available to MWH by Professor M Kassas.
15   Michael J Cockerell (1981) Memo to Commission Executive Officers/Regional Officers/Project Management, 18 June. Supplied to MWH by M J Cockerell.
16   Michael J Cockerell (1998) Letter to MWH, 22 June, with detailed comments on near-final text of this book.
17   Jacobs, P and Munro, D A (Eds) (1987) *Conservation with Equity: Strategies for Sustainable Development. Proceedings of the Conference on Conservation and Development: Implementing the World Conservation Strategy.* Gland, Switzerland and Cambridge, UK: IUCN.
18   Government of Pakistan (1992) *The Pakistan National Conservation Strategy.* Karachi: Environment and Urban Affairs Division, Government of Pakistan and IUCN–Pakistan.
19   Nature Conservancy Council UK (1981) *Earth's Survival. A Conservation and Development Programme for the UK.* London: The Nature Conservancy Council.
20   Barney, G O (Programme Director) (1980) *The Global 2000 Report to the President.* Washington DC: US Government Printing Office, O–256–752.
21   Miller, Kenton R (1987) *Director General's Report on the Work of the Union since the 16th Session of the IUCN General Assembly Held in Madrid*, November 1984. Gland: IUCN.
22   Aban Marker Kabraji (1993) What can IUCN deliver? In: Holdgate, M and Synge, H (Eds) *The Future of IUCN.* Gland, Switzerland and Cambridge, UK: IUCN.

23   Lee M Talbot. Commentary to MWH, 24 June 1998.
24   Mersie Ejigu (former Director of Central Planning, Ethiopia). Discussion with MWH on 18 March 1998.
25   Miller, Kenton R (1984) *Report of the Director General to the Sixteenth Session of the IUCN General Assembly, Madrid*, November 1984.
26   Minutes, IUCN Bureau, fourteenth meeting, London, 11–12 June 1982. In IUCN archives.
27   Proposal for the establishment of a Regional Conservation for Development Centre in Zimbabwe. Annex 3 to op cit Note 10.
28   Minutes, IUCN Bureau, thirteenth meeting, Gland, 18–19 January 1982. In IUCN archives.
29   Per Ryden. Interview with MWH, 30 May 1997.
30   Tony Mence. Discussion with MWH, 3 February 1998.
31   Mohamed Kassas (1982) Letter to all IUCN Commission Chairmen dated 15 July 1982. Copy made available to MWH by Professor M Kassas.
32   Hal Eidsvik (1998) Letter to MWH dated 28 January.
33   Marc Dourojeanni (1998) Letter to MWH, 8 April.
34   Holdgate, M W, Kassas, M and White, G F (1982) *The World Environment, 1972–1982.* Dublin: Tycooly International for UNEP.
35   UNEP (1987) *Environmental Perspective to the Year 2000 and Beyond.* Nairobi: UNEP.
36   Minutes, IUCN Council, thirteenth meeting, Gland, 8–11 November 1983. In IUCN archives.
37   Hal Eidsvik. Discussion with MWH, 23 March 1998. Hal Eidsvik was elected to IUCN Council at Christchurch in 1981, a year after stepping down as Executive Officer for CNPPA.
38   Minutes, IUCN Council, nineteenth meeting, Gland, 14–15 November 1985. In IUCN archives.
39   Minutes, IUCN Bureau, twenty-first meeting, Gland, 10–11 November 1986. In IUCN archives.
40   IUCN/UNEP/WWF (1991) *Caring for the Earth, A Strategy for Sustainable Living.* Gland, Switzerland: IUCN, UNEP and WWF.
41   Monkombu Swaminathan. Address to the Ottawa Conference on Conservation and Development. In Jacobs, P and Munro, D A op cit Note 17.
42   McNeely, J A and Miller, K R (Eds) (1984) *National Parks, Conservation and Development.* Washington DC: Smithsonian Institution Press. This volume reports on the Third World Conference on National Parks and Protected Areas, Bali, 1982.
43   Kenton Miller. Discussion with MWH, 17 March 1998.
44   Minutes, IUCN Bureau, fifteenth meeting, Gland, 20 January 1983. In IUCN archives.
45   IUCN-CEC historical notes. Document in IUCN archives.
46   Mohamed Kassas (1983) Letter to Dr Al Baez, 24 June. Copy made available to MWH by Professor M Kassas.
47   Harold J Coolidge (1983) Letter to Dr Albert V Baez, 5 October. Copy made available to MWH by Professor M Kassas.
48   Albert V Baez (1983) Letter to Kenton Miller, 3 October. Copy made available to MWH by Professor M Kassas.
49   Albert V Baez (1983) Letter to Kenton Miller, 17 August. Copy made available to MWH by Professor M Kassas.
50   Mohan Mathews, World Secretary – International Youth Federation. Letter to Professor Mohamed Kassas, 18 September 1983. Copy made available to MWH by Professor M Kassas.
51   Report of the working group to establish a task force to review IUCN's work with respect to influencing government policy. Annex 4 to the minutes of the seventeenth meeting of the IUCN Council, Madrid, 15 November 1984.
52   Mike McCloskey (1998) Letter to MWH, 2 July, with comments on near-final text of this book.
53   World Resources Institute and others. *World Resources* (volumes produced in 1986, 1987 and then biennially by WRI with a range of partner organizations, not including IUCN).

54 Minutes, IUCN Council, eighteenth meeting, Gland, 15–16 May 1985. In IUCN archives.
55 Wolfgang Burhenne. Discussion with MWH, 16–17 February 1998.
56 IUCN (1991) *A Strategy for Antarctic Conservation.* Gland, Switzerland and Cambridge, UK: IUCN.
57 IUCN (1989) The Sahel: out of the myths. Special report, *IUCN Bulletin*, vol 20, 7–9, pp 16–29.
58 Lee M Talbot (1998) Detailed written commentary and discussion with MWH,18 March.
59 Robert E Boote. Discussion with MWH,19 February 1998.
60 E M Nicholson (1980) Letter to R E Boote, 30 December 1980. Copy supplied to MWH by R E Boote.
61 Note of a special meeting for the General Assembly group on 14 January 1981. Copy supplied to MWH by R E Boote.
62 Minutes, IUCN Council, twentieth meeting, Ottawa, 7–8 June 1986. In IUCN archives.
63 Minutes, IUCN Council, twenty-first meeting, Gland, 6–8 May 1987. In IUCN archives.
64 Harold J Coolidge (1983) Letter to Mohamed Kassas,1 September. Copy made available to MWH by Professor M Kassas.
65 Mohamed Kassas (1983) Conservation NGOs. Memorandum to IUCN Councillors,10 July. Copy made available to MWH by Professor M Kassas.
66 IUCN (1990) *Triennial Report. The Work of the Union since the 17th Session of the General Assembly Held in San Jose, Costa Rica, in February 1988.* Gland: IUCN.
67 Delmar Blasco. Conversation with MWH, 30 May 1997.
68 Minutes, IUCN Bureau, sixteenth meeting, Gland, 22–23 June 1983. In IUCN archives. The annex is a decision of Council in closed session on 8–10 June 1981 recording the intention to apply 'United Nations rules' to the hosting of sessions of the General Assembly.
69 Minutes, IUCN Bureau, twentieth meeting, Ottawa, 4 June 1986. In IUCN archives.
70 Minutes, IUCN Council, fifteenth meeting, Madrid, 5 and 13 November 1984. In IUCN archives.
71 Michael J Cockerell (1998) Letter to MWH, 21 February.
72 The Hon Russell Train. Discussion with MWH,18 March 1998.
73 Mark Halle. Interview with MWH, 30 May 1997.
74 Claude Martin (1998) Letter to David McDowell, 24 June, with comments on the near-final text of this book and details of WWF financial support to IUCN.
75 Leonard Hentsch's predecessor, Dietrich von Hegel, the WWF Treasurers, Louis Franck and John Nash, and the Finance Director, Conrad von Ulm-Erbach seem to have worked in close harmony. The main friction had been over how IUCN used the money passed to them by WWF (HRH The Duke of Edinburgh, as reported by his Private Secretary, Brigadier Miles Hunt-Davis, in a letter to MWH, 2 July 1998). However, Leonard Hentsch clearly took a more challenging line. He had antagonized Prince Bernhard by demanding a statement accounting for the use of his first contribution to the WWF '1001' Trust (Kenton Miller[43]). Reports of confrontation between Prince Philip and Leonard Hentsch were current 'in the corridors' of the IUCN General Assembly in Costa Rica in February 1988, although Prince Philip, in discussion with MWH on 25 July 1997, said that he did not recall this. However he did feel that Hentsch's 'uncompromising attitude' made the situation more difficult.
76 WWF accepted that these changes in financial services were prudent. In May 1987 Luc Hoffmann stressed that the Fund still looked on itself as IUCN's closest partner, and suggested that the problems that had arisen had been '*due to the fact that both organizations were expanding their activities*'.[63] Claude Martin, Charles de Haes' successor, accepts that by 1986 '*the joint services didn't really serve IUCN*' (discussion with MWH, 4 December 1997). Curtis 'Buff' Bohlen, who was Financial Comptroller for WWF–US and attended IUCN Councils as an observer for WWF, also criticized the joint financial services in discussion with MWH on 19 March 1998. Christine Buhler, who joined the Common Services as Assistant Personnel Officer in 1984 noted that the IUCN administrative procedures were poor and the joint services with WWF were inefficient (discussion with MWH, 29 May 1997). Per Ryden, who came from SIDA to run the Sahel programme in 1987 was also surprised to find IUCN less efficient than he had expected (interview with MWH, 30 May 1997).

77   Kenton Miller (1986) Letter to Lee M Talbot, April. Copy supplied to MWH by Dr Talbot.
78   Status of IUCN, June 1987. Memo from Mike Cockerell to Kenton Miller, 2 June. Supplied to MWH by M J Cockerell.
79   Letter from Michael J Cockerell to Russell Peterson, Chairman, IUCN Budget Advisory Committee, 24 January 1988. Supplied to MWH by M J Cockerell.
80   Martin Holdgate. Personal recollection and personal papers.
81   Kenton Miller. Account of the meeting of former Director-Generals, in discussion with MWH, 17 March 1998.
82   Minutes, IUCN Bureau, twenty-second meeting, Gland and Hotel Clos de Sadex, Nyon, 5 May 1987. In IUCN archives.
83   Minutes, IUCN Council, twenty-second meeting, Gland, 3–4 September 1987. In IUCN archives.
84   Minutes, IUCN Council, twenty-third meeting, San Jose, Costa Rica, 1–8 February 1988. In IUCN archives.
85   Conrad von Ulm-Erbach (1998) Letter to MWH, 7 August. Dr von Ulm-Erbach states that one cause of IUCN's deficit was a differing approach on the part of the two Treasurers. The US dollar fell sharply against the Swiss franc in 1985–86. With the backing of the WWF Treasurer, John Nash, von Ulm-Erbach sold WWF dollars in 1985, but did not touch the IUCN dollar account because of the lack of support from Leonard Hentsch. As a result the WWF's exchange loss at the end of 1986 was only SFr60,000 while IUCN lost SFr400,000.

Chapter 10: The Web Extends

1   Special report, General Assembly. *IUCN Bulletin*, vol 19, 1–3, pp SR1–16.
2   Miller, K R (1987) *Director General's Report on the Work of the Union since the 16th Session of the IUCN General Assembly Held in Madrid, November 1984*. Gland: IUCN.
3   Oscar Arias Sanchez. Conserve diversity or face ruin. Extract from opening address to the IUCN General Assembly in San Jose, Costa Rica. *IUCN Bulletin*, 19, vol 1–3, p SR3.
4   Monkombu Swaminathan. Closing statement to IUCN General Assembly, San Jose, Costa Rica. *IUCN Bulletin*, vol 19, 1–3, pp SR2–3.
5   HRH Prince Philip, Duke of Edinburgh. Statement to the IUCN General Assembly, San Jose, Costa Rica. *IUCN Bulletin*, vol 19, 1–3, p SR2.
6   Fourteen expert workshops address conservation's main challenges. *IUCN Bulletin*, vol 19, 1–3, pp SR4–7.
7   Michael J Cockerell. Status of IUCN, June 1987. Memo to Kenton Miller, 2 June 1987. Supplied to MWH by M J Cockerell.
8   Michael J Cockerell (1998) Letter to MWH, 22 June, with comments on near-final text of this book.
9   Kenton R Miller. Discussion with MWH, 17 March 1998.
10   Leonard Hentsch had been coopted to the Council, and his term of office ended at the General Assembly. He was asked to continue, but stood down in 1989 and was succeeded by Richard Steele of the UK.
11   Minutes, IUCN Council, thirty-first meeting, Gland, 8–10 April 1991. In IUCN archives.
12   Minutes, IUCN Bureau, twenty-second meeting, Gland and Hotel Clos de Sadex, Nyon, 5 May 1987. In IUCN archives.
13   Minutes, IUCN Council, twenty-second meeting, Gland, 3–4 September 1987. In IUCN archives.
14   IUCN (1990) *Triennial Report, 1988–1990*. Gland, Switzerland: IUCN.
15   E U Curtis ('Buff') Bohlen. Discussion with MWH on 19 March 1998.
16   Yolanda Kakabadse. Conversation with MWH on 2 December 1997.
17   Minutes, IUCN Council, thirty-second meeting, Gland, 25–27 November 1991. In IUCN archives.
18   Minutes, IUCN Council, twenty-fifth meeting, Gland, 8–10 June 1988. In IUCN archives.

19 Elliott, H F I (Ed) (1968) *Proceedings of the Latin American Conference on the Conservation of Renewable Natural Resources. San Carlos de Bariloche, Argentina, 27 March–2 April 1968*. Morges: IUCN.

20 Ramphal, Shridath (1992) World environment and world environmental concerns: a perspective of the past 20 years. In: Holdgate, M W and Synge, H (Eds) *The Future of IUCN*. Gland, Switzerland and Cambridge, UK: IUCN.

21 Marc Dourojeanni (1998) Letter to MWH, 8 April.

22 Russell Mittermeier. Discussion with MWH on 20 March 1998.

23 Minutes, IUCN Bureau, twenty-third meeting, Gland, 6–7 February 1989. In IUCN archives.

24 Growth and diversity in Latin America. Special report. *IUCN Bulletin*, vol 25, no 1, 1994, pp 9–31.

25 Juan Mayr, M Conversation with MWH, 2 December 1997.

26 Juan Mayr, M (1998) Letter to David McDowell, 23 June, with comments on the near-final text of this book.

27 Martin Holdgate (1988) Six Months of Glandular Fever. A personal note to senior staff, 24 October.

28 Minutes, IUCN Council, twenty-seventh meeting, Gland, 12–14 June 1989. In IUCN archives.

29 Tight management caused problems. The marine programme needed another SFr200,000 and SFr250,000 in 1988 and 1989 respectively to cover its planned activities. In June 1989 three important programmes – the East European Programme, the Plants Programme and the 1992 World Parks Congress – were held back until supporters could be found.

30 Minutes, IUCN Council, twenty-sixth meeting, Paris, 7 October 1988. In IUCN archives.

31 Portas, P (Ed) *Forty Years in Conservation. IUCN Bulletin Special Issue,* vol 19, 7–12, pp 1–40.

32 Reunion at Fontainebleau. *IUCN Bulletin*, vol 20, no 1–3, p 4.

33 Declaration of Fontainebleau and goals and objectives for world conservation. *IUCN Bulletin*, vol 20, no 1–3, pp 7–8.

34 A day of prospect and retrospect and prospects for the future. *IUCN Bulletin*, vol 20, no 1–3, pp 5–7, 9–10.

35 Minutes, IUCN Council, twenty-eighth meeting, Gland, 1–3 May 1990. In IUCN archives.

36 Amending the Statutes. *IUCN Bulletin*, vol 22, no 1–2, June 1991, p 30.

37 Resolution 18.1. Mission, objectives and approach of the World Conservation Union. In: IUCN (1991) *18th General Assembly. Resolutions and Recommendations*. Gland: IUCN.

38 The General Assembly. *IUCN Bulletin*, vol 22, no 1–2, June 1991, pp 4–5.

39 The Sahel: out of the myths. Special report. *IUCN Bulletin*, vol 20, no 7–9, July–September 1989.

40 Per Ryden. Discussion with MWH, December 1997.

41 McNeely, J A (1988) *Economics and Biological Diversity: Developing and Using Economic Incentives to Conserve Biological Resources*. Gland, Switzerland: IUCN.

42 Using wildlife wisely. Special report. *IUCN Bulletin*, vol 21, no 4, December 1990.

43 Ian McTaggart Cowan (former Canadian Council member and Vice-President, IUCN). Discussion with MWH, 21 March 1998.

44 Recommendation 18 26. Conservation of wildlife through wise use as a Renewable Natural Resource. *Resolutions and Recommendations of the 18th Session of the General Assembly of IUCN – The World Conservation Union, Perth, 28 November–5 December 1990*. Gland, Switzerland: IUCN.

45 Minutes, IUCN Bureau, twenty-fifth meeting, Gland, 22–23 February 1990. In IUCN archives.

46 Monkombu Swaminathan (1991) Opening address to the eighteenth session of the General Assembly. *IUCN Bulletin*, vol 22, no 1–2, p 8.

47 Monkombu Swaminathan (1990) President's message. In: *Triennial Report on the Work of the Union since the 17th Session of the General Assembly Held in San Jose, Costa Rica*. Gland, IUCN.

48   HRH Prince Philip, Duke of Edinburgh. Address to the Eighteenth General Assembly. *IUCN Bulletin*, vol 22, no 1–2, p 9.
49   Phillip Toyne (1991) Remarks quoted in *IUCN Bulletin*, vol. 22, no 1–2, June, p 15.
50   Shridath Ramphal (1991) A question of survival. *IUCN Bulletin*, vol 22, no 1–2, June, p 3.
51   Rob Malpas (1988) Turning goals into realities. *IUCN Bulletin*, vol 19, no 4–6, April/June.
52   Special report, East Africa. *IUCN Bulletin*, vol 19, no 4–6, April/June 1988.
53   Branching out. *IUCN Bulletin*, vol 23, no 1, March 1992.
54   IUCN in Pakistan. *IUCN Bulletin*, vol 20, 10–12, October/December 1989.
55   Progress in Pakistan. *IUCN Bulletin*, vol 23, no 1, March 1992.
56   Enrique Lahmann. IUCN in Meso-America. From hope to determination. *IUCN Bulletin*, vol 25, 1/94, pp10–12.
57   Luis M Castello (1994) IUCN in South America: connecting a continent. *IUCN Bulletin*, vol 25, no 1, p 17.
58   The Asia-Pacific region: crisis and challenge. *IUCN Bulletin*, vol 24, no 2, 1993.
59   IUCN in West Asia, North Africa and Pakistan. *IUCN Bulletin*, vol 24, no 3, 1993.
60   Jan Cerovsky. IUCN and Eastern Europe: an end to isolation. *IUCN Bulletin*, vol 21, no 4, December 1990.
61   IUCN East European Programme. *IUCN Bulletin*, vol 19, 1–3, January/March 1988.
62   Europeans and their land. *IUCN Bulletin*, vol 24, no 4, December 1993.
63   Holdgate, M W (1994) Director-General's Report on the Activities of the Union since the 18th Session of the General Assembly. General Assembly Paper GA/19/94/4. IUCN–The World Conservation Union. Nineteenth session of the General Assembly, Buenos Aires, Argentina, 17–26 January 1994.
64   IUCN/UNEP/WWF(1991) *Caring for the Earth: a Strategy for Sustainable Living.* Gland, Switzerland: IUCN.
65   Holdgate, M W (1996) *From Care to Action. Making a Sustainable World.* London: Earthscan. (Chapter 3 of this book looks at actions to implement *Caring for the Earth*.)
66   Monkombu Swaminathan. Address to the Ottawa Conference on Conservation and Development. In Jacobs, P and Munro, D A (Eds) (1987) *Conservation with Equity: Strategies for Sustainable Development. Proceedings of the Conference on Conservation and Development: Implementing the World Conservation Strategy.* Gland, Switzerland and Cambridge, UK: IUCN.
67   *Caring for the Earth* – the launch. *IUCN Bulletin*, vol 22, no 4, December 1991, pp 12–15.
68   Eiser, Pam (1991) What on Earth can I do? A personal action guide to sustainable living. *IUCN Bulletin*, vol 22, no 4, December 1991, pp 15–16.
69   Robinson, J G (1993) The limits to caring: sustainable living and the loss of biodiversity. *Conservation Biology*, 7, no 1, March.
70   United Nations (1993) *Report of the United Nations Conference on Environment and Development, Rio de Janeiro, 3–14 June 1992. Volume 1: Resolutions Adopted by the Conference.* Document A/CONF151/26/Rev1. New York: United Nations. (Chapter 15 addresses biological diversity.)
71   Shridath Ramphal (1993) Para nostros la patria es el planeta tierra. Opening address. In: *Parks for Life, Report of the IVth World Congress on National Parks and Protected Areas, Caracas, Venezuela, 10–21 February 1992.* Gland: IUCN.
72   Parks for life: a new beginning. Special section. *IUCN Bulletin*, vol 23, no 2, June 1992.
73   McNeely, J (Ed) (1992) *Parks for Life, Report of the IVth World Congress on National Parks and Protected Areas, Caracas, Venezuela, 10–21 February 1992.* Gland: IUCN.
74   Walter Lusigi (1992) Remarks quoted in *IUCN Bulletin*, vol 23, no 2, June, p 13.
75   Shridath Ramphal (1992) Remarks quoted in *IUCN Bulletin*, vol 23, no 2, June, p 14.
76   Claude Martin (1992) Remarks quoted in *IUCN Bulletin*, vol 23, no 2, June, p 13.
77   Maurice Strong (1992) Remarks quoted in *IUCN Bulletin*, vol 23, no 2, June, p 25.
78   Resolution 16/24. World Genetic Resources and Endangered Species Habitat Protection. In: IUCN (1984) *Resolutions, 16th Session of the General Assembly of IUCN, Madrid, Spain, 5–14 November 1984.* Gland: IUCN.

79   Glowka, L, Burhenne-Guilmin, F and Synge, H (1994) *A Guide to the Convention on Biological Diversity.* Environmental Policy and Law Paper No 30. Gland, Switzerland and Cambridge, UK: IUCN.

80   Minutes, IUCN Bureau, twenty-fourth meeting, Gland, 20–21 November 1989. In IUCN archives.

81   Repetto, R (1985) *The Global Possible. Resources, Development and the New Century.* New Haven and London: Yale University Press.

82   Reid, W V and Miller, K R (1989) *Keeping Options Alive. The Scientific Basis for Conserving Biodiversity.* Washington DC: World Resources Institute.

83   McNeely, J A, Miller, K R, Reid, W V, Mittermeier, R A and Werner, T B (1990) *Conserving the World's Biological Diversity.* Gland, Switzerland and Washington DC: IUCN, WRI, CI, WWF–US and the World Bank.

84   WRI, IUCN and UNEP (1992) *Global Biodiversity Strategy. Guidelines for Action to Save, Study and Use Earth's Biotic Wealth Sustainably and Equitably.* Washington DC: WRI.

85   Groombridge, B (Ed) *Global Biodiversity. Status of the Earth's Living Resources.* London: Chapman and Hall.

86   Groombridge, B and Jenkins, M (Eds) (1994) *Biodiversity Data Sourcebook. WCMC Biodiversity Series No 1.* Cambridge: World Conservation Press.

87   Heywood, V H (Ed) (1995) *Global Biodiversity Assessment.* Cambridge University Press for UNEP.

88   Ramphal, Shridath (1992) *Our Country the Planet.* Washington DC: Island Press.

89   Minutes, IUCN Council, thirty-fourth meeting, Gland, 2, 5 and 6 November 1992. In IUCN archives.

90   Martin Holdgate (1992) Extracts from address to UNCED. *IUCN Bulletin*, vol 23, no 3.

91   Tolba, M K, Ek Kholy, O, El Hinnawi, E, Holdgate, M W, McMichael, D F and Munn, R E (Eds) *The World Environment, 1972–1992.* London: Chapman and Hall.

92   Runnalls, D (1992) A duty to hope. Comments on UNCED, quoted in *IUCN Bulletin*, vol 23, no 3, pp 19–20.

93   Angela Cropper (1992) View from the South. Comments on UNCED, quoted in *IUCN Bulletin*, vol 23, no 3, p 21.

94   New headquarters. *IUCN Bulletin*, vol 22, no 1–2, June 1991.

95   IUCN and WWF policy on joint projects. Memorandum of agreement. Annex 2 to the minutes of the twenty-sixth session of the IUCN Council, Paris, 1988. In IUCN archives.

96   Shridath Ramphal (1991) Remarks at the laying of the foundation stone for the new IUCN Headquarters, April 9 1991. *IUCN Bulletin*, vol 22 no 3, September, p 4.

97   The inauguration. *IUCN Bulletin*, no 4/92, pp 2–7.

98   Holdgate, M W and Synge, H (Eds) (1993) *The Future of IUCN, the World Conservation Union.* Gland, Switzerland and Cambridge, UK: IUCN.

99   Charles de Haes (1992) What does the world expect of IUCN? In Holdgate, M W and Synge, H (Eds) op cit Note 98.

100   Aban Marker Kabraji (1992) What can IUCN deliver? In Holdgate, M W and Synge, H (Eds) op cit Note 98.

101   Mark Halle (1992) Building the worldwide union. In Holdgate, M W and Synge, H (eds) op cit Note 98.

102   Proceedings, 19th session of the General Assembly of IUCN – The World Conservation Union, Buenos Aires, Argentina, 17–26 January 1994. Gland, Switzerland: IUCN.

103   Minutes, IUCN Council, thirty-seventh meeting, Sheraton Hotel, Buenos Aires, 17 January 1994. In IUCN archives.

104   Report on membership and constituency development. Congress paper CGR/1/96/3. In *World Conservation Congress Agenda and Documentation, 13–23 October 1996, Montreal, Canada.* Gland: IUCN.

105   Minutes, IUCN Council, thirty-sixth meeting, Gland, 14–15 October 1993. In IUCN archives.

106   The finances of IUCN in the 1994–1996 triennium. Paper CGR/1/95/6. World Conservation Congress Agenda and Documentation, Montreal, Canada, 13–23 October 1996. Gland: IUCN.

107 IUCN (1995) *Annual Report, 1994.* Gland, Switzerland and Cambridge, UK: IUCN.
108 David McDowell (1996) The report of the Director-General on the work of the Union
     since the 19th Session of the IUCN General Assembly. Congress paper CGR/1/96/2,
     World Conservation Congress Agenda and Documentation, Montreal, Canada, 13–23
     October 1996. Gland: IUCN.
109 Minutes, IUCN Council, thirty-fifth meeting, Gland, 26–28 May 1993. In IUCN archives.
110 Tariq Banuri. Conversation with MWH, 3 December 1997.
111 Royston, M G (1979) *Pollution Prevention Pays.* Oxford: Pergamon.
112 Schmidheiny, S (1992) *Changing Course: Report of the World Business Council for
     Sustainable Development.* Cambridge, Mass. and London: MIT Press.
113 Greene, G and Picciotto, R (Eds) (1997) *Large Dams: Learning from the Past. Looking
     at the Future.* Gland, Switzerland and Cambridge, UK: IUCN. Washington DC: The
     World Bank.
114 The strategy of IUCN, as adopted following the 19th session of the IUCN General
     Assembly. Gland: IUCN, 1994.
115 Allen, Thomas B (1987) *Guardian of the Wild. The Story of the National Wildlife
     Federation, 1936–1986.* Bloomington and Indianapolis: Indiana University Press.
116 Shabecoff, Philip (1993) *A Fierce Green Fire. The American Environmental Movement.*
     New York: Hill and Wang.

Chapter 11: Power to the Members

1   Holdgate, M W (1996) *From Care to Action: Making a Sustainable World.* London:
     Earthscan.
2   de Mattos-Shipley, H, Lyons, J, Belsham, C, Harding, D and Johnston, M (Eds) (1996)
     WWF. Changing Worlds: 35 Years of Conservation Achievement. London: Banson for
     WWF.
3   David McDowell (1998) Letter to MWH, 21 January.
4   David McDowell (1996) The report of the Director-General on the work of the Union
     since the 19th Session of the IUCN General Assembly. Congress paper CGR/1/96/2,
     World Conservation Congress Agenda and Documentation, Montreal, Canada, 13–23
     October 1996. Gland: IUCN.
5   Minutes, IUCN Council, fortieth meeting, Gland, 30 November–1 December 1994. In
     IUCN archives.
6   Report of the Task Force on Regionalization and Decentralization. IUCN Council Paper
     UC 40/94/40. In IUCN archives.
7   See, for example, the detailed account of regional and country activities in the special
     report entitled 'Branching out' in *IUCN Bulletin*, vol 23, no 1, March 1992.
8   Yolanda Kakabadse. Discussion with MWH, 2 December 1997.
9   Jan Mayr, M. Discussion with MWH, 2 December 1997.
10   Dan Martin (IUCN Council member and senior staff member of the MacArthur
     Foundation). Discussion with MWH, 3 December 1997.
11   IUCN (1997) *A Pocket Guide to IUCN – the World Conservation Union.* Gland,
     Switzerland and Cambridge, UK: IUCN. As comparison, WWF, by the end of 1987, had
     26 national organizations, 22 programme offices (of which 16 were in developing
     countries), 4.7 million regular supporters and activities in 96 countries – WWF *Annual
     Report*, 1997.
12   Wasaa Centre hosts meeting of IUCN's East African members. *IUCN Bulletin*, vol 26,
     no 2, 1995, p 9.
13   World round-up. *IUCN Bulletin*, vol 26, no 2, 1995, p 10.
14   Hulm, Peter (1997) *IUCN – The World Conservation Union.* Gland, Switzerland and
     Cambridge, UK: IUCN.
15   Holdgate, M W (1992) Where now? Concluding comment in the special report entitled
     'branching out' in *IUCN Bulletin*, vol 23, no 1, March.
16   Jay Hair (1994) Building a strong team. Editorial. *IUCN Bulletin*, no 3, p 2.
17   Minutes, IUCN Council, forty-first meeting, Gland, 22–24 May 1995. In IUCN archives.

18 David McDowell (1998) Letter to MWH,18 June 1998.
19 IUCN (1995) *Annual Report,1994*. Gland, Switzerland and Cambridge, UK: IUCN.
20 Minutes, IUCN Council, forty-second meeting, Gland, 27–29 November 1995. In IUCN archives.
21 Minutes, IUCN Council, forty-third meeting, Gland, 16–17 April 1996. In IUCN archives.
22 David McDowell. Introduction to Hulm, P (1997) op cit Note 14.
23 WWF (1998) *The Living Planet Campaign. Celebrating Gifts to the Earth*. Vienna: WWF.
24 WWF (1998) *Annual Report, 1997*. Gland: WWF.
25 Commission on Ecosystem Management (1998) *Principles of Ecosystem Management. Report of a Seminar held at Royal Holloway College, University of London, June 1996* (in press).
26 Ecosystem management. Special report. *World Conservation (formerly IUCN Bulletin)*, no 3/97, September 1997.
27 IUCN (1996) *Red List of Threatened Animals*. Gland, Switzerland and Cambridge, UK: IUCN.
28 IUCN (1998) Invaders from Planet Earth. *World Conservation (formerly IUCN Bulletin)* special number, 4/97 and 1/98.
29 IUCN (1995) *Parks for Life. Action Plan for Protected Areas in Europe*. Gland, Switzerland and Cambridge, UK: IUCN.
30 IUCN (1995) *A Global System of Marine Protected Areas*. Gland, Switzerland and Cambridge, UK: IUCN.
31 Making the most of forests. Special report. *IUCN Bulletin*, vol 25, no 3, July/September 1994, pp 13–20.
32 Minutes, IUCN Council, thirty-ninth meeting, Gland, 31 May–1 June 1994. In IUCN archives.
33 The finances of IUCN in the 1994–1996 triennium. Paper CGR/1/95/6. World Conservation Congress Agenda and Documentation, Montreal, Canada, 13–23 October 1996. Gland: IUCN.
34 Statutes Review Committee. Documentation for the meetings of the committee. In IUCN archives.
35 *IUCN – the World Conservation Union* (1997) *Statutes of 5 October 1948 revised on 22 October 1996 (including Rules of Procedure of the World Conservation Congress) and Regulations revised on 22 October 1996*. Gland: IUCN.
36 IUCN (1997) *Making the Union Relevant*. Special double issue on the Montreal Congress. *World Conservation (formerly the IUCN Bulletin)*, no 1–2. Gland: IUCN.
37 Trzyna, T. Commission on Environmental Strategy and Planning (CESP). Triennial report, 1994–1996. Annex 4 to Congress paper CGR/1/96/2. World Conservation Congress Agenda and Documentation, Montreal, Canada, 13–23 October 1996. Gland: IUCN.
38 Hassan, Parvez (1996) Commission on Environmental Law (CEL). Triennial report, 1994–1996. Annex 3 to Congress paper CGR/1/96/2. World Conservation Congress Agenda and Documentation, Montreal, Canada, 13–23 October 1996. Gland, IUCN.
39 Martin, Rowan (1997) Guardians of Eden. Account of the dramatic presentation at the Montreal Congress. In Note 36, pp 15–17.
40 Holdgate, M W (1997) Parting thoughts. Roll on World Congress II. In Note 36, p 57.
41 McNeely, J (1997) Charting a course. Account of the workshops. In Note 36, pp 18–24.
42 The Panel of Panels. Summary of discussion. In Note 36, p 25.
43 Michael McCloskey. Discussion with MWH, 19 March 1998.
44 Stephen Edwards. Summary and analysis of resolutions adopted at IUCN General Assemblies, 1948–1994. Tabulation made available to MWH by Dr Stephen Edwards.
45 Resolutions proposed for adoption at the World Conservation Congress, Montreal, Canada. Congress documents CGR/1/196/17 together with Addenda 1, 2 and 3. In IUCN archives.
46 Greene, George (1997) Resolutions, recommendations and the 50th anniversary. In Note 36, pp 30–31.

47   Castano, Juanita (1997) Communicating the environment. Summary of panel discussion. In Note 36, pp 6–7.
48   Hajost, Scott (1997) Caring for the earth: from advertising strategy to business proposition. Summary of panel discussion. In note 36, p 8.
49   Vorhies, Frank (1997) Financing sustainable development. Summary of panel discussion. In Note 36, pp 9–10.
50   Nature in the 21st century. Summary of panel discussion. In Note 36, pp 10–11.
51   McNeely, J A (1997) *Conservation and the Future: Trends and Options beyond the Year 2025.* Gland, Switzerland and Cambridge, UK: IUCN.
52   David McDowell (1997) Lifting the Union's game. Internal paper IUCN, 12 September.
53   Hair, Jay (1997) Some good news too…Edited summary of concluding remarks and remarks at press conference in Montreal, October 1996. In Note 36, p 63.
54   Kakabadse, Yolanda (1997) A matter of life and death. Remarks at her incoming news conference as President, Montreal, October 1996. In Note 36, p 63.

Chapter 12: The Balance Sheet

1   Trends in the world environment have been reviewed by Holdgate, M W, Kassas, M and White, G F (Eds) (1982) *The World Environment, 1972–1982.* Dublin: Tycooly International for UNEP and Tolba, M K, El Kholy, O, El Hinnawi, E, Holdgate, M W, McMichael, D F and Munn, R E (Eds) *The World Environment, 1972–1992.* London: Chapman and Hall. The various *World Resources Reports* published by the World Resources Institute in partnership with UNEP and the *State of the World Reports* by the Worldwatch Institute provide overviews and interpretations of the situation.
2   For an evaluation of the impact of species translocation see Invaders from Planet Earth. *World Conservation*, no 4/97 and 1/98, 1998.
3   Some attempt at evaluating the successes and failures is to be found in Holdgate, M W (1996) *From Care to Action.* London: Earthscan.
4   A convenient summary of the massive volume of international environmental law is given in IUCN (1993) *Status of Multilateral Treaties in the Field of Environmental Conservation.* IUCN Environment and Law Occasional Papers, No 1. Gland, Switzerland: IUCN.
5   Charles de Haes (1993) What does the world expect of IUCN? In: Holdgate, M W and Synge, H (Eds) *The Future of IUCN, the World Conservation Union.* Gland, Switzerland and Cambridge, UK: IUCN.
6   Nicholas Robinson. Discussion with MWH, December 1997.
7   Aban Marker Kabraji (1993) What can IUCN deliver? In: Holdgate, M W and Synge, H (Eds) op cit Note 5.
8   David Bellamy (1997) Communicating the environment. *World Conservation*, no 1–2/97, 1997.
9   Kevin Grose (1997) BCIS: Better Data for Better Decisions. *World Conservation*, 1–2/97, p 49.
10   Edward Maltby (1997) Linking science with society. *World Conservation*, 1–2/97, pp 37–38.
11   Richard Sandbrook (1997) Excelling as a knowledge-based institution. *World Conservation*, 1–2/97, p 32.
12   Hulm, Peter (1997) *IUCN – the World Conservation Union.* Gland, Switzerland and Cambridge, UK: IUCN.
13   IUCN at CITES: a triumph of teamwork. *IUCN Bulletin*, vol 267, no 1, January–March 1995, pp 13–24.
14   Strategies for sustainable livelihood. Special report. *IUCN Bulletin*, vol 26, no 2, April–June 1995, pp 13–20.
15   Anis Mouasher (President, Royal Society for the Conservation of Nature, Jordan). Letter to MWH,15 April 1998.
16   Paulo Nogueira-Neto (Professor of Ecology and former IUCN Council member). Letter to MWH,16 April 1998.

17 Roger McManus. Discussion with MWH,19 March 1998.
18 IUCN Commission on Education and Communication. Statement on Agenda 21, chapter 36, to the United Nations Commission on Sustainable Development.
19 Dan Martin. Discussion with MWH, 3 December 1997.
20 Hal Eidsvik (1998) Letter to MWH, 27 January.
21 Walter Lusigi. Discussion with MWH,18 March 1998.
22 David McDowell (1998) Letter to MWH, 21 January.
23 Claude Martin. Discussion with MWH, 4 December 1997.
24 Kenton Miller (1998) Letter to David McDowell, 24 June, with detailed commentary on the near-final text of this book.
25 Mark Halle (1993) Building the worldwide Union. In: Holdgate, M W and Synge, H (Eds) op cit Note 5.
26 Mike McCloskey (1998) Letter to MWH, 2 July, with comments on the near-final text of this book.
27 Resolution 19.1: The strategy of IUCN – the World Conservation Union. *Resolutions and Recommendations of the 19th Session of the General Assembly of IUCN – the World Conservation Union, Buenos Aires, Argentina, 17–26 January 1994.* Gland, Switzerland: IUCN.
28 Marshall Murphree and John Robinson (1997) IUCN's sustainable use initiative. *World Conservation*, 1–2/97, pp 41–42.
29 Minutes, IUCN Council, fortieth meeting, Gland, 30 November–1 December 1994. In IUCN archives.
30 Eskandar Firouz (former IUCN Vice-President: former Deputy Prime Minister and minister responsible for environment in Iran). Letter to MWH,12 April 1998.
31 Goldemberg, Jose (1998) What is the role of science in developing countries? *Science*, vol 279, 20 February.
32 Guha, Ramachandra (1997) The authoritarian biologist and the arrogance of anti-humanism. Wildlife conservation in the Third World. *The Ecologist*, vol 27, no 1, 14–20.
33 Zafar Futehally (1998) Letter to MWH, 9 June.
34 Marc Dourojeanni (former IUCN Council Member and Vice-President). Letter to MWH, 8 April 1998.
35 *A Pocket Guide to IUCN – the World Conservation Union, 1996/1997.* Gland, Switzerland: IUCN.
36 Tariq Banuri. Quoted in *IUCN Bulletin*, vol 25, no 2, 1994, p 6.
37 IUCN Management Board. Interim draft terms of reference and record of meeting held on 4–5 March 1998. In IUCN archives.
38 Claude Martin (1998) Letter to David McDowell, 24 June, with comments on near-final text of this book, and including details of WWF payments to IUCN.
39 de Mattos-Shipley, H, Lyons, J, Belsham, C, Harding, D and Johnston, M (eds) (1996) *WWF. Changing Worlds: 35 Years of Conservation Achievement.* London: Banson for WWF.
40 The finances of IUCN in the 1994–1996 triennium. Paper CGR/1/95/6. World Conservation Congress Agenda and Documentation, Montreal, Canada, 13–23 October 1996. Gland: IUCN.
41 Charles de Haes (1998) Letter to MWH, 26 July 1998.
42 Robert Prescott-Allen (1998) Letter to David McDowell and Martin Holdgate,15 July, with comments on the near-final text of this book.
43 David McDowell (1998) Letter to MWH,15 August.

Acronyms and Abbreviations

ACIC	American Committee for International Conservation
ASEAN	Association of South East Asian Nations
ASOC	Antarctica and Southern Oceans Coalition
ASP	Africa Special Project
BCIS	Biodiversity Conservation Information System
BCSD	Business Council for Sustainable Development (now WBCSD)
BGCS	Botanic Gardens Conservation Secretariat
CATIE	Tropical Agricultural Research and Training Center
CBD	Convention on Biological Diversity
CCAMLR	Convention on the Conservation of Antarctic Marine Living Resources
CCTA	Commission for Technical Cooperation in Africa South of the Sahara
CDC	Conservation for Development Centre
CEC	Commission on Education and Communication
CEESP	Commission on Environmental Economics, Strategy and Policy
CEL	Commission on Environmental Law
CEM	Commission on Ecosystem Management
CEP	Commission on Environmental Planning
CEPLA	Commission on Environmental Policy, Law and Administration
CESP	Commission on Environmental Strategy and Planning
CFE	Caring for the Earth
CIC	Conseil International de la Chasse
CITES	Convention on International Trade in Endangered Species of Wild Fauna and Flora
CMC	Conservation Monitoring Centre (now WCMC)
CNPPA	Commission on National Parks and Protected Areas
COE	Commission on Ecology
CP	Comparative Physiology
CSD	Commission on Sustainable Development (IUCN)
CSIRO	Australian Commonwealth Scientific and Industrial Research Organization
CT	Conservation Terrestrial
ECE	Economic Commission for Europe
ECG	Ecosystems Conservation Group
ECOSOC	Economic and Social Council (of the United Nations)
ELC	Environmental Law Centre
ELIS	Environmental Law Information System
FAO	Food and Agriculture Organization (of the United Nations)
GEMS	Global Environmental Monitoring System

GONGO	Governmental and Non-governmental Organization
HA	Human Adaptability
IBP	International Biological Programme
ICBP	International Council for Bird Preservation (now BirdLife International)
ICEL	International Council for Environmental Law
ICOMOS	International Committee on Monuments, Artistic Sites and Archaeological Excavations
ICSU	International Council of Scientific Unions
ICTSD	International Centre for Trade and Sustainable Development
IEEP	International Environmental Education Programme
IIED	International Institute for Environment and Development
IMCO	Intergovernmental Maritime Consultative Organization
IMO	International Maritime Organization
INFOTERRA	International Environmental Information System
INTECOL	International Association of Ecology
IOPN	International Office for the Protection of Nature
IRPTC	International Register of Potentially Toxic Chemicals
IRSAC	Belgian Institute for Scientific Research in Central Africa
IUBS	International Union of Biological Sciences
IUCN	International Union for Conservation of Nature and Natural Resources
IUPN	International Union for the Protection of Nature
IWRB	International Wildfowl Research Bureau
MAB	Man and Biosphere programme (UNESCO)
MAR	A joint ICBP/IWRB project to study and assess the conservation priority for wetlands (Marecages)
MERCASUR	Common Market of the Southern Cone of South America
NCS	National Conservation Strategy
NEAP	National Environmental Action Plan
NGO	Non-governmental Organization
NORAD	Norwegian Agency for International Development
OAU	Organization of African Unity
PADU	Protected Areas Data Unit
PF	Productivity Freshwater
PP	Production Processes
PPAG	Programme Planning Advisory Group
PR	Public Relations
PSO	Professional Services Organization
PT	Productivity Terrestrial
SB	Systematics and Biogeography
SCAR	Scientific Committee on Antarctic Research
SCIBP	Scientific Committee for the International Biological Programme
SCMU	Species Conservation Monitoring Unit
SCOPE	Scientific Committee on Problems of the Environment
SCOR	Scientific Committee on Oceanic Research
SIDA	Swedish International Development Agency
SPNR	Society for the Promotion of Nature Reserves
SSC	The Survival Service Commission (subsequently Species Survival Commission)

SWMTEP	System Wide Medium Term Environmental Programme (United Nations)
TRAFFIC	Trade Records Analysis of Fauna and Flora in Commerce
UM	Use and Management
UNCED	United Nations Conference on Environment and Development
UNCSD	United Nations Commission on Sustainable Development
UNDP	United Nations Development Programme
UNEP	United Nations Environment Programme
UNESCO	United Nations Educational, Scientific and Cultural Organization
UNSCCUR	United Nations Scientific Conference on the Conservation and Utilization of Natural Resources
WBCSD	World Business Council for Sustainable Development
WCED	World Commission on Environment and Development
WCMC	World Conservation Monitoring Centre
WCPA	World Commission on Protected Areas
WCS	World Conservation Strategy
WRI	World Resources Institute
WWF	World Wide Fund for Nature (World Wildlife Fund – in North America)

Index

Page numbers in **bold** refer to figures